The Marrying Kind?

Ch.1, II, Either 4 or 6

The Marrying Kind?

Debating Same-Sex Marriage within
the Lesbian and Gay Movement

Mary Bernstein and Verta Taylor, Editors

University of Minnesota Press
Minneapolis • London

Chapter 6 was previously published as "Culture and Mobilization: Tactical Repertoires, Same-Sex Weddings, and the Impact on Gay Activism," *American Sociological Review* 74, no. 6 (December 2009): 865–90.

Published by the University of Minnesota Press
111 Third Avenue South, Suite 290
Minneapolis, MN 55401-2520
http://www.upress.umn.edu

Library of Congress Cataloging-in-Publication Data

The marrying kind? debating same-sex marriage within the lesbian and gay movement / Mary Bernstein and Verta Taylor, editors.
Includes bibliographical references and index.
ISBN 978-0-8166-8171-6 (hc : alk. paper)—ISBN 978-0-8166-8172-3 (pb : alk. paper)
1. Same-sex marriage—United States. 2. Gay rights—United States. I. Taylor, Verta A. II. Bernstein, Mary.
HQ1034.U5M38 2013
323.3'264—dc23

2013010127

Printed in the United States of America on acid-free paper

The University of Minnesota is an equal-opportunity educator and employer.

20   19   18   17   16   15   14   13   10   9   8   7   6   5   4   3   2   1

Contents

Abbreviations

ACLU	American Civil Liberties Union
AIDS	acquired immune deficiency syndrome
BFP	*Burlington Free Press*
CLUES	Comunidades Latinas Unidas en Servicio
CTAC	Connecticut TransAdvocacy Coalition
CWEALF	Connecticut Women's Education and Legal Fund
DOMA	Defense of Marriage Act
EQCA	Equality California
FIC	Family Institute of Connecticut
GLAD	Gay and Lesbian Advocates and Defenders
GLBT	gay, lesbian, bisexual, and transgender
GLSEN	Gay, Lesbian and Straight Education Network
GLVF	Gay and Lesbian Victory Fund
GSS	General Social Survey
HIV	human immunodeficiency virus
HRC	Human Rights Campaign
IGF	Independent Gay Forum
LDS	Church of Jesus Christ of Latter Day Saints
LGBT	lesbian, gay, bisexual, and transgender
LGBTQ	lesbian, gay, bisexual, transgender, and queer
LISM	lifelong, internally stratified marriage
LMF	Love Makes a Family
MECA	Marriage Equality California
NCLR	National Center for Lesbian Rights
NHSLS	National Health and Social Life Survey
NOM	National Organization for Marriage
OITM	*Out in the Mountains*

PAC	Pacte Civil de Solidarité
PFLAG	Parents, Families, and Friends of Lesbians and Gays
PMC	Protect Marriage Coalition
SMO	social movement organization
TANF	Temporary Assistance for Needy Families
Task Force	National Gay and Lesbian Task Force
UCLA	University of California, Los Angeles
VFM Task Force	Vermont Freedom to Marry Task Force

Acknowledgments

Perhaps no issue in contemporary American society has provoked such polarized responses as same-sex marriage. The national debate over gay marriage has been heard in the halls of the U.S. Congress, at the White House, in state legislatures and courtrooms, and in the rhetoric of election campaigns at the national, state, and local levels. The right to marry has also been a polarizing issue within the gay and lesbian movement. Thus far, much of the debate over gay marriage has been ideological and theoretical. We undertook this project out of a desire to understand why gay and lesbian activists have been so divided over marriage, how this has affected campaigns for same-sex marriage across the United States, and whether and how marriage has changed gay and lesbian communities, identity, and activism. We view this book as an attempt to ease the ongoing tension over this issue that is taking place among activists on the ground.

We also hope to bridge the disconnect between theorists and activists. Theorists too often speak to themselves, rarely reaching beyond the narrow confines of academic journals, periodicals, and conferences, isolated from social movement struggles and unable to capture the vibrant hearts of activists and the subtle nuances of social movement efforts. At the same time, activism is often uninformed by broader theories of power and by social movement research on strategies and tactics. We believe there is a price to be paid for the chasm that exists between scholars and activists. Both activism and theory are diminished by the failure to integrate the two. Over the course of our careers, we have sought through our research to learn lessons from activists in the hope of bridging the divide between theory and activism. So, too, have the contributors to this volume. We are enormously indebted to them for believing in this project and for writing essays that we hope will contribute to fruitful conversations between activists and scholars concerned with one of the most divisive issues in American society today.

We are grateful to many people who helped with this project. Mary's life partner, Nancy Naples, has provided consistent support throughout the years, serving as an in-house reviewer and sounding board. Their daughters Alexandra and Samantha, to whom we dedicate this book, have already seen the legalization of same-sex marriage in their home state of Connecticut. While some of their friends express surprise that they have two moms, others say, "You're lucky!" or "That's not fair. I have only one mom." Alexandra and Samantha know that the law is important, but they also know that families come in all shapes and sizes and that love, commitment, and courage are what matter most.

We began this book in earnest in 2008, the same year that Verta's mother died. Verta's mother—a staunch Democrat and one of the first women to hold political office in rural and politically conservative northeastern Arkansas—whispered shortly before she died that she believed that during their lifetime Verta and Leila would have a chance to marry. Like many lesbians who came of age during the second wave of feminism, marriage was not something Verta and Leila aspired to because of its fundamental role in women's subordination. They had chosen not to rush to San Francisco in 2004 when more than 4,000 couples lined up at City Hall for marriage licenses over a month-long period. But they finally married in 2008 at the Santa Barbara Courthouse during what came to be known in lesbian and gay circles in California as the "summer of love," when more than 18,000 couples tied the knot between the time the California Supreme Court ruled it unconstitutional to exclude same-sex couples from marriage and Proposition 8, banning same-sex marriage in California, went into effect. They married on their thirtieth anniversary as part of the collective effort to halt the Religious Right's campaign to overturn marriage equality in California. This book is dedicated to Verta's late mother, Alice Taylor Houston, and to Verta's life partner, collaborator, and inspiration for nearly thirty-five years, Leila J. Rupp. Alice chose finally to come out as the mother of a lesbian daughter in her obituary, which she insisted on writing herself, and she requested no service so that Leila and Verta, who had been her caretakers, would not have to face the outright hatred and hostility they had been subjected to at Verta's brother's funeral in Tennessee more than a decade earlier. They decided to have a service anyway, where Verta spoke about her mother's courage that taught her about the politics of visibility.

The idea for this volume was sparked at the 2008 reception of the Sexualities section of the American Sociological Association, where we approached Jason Weidemann, senior acquisitions editor at the University of Minnesota Press. Jason has stood by this project from the beginning, making the book better with his insights and experience. We would also like to thank our colleagues, students, and the external reviewers who commented on all or parts of the manuscript and provided needed advice: Michael Bourgeois, Jennifer Earl, Peter Hennen, Jason Hopkins, Nancy Naples, Brian Powell, Leila J. Rupp, Anna Sorenson, Shannon Weber, and Nancy Whittier. We are also grateful to our student research assistants who helped collect materials that play a major role in the analysis: Mary Burke, Alison Crossley, Heather Hurwitz, Katrina Kimport, Shae Miller, and Kristine Olsen.

The most important acknowledgment we have to make is to the activists around the country, gay and straight, who believe that the freedom to marry must prevail over fear and discrimination and whose stories we tell here during an extraordinary moment in the history of marriage in the United States.

Marital Discord

Understanding the Contested Place of Marriage in the Lesbian and Gay Movement

Mary Bernstein and Verta Taylor

> *Traditional marriage is a rotten, oppressive institution . . . marriage is a contract which smothers both people, denies needs, and places impossible demands on both people . . . Gay people must stop gauging their self-respect by how well they mimic straight marriages . . . To accept that happiness comes through finding a groovy spouse and settling down, showing the world that "we're just the same as you" is avoiding the real issues, and is an expression of self-hatred.*
>
> —Carl Wittman, "A Gay Manifesto," 1970

IT WOULD BE HARD TO IMAGINE a more heated condemnation of the institution of marriage than this. In isolation, such a manifesto suggests that gay men and lesbians have no use for matrimony. But contrasted to the nationwide campaign for same-sex marriage raging in states across the United States and the crowds of same-sex couples rushing to marriage license counters, Carl Wittman's statement points to just how contested the issue of marriage is within gay and lesbian communities and the movement. Social movements generally face the most visible opposition from their opponents, but the battle for same-sex marriage is an exception. Rarely has a social movement goal so central to a movement's political agenda been so fraught. At the same time that antigay forces fight to preserve marriage for one man and one woman, lesbian and gay activists argue with passion about the viability and the social consequences of same-sex marriage. Why is the campaign for marriage equality so controversial *within* lesbian, gay, bisexual, and transgender (LGBT) communities? What are the main critiques of marriage and of same-sex marriage that divide LGBT communities, and are these criticisms and fears justified? What does this debate suggest about the shifting meaning of lesbian and gay identity? And how does the debate over marriage within LGBT communities help us understand where gay marriage is headed in the future? All social movements experience conflict over identity and strategy, and how conflict gets resolved is critical for understanding whether a movement succeeds or fails (Ghaziani 2008).

The goal of this book is to understand the debate within LGBT communities over same-sex marriage; how this conflict has influenced the nationwide campaign for same-sex marriage; and the extent to which disputes and fears that surround same-sex marriage are justified. The essays in this volume analyze the discourses, strategies, and composition of LGBT social movement organizations pursuing same-sex marriage. They also explore the complexity of the LGBT movement's opposition to marriage by addressing the dire predictions of LGBT activists that same-sex marriage will spell the end of queer identity and community. Case studies of Oklahoma, California, Vermont, Massachusetts, Connecticut, New Jersey, and Canada illuminate the complex politics of same-sex marriage, making it clear that the current debate among LGBT activists over whether marriage is assimilationist or transformative is far too simplistic. Many gay marriage activists are motivated by a desire to build bridges toward the dominant group. At the same time, others, both within and outside the marriage-equality movement, maintain a sustained critique of heteronormativity (the social system of heterosexual privilege). In short, these positions are not always opposed. While infighting is often seen as weakening a movement, the essays in this book reveal that conflict is one of the major ways activists make decisions about goals and strategies (Ghaziani 2008).

In this introduction, we begin with a history of same-sex marriage in the United States. We then examine the various arguments that have been advanced by activists as well as queer scholars and commentators to question and, in some instances, to oppose the LGBT movement's pursuit of marriage equality. Drawing on the empirical analyses presented in subsequent chapters, we argue that the marriage-equality movement is neither fully assimilationist nor fully oppositional and critical of heteronormativity. Instead, the impact of the marriage-equality movement and the meaning of marriage-equality activism is complex, often marked by contradictory impulses and unintended consequences. We conclude by reflecting on the ways that battles within the LGBT movement may prove both beneficial and deleterious to the campaign for marriage equality, which continues to be fought in states across the United States.

THE HISTORY OF SAME-SEX MARRIAGE

The first time that the lesbian and gay movement publicly put marriage on its agenda was in 1987 at the third national March on Washington for Lesbian and Gay Rights. Couples, Inc., a Los Angeles–based organization fighting for recognition of lesbian and gay couples, organized "The Wedding," a ceremony celebrating gay relationships and demanding that gay partnerships be accorded the same legal rights as married heterosexual couples (Ghaziani 2008). Although several thousand gay and lesbian couples participated in The Wedding, it turned out to be the most controversial event of the march. Critics argued that, despite its campy in-your-face quality, The Wedding promoted traditional relationships and patriarchal family forms that are inconsistent with, even opposed to, the gay lifestyle and signaled a dangerous redirection of the movement toward a more mainstream agenda. The 1987 March also sparked a movement to achieve domestic partnership laws and policies designed to provide some recognition to same-sex couples by employers and local and state governments. Such recognition would result in the achievement of a limited set of benefits for same-sex partners, including health insurance, family leave, and so on (Raeburn 2004). Regardless of whether or not it was considered desirable, LGBT activists believed at the time that same-sex marriage was a political impossibility.

By the early 1990s, almost by accident, same-sex marriage emerged on the lesbian and gay political agenda. Three same-sex couples, with the aid of a private lawyer, sued the state of Hawaii for the right to marry. National lesbian and gay organizations wanted nothing to do with the case, since they believed it had no chance of winning. Despite expectations to the contrary, the *Baehr v. Lewin* decision of 1993 found that denying same-sex couples the right to marry violated equal protection based on sex according to the Hawaii state constitution and remanded the case back to the trial court to determine whether or not it could find a compelling state interest to legitimately deny the right to marry to same-sex couples. National organizations such as the Lambda Legal Defense and Education Fund quickly joined the cause (Andersen 2006).

Hawaii proved to be a catalyst for renewed Religious Right organizing at both the federal and state levels. The result was the passage of the federal Defense of Marriage Act (DOMA) in 1996, which defined marriage as being between one man and one woman, and, in possible violation of the full faith and credit clause of the U.S. Constitution, allowed both states and the federal government to refuse to recognize same-sex marriages performed in other states (Andersen 2006; Bernstein 2001). Since it looked as if same-sex marriage might become lawful in Hawaii, the Hawaii legislature introduced its own DOMA in the form of an amendment to the state constitution that was approved by the voters in 1998 (Andersen 2006). The Religious Right continued to pass an avalanche of state-level DOMAs similarly restricting marriage and precluding the recognition of lesbian and gay relationships. As time went by, these laws became more expansive and even had the effect of overturning existing domestic partnership laws granting benefits to "marriage-like" relationships (Gossett 2009).

In 1999, the Vermont Supreme Court ruled in *Baker v. State of Vermont* that same-sex couples must be granted the same benefits as heterosexual married couples and ordered the legislature to remedy the situation. The result was a compromise that granted all of the benefits of marriage but denied symbolic equality to same-sex relationships by creating a separate term, "civil unions," for same-sex relationships (Bernstein and Naples 2010; chapter 9 herein).

After Vermont, the campaign for same-sex marriage languished nationally until 2003, when the Massachusetts Supreme Judicial Court ruled it unconstitutional to deny same-sex couples the right to marry. The court gave the Massachusetts legislature 180 days to change its laws to provide marriage rights to same-sex couples. Having learned from Vermont, however, the Massachusetts Supreme Judicial Court said that a separate institution, such as civil union, would not be an acceptable remedy. But the legislature deadlocked, and same-sex marriage ultimately went into effect by court order.

Strongly opposing this decision, then-President George W. Bush proposed a constitutional amendment to ban same-sex marriage. This move provoked San Francisco's Democratic mayor, Gavin Newsom, whose constituency comprised large numbers of LGBT people, to direct the City of San Francisco's assessor-recorder's office to begin issuing marriage licenses to same-sex couples. This set off a new wave of protests at marriage counters around the country (see chapters 6 and 8 herein) in which same-sex couples showed up and demanded marriage licenses. The largest of these demonstrations occurred in San Francisco in 2004 (Taylor et al. 2009). Over a month-long period, 4,037 same-sex couples received marriage licenses, waiting in long lines to marry on the steps of San Francisco City Hall, until the marriages were shut down by the California Supreme Court. LGBT organizations joined the American Civil Liberties Union and others to appeal the court's action, and in 2008 the California Supreme Court ruled it unconstitutional to exclude same-sex couples from marriage.

That summer, which came to be known among LGBT activists as the "summer of love," an estimated 18,000 couples married until Proposition 8 passed, banning same-sex marriage in California. During the course of the summer, as gay couples sought visibility and recognition for their partnerships and families by marrying openly across the state, it became evident that the Religious Right's campaign to ban same-sex marriage was gaining ground. Proposition 8, the most highly funded campaign on any state ballot in history, was heavily supported by the Religious Right (see chapter 5 herein). Same-sex couples and even elected California officials, including then-Governor Arnold Schwarzenegger and California Attorney General Jerry Brown, filed numerous lawsuits with the California Supreme Court challenging the proposition's validity and its effect on the same-sex marriages that had occurred prior to the passage of Proposition 8. In 2010, United States District Court Judge Vaughn R. Walker overturned Proposition 8 in *Perry v. Schwarzenegger*. The federal appeals court upheld his ruling in 2012, stating that Proposition 8 "serves no purpose and has no effect, other than to lessen the status and human dignity of gays and lesbians in California, and to officially reclassify their relationships and families as inferior to those of opposite sex couples" (Bessent 2012, 9). Showing just how far the backers of California's same-sex marriage ban will go, they petitioned a federal appeals court to review the decision, but the court declined to reconsider the case. The case will now be heard by the U.S. Supreme Court. The marriages of the more than 18,000 couples who managed to acquire marriage licenses before the court banned same-sex marriage in 2008 still stand. But lesbian and gay citizens of California, the nation's most populous state, do not yet have legal access to marriage, only domestic partnerships authorized by the legislature in 2003.

As of this writing, the lesbian and gay movement has achieved the right to marry for same-sex couples in nine states: Connecticut, Iowa, New Hampshire, Maine, Maryland, Massachusetts, New York, Vermont, and Washington, as well as the District of Columbia. Although six states and the District of Columbia legalized same-sex marriage through court or legislative decisions, Maine, Maryland, and Washington's laws, which passed in 2012, were the first time that marriage for gay men and lesbians was approved by voters at the ballot box. This was a major turning point, since in the thirty-two states in which marriage bans had been previously put to the ballot box, voters had passed them. The only exception was in Arizona in 2006, when voters defeated Proposition 107, a ban on same-sex marriage, by arguing that it would adversely affect heterosexual senior citizens who chose not to marry for fear that it would negatively affect their retirement income (Geis 2006). But in 2008, Arizona voters approved a marriage ban more specifically tailored to target same-sex couples. Forty states have officially banned same-sex marriage through sixty-seven statutes, amendments to state constitutions, or both. But in a stunning turnaround in 2012, a proposed amendment to the state constitution that would have defined marriage as solely between a man and a woman was defeated by Minnesota voters.

Support of same-sex marriage has been stronger among Democrats than Republicans. In 2012, President Barack Obama, who had gone on record opposing gay marriage, finally expressed the belief that same-sex couples should be able to legally marry after Vice President Joseph Biden forced his hand by embracing same-sex unions in a talk show interview. That Obama was reelected on a platform supporting same-sex marriage reflects nothing short of a sea change in public opinion. Previously no presidential candidate who supported same-sex marriage had made it to the primaries. Opponents of same-sex marriage, often backed by right-wing and religious organizations, have frequently targeted Democratic candidates and judges who support same-sex marriage in statewide elections. Recent court actions and the ballot victories won in four states in 2012 suggest that it may be difficult to halt lesbians' and gay men's long slow march to the altar. In 2012, a federal appeals court in Boston declared that the Defense of Marriage Act unconstitutionally denies federal benefits to gay couples, including the ability to file joint tax returns. In the same year, two U.S. district judges in California also ruled that DOMA is unconstitutional because it violates the civil rights of legally married couples, and the Obama administration has indicated that it would no longer defend DOMA in court. The U.S. Supreme Court will hear a challenge to the Federal Defense of Marriage Act in 2013 in addition to the challenge to Proposition 8 (*United States v. Windsor* 2012; *Hollingsworth v. Perry* 2012). The importance of these cases for contouring future marriage rights and marriage-equality activism cannot be underestimated. The wave of state-sanctioned same-sex marriages has led to an increasing emphasis on marriage equality within the LGBT movement, even though many activists have also supported domestic partnership laws, especially those that provide recognition to unmarried heterosexual partners as well as same-sex couples. Public attitudes toward gays and lesbians have shifted so sharply over the past decade that opinion polls consistently report that more than half of Americans believe that being gay is morally acceptable, that gay relations ought to be legal, and that gay and lesbian couples should have the right to legally marry (Powell 2012). It is ironic that, as public opinion is growing more favorable toward same-sex marriage, the LGBT movement's increasing focus on marriage equality has generated even stronger debate from within LGBT communities.

THE END OF QUEERS? A GENEALOGY OF
CONCERN OVER SAME-SEX MARRIAGE

Different intellectual and political traditions within the LGBT movement, along with sociological analyses of the movement, have led to six sets of overlapping arguments about the wisdom of the movement's pursuit of same-sex marriage. Three of the six clusters of overlapping arguments (which we term liberationist, queer, and homonormative) can be characterized as both speculative, in the sense that they raise fears about what might happen if lesbian and gay couples are allowed to marry, and normative, in the sense that they make assessments based on particular sets of values. Feminist and lesbian feminist critiques of marriage, a fourth cluster, are based more concretely on empirical studies that illustrate how marriage systematically disadvantages women. The other two clusters of arguments, "beyond the closet" (Seidman 2003) and "post gay" (Ghaziani 2011), are more sociological in nature, in that they try to assess the extent to which the LGBT movement has moved into a new phase where LGBT identities are no longer dispositive of a movement. We consider the extent to which the politics of same-sex marriage symbolizes such a shift.

Gay Liberation

The late 1960s saw a shift from a more cautious homophile movement that advocated legal and social tolerance for lesbians and gay men to a more radical politics that sought to challenge dominant cultural norms as oppressive. The gay liberation movement that emerged in force in the early 1970s faced an inhospitable political climate and a nearly complete lack of political access (Bernstein 2002). Building on the hippie and free-love movements, gay liberationists sought to challenge dominant cultural norms about gender, sexual identity, and relationship forms (Teal 1971; Marotta 1981).

In the eyes of gay liberationists, relationships, instead of being shackled by the dominant norms of society, presented an opportunity to produce new, more voluntary and egalitarian forms of intimacy. In "A Gay Manifesto," one of the defining statements of the gay liberation movement, Carl Wittman (1970) laid out a cogent argument for why lesbians and gay men should avoid marriage. Wittman discussed the need for alternatives to marriage that recognize a variety of types of intimate relationships:

> People want to get married for lots of good reasons, although marriage won't often meet those needs or desires. We're all looking for security, a flow of love, and a feeling of belonging and being needed. These needs can be met through a number of social relationships and living situations. Things we want to get away from are: 1. exclusiveness, propertied attitudes toward each other, a mutual pact against the rest of the world; 2. promises about the future, which we have no right to make and which prevent us from, or make us feel guilty about, growing; 3. inflexible roles, roles which do not reflect us at the moment but are inherited through mimicry and inability to define equalitarian relationships. We have to define for ourselves a new pluralistic, rolefree [sic] social structure for ourselves. It must contain both the freedom and physical space for people to live alone, live together for a while, live together for a long time, either as couples or in larger numbers; and the ability to flow easily from one of these states to another as our needs change. Liberation for gay people is defining for ourselves how and with whom we live, instead of measuring our relationship in comparison to straight ones, with straight values.

Wittman painted a picture of sexual liberation as fluidity in relationship form, a depriviledging of monogamy, equality between partners with an end to inflexible gender roles, and the development of a new set of values. However, gay liberation was short-lived, and by the mid-1970s had given way to an LGBT politics focused more on obtaining legal and political rights (Bernstein 2002).

Lesbian Feminism

Feminists in the 1970s presented another related set of critiques of marriage, with lesbian feminists at the forefront of the campaign to undermine traditional heterosexual marital relationships (Echols 1989; Taylor and Whittier 1992; Stein 1997). Their foremost argument was that marriage is a patriarchal institution—that is to say, it benefits men. Until the mid-1800s, married women could not own property; any property that a woman owned before marriage became her husband's (Kerber 1998). If a married woman worked, her wages belonged to her husband, and if she divorced, which was not easy, a woman lost the right to her own children. Married men could beat their wives, and there was no such thing as marital rape, since a man owned his wife's body. In more contemporary times, states have cited a right to marital privacy as a justification for not intervening in domestic violence cases (Gagne 1998). Equally abhorrent to feminists is the gendered structure of marriage in which wives and husbands have different duties and privileges and therefore must be "gender opposites." Traditional assumptions about the gender division of labor within marriage are deeply embedded in long-standing practices; for example, most Americans continue to endorse the practice of women taking their husband's name at marriage (Powell et al. 2010) [Although most of the legal inequalities in marriage associated with gender have been overturned, the tax structure and the benefits of the welfare state (including social security) continue to privilege economically heteronormative family structures where one partner works and the other stays at home (Chambers 2001).]

If the gender biases inherent in the legal definition of marriage, at least to some extent, have been redressed, marriage as a social institution and practice continues to disadvantage women in other ways. For example, married women perform more housework and childcare than their husbands, even when they have a full-time job. The salaries of men tend to increase upon marriage, while their wives' salaries and careers often decline. The pay gap between mothers and childless women is actually larger than the pay gap between women and men. Mothers are judged by a harsher standard, which leads to a 'motherhood penalty' in getting hired and being offered a good salary (Correll, Benard, and Paik 2007). Married women also tend to have higher rates of depression, anxiety, and other forms of mental illness and are more likely to commit suicide (Ross, Mirowsky, and Huber 1983; Ross, Mirowsky, and Goldsteen 1990; Taylor 1996). For a long time, scholars believed that women's higher rates of depression were not real but could be explained by women's greater willingness to express their feelings. However, a study by John Mirowsky and Catherine Ross (2003) based on interviews with both women and men helped dispel this myth. They found that married women do, in fact, suffer more symptoms of psychological distress as a result of the stresses associated with trying to combine employment with motherhood, and this finding holds across all racial, ethnic, and class groups. Thus, feminists raise the question as to why same-sex couples would want to enter into an institution with such a negative history, rather than create new forms of intimacy.

Despite strong opposition from gay liberationists and lesbian feminists, LGBT communities were not unanimously opposed to marriage during the 1970s. The gay and lesbian Metropolitan Community Church performed "marriages" for lesbian and gay couples, even though they were not recognized by the law (Chauncey 2004). In the early 1970s, there was a spate of attempts by same-sex couples to file for marriage licenses, and two couples who were denied licenses sued, claiming that their state's laws did not limit marriage to one man and one woman. Nonetheless, the courts simply dismissed these cases, "concluding that marriage could not mean anything else" (Chauncey 2004, 91). Regardless of lesbian and gay feelings about marriage, during the 1970s LGBT people faced such a hostile climate that achieving the legal recognition of same-sex marriage was virtually unthinkable. Although there were isolated attempts by couples and activist groups to gain recognition for same-sex relationships beginning in the 1980s, marriage would not appear on the political agenda of the organized LGBT movement until the 1990s.

Queer Activism

In the late 1980s, queer activism emerged as the heir to the gay liberation movement of the 1970s. Several important events set the stage for the emergence of queer activism. First, the government had neglected the epidemic of acquired immune deficiency syndrome (AIDS) that emerged in the 1980s; AIDS was vilified as a "gay disease," ignored by the government, and received almost no funding (Epstein 1996). In 1980, Ronald Reagan was elected president, ushering in twelve years of Republican rule. During this time, LGBT people were denied political access at the federal level. In 1986, the U.S. Supreme Court ruled in *Bowers v. Hardwick* that there was no constitutional right to privacy for homosexual sodomy to be found in the U.S. Constitution (see Rubenstein 1993). This decision sent a symbolic message to LGBT people that they were inferior to heterosexuals (Bernstein 2003), sparking widespread outrage in LGBT communities and culminating the following year in a national March on Washington (Ghaziani 2008). The decision also shifted the focus of AIDS advocacy from timid tactics and service provision for people with AIDS to a radical politics that challenged heteronormativity as an institution (Gould 2009). Heteronormativity, according to Schilt and Westbrook (2009, 441), is "the suite of cultural, legal, and institutional practices that maintain normative assumptions that there are two and only two genders, that gender reflects biological sex, and that only sexual attraction between 'opposite' genders is natural or acceptable." Activists also began responding to the domination of the LGBT movement by white middle-class gay men and to challenge exclusions based on race, bisexuality, and gender identity (Seidman 1993). As LGBT activists formed new organizations to redress their grievances, they began to reframe the discourse around sexual orientation and to employ new performative tactics, such as drag, kiss-ins, die-ins, and performances of genderqueer identity, that drew on Foucauldian understandings of sexuality and identity to challenge and deconstruct the very categories of identity (gay and straight) that had previously motivated gay activism. Self-proclaimed queer activists sought alliances with people of color, bisexual and transgendered people, and anyone else defined by mainstream discourse as somehow transgressing dominant cultural norms. Debates over queer politics versus gay rights seeped into lesbian and gay communities across the country (Warner 1993; Seidman 1993; Gamson 1995).

Like queer theory, its academic counterpart, queer politics saw the transformative potential of LGBT people not in terms of sheer political and policy gains. Rather, queer activists hold out the hope that queer—which by definition is whatever is at odds with the normal, the legitimate, or the dominant (Halperin 1997, 62)—carves out a space where LGBT people can pose challenges to dominant cultural norms regarding gender identity and practice, create new forms of intimate relationships that overcome the problems associated with traditional marriage, and resist and reject the very categories of sex, gender, and sexual orientation that were used by the mainstream LGBT movement as a basis from which to gain recognition and legal rights.

Queer activists developed a cogent critique of same-sex marriage, echoing both feminist and gay liberationist concerns. In 2006, for example, a new organization of academics and activists calling themselves "BeyondMarriage.org" formed in response to growing dissatisfaction with the emphasis on marriage equality taking hold in the LGBT movement (Hartocollis 2006). Decrying the marriage-equality movement's focus on marriage as a way to obtain rights and benefits (including tax relief, benefit sharing, and inheritance rights), Beyond Marriage.org states on its website that "we believe the LGBT movement should reinforce the idea that marriage should be one of many avenues through which households, families, partners, and kinship relationships can gain access to the support of a caring civil society" (BeyondMarriage.org, 2006). San Francisco's Gay Shame collective is even more outspoken in their "End Marriage" statement:

> What we are calling for is an abolishment of State sanctioned coupling in either the hetero or homo incarnation. We are against any institution that perpetuates the further exploitation of some people for the benefit of others. Why do the fundamental necessities marriage may provide for some (like healthcare) have to be wedded to the State sanctioned ritual of terror known as marriage? (Gay Shame 2009)

Commentators (e.g., Warner 2000; Duggan and Kim 2005; Duggan 2002) outline a host of fears about the problems with the pursuit of same-sex marriage, ranging from charges that marriage is a white, middle-class issue that marginalizes poor queers and LGBT people of color; that same-sex marriage will further marginalize those who choose not to be in marital relations by giving the stamp of normality to "good" gays at the expense of "bad" gays; that same-sex marriage will produce a new "homonormativity" that will sound the death knell of LGBT/queer culture; that same-sex marriage marks the final assimilation of LGBT people into mainstream culture and its most conservative and patriarchal of institutions, marriage; and that same-sex marriage would result in the containment and control of queer sexuality within monogamous, state-sanctioned relationships.

Homonormativity

One of the most vocal queer opponents of same-sex marriage, who represents what we term the "homonormative critique," is Lisa Duggan. In "The New Homonormativity: The Sexual Politics of Neoliberalism" (2002), she raises serious concerns about the long-term implications of same-sex marriage on the LGBT movement itself. Duggan analyzes the meaning of the quest for same-sex marriage by a relatively new gay organization, the Independent Gay Forum (IGF), which seeks a "third way" approach to LGBT politics. The group holds conservatives accountable for their moralizing antigay stance while simultaneously criticizing "'progressive claims that gays should support radical social change or restructuring of society'" (quoted in Duggan 2002, 176). IGF is composed of gay conservatives, such as Andrew Sullivan, who place priority on goals such as same-sex marriage and the right to serve openly in the military. Duggan argues that for LGBT organizations like IGF, "Marriage is a strategy for privatizing gay politics and culture for the new neoliberal world order" (Duggan 2002, 188). She continues:

> The new neoliberal sexual politics of the IGF might be termed the *new homonormativity*—it is a politics that does not contest dominant heteronormative assumptions and institutions but upholds and sustains them while promising the possibility of a demobilized gay constituency and a privatized, depoliticized gay culture anchored in domesticity and consumption (179). . . . There is no vision of a collective, democratic public culture or of an ongoing engagement with contentious, cantankerous queer politics. Instead we have been administered a kind of political sedative—we get marriage and the military[1] then we go home and cook dinner, forever. (189)

Those who hold this position are also highly critical of large mainstream gay and lesbian organizations, especially the Human Rights

Campaign, for emphasizing marriage equality at the expense of what they see as more pressing issues such as health care, transgender discrimination, adoption rights, HIV/AIDS, immigration, and racism. They believe that the fight for same-sex marriage and the new homonormativity associated with pursuing this strategy for achieving equality will leave heteronormative assumptions and institutions intact, will remove homosexuality from the public's eye through promotion of domesticated, private marriage, and ultimately will demobilize the movement. In short, queer critics believe that marriage is much too narrow and confining a status to accommodate the different kinds of families and households and the innovative forms of intimacy, kinship, interconnection, and family that characterize queer communities (Duggan 2012).

Beyond the Closet?

Queer critiques of the marriage-equality movement overlap with scholarly analyses that contend that contemporary lesbian and gay life can be described as "postgay" (Ghaziani 2011) or "beyond the closet" (Seidman 2003; see also Valocchi 1999; Vaid 1995; Ward 2008). Steven Seidman (2003) argues that the "closet" once structured lesbian and gay life. Gay men and lesbians constantly had to monitor and conceal their identity and to negotiate if, when, and how to disclose their sexual identity for fear of repression. Ironically, this state of fear led to the creation of separate lesbian and gay institutions, such as bars, bookstores, churches, bicycle rides, fundraising events, and sports teams that served as "free spaces," or incubators for the creation of lesbian and gay identities and a lesbian and gay political movement. While lesbians and gay men faced the loss of jobs, homes, and family and were subjected to ostracism and violence, the era of the closet was also productive in that it helped to establish a collective identity that served as a basis for political mobilization.

Although Seidman admits that the closet door still remains shut in many parts of the United States, he contends that contemporary gay life has become both normalized and routinized—that is, homosexuality is an integral part of oneself that is accepted and integrated as an ordinary part of routine interactions. Concealment and disclosure, he argues, are no longer primary concerns. But by normalizing homosexuality, a gay identity also becomes decentered, a less significant marker of self. In this way, a gay or lesbian identity and a connection to lesbian and gay communities becomes, according to Seidman, optional, partial, and symbolic. Arlene Stein (1997) has argued, for example, that the meaning of lesbian identity has shifted over the past two decades as young women have found it more acceptable to adopt labels such as queer, genderqueer, and pansexual to signify a variety of more fluid sexual and gender identities. In other words, in the absence of the closet, there is both a decline in the centrality and meaning of gay identity and a privileging of certain ways of organizing intimacies—for example, same-sex marriage—to the exclusion of others. While this position has been most closely associated with queer scholars and espoused in academic writings, many of its advocates are public intellectuals and spokespersons for the movement. As a result, the belief that gay life has moved beyond the closet has been influential in the way radical activists have framed identity and strategy in the LGBT movement (Ghaziani 2008).

Postgay?

The concept "postgay," like "beyond the closet," implies that a gay or lesbian identity may no longer be central to a lesbian or gay person's self-definition. Assimilation into the mainstream and increasing diversification of LGBT communities characterize postgay life. Postgay collective identity construction, then, is less oppositional and confrontational as political struggle in the postgay world becomes secondary, not an assumed aspect of being gay or lesbian. However, this assimilation has only taken place among a segment of the lesbian and gay population, creating a politics that reinforces white, male, gender-conforming middle-class standards of sexuality—in other words, those best positioned to take advantage of the privileges of normalization and assimilation. For example, Bernadette Barton's account of gay life in the "Bible Belt" region of the southern United States reveals that gays continue to be subject to ostracism, hatred, and violence in some parts of the country (Barton 2012). For Bible Belt gays, embracing lesbian and gay identity is a means of overcoming their shame and isolation.

According to Amin Ghaziani (2011), a postgay politics can be characterized as building bridges to the dominant culture. Rather than forging collective identity on the basis of "us versus them," postgay politics emphasizes perceived similarities to the majority, framed as "us and them," muting differences and suppressing what is distinctive about gay identity (Bernstein 1997). The use of postgay-identity claims to justify the campaign for same-sex marriage is reflected in the words of one of the activists who initiated the court case that resulted in the California Supreme Court's March 2008 decision to open access to same-sex marriage prior to the passage of Proposition 8: "With this ruling, in the eyes of the government, my family is finally normal." In the postgay context, LGBT organizations have the potential to become privatized and depoliticized social groups, rather than political groups based in shared and distinct oppositional identities.

THE TROUBLE WITH MARRIAGE

These anxieties over the direction of LGBT politics are most pronounced in debates over the wisdom of pursuing same-sex marriage and its possible effects on the movement, LGBT communities, and LGBT individuals. Within LGBT communities, the marriage-equality movement has become a flashpoint for concerns about the future of LGBT culture, communities, and politics. While for some, marriage is a simple matter of equality and a sign of progress toward achieving that goal, for others, it is an alarm signaling the death of what makes queer people unique. The concerns over same-sex marriage expressed by lesbian and gay activists can be condensed into three main arguments that we term "normalization," "decentering and privatizing lesbian and gay identity," and "misguided energy." We discuss each of these in turn and draw on the chapters in this book to assess the validity of these concerns. To what extent does the campaign for same-sex marriage represent a broader shift in the meaning of lesbian and gay identity and in the goals and direction of the LGBT movement in the United States?

Normalization

There are multiple fears among LGBT activists associated with the charge that the marriage-equality movement uses strategies and tactics designed to represent same-sex couples as basically the same as heterosexual couples. For gay liberationists, lesbian feminists, and queer critics, marriage will reproduce traditional gender roles and hierarchy within marriage and continue to privilege monogamy. Underlying these concerns is the fear that these strategies will lead to the assimilation of LGBT culture into the mainstream, resulting in the disappearance of LGBT culture and identity altogether (e.g., Ettelbrick 1989). Furthermore, critics charge that such strategies benefit couples who are "homonormative" (Duggan 2002) but will further marginalize those who are already marginal to the movement, such as the working class, people of color, or those who prefer other forms of intimacy (Warner 2000).

In chapter 8, Katrina Kimport challenges this position by demonstrating that same-sex marriages do in fact disrupt heteronormativity. Drawing on Mary Bernstein (2001), who argues that the inherently sexual nature of marriage challenges heteronormativity by foregrounding the (same-sex) marital couple as sexual, Kimport reveals how the wedding pictures of lesbians who married in San Francisco when Mayor Gavin Newsom defied California law and allowed marriages for same-sex couples challenge heteronormativity. Specifically, she argues that wedding pictures force the onlooker to read the couple as a *sexual* couple, linked to each other. These images of lesbian couples challenge deeply held assumptions about normative sex, gender, and sexuality, mixing up and questioning the meanings of the ritual and institution of marriage. In chapter 1, Arlene Stein argues that, at least for middle-class same-sex couples living in the suburbs, same-sex marriage implies a commitment to non-normative sexuality and forces people to be out in multiple areas of their lives.

In chapter 11, Adam Isaiah Green draws on interviews with same-sex couples who have been legally married in Canada to assess the impact of marriage on their relationships. Rather than the dire, normalizing outcomes predicted by both social conservatives and queer critics of same-sex marriage, Green finds that same-sex married couples have not assimilated into homonormatively structured forms of marriage. Rather, Green finds a complex mix of marital forms. On the one hand, marriage strengthens the couple dyad for same-sex married couples, facilitates parenting, and generates broad community support for relationships. On the other hand, same-sex married couples challenge and subvert contemporary marital norms such as monogamy and the gendered division of labor that characterizes most marital relations. Green finds that, especially for gay male couples, marriage provides a framework of safety and trust in relationships that, for many, facilitates the development of open, less monogamous relationships. Relationships among same-sex couples are also more egalitarian and negotiated according to the needs of the couples. In fact, these married same-sex couples seem to be creating their own rules for their marriages, much as Wittman (1970) called for more than four decades ago. Green argues that practices that challenge the conventions of marriage are the result of gay couples' connections to queer constitutive communities that interrogate and reconfigure conventional relationship forms, rather than take them for granted. However, Green also cautions that as same-sex marriage becomes increasingly accepted, both socially and legally, younger same-sex couples may lack a connection to a queer tradition that inspires creativity in relationships. As a result, future generations may indeed become homonormative.

In chapter 9, Mary Bernstein and Mary C. Burke argue that cultural representations of and discourse about gay marriage in mainstream and LGBT newspapers is one way to gauge the extent to which normalization has been an outcome of the marriage-equality movement. They demonstrate that the marriage-equality movement in Vermont and the *Baker v. State of Vermont* decision that resulted in civil unions opened up space for a critical discussion of marriage as an institution. They find that willingness to engage with queer ideas in Vermont newspapers depended on the standing given to same-sex marriage opponents. Because *Baker* did not mandate marriage, but instead called on the Vermont state legislature to provide equal benefits to same-sex and different-sex couples, the ruling (however unintended) granted standing to queer positions on gay marriage. Yet Bernstein and Burke make clear that, although normalizing arguments predominated in mainstream newspapers, marriage-equality activism was ultimately responsible for making the public aware of the criticisms that have been leveled against marriage by LGBT activists.

In chapter 3, Jeffrey Kosbie argues that for many marriage-equality activists, the extent of opposition along with the passion of opponents means that same-sex marriage must pose a fundamental challenge to heteronormativity. Kosbie examines the ways in which the meaning of marriage is constructed by MassEquality, the social-movement organization behind the campaign to protect marriage equality after it was legalized by the *Goodridge v. Department of Public Health* decision in Massachusetts. He finds that MassEquality defined same-sex marriage as a "battleground" issue that was important not because it represented the assimilation of same-sex couples into the mainstream, but because it garnered significant opposition among the general public. Similarly, Amy L. Stone, in chapter 4, finds that the Christian Right has developed anti-same-sex marriage discourse that appeals not just to conservative voters, but also to liberal and undecided voters. While same-sex marriage may seem to some like assimilation, the strong opposition it has generated suggests that it continues to challenge dominant cultural norms. Lisa Duggan and Richard Kim (2005) suggest that part of the challenge of same-sex marriage and part of the success of groups opposed to same-sex marriage arise from a generalized anxiety that results from neoliberal economic policies that have divested the state of its responsibilities for providing economic support for individuals, families, and the poor, while simultaneously viewing marriage as the panacea for poverty, a lack of health care, and declining pensions. It may very well be that opposition to same-sex marriage is as much if not more a response to economic insecurity than to homophobia.

The essays in this volume suggest that the same-sex marriage movement has had a variety of impacts that are not normalizing. By signifying the marital couple as a sexual couple, same-sex couples make visible lesbian and gay sexuality, thus challenging heteronormativity. Married same-sex couples create a whole host of different types of relationships that are reminiscent of the variety that Wittman called for in 1970. So, rather than thoughtlessly aping dominant monogamous, nonegalitarian heterosexual marital relationships, same-sex couples are creating a variety of types of relationships. Finally, the marriage-equality movement has opened up an important discursive space for a discussion of the pros and cons of marriage and for a public recognition that marriage does not provide the only blueprint for intimate relationships.

Decentering and Privatizing Lesbian and Gay Identity

Related to the charge that the marriage-equality movement is normalizing and assimilationist is the allegation that fighting for same-sex marriage will decenter a lesbian and gay identity and that this may have a deleterious impact on LGBT political organizing, culture, and communities. For example, Ghaziani (2011) argues that a postgay sensibility motivates how college LGBT organizations name themselves. Because there is no longer an "us versus them" mentality, LGBT college groups struggle to be inclusive of everyone, including LGBT people, queer and questioning people, people of color, and so on. As a result, such organizations adopt generic names such as the "Pride Alliance," devoid of any but an oblique association with homosexuality. The same-sex marriage movement frequently has adopted similar naming practices; consider, for example, LGBT activists' decision to name one of the key social-movement organizations in California "Equality California." Yet groups who eschew the use of "gay" in their organizational titles, such as "Join The Impact," "Courage Campaign," and "GetEQUAL," often employ radical in-your-face tactics in their struggle for same-sex marriage and other social justice goals. Certainly, not everyone agrees that we have moved into a postgay period. Separate gay institutions, such as bars, coffeehouses, and clubs, which have historically been central to the mobilization of lesbian and gay activism (D'Emilio 1983), remain vibrant and active in most regions of the country, belying the decline of gay culture and community. Is same-sex marriage another move toward decentering a lesbian and gay identity, with the implication that it spells the beginning of the end of the LGBT movement? Duggan (2002) raises a serious question as to whether the movement more generally is becoming depoliticized and privatized as it becomes increasingly assimilated through pursuing the normalizing goal of same-sex marriage.

The term "privatizing" can be understood in several ways: First, marriage privatizes many of the economic functions of the state, such as providing health-care services for the elderly, and promoting marriage has often been a substitute for providing welfare to the poor (Heath 2012). This is undeniably the case in the contemporary U.S.

context, where there has been a heated political debate over health-care access and reform. Second, Lisa Duggan (2002), Michael Warner (2000), Nancy Cott (2000), and others argue that romantic notions of love currently associated with marriage reinforce the belief that marriage is a private act by concealing the fact that married people have greater access to citizenship rights than those who are unmarried, thus making marriage a public institution that is exclusionary, with profound civic implications. Finally, Duggan is also concerned that same-sex marriage will privatize LGBT people behind a white picket fence, where they no longer present a challenge to heteronormativity.

Is same-sex marriage activism ultimately depoliticizing and privatizing, in the sense that it will render lesbian and gay life invisible and lesbian and gay politics inactive? What is the relationship between activism around same-sex marriage and lesbian and gay identities? Chapters 3 and 10 examine this relationship at the organizational level, while chapters 6 and 7 examine these issues at the individual level. In chapters 3 and 10, Jeffrey Kosbie and Kristine A. Olsen, respectively, argue that the political and cultural context in which same-sex marriage activism takes place influences how activists view same-sex marriage and whether or not its achievement will be demobilizing or mobilizing. In chapter 10, Olsen examines why Connecticut's highly successful marriage-equality organization, Love Makes a Family (LMF), decided to close its doors after the 2008 *Kerrigan v. Commissioner of Public Health* ruling made Connecticut the second state to legalize same-sex marriage. Olsen argues that the exclusive collective identity of LMF equated same-sex marriage with complete equality for gay men and lesbians. The closing of LMF reflects the worst fears of queer critics and others who argue that the achievement of same-sex marriage will signal an end of the LGBT movement. In contrast, and perhaps counterintuitively, Kosbie finds that many MassEquality activists were critical of the institution of marriage, yet continued to fight to protect same-sex marriage because the opposition had turned it into a battleground issue and because of its constitutional implications. In other words, activists did not view same-sex marriage as the final marker of equality for LGBT people. As a result, MassEquality continued to thrive, even after the passage of same-sex marriage. Taken together, these chapters suggest that there are multiple ways to construct the meaning of same-sex marriage and that this will influence the potential for both organizations and the movement to address other issues besides marriage. If LGBT organizations view same-sex marriage as the ultimate solution to inequality, then its achievement will indeed be demobilizing. However, in cases where activist organizations have pursued same-sex marriage but have not treated it as the ultimate movement goal, winning same-sex marriage has not led to organizational decline.

In chapter 6, Verta Taylor, Katrina Kimport, Nella Van Dyke, and Ellen Ann Andersen draw on interviews and a random survey of couples who married in San Francisco when Mayor Gavin Newsom defied California's Defense of Marriage Act (Proposition 22) by ordering the city clerk to issue marriage licenses to same-sex couples to examine the impact of marriage-equality activism on activists themselves. Their study shows that the lesbian and gay couples who participated in this event viewed their weddings as acts of civil disobedience and that two-thirds remained active in the marriage-equality movement two-and-a-half years after the San Francisco demonstration. Taylor and her collaborators demonstrate how the solidarity and collective identity created among participants sparked court action and other forms of collective action geared toward policy change. This study also provides empirical evidence about whether or not the campaign for marriage has had a deleterious effect on the LGBT movement as a whole by diverting resources away from other movement goals. In a sample that reported very high rates of participation in a broad spectrum of social movements, less than half of the approximately 8,000 individuals who married during the "month of marriages" in San Francisco indicated that they had channeled their activism away from other causes, such as LGBT and women's rights, to focus primarily on marriage equality. So rather than demobilizing, marrying made these couples significantly more political than they had been before, as well as more visible.

In chapter 7, Melanie Heath turns our attention to couples who traveled across the United States to participate in the historic San Francisco wedding protest. These couples came from Oklahoma, unquestionably one of the most politically and religiously conservative states in the Bible Belt, with a long history of legislating against lesbians and gay men. She examines the deeply personal stories of these couples, who struggle on a day-to-day basis to survive in such a hostile environment. She finds that rather than using marriage as a way to assimilate into dominant heterosexual culture, lesbian and gay couples viewed marrying as a political act to resist conservative backlash and discrimination in an environment that is decidedly not postgay. For the couples discussed in both chapters 6 and 7, choosing to marry was anything but a private decision to trade tolerance for marital privacy. Instead, marrying actually made these couples more active and more public about their identities and relationships, even in environments where simply being out was a challenge to heteronormativity. However, Heath also points out that the marriage-equality movement that began in other states may have harmed LGBT people in Oklahoma more than helped them, since it sparked a strong countermovement that the LGBT movement was not in a position to resist.

Katie Oliviero argues in chapter 5 that much of the opposition to marriage comes from the conservative view that marriage *is* a public institution that is under threat. She shows that the opponents of same-sex marriage share with supporters the insistence that marriage is not simply a private act between two people. Analyzing the campaign for Proposition 8 in California, she suggests that the Protect Marriage Coalition defeated marriage-equality activists by framing "marriage as an exceptional relationship endowed with special governmental rights to promote conservative social responsibilities and public morals." Ironically, defenders of traditional marriage mimicked the performative tactics used by LGBT activists—including staging public weddings—with the goal, however, of depicting same-sex marriage as a threat to traditional American values. Once again, the strong opposition to same-sex marriage played out in California since 2008 points to the threat that it holds to heteronormativity.

Whether or not the goal of marriage equality promotes or inhibits mobilization depends on how the meaning of marriage is constructed. In two liberal Northeastern states, Massachusetts and Connecticut, attaining marriage equality has had very different implications for social-movement organizations, stemming from the ways in which the meaning of marriage was constructed within the organization and by the opposition. These two campaigns demonstrate that it is far from certain that marriage will function as a political sedative for LGBT people. Same-sex couples who married knowing those unions might not be legally sanctioned if their marriages got struck down were more politicized after they were married and became more visible and more active. While increased social acceptance may be making a lesbian or gay identity less consequential and less salient as a central aspect of the self than in the past, same-sex marriage may be more a symptom than a cause of this change. And the fight for marriage equality may have politicizing effects, at least in the short term, while at the same time having disparate meaning and disparate impact on activist organizations depending on the local political context and on local constructions of meaning.

Misguided Energy

Embedded in the critique that the marriage-equality movement normalizes and depoliticizes by decentering and privatizing lesbian and gay identities within marriage is the view that in pursuing same-sex marriage, activists are focusing energy on the wrong issue. Some critics argue that marriage will primarily benefit those who already have the most, namely, white middle-class gay men (Warner 2000; Duggan 2002). Others argue that activist energy would be better spent pursuing the legal recognition of a variety of family forms, including unmarried partners (whether or not they are romantically attached) who care for each other and/or their children, and nonspousal relatives (including siblings) who together care for parents and children (Ettelbrick 1989; Duggan and Kim 2005; Wittman 1970; Warner 2000).

In chapter 2, Kathleen E. Hull and Timothy A. Ortyl examine whether LGBT people support the movement's focus on the right to marry in order to respond to critics' claims that the movement should not be advocating for marriage, but rather for civil unions or other forms of legal recognition that maintain the tangible benefits of marriage. This chapter also examines whether the focus on marriage has resulted in the "secondary marginalization" (Cohen 1999) of poor queers, queers of color, and bisexual and transgender people. Through in-depth interviews with LGBT community members, Hull and Ortyl argue that the situation is more complicated than the queer critique suggests. They find substantial support among lesbian and gay constituents for the movement's broad goals, including the focus on marriage and family concerns. Genderqueer and transgender people are slightly more critical of the movement's focus on marriage. Those who identified as gender transgressors also had higher educational levels than the general population, suggesting that they are more elite, countering the queer critique that marriage is predominantly of interest to white, middle-class people. Still others consider the LGBT movement's strategies as either too radical or too timid, leading to a sense of exclusion. But this sense of exclusion does not stem from the movement's focus on marriage, as queer theorists have suggested.

Arlene Stein raises the question in chapter 1 about whether or not the pursuit and achievement of same-sex marriage will benefit poor people, especially poor people of color, to the same extent that it will benefit middle-class people living in the suburbs (a separate question from who desires the right to marry). Comparing two cities—Newark, New Jersey, a low-income, predominantly black city, and Maplewood, New Jersey, an ethnically diverse middle-class suburb—Stein argues that poor people often produce different family formations that would not be served by same-sex marriage. Furthermore, she illustrates that demographically, LGBT people in Newark are less likely to benefit from marriage, since statistically they are less likely to get married. When they do marry, their marriages are less likely to last, although some scholars have argued that marriage might conceivably be a benefit in those cases by providing access to divorce (e.g., Andersen 2009).

Stein also argues that the LGBT movement's focus on marriage takes away energy from movement initiatives and tactics geared toward supporting other family forms. Duggan and Kim (2005) acknowledge that the pursuit of same-sex marriage has produced legal recognition for a variety of household forms, including domestic partnerships, unmarried cohabiting couples (straight or gay), and other forms of families and households capable of providing care and nurturance to their members (see also Bernstein and Naples 2010; Gossett 2009). They take issue with the fact that the LGBT movement now sees those as poor substitutes for marriage, arguing that the movement should, instead,

broaden its membership to include progressives who support legal recognition of a variety of household types. As Bernstein and Burke argue
in chapter 9, the marriage-equality movement has sparked conversations that question the sacred place of marriage in U.S. culture. In Arizona, the state's proposed Defense of Marriage Act in 2006 would have
taken away any legal rights granted to unmarried heterosexual partners
through civil unions and domestic partnerships. The LGBT movement
in Arizona was able to garner enough support to defeat this bill because
activists were able to broaden their plea to a defense of the rights of
all unmarried couples, not just the rights of same-sex couples (Geis
2006). However, in 2008, Arizona passed by referendum a more narrow
constitutional amendment that defined marriage as a union between
one man and one woman but did not take rights away from unmarried heterosexual couples.[2] For the most part, however, LGBT support
for broader forms of relationship recognition are not foremost on the
LGBT political agenda, and the Religious Right has, until the 2012
election, defined the agenda when it comes to referenda on same-sex
marriage (Fetner 2008). Mary Bernstein and Nancy A. Naples (2010)
argue that the LGBT movement's lack of emphasis on pursuing recognition of broad forms of relationships is largely due to the opposition's
effort to symbolically devalue LGBT relationships by grouping them
with other types of relationships that cannot be legally recognized,
such as two unmarried sisters who live together who want legal protection (see also Gossett 2009). Strategically, marriage-equality opponents
put forward proposals to recognize a variety of different relationships,
including same-sex couples, while simultaneously advocating to deny
same-sex couples the right to marry. Pursuing these alternatives to civil
marriage ironically aligns LGBT activists with those who seek to de-
prive same-sex couples of the symbolic significance of marriage.

Furthermore, many same-sex couples want the same social and
legal support for their relationships that heterosexual married couples receive. Given the importance of marriage in the U.S. context[3]
and the Religious Right's sustained efforts to deny rights and recognition to same-sex couples, we think it is unlikely that the LGBT
movement in the United States will be at the forefront of such a broad
progressive movement. Therefore, the same-sex marriage movement's

pursuit of marriage equality may reproduce legal exclusions while simultaneously, and perhaps unintentionally, opening the door both legally and socially to recognizing a variety of relationship forms.

The argument that the LGBT movement should fight to recognize a variety of relationship forms has also been used against the LGBT movement. For example, as Stone (chapter 4) and Oliviero (chapter 5) contend, marriage-equality opponents have argued that as long as same-sex couples have the same legal benefits as heterosexual couples—for example, in the form of domestic partnerships or civil unions—then it is all right to deny them the right to marry. In the recent court case on Proposition 8 (*Perry v. Schwarzenegger* 2010), expert witness and historian George Chauncey was asked multiple questions about whether same-sex couples needed the benefits of marriage and whether or not lesbians and gay men actually supported marriage given California's domestic partnership laws.

Whether or not one thinks that the LGBT movement should place so much energy in pursuing same-sex marriage is of course a matter of personal opinion. But it appears that the focus on marriage itself is generally supported across LGBT communities. However, the achievement of marriage may not benefit all groups within LGBT communities to the same extent. Furthermore, the marriage-equality movement itself has led to the recognition of a variety of types of relationships, although these were not always the goal of the movement but rather a result of a complex mix of dynamics between opponents and proponents. It is unlikely that the LGBT movement in the United States will spearhead a broad-based movement for diverse forms of relationship recognition as its ultimate goal.

CONCLUSION

By the time this book is published, undoubtedly another state will have become the latest flashpoint in the culture war over gay civil rights. The 2012 elections were a milestone at which the LGBT movement experienced ballot victories in four states. It seems likely that advocates of same-sex marriage rights will push legislatures in at least half a dozen other states toward legalization in the near future, at the same time that they press their cause in federal courts. A rapid shift in public opinion favoring same-sex marriage is bolstering the movement, as more and more people in the United States grow accustomed to the idea of same-sex marriage and become personally acquainted with openly gay people, couples, and families. Most advocates of marriage equality, nevertheless, believe that broad national change is most likely to happen through the courts, and the U.S. Supreme Court will decide on the constitutionality of both DOMA and Proposition 8 in 2013. But perhaps the most important outcome of the 2012 elections is symbolic: the discovery that the fear and confusion over the changing definition of marriage used by right-wing, religious, and other opponents of same-sex marriage did not seem to work this time around. In prior elections, Republican strategists have often used state ballot initiatives to turn out the conservative vote for the party, yet this strategy failed to achieve the desired results in 2012.

What does all of this mean for the future of the LGBT movement? Is the pursuit of same-sex marriage an indicator that we find ourselves in a postgay world? Have LGBT people forsaken their uniqueness in favor of assimilation and normalization? Are they pursuing a goal that will signify the end of the LGBT movement, communities, and culture? Are those who choose not to be in long-term monogamous marital relationships going to be left behind?

In this introduction, we have argued that the consequences of same-sex marriage and of the marriage-equality movement are far more complex and challenging than queer critics fear. Same-sex married couples make their sexuality visible and organize their intimate lives in a variety of ways, some more normative and others less so. There can be little question that the institution of marriage was changed when gay people earned the right to marry, even if, as Lee Badgett (2009) argues, "the evidence from around the world suggests that marriage changes gay people more than gay people change marriage." The extent of opposition to same-sex marriage and the sustained attempt of opponents to preserve marriage as a "timeless, universal, unique union between husband and wife" (Bolton and Fernandez 2012, 6) is a testament to the fundamental challenge that gay marriage presents to the cherished beliefs of many. The claim of queer activists that achieving the right to marry will exclude those who are not in such relationships is certainly correct legally, but socially it assumes that all heterosexuals have similar lifestyles. Given high rates of divorce, remarriage, living alone, the development of polyamorous communities, and so on, it is clear that there is not one heterosexuality and that the law itself has not kept heterosexuals from forming a variety of types of relationships, many of which are anything but heteronormative. In fact, legal scholar Mary Ann Glendon (1997) argues that the law generally lags behind the ways that people actually organize their intimate lives, including whom they call family. So it may be that in allowing same-sex marriage, the law is simply catching up to how some same-sex couples are organizing their lives and to the changing meaning of gay identity and community.

It seems fitting to conclude by asking the question that led us to this project in the first place: how might the debate among LGBT activists over the merits of pursuing marriage be affecting movement success? Disagreement and conflict in any movement is generally about what sort of politics people should promote and who the "we" is on behalf of whom activists claim to speak. As we have suggested, there remains much disagreement among LGBT people about movement goals and strategies and where the movement as a whole is headed. Some of the chapters in this book (e.g., chapters 4 and 7) suggest that internal debates among activists may be weakening the campaign for equality in states where the antigay opposition has greater organizational strength and political support. Others (chapters 6 and 8) demonstrate how debates over strategy and tactics (for example, the use of institutional strategies such as court action and electoral politics as opposed to civil disobedience, new media, and other forms of direct action) often lead to the formation of new social-movement organizations, resulting in the deployment of a larger and more varied battery of tactics and strategies.

We also learn that activists use conflict and dissent to come to terms with their commonalities and connectedness, as well as to understand their differences and to establish boundaries between "us" and "them." As Ghaziani (2008) has shown, movement infighting has played a critical role in defining and redefining gay identity over the past several decades. But as Kosbie reveals in his analysis of the marriage-equality movement in Massachusetts (chapter 3), identity differences and disputes can sometimes be overcome through participation in a common struggle, even if activists' initial motivations for participating were very different.

Although there is little consensus among scholars or activists about how to measure the success or failure of a social movement, we contend that the essays in this book provide insight into the role that lesbian and gay activists and the marriage-equality movement specifically have played in moving public opinion so dramatically and so rapidly on this issue in such a short period of time. After the passage of Proposition 8 in California, LGBT activists increasingly advocated "coming out" as a strategy to educate friends, neighbors, work associates, families, and the general public about the personal costs to their families, particularly children, of being denied the right to marry, as well as to criticize the social and economic injustices written into marriage law (see chapters 5 and 7, Barton 2012; and Kimport forthcoming). Visibility politics may have limited success as a strategy for winning policy gains and ameliorating fundamental structural and economic injustices (Whittier 2009). But the shift in public opinion on the issue of same-sex marriage in such a short period of time clearly suggests that, as lesbian and gay individuals and couples have come out to friends and strangers in the long march to marriage equality, they have changed the hearts and minds of others.

It remains to be seen where the movement for marriage equality is headed. But there is little question that the battle for and against same-sex marriage will continue to be waged in states across the United States, and that the U.S. Supreme Court will ultimately rule on whether or not bans on same-sex marriage are constitutional, as well as on whether states without same-sex marriage will be forced to recognize such unions performed in states where it is legal. The essays in this volume shed light, however, on a much larger debate that has long been waged in lesbian and gay communities about the benefits and costs of greater inclusion in society. Marriage undoubtedly will remain a contested issue as the lesbian and gay movement continues the long march to equality. The future of the movement will depend, at least in part, on how activists themselves respond as public support for the right of lesbians and gays to marry grows and conservative opponents find that their scare tactics are falling short.

NOTES

1. At the time, the military could still expel lesbians and gay men under the "Don't Ask, Don't Tell" policy that has since been repealed (Bernstein 2011).
2. Arizona State Legislature, Senate Concurrent Resolution 1042 (2008). http://www.azleg.gov//FormatDocument.asp?inDoc=/legtext/48leg/2r/bills/scr1042h.htm&Session_ID=86.
3. Cross-national evidence from Australia (Bernstein and Naples 2010), Canada (Smith 2008), and Denmark (Eskridge and Spedale 2006) suggests that marriage is a less significant marker of status in those countries than it is in the United States.

REFERENCES

Andersen, Ellen Ann. 2006. *Out of the Closets and into the Courts: Legal Opportunity Structure and Gay Rights Legislation.* Ann Arbor: University of Michisgan Press.
———. 2009. "The Gay Divorcée: The Case of the Missing Argument." In *Queer Mobilizations: LGBT Activists Confront the Law,* edited by Scott Barclay, Mary Bernstein, and Anna-Maria Marshall, 281–302. New York: New York University Press.
Badgett, M. V. Lee. 2009. *When Gay People Get Married: What Happens When Societies Legalize Same-Sex Marriage.* New York: New York University Press.
Barton, Bernadette. 2012. *Pray the Gay Away.* New York: New York University Press.
Bernstein, Mary. 1997. "Celebration and Suppression: The Strategic Uses of Identity by the Lesbian and Gay Movement." *American Journal of Sociology* 103 (3): 531–65.
———. 2001. "Gender, Queer Family Policies, and the Limits of the Law." In *Queer Families, Queer Politics: Challenging Culture and the State,* edited by Mary Bernstein and Renate Reimann, 420–46. New York: Columbia University Press.
———. 2002. "The Contradictions of Gay Ethnicity: Forging Identity in Vermont." In *Social Movements: Identity, Culture, and the State,* edited by David S. Meyer, Nancy Whittier, and Belinda Robnett, 85–104. New York: Oxford University Press.
———. 2003. "Nothing Ventured, Nothing Gained? Conceptualizing Social Movement 'Success' in the Lesbian and Gay Movement." *Sociological Perspectives* 46 (3): 353–79.
———. 2011. "United States: Multi-Institutional Politics, Social Movements and the State." In *The Lesbian and Gay Movement and the State: Comparative Insights into a Transformed Relationship,* edited by Carol Johnson, David Paternotte, and Manon Tremblay, 197–212. Burlington: Ashgate Publishing Ltd.
Bernstein, Mary, and Nancy A. Naples. 2010. "Sexual Citizenship and the Pursuit of Relationship Recognition Policies in Australia and the U.S." *Women's Studies Quarterly* 38 (1–2): 132–56.
Bessent, Alvin. 2012. "Proposition 8 Win Feels Like a Step Back." *Santa Barbara News-Press,* February 15, A-9.
BeyondMarriage.org. 2006. "Beyond Same-Sex Marriage: A New Strategic Vision for All Our Families and Relationships." http://www.beyondmarriage.org/full_statement.html.
Bolton, Carolyn, and Sonia Fernandez. 2012. "Federal Appeals Court Rules Proposition 8 Unconstitutional." *Santa Barbara News-Press,* February 8.

Chambers, David L. 2001. "'What If?' The Legal Consequences of Marriage and the Legal Needs of Lesbian and Gay Male Couples." In *Queer Families, Queer Politics: Challenging Culture and the State*, edited by Mary Bernstein and Renate Reimann, 306–37. New York: Columbia University Press.

Chauncey, George. 2004. *Why Marriage? The History Shaping Today's Debate over Gay Equality*. New York: Basic Books.

Cohen, Cathy J. 1999. *The Boundaries of Blackness: AIDS and the Breakdown of Black Politics*. Chicago: University of Chicago Press.

Correll, Shelley, Stephen Benard, and In Paik. 2007. "Getting a Job: Is There a Motherhood Penalty?" *American Journal of Sociology* 112: 1297–338.

Cott, Nancy. 2000. *Public Vows: A History of Marriage and the Nation*. Cambridge, Mass.: Harvard University Press.

D'Emilio, John. 1983. "Capitalism and Gay Identity." In *Powers of Desire: The Politics of Sexuality*, edited by Ann Snitow, Christine Stansell, and Sharon Thompson, 100–113. New York: Monthly Review Press.

Duggan, Lisa. 2002. "The New Homonormativity: The Sexual Politics of Neoliberalism." In *Materializing Democracy: Toward a Revitalized Cultural Politics*, edited by Russ Castronovo and Dana Nelson, 175–94. Durham, N.C.: Duke University Press.

———. 2012. "Beyond Marriage: Democracy, Equality, and Kinship for a New Century." *The Scholar and Feminist Online* 10 (Fall/Spring). http://sfonline.barnard.edu/a-new-queer-agenda/.

Duggan, Lisa, and Richard Kim. 2005. "Beyond Gay Marriage." *The Nation*, July 28. http://www.thenation.com/doc/20050718/kim.

Echols, Alice. 1989. *Daring to Be Bad: Radical Feminism in America 1967–1975*. Minneapolis: University of Minnesota Press.

Epstein, Steven. 1996. *Impure Science: AIDS, Activism, and the Politics of Knowledge*. Berkeley: University of California Press.

Eskridge, William Jr., and Darren Spedale. 2006. *Gay Marriage: For Better or for Worse? What We've Learned from the Evidence*. Oxford: Oxford University Press.

Ettelbrick, Paula. 1989. "Since When Is Marriage a Path to Liberation?" *Out/Look* 6: 9.

Fetner, Tina. 2008. *How the Religious Right Shaped Lesbian and Gay Activism*. Minneapolis: University of Minnesota Press.

Gagne, Patricia. 1998. *Battered Women's Justice: The Movement for Clemency and the Politics of Self-Defense*. New York: Twayne.

Gamson, Joshua. 1995. "Must Identity Movements Self-Destruct? A Queer Dilemma." *Social Problems* 42 (3): 390–407.

Gay Shame. 2009. "End Marriage." www.gayshamesf.org/endmarriage.

Geis, Sonya. 2006. "New Tactic in Fighting Marriage Initiatives." *The Washington Post*, November 20. http://www.washingtonpost.com/wp-dyn/content/article/2006/11/19/AR2006111901168.html.

Ghaziani, Amin. 2008. *The Dividends of Dissent: How Conflict and Culture Work in Lesbian and Gay Marches on Washington*. Chicago: University of Chicago Press.

———. 2011. "Post-Gay Collective Identity Construction." *Social Problems* 58 (1): 99–125.

Glendon, Mary Ann. 1997. *The Transformation of Family Law: State, Law, and Family in the United States and Western Europe*. Chicago: University of Chicago Press.

Gossett, Charles W. 2009. "Pushing the Envelope: Dillon's Rule and Local Domestic Partnership Ordinances." In *Queer Mobilizations: LGBT Activists Confront the Law*, edited by Scott Barclay, Mary Bernstein, and Anna-Maria Marshall, 158–86. New York: New York University Press.

Gould, Deborah B. 2009. *Moving Politics: Emotion and ACT UP's Fight against AIDS*. Chicago: University of Chicago Press.

Halperin, David. 1997. *Saint Foucault: Towards a Gay Hagiography*. New York: Oxford University Press.

Hartocollis, Anemona. 2006. "For Some Gays, a Right They Can Forsake." *New York Times*, July 30. http://www.nytimes.com/2006/07/30/fashion/sundaystyles/30 MARRIAGE.html?scp=2&sq=%22For+Some+Gays%2C+A+Right+They+Can+ Forsake%22&st=nyt.

Heath, Melanie. 2012. *One Marriage under God: The Campaign to Promote Marriage in America*. New York: New York University Press.

Kerber, Linda K. 1998. *No Constitutional Right to Be Ladies: Women and the Obligations of Citizenship*. New York: Hill and Wang.

Kimport, Katrina. Forthcoming. *Queering Marriage*. New Brunswick, N.J.: Rutgers University Press.

Marotta, Toby. 1981. *The Politics of Homosexuality*. Boston: Houghton Mifflin.

Mirowsky, John, and Catherine E. Ross. 2003. *The Social Causes of Psychological Distress*. New York: Walter de Gruyter.

Perry v. Schwarzenegger. 2010. 704 F.Supp. 2d 921.

Powell, Brian. 2012. "Counted Out: Same-Sex Relations and Americans' Definitions of Family." Paper presented at the University of California, Santa Barbara.

Powell, Brian, Catherine Bolzendahl, Claudia Geist, and Lala Carr Steelman. 2010. *Counted Out: Same-Sex Relationships and Americans' Definition of Family*. New York: Russell Sage Foundation.

Raeburn, Nicole. 2004. *Changing Corporate America from Inside Out: Lesbian and Gay Workplace Rights*. Minneapolis: University of Minnesota Press.

Ross, Catherine E., John Mirowsky, and Karen Goldsteen. 1990. "The Impact of the Family on Health: The Decade in Review." *Journal of Marriage and the Family* 52: 1059–78.

Ross, Catherine E., John Mirowsky, and Joan Huber. 1983. "Dividing Work, Sharing Work, and In-Between: Marriage Patterns and Depression." *American Sociological Review* 48: 809–23.

Rubenstein, William B. 1993. *Lesbians, Gay Men, and the Law*. New York: New Press.

Seidman, Steven. 1993. "Identity and Politics in a 'Postmodern' Gay Culture: Some Historical and Conceptual Notes." In *Fear of a Queer Planet: Queer Politics and Social Theory*, edited by Michael Warner, 105–42. Minneapolis: University of Minnesota Press.

———. 2003. *Beyond the Closet: The Transformation of Gay and Lesbian Life*. New York: Routledge.

Schilt, Kristen, and Laurel Westbrook. 2009. "Doing Gender, Doing Heteronormativity: 'Gender Normals,' Transgender People, and the Social Maintenance of Heterosexuality." *Gender and Society* 23: 440–64.

Smith, Miriam. 2008. *Political Institutions and Lesbian and Gay Rights in the United States and Canada*. New York: Routledge.

Stein, Arlene. 1997. *Sex and Sensibility: Stories of Lesbian Generation*. Berkeley: University of California Press.

Taylor, Verta. 1996. *Rock-a-by Baby: Feminism, Self-Help, and Postpartum Depression*. New York: Routledge.

Taylor, Verta, Katrina Kimport, Nella Van Dyke, and Ellen Ann Andersen. 2009. "Culture and Mobilization: Tactical Repertoires, Same-Sex Weddings, and the Impact on Gay Activism." *American Sociological Review* 74: 865–90.

Taylor, Verta, and Nancy E. Whittier. 1992. "Collective Identity in Social Movement Communities: Lesbian Feminist Mobilization." In *Frontiers in Social Movement Theory*, edited by Aldon Morris and Carol McClurg Mueller, 104–30. New Haven, Conn.: Yale University Press.

Teal, Donn. 1971. *The Gay Militants*. New York: Stein and Day.

Vaid, Urvashi. 1995. *Virtual Equality: The Mainstreaming of Gay and Lesbian Liberation*. New York: Anchor.

Valocchi, Stephen. 1999. "Riding the Crest of the Protest Wave? Collective Action Frames in the Gay Liberation Movement, 1969–1973." *Mobilization* 4: 59–73.

Ward, Jane. 2008. *Respectably Queer: Diversity Culture in LGBT Activist Organizations*. Nashville, Tenn.: Vanderbilt University Press.

Warner, Michael. 1993. Introduction to *Fear of a Queer Planet: Queer Politics and Social Theory*, edited by Michael Warner, vii–xxxi. Minneapolis: University of Minnesota Press.

———. 2000. *The Trouble with Normal: Sex, Politics and the Ethics of Queer Life*. Cambridge, Mass.: Harvard University Press.

Whittier, Nancy. 2009. *The Politics of Child Sexual Abuse: Emotion, Social Movements, and the State*. New York: Oxford University Press.

Wittman, Carl. 1970. "A Gay Manifesto." http://library.gayhomeland.org/0006/EN/A_Gay_Manifesto.htm.

PART **I** Marital Discord

1 What's the Matter with Newark?

Race, Class, Marriage Politics,
and the Limits of Queer Liberalism

Arlene Stein

TWENTY YEARS AGO, an attorney specializing in the rights of same-sex couples wrote that "no American jurisdiction recognizes the right of two women or two men to marry one another," and there is "little discussion within the gay rights movement about whether such a right should exist." Moreover, he lamented, "no gay organization of any size, local or national, has yet declared the right to marry as one of its goals" (Stoddard [1989] 1998, 477). He could hardly have predicted the groundswell of support for same-sex marriage today. Nearly every national gay and lesbian activist organization lists same-sex marriage rights as among its primary goals. The marriage-equality movement has succeeded in gaining significant legal recognition for same-sex couples in states that compose a quarter of the country's population (Badgett 2009, 121). As historian George Chauncey has written, "it is hard to think of another group whose circumstances and public reputation have changed so decisively in so little time. . . . [E]specially since the 1990s," he says, "Americans have become more familiar with their lesbian and gay neighbors and more supportive of them" (2004, 166). Marriage has become the central symbolic axis around which the inclusion and participation of lesbians and gay men turns (Adam 2003, 274, paraphrasing Calhoun 2000).

It should come as little surprise, then, that the fight for marriage equality has captured the imagination of many lesbians and gay men who never before saw themselves as activists—people like those who live in Maplewood, New Jersey, a racially and ethnically diverse, middle-class suburb located in the northern part of the state. Since the 1980s, Maplewood—affectionately called "Gayplewood"—and its sister town, South Orange, have become a magnet of sorts for same-sex couples, the majority of whom are middle-class men and women who are in long-term relationships and who have children. Much like their heterosexual neighbors, the most pressing issues on their minds are the quality of their children's educations and the robustness of their property values. Raising children has required them to think beyond questions of coming out—to consider how to maintain family stability and how to equitably dissolve these structures if necessary. So in 2003, when New Jersey first began to register domestic partnerships, the fourth state in the United States to do so, many Maplewood residents lined up to get their certificates, viewing it as the first step in the evolution toward full marriage rights. In 2006, when the legislature passed a bill providing for civil unions and offering same-sex couples nearly all of the rights granted to married couples under New Jersey state law, they followed suit.

For Maplewood's lesbian, gay, bisexual, and transgender (LGBT) residents, being able to marry represents the culmination of a decades-long fight for equality and is a measure of hard-won progress. As "queer liberals," they champion a politics of inclusion—access to marriage, custody, inheritance, and service in the military—and a color-blind and classless politics of identity (Duggan 2003; Eng 2010). That is, they believe the right to marry will benefit all members of the LGBT community, regardless of race or class, and will advance the cause of social justice, which they interpret as the expansion of rights and recognition for underrepresented groups in American society. Since marriage is a primary means of distributing symbolic and economic capital, those who are denied the right to marry are therefore excluded from the promise of respectability, belonging, and material benefits accrued through marriage.

During the past twenty years, under the sign of queer theory, a number of critics have lodged a sustained and spirited critique of the increasing dominance of marriage politics within gay and lesbian movements in the United States, arguing that it sacrifices and diffuses radical challenges to heteronormativity by privatizing sexuality, forces queer people to conform to a fundamentally heterosexual script, and negates the ways lesbians, gay men, and other queer people create alternative relational forms and intimacies (see, e.g., Warner 1999). I do not need to rehearse these arguments, which are by now familiar. Rather, my goal is to look at how the aspirations these debates signal play out in two very different LGBT worlds—a low-income, predominantly black city, and a nearby mixed-race, largely middle-class suburb—and what that tells us about the politics of marriage equality.

As we know, racial, economic, gender, *and* sexual inequalities profoundly structure life chances in overlapping, multiply determined, intertwined, and complex ways (Choo and Ferree 2010; McCall 2001; Stein 2008). These "complex inequalities" also play out in social space. A comparison of the middle-class suburb of Maplewood, New Jersey, and its close, much larger, and much-maligned postindustrial urban cousin, Newark, offers a clear illustration of this. Despite their proximity, they are profoundly culturally isolated from each other yet deeply structurally linked as well—much like the LGBT populations that inhabit them.

During 2001–2009 I lived in the suburb of South Orange, which shares a school district with Maplewood. The following account is based on my membership in and knowledge of those towns, where I was both a participant and observer in the gay and lesbian community, which comprised a loosely organized series of friendship networks and somewhat more institutionalized groupings of gay and lesbian families, both virtual and face-to-face. In Newark, I was a participant-observer in the burgeoning LGBT community during 2008–2011, attending gay pride activities, planning meetings for educational reform efforts and events sponsored by the newly formed Mayor's Lesbian, Gay, Bisexual, Transgender, and Questioning (LGBTQ) Advisory Commission, and was in conversation with a number of community leaders. A comparison of these two places forces us to question the liberal universalism at the heart of same-sex marriage politics, and the progressive narrative it embodies. Yet my goal is not to bury marriage (if that were even possible!) but to provide a modest opening for thinking more expansively about "actually existing" intimacies and the role that the state might play in supporting them.

GET THEE TO A SUBURB?

The "gay couple from New Jersey," a recurring skit on the television comedy show *Saturday Night Live*, features "Vinnie" and "Joey," Italian Americans with thick accents, big hair, matching track suits, and gold medallions. They have major attitude, two adopted children, and, in a nod to *The Sopranos* and the state's mafioso reputation, they threaten to "whack" anyone who doesn't support same-sex marriage. The skit's humor lies in the absurd pairing of machismo and gay domesticity, and the suggestion that "gays are everywhere"—*even* in unsophisticated New Jersey, in the shadow of its bigger, flashier neighbor, New York City.

There have long been queers in New Jersey, of course—in urbanized areas such as Jersey City, Hoboken, and Plainfield and in arts centers such as Lambertville, as well as numerous men and women living quiet lives in suburban communities who "commute" to the city to be gay—and who are often disparaged by New Yorkers, much like their heterosexual counterparts, as "bridge and tunnel" (Brekhus 2003; Bruck 2008). In 2000, 16,604 New Jersey couples identified themselves as same-sex partnerships on the census short form, and 21,405 did so in 2006, according to the American Community Survey (Alaya 2001; see also Gates 2007). Gay and lesbian couples live in nearly all of New Jersey's 566 towns; at least one hundred same-sex households reside in each of the twenty-one counties, according to latest census figures— low estimates that undercount same-sex intimacies. The state has, in fact, been on the forefront of gay and lesbian civil rights: it was one of the first to end crackdowns on gay bars, to decriminalize sodomy and gay pornography, to prohibit workplace discrimination, and to grant legal rights to nonbiological parents in same-sex families (Bruck 2008).

More recent is the "queering" of suburban communities by out gays and lesbians—a trend that began in the 1980s.[1] The "great gay migration" of the 1970s, as Kath Weston (1995) termed it, brought young men and women from rural areas, suburbs, and smaller cities into gay meccas such as New York and San Francisco, but by the following decade, as this cohort aged, their residential patterns shifted as the result of life-cycle changes, the mainstreaming of gay and lesbian politics, and rising urban real-estate values. The first post–gay liberation cohort began to form families and seek out living space, backyards, and suburban lifestyles that resembled those of their youth. In the northern part of the state, where Maplewood is located, LGBT New Jerseyans tend to work in New York City, where rising property values have shut out most middle-class families, and where approximately half of all rental units are one-bedroom or studio apartments (Klinenberg 2010).

One gay male couple moved to Maplewood in 1980 knowing "they would be alone," and, they recalled, "to a large extent we were" (Alaya 2001). But over the next two decades, many more gay men and lesbians, drawn by word-of-mouth contacts and aided by realtors seeking to market suburban communities as gay-friendly, multicultural havens, bought houses in the community. A 2001 article in the *Newark Star-Ledger* quotes a man who moved to Maplewood in 1997 with his male partner:

> "The key to us is the comfort level," said [Jerry] Clifford, a physics professor. . . . "Our neighbors are comfortable with us and they're mostly straight, although there are a few gay couples. There is no stigma. I found the openness unique, and I've lived in Colorado Springs, Sacramento, Washington, D.C., San Diego, Chicago and Albuquerque."

The article proceeds to describe Clifford and his partner, a scientist, as "a popular couple in their neighborhood," who, on "most nights . . . stroll hand-in-hand down their tree-lined street, chatting with their neighbors as they go." Clifford asserts: "'The way you change attitudes is one on one. I'm sure that is happening here. I'm sure the neighbors . . . begin to see us just like themselves as opposed to 'the GAY couple.' That's the advantage, when you can be totally integrated into the community'" (Alaya 2001).

According to ethnographic evidence and informal polling, today the "typical" LGBT Maplewoodian is a middle-aged female in a long-term primary relationship, with one or more children, who grew up in a suburban community in the New York metropolitan area, left to attend college, and subsequently spent several years living on her own, or with friends or intimates, in an urban area, especially New York City. Lesbian Maplewoodians generally bear children through donor insemination, while their gay male counterparts parent via adoption. Indeed, there are so many adopted Chinese children in the community that local parents have formed play groups to support one another and offer their children the chance to socialize with other Chinese adoptees.

These are "chosen families" who are creating forms of intimacy that borrow from nuclear families and also depart from them, embodying a protean view of family formation. In terms of their self-understandings and the ways they structure their families, they are hardly radical. As members of the post-Stonewall generation, the first generation of men and women who are publicly out as gays and lesbians, these LGBT suburbanites possess a sense of entitlement to public acceptance for their sexual difference—a difference they would like to see writ relatively small. They want to be out, they want to be able to raise children in an open, diverse community (which they define almost exclusively in terms of sexual and racial composition), and they want their sexual identities to be affirmed by politicians, religious leaders, and their kids' teachers. At the same time, because they wish to be seen as complex human beings whose sexuality does not define them, "gay ghettos"— predominantly gay neighborhoods such as those in San Francisco and New York—hold little appeal for them.

For most of the twentieth century, the power of "the closet" necessitated that gays and lesbians assiduously manage their identities in order to survive, prompting many to move to cities such as San Francisco, New York, and Chicago, where those possessing same-sex desires could find each other and create social networks and supportive communities. The politics of "coming out" in the post-Stonewall era led to the growth and consolidation of urban gay enclaves such as San Francisco's Castro district in the 1970s and 1980s, where gays and lesbians—primarily gay men—could live surrounded by other gay people, shop in gay-owned stores, and frequent gay bars, restaurants, and other commercial establishments (Castells 1983; Fitzgerald 1987). In the "postgay" era—characterized by Lisa Duggan (2003) as "homo-normative"—diminished sexual stigma has made the "gay ghetto" a less attractive option (Ghaziani 2010). Concentrating in "gayborhoods" was always a less desirable (and less readily available) option for women than for men, who have historically had less access to the sort of capital that the colonization of urban space requires, and for whom establishing a subculture based on sexuality has arguably been less important. Still, as I have observed, the lesbian community, which was always more of a cultural and symbolic entity than a commercial one, began to unravel in the 1980s with the fragmentation of lesbian-feminist collective identities and the aging of the baby boom cohort (Stein 1997). The rush toward parenting exacerbated this trend as many lesbians and gay men of the first post-Stonewall generation began to age out of their commitment to sexual subcultures, often prioritizing nuclear family formation instead.

That the residential patterns of this cohort were shifting alongside these changes was acknowledged and even celebrated by *The Advocate*, a standard-bearer for the gay consumer lifestyle, in 2007: "'As the country opens its arms to openly gay and lesbian people, the places we call home have grown beyond urban gay ghettos. [This magazine] welcomes you to this new American landscape.' When the magazine polled its readers, asking if they'd 'prefer to live in an integrated neighborhood rather than a distinct gay ghetto,' 69 percent said yes" (quoted in Ghaziani 2010, 65).

Suburban queer enclaves like Maplewood, a far cry from New York's Chelsea neighborhood or even Brooklyn's Park Slope, with their much larger, more densely concentrated, and visible populations of gay men and lesbians, respectively, are products of this history. There are no gay and lesbian bars or other gay commercial establishments, no gay and lesbian publications, and few if any rainbow flags boldly announcing the identities of their queer residents. If there is a "gay community," it consists of informal social networks, such as "Rainbow Families," a group of queer parents and children that meets virtually on the Internet, and only occasionally in person. Indeed, pressed for time, devoted to their partners and children, and having little in common with the

"Castro Clone" or "Chelsea Boy," that's the way their gay and lesbian residents like it.

"One of the things I loved about this area was that it was not just gay," said one resident. "It wasn't like I was looking for a gay haven, like I needed the protection. It was more about the diversity of the neighborhood and the fact that people are open and everyone is celebrated"—everyone, that is, who shares a set of middle-class resources and dispositions (Alaya 2001). With its high property taxes and housing costs, Maplewood (whose median household income exceeded $100,000 in 2009) is far more diverse racially than economically.[2] Its residents value living in a "good" suburban area, one that is not only racially diverse (58 percent of its residents are white; 30 percent are black) but also relatively safe, where they can dip into urban life in order to work or recreate, but where they are relatively insulated from urban problems—poor schools, crime, random violence, and drugs.[3] Indeed, most same-sex parents in Maplewood tend to embrace a sense of themselves as "ordinary," and as similar, in nearly all respects, to their heterosexual neighbors. Ethnographic evidence suggests that they are, collectively, somewhat less diverse racially than the community that surrounds them.

In my 1997 book *Sex and Sensibility*, a study of sexual identities among women, I documented what I called the "decentering" of lesbian communities, showing that the movement of baby boomers through the life cycle was leading to the increasing salience of motherhood and/or career as shapers of identities—rather than subcultural identifications in which sexual identities were primary. Deciding to raise children requires individuals to think beyond questions of coming out. Particularly for middle-class gays and lesbians with children, who choose to locate in child-centric suburban communities such as Maplewood, having kids in the public schools makes being closeted difficult, if not impossible. One must be out to one's children, their friends, the neighbors on one's block, one's children's teachers, dentists, pediatricians, and so forth.

Same-sex parents in Maplewood tend to be highly committed to their children, expending vast amounts of emotional labor, economic capital, time, and attention to cultivating their children's talents (Hays

1996; Lareau 2003). At dinner parties, LGBT Maplewoodians discuss their children's school performance and athletic pursuits, assess their children's teachers, and debate recent school controversies. On a "Rainbow Families" e-mail list they solicit advice on the best local daycare centers, compare the performances of local schools, post notices about upcoming gatherings (such as the annual Easter egg hunt for LGBT families), and exchange information about gay-friendly vacation spots.

Suburban queer couples tend to believe that "good" childrearing requires parents to devote considerable resources and personal energy to it. At least one gay male couple whom I knew when I lived in suburban New Jersey were rarely, if ever, seen in public without their children, a teenage boy and a younger girl, both adoptees from China, in tow, and they readily admitted that they had not had a date with each other in years. Firmly committed to "intensive parenting," a strategy that requires middle-class resources, the two men devoted enormous amounts of time and energy to their kids, scheduling a myriad of organized after-school activities, using everyday conversations as opportunities to develop their kids' cognitive and language skills, and regularly intervening with teachers on their behalf. They were fairly typical of gay- and lesbian-headed households I knew in that middle-class suburban community, and closely resembled their straight neighbors in this respect. Perhaps their commitment to the "concerted cultivation" (Lareau 2003) of their children is a sign of their basic similarity to the dominant culture. At the same time, one wonders whether it is a strategy designed to minimize stigma, overcompensating for the widespread belief that gays and lesbians make "bad" parents.

In a community oriented around heterosexual nuclear families with children, sexuality is a salient aspect of identity for these same-sex couples. In a place where face-to-face relationships are key, and where neighbors know each other, they are marked as visibly "queer." At the same time, their homosexual identities are fairly "routinized" (Seidman, Meeks, and Traschen 2002); they do not engage in the forms of identity management that characterize a closeted life; nor do they see the assertion of their sexual identities as a radical act, or even as the primary way they see themselves or wish to be seen by others. Just as these queer suburbanites seek to integrate their homosexuality into the rest of their lives, so do they wish to become integrated into the neighbor-hoods in which they live, echoing the ongoing process of racial integra-tion of African American families in surrounding middle-class suburbs. Resources of economic and social class, perhaps even more than racial privilege—though, at times, linked to it—afford homosexual suburban-ites opportunities to achieve the ordinariness they desire, and to live lives that are distinct from their neighbors down the road in Newark.

QUEERING BRICK CITY

Driving from Maplewood to Newark—"Brick City"—only eight miles away, one passes through a dramatic tableau of the American class sys-tem, moving from leafy suburbs filled with older homes, some of them quite grand, to working-class and poor neighborhoods, broken-down buildings, and men idling in the street. Newark is one of the poor-est cities in the country, a "majority minority" city whose population is more than half African American and about a third Latino. While Maplewood's median household income exceeded $100,000 in 2009, Newark's was about $35,000, and nearly a third of its residents lived below the poverty line.[4]

Despite their relative geographic and cultural isolation from each other, Newark and Maplewood in fact have been deeply structurally linked at least since the 1920s, when improved transportation and a booming economy turned Maplewood, South Orange, and other nearby towns into bedroom communities for Newark. Wealthy fami-lies built large houses and tennis clubs, and a burgeoning middle class came to inhabit more modest foursquare houses that filled the surrounding suburbs. By the 1950s, Newark, a port city, had a popula-tion of about 500,000, mostly middle- and working-class people.[5] But the development of surrounding suburban communities, coupled with the economic decline of the city, led to white out-migration. In his novel *American Pastoral*, Philip Roth's narrator describes the exodus of middle-class Jews and Italians from Newark to the suburbs: "Everybody else who was picking up and leaving Newark was headed for one of the cozy suburban streets in Maplewood or South Orange" (1997, 307). After the riots of 1967, which left twenty-six people dead, more than fifteen hundred wounded, and millions of dollars worth of property destroyed, Newark's middle-class population deserted the city (Mumford 2007, 98). Still, with 277,000 residents (according to the 2010 U.S. Census), Newark is today New Jersey's most populous city.

White flight, coupled with decades of incompetent and corrupt leadership and deindustrialization, has resulted in high levels of crime, inadequate provision of social services, and a diminished middle-class population. Less than 10 percent of those older than twenty-five hold a college degree; half of employed Newark residents work in lower-tier service occupations, and the remaining half work in transportation and construction, or for federal, state, or local government. Since becoming mayor in 2006, Cory Booker has made a valiant effort to attract new investment and reduce crime in the city, but the recent recession has slowed the pace of change. Newark continues to be a place where most people have barely tasted the American dream.

Though they see themselves as having little connection with each other, a sizeable minority of Maplewoodians work in downtown Newark, the county seat, in education, law, and social services, as well as in health care and other industries. They occasionally venture downtown for dinner in the Ironbound district, a Portuguese- and Spanish-speaking enclave, or to attend a cultural event at the nearby state-of-the-art performing arts center. Hundreds of service workers commute from Newark to Maplewood and other nearby suburbs every day to clean homes, care for aging residents, and work as nannies. To a lesser extent, the "care work" connections extend in the opposite direction as well: a number of Maplewoodians, some of whom are LGBT, have foster-parented and/or adopted children from Newark.

Census figures, which suggest that 0.4 percent of Newark households consist of self-reported same-sex unmarried-partner households, fail to capture the diversity of LGBT life in the city, which has long had a queer community, though it is largely invisible to outsiders.[6] Though a couple of neighborhoods have become middle-class gay and lesbian enclaves, high crime levels and underperforming schools have limited the appeal of the city to outsiders seeking inexpensive real estate, and, unlike neighboring cities close to Manhattan, such as Jersey City, Newark has yet to experience gentrification to any considerable extent.

Nonetheless, there are LGBT individuals as well as several loosely defined, overlapping LGBT communities in the city.

A small enclave of relatively affluent, racially mixed gay men, who are mainly childless, has emerged in the Forest Hill section of the city. There one can buy a large historic home for half a million dollars—a steal by New York metropolitan area standards, which is why the neighborhood has attracted, in the words of the *New York Times*, "older professionals, families with no kids, and the gay community"—in other words, people who may not have children in the public school system (Capuzzo 2007).

A burgeoning population of young, mainly low-income LGBT Newarkers also live in neighborhoods scattered throughout the city: they are the most visibly "queer," and can be seen congregating at the central intersection of Broad and Market Streets downtown. On weekend nights, groups of young lesbians, often embodying femme and butch self-presentations, and gay men of color, ranging from those who perform hegemonic masculinity to those in full drag, make their way into Manhattan, spilling out of the Christopher Street transit stop and fanning out into nearby bars or the Hudson River Park to socialize with one another in ways that are not possible in Newark under the watchful eyes of their families and neighbors.

Less publicly visible are the same-sex couples and single lesbians who are raising children; they live a more domestic existence, and their numbers are impossible to estimate. Informal surveys and anecdotal evidence suggest that these families, lacking the social and economic capital of their middle-class LGBT neighbors in Maplewood, consist predominantly of women who have children from former marriages or heterosexual liaisons. As surveys suggest, LGBT people of color are twice as likely to have children than their white counterparts (Tavernise 2011). But since many Newark lesbian mothers, like other lesbians of color, are single mothers or live apart from their intimate partners, they do not show up as same-sex couples on census data and they are also less likely to be read as identifiably "queer" in public.[7]

Finally, there are men who have sex with men, some of whom are married to women, but who do not identify as homosexual. Labeled "down low," they have at times attracted notoriety and some oppro-

brium from more openly identified gay men as well as from heterosexual women, and they compose the least visible of Newark's "queer"
communities.[8]

In sum, in Newark there are same-sex couples, but also those who
live alone, single gay men and lesbians raising children, families with
transgender people, people who do not live with their partner, people
who count more than one other adult as a family member—to name
but a few of the intimate arrangements—and a sizeable population of
men who have sex with men who do not identify as gay. Newark queers
negotiate multiple identity statuses based on race, gender, class, and
sexuality (and, frequently, for Latino residents, citizenship status). They
construct identities in the interstices between the dominant "white"
culture and the cultures of their peers and families; they navigate between a hegemonic "coming out" script that privileges the conscious,
public formation of queer identities and family forms, and membership
in racial and ethnic minority communities, where homosexuality is
frequently seen as "acting white" (Carter 2011).

As a number of recent studies document, people of color negotiate varied linkages between their "home" communities, defined in relation to biological families and racial and ethnic identities, and the
queer communities they fashion to nurture same-sex relationships. On
the basis of in-depth interviews with fifty black gay men in Philadelphia and New York, Marcus Hunter (2010) found that some black gay
men privileged a racial identity over a sexual identity, others situated
race and sexuality as equally important, and a minority viewed their
sexual identities as most salient. Carlos Decena (2011) suggests that
the "closet," and the public/private dichotomy it implies, does not adequately describe the "tacit subjectivities" of queer Dominican immi-
grant men in New York. They are neither secret nor silent, yet they tend
to refuse to engage in public acts of disclosure about their sexuality,
in part because their survival and (real or imagined) upward mobility
are at stake, but also because they refuse to reduce their complexity of
identities to center upon homosexuality.

Looking at the ways black gays and lesbians in Los Angeles "negotiate multiple identity statuses based in race and sexuality," Mignon
Moore (2010, 316) finds salient generational differences. Those born

before 1954 tend to prioritize racial over sexual identities; those born in the 1960s and '70s struggle to construct identities in which both race and sexuality are salient and linked; black gays and lesbians born after the 1980s, she argues, are less likely to "de-emphasize a gay sexuality in Black social environments" (2010, 317). What these and other studies suggest is that queer people of color are, for a variety of reasons—including lack of access to capital, greater embeddedness in nonnuclear familial networks, feelings of loyalty to and belonging to racial and ethnic minority groups, fear of stigma, and higher rates of religiosity, among others—less likely than their white middle-class counterparts to make sexuality a primary identity.

While there is little evidence to suggest that low-income people of color are more homophobic than white Americans at similar educational and income levels, pressures for gender and sexual conformity within black and Hispanic communities can be considerable (Mumford 2007, 168–69).[9] The reasons are at least partially defensive: white policymakers have long pronounced that female-headed African American families are a "tangle of pathology." Seeking respectability (and political power), moral entrepreneurs within communities of color, fueled by black nationalism and Christian theology, privilege heterosexual nuclear families and view homosexuality as a threat to the family, charging gay men and lesbians with being "race traitors." In the early 1970s, during the rise of the gay liberation movement, famed Newark-based writer and activist Amiri Baraka repudiated homosexuality, proclaiming that it was a disease of white Western culture. In the aftermath of the Million Man March twenty-five years later, which mobilized a more subtle homophobia, churches in Newark and other black communities across the nation established "Fatherhood Programs" to encourage men to stay attached to their children and families.[10] This politics of "respectability" decried the supposed breakdown of the family and called for its restoration, with the father at the helm (Collins 2004; Cohen 1997, 1999; Alexander-Floyd 2007). Today, crusaders for sexual "respectability" in and outside of black communities target homosexuals as well as unmarried heterosexual women.

Sexual stigma and violence is also enacted in the streets against gender nonconforming youth. The brutal slaying in 2003 of fifteen-year-old African American butch lesbian Sakia Gunn is a case in point. Gunn was on her way home to Newark from Greenwich Village when two men got out of a car and made sexual advances to her and her friends. When Gunn told them she was a lesbian, she was stabbed in the chest (Collins 2004, 115). Clearly, being out in places like Newark can be dangerous. That's true in many other places too, of course, but in a poor city like Newark, because of the density of the population, the level of economic desperation, and the influence of religious traditionalism, this risk is amplified. No wonder, then, that Newark queers construct identities that may not conform to the hegemonic "coming out" script that privileges sexuality over other forms of identification and sees public recognition as key.

While Maplewood and Newark are just down the road from each other, culturally and socioeconomically they are clearly very different places. Their LGBT communities consequently look very different and have different political priorities. Maplewood's middle-class gays and lesbians want their neighbors to recognize them as different but also similar and to accord their homosexuality a kind of "ethnic" rather than a "master" status; they also want the state to grant them the legal rights and economic benefits enjoyed by their heterosexual neighbors. For them, the prospect of marrying represents the culmination of a decades-long fight for equality and is a measure of hard-won progress.

While their middle-class neighbors view same-sex marriage as the most important issue facing LGBT Americans, few queer Newarkers have been committed to the fight for marriage equality. A vivid illustration of this is the fact that, as of June 2011, eight times as many Maplewood couples have obtained civil unions as in Newark, although the population of Newark is twelve times that of Maplewood.[11] While there are certainly marriage advocates within black communities nationally, in Newark there are few.[12] "[A]ll this talk of marriage is just a luxury," says longtime Newark queer activist James Credle. "For us, it's about survival" (Joe.My.God. 2007). At the top of his and other activists' agendas are safe streets, decent jobs, and access to quality health care.

Newarkers' reticence to sign on to the fight for same-sex marriage rights has been a source of some frustration for New Jersey LGBT activists, who can't quite understand why they can't encourage those who seemingly have so much to benefit from and so little to lose by joining the fight.[13] Yet from a sociological perspective, there may be very good reasons for Newarkers to have been less committed to the issue than their middle-class neighbors down the road.

WHAT IS MARRIAGE FOR?

A number of observers have noted ironically that gays and lesbians are seeking membership in an institution that heterosexuals are defecting from in droves—as the decline in marriage rates, rise in divorce rates, and huge increases in the number of single-person households indicate. Even though marriage as an institution may be losing some of its staying power, however, the marital bond continues to exert profound symbolic importance, signifying adulthood, security, and normalcy. Marriage is indelibly linked to romantic love, which remains a crucial repository of emotional meaning in our culture, and also provides numerous economic benefits to couples.

Research suggests that lesbians and gay men who wish to marry do so for the following reasons: to express a commitment to the relationship and an intention to stay together; to express that commitment both to each other and to their families and friends; to establish a legal bond that addresses the practical issues related to living a joint economic life together and pooling some or all of their financial resources; to ensure the well-being of their current or future children; and to make a political statement about the equality of gay men and lesbians or a feminist statement related to the equality of men and women (Badgett 2009, 89). With the exception of the desire to make a political statement, none of these considerations are unique to same-sex couples. They express desires for social recognition, emotional well-being, and economic security.

For lesbians and gay men, declaring a commitment to another person also entails declaring a very public commitment to a nonnormative sexual identity. Lesbians and gay men who marry must be out in most if not all aspects of their lives, making the ritual of marriage not only an affirmation of a relationship, but also a proclamation of one's sexuality. (Of course this is true of heterosexual marriages as well, but we tend not to understand it in those terms.) The existence of millions of individuals engaged in same-sex relationships who are willing to publicly profess their love and commitment and their sexual identities is a relatively new development. For many Americans today, homosexuality is less likely to be a source of shame and stigma that requires individuals to live a double life and engage in the kinds of identity management practices that were so common only a few decades ago. The closet is no longer the central organizing principle, marking a clear distinction between "a private life where one can be oneself and a public life where one has to conceal one's stigma" (Seidman, Meeks, and Traschen 2002, 435).

In addition to professing their commitment to their partners and seeking recognition for their families, gays and lesbians also wish to be married for material reasons—to establish legal economic bonds and ensure the well-being of current or future children. This is particularly the case in the United States, where economic rights are organized around the couple, and where marital status often determines whether one receives health insurance and other benefits, even citizenship. Heteronormativity has been inscribed into welfare, immigration, and military policy, and actively excludes gay and lesbian people (Canaday 2009). The "straight state" ensures that people with same-sex partners are almost twice as likely as married people to be uninsured (Badgett 2009, 121). Their inability to marry also means that approximately 35,000 binational same-sex couples in the United States must live in fear of the Immigration and Naturalization Service, and untold others must live separated by national borders or emigrate elsewhere in order to remain together (Epstein 2009).

For all of these reasons, marriage is a no-brainer for gays and lesbians in committed relationships. A compelling recent study touting the benefits of same-sex marriage offers the Netherlands as a test case (Badgett 2009). But the United States, lacking a strong welfare state, and with a growing gap between rich and poor, is not the Netherlands. So while middle-class gays and lesbians, such as the LGBT population of Maplewood, have embraced the fight for marriage equality, when we introduce class and racial diversity into the mix, the story becomes considerably more complicated.

First, if marriage offers economic benefits, it does so mainly for those who possess considerable economic resources. A number of studies that have tried to account for lower rates of marriage among working-class and poor people of color conclude that the reasons that single parenthood is more pervasive in low-income communities is largely economic. Low-income women continue to embrace motherhood while postponing marriage because they face difficulties finding partners who can support them economically (Edin and Kefalas 2005). Workers in the lowest ranks of the workforce are less likely to have jobs with benefits, and more likely to be coupled with people who either are unemployed or hold jobs without benefits (Cahn and Carbone 2010; Chauncey 2004, 118). Testifying to the economic underpinnings of marriage is the fact that during the last ten or twenty years increasing numbers of cohabiting couples in their twenties or early thirties who are not economically secure enough to get married are having children out of wedlock, a trend that is exacerbated by the current economic recession (Cherlin 2010).

Lower-income same-sex couples are less likely to have health insurance, or be able to transfer their health insurance to a partner lacking insurance. They are less likely to own property and be concerned with questions of inheritance. Concentrated in lower-level service jobs, which often lack benefits, it's no wonder Newark's gays and lesbians generally have less economic incentive to marry than their middle-class counterparts.

Second, marriage, by definition, requires individuals to be able and willing to declare their relationships publicly; in Newark and places like it, "coming out" as gay or lesbian, as I have argued, often looks different. Queers of color live at the intersection of racial, sexual, and gender marginality and they exercise agency in relation to the complex inequalities that pattern their lives. While they are just as likely to be embedded in family networks as their middle-class peers, they are somewhat less likely to move away from their families of origin in order to act on their homosexuality and are less likely to construct identities in which sexuality is primary (Decena 2011; Hunter 2010; Moore 2010).

Much like their national counterparts, Newark's LGBT activists see the threat of violence and lack of access to good jobs as the most important issues facing them, rather than the inability to marry (Albelda et al. 2009, i–ii). The combined effects of sexual stigma, lack of access to the economic benefits accrued through marriage, weaker symbolic commitment to marriage, and a more complex and multilayered conception of identity make the prospect of marrying simultaneously less accessible and less appealing for queer Newarkers.

THE LIMITS OF QUEER LIBERALISM

When local television stations cover the issue of same-sex marriage in New Jersey, they send film crews to Maplewood or places like it, finding news value in "ordinary" gays and lesbians and their families, and reinforcing the belief that gays and lesbians are predominantly white and middle class. Mainstream gay and lesbian organizations tend to reproduce this view, along with most social scientists—and I am among those who have been guilty of this on occasion. But the preceding "tale of two cities" forces us to recognize that there is no one queer America; studies that conceptualize sexuality in class and race-neutral ways are incomplete (Vaid 2010).[14] This is an intellectual as well as a political problem. It leads us, for example, to overgeneralize about support for marriage equality and universalize its potential benefits. While the right to marry will certainly benefit my Maplewood neighbors, whether it will be equally beneficial to low-income lesbians and gay men such as those in Newark is less certain. Indeed, recent work (Stacey 2011) suggests that expanding access to marriage to same-sex couples is likely to increase race and class inequality.

Queer liberalism, framed by the rhetoric of "choice," emphasizes the importance of coming out and creating "chosen families." It embodies late modernity's "reflexive individualism," a self-consciousness committed to self-creation, common among relatively privileged members of advanced capitalist societies (Giddens 1991). Middle-class gay and lesbian families exercise greater choice over a wider array of areas—reproduction, their children's educational experiences, and the kinds of extracurricular activities their children engage in, and so on—than their less economically privileged counterparts. In other words, it takes resources for middle-class families to achieve the "ordinariness" they desire. In middle-class Maplewood, "things [are] negotiated, re-sourced, and planned"; in low-income Newark, things "just happen" (Taylor 2009, 67). That is, in Newark so many of the decisions that structure one's life—about where to live, what kinds of jobs to labor in, how to get to work in the morning, and so forth—are beyond one's control.

Those who view queer communities of color within liberal frame-works tend to find them wanting. They see gays and lesbians of color, who are less likely to embrace public identifications and frame their identities as "chosen," as less capable of carving out social spaces and as victims of oppression, shame, duplicity, and the persistence of the closet. Privileging "chosen families" over "families that just happen," liberals suggest that the most "advanced" form of same-sex partner-ship is the one that unites monogamous couples and is blessed by the state. But this queer-liberal narrative, as I have suggested, presupposes access to cultural and economic capital and is much better suited to the lives of middle-class gays and lesbians than to lower-income peo-ple of color who have, by choice or necessity, pursued different family formations.

Being "just like everyone else" requires economic and cultural capi-tal that is out of reach for many low-income people of color and may not hold the same allure or meaning. The combined effects of racism, classed hierarchies, and cultural differences make the process of sexual identification more complex, and the potential benefits of marriage—both material and symbolic—fewer. Newarkers express a diverse range of same-sex intimacies that do not conform to the hegemonic "coming out" script and "families we choose" model with which it is linked. While these and other race/class/gender identities may look different from the hegemonic model embraced mainly (but not exclusively) by white middle-class gays and lesbians, they are no less "queer." (Indeed one might argue that the range of same-sex intimacies in Newark is in fact more diverse and even "queerer" than those of middle-class sub-urbs such as Maplewood.)

Advocates for same-sex marriage suggest that Newark gays and les-bians are simply at an earlier stage in their fight for equality, and that

once they solve more pressing issues, such as ensuring safe streets, creating decent jobs, or improving provisions for health care, they will be
able to take full advantage of the benefits of marriage. In the mean-
time, access to marriage will normalize same-sex relationships, bringing them more fully out into the open (see, for example, Moore 2010).
It will change social attitudes and mean that fewer gay youth in Newark
are kicked out of their homes or attacked in the streets. It will allow
those who are partnered with individuals who have benefits to be able
to share them and potentially move two relatively low-income households into one higher-income family. In short, they argue that marriage
equality will not make our profoundly unequal society suddenly fair,
but that it will close some of the gaps.

On the other side are those who argue that marriage in fact exacerbates inequalities rather than alleviates them. Marriage, according
to sociologists, tends to bring together people who are very much like
each other. This pull toward similarity has accelerated during the past
few decades among heterosexuals: highly educated men are now even
more likely to marry highly educated women than they once were, and
high-income men increasingly marry high-income women (see, for example, Blackwell and Lichter 2004; Kalmijn 1994; and Gardyn 2002).
While there is a somewhat higher incidence of interracial coupling
among gays and lesbians, there is little evidence that, when it comes to
socioeconomic class, they are much different from heterosexuals: they
tend to choose partners who are fairly similar to themselves.[15] Following this logic, one might conclude that access to marriage will not be
as beneficial to the men and women engaged in same-sex relationships
in low-income Newark as it would be for their middle-class counterparts. Moreover, without alleviating barriers to economic opportunity,
increasing access to marriage may well contribute to the widening income gap in our country (see also Farrow 2004; Cahill 2005).

Maplewood's LGBT community, much like national mainstream
LGBT activists generally, tends to subscribe to the former position,
believing that they champion a stance that will ultimately benefit all
queers, and, by implication, all Americans. However, Newark's LGBT
activists are divided: while a relatively small number have placed the

fight for marriage equality high on their agenda, most prioritize community building, combating street violence, and integrating queer-friendly educational curricula in the secondary schools over the right to marry.[16]

The queer-liberal progress narrative, which makes the fight for marriage equality its centerpiece, makes a great deal of sense if one imagines that Maplewood *is* queer America. But it's not. A century ago, classical liberals formulated the belief that capitalist economic development is tantamount to progress, and that modernization would lead to a better life for all of the world's peoples. Over the last fifty years, a host of critiques have called into question the universality of such claims, revealing that economic development has had mixed results, wildly varying across and within cultures. Much the same could be said of the progress narrative embedded in liberal same-sex marriage discourse: it will benefit some queer people, diminish many of those who cannot or do not wish to marry, and have a negligible impact upon others. It is particularism masquerading as universalism. The LGBT movement's overriding focus on marriage equality may prevent us from thinking more expansively about how to protect and nurture alternative family forms—including the kinds of nonnuclear families that many low-income people, such as those in Newark, create.[17]

Those who wish to marry should be entitled to do so. But rather than working solely to open membership to comparatively privileged same-sex couples, a transformational queer politics would support the diversity of family structures—not only those living in couples, but also people living alone, singles raising children, people who do not marry their partners, families with transgender people, people who do not live with their partner, people who count more than one other adult as a family member—to name but a few of the forms of family that make up our communities today. It would see the struggle for same-sex marriage not simply as the culmination of the fight for social justice but as one strategy in a more comprehensive menu of activism that addresses racial and economic inequality, including access to decent jobs, health-care benefits, and social services. Addressing the ways that marriage exacerbates economic inequality, it would decouple benefits and privileges from marital status. It would embrace an expansive conception of what makes "good" parents, children, and citizens. And it would reimagine queer America in more inclusive ways, as a place that includes Newark, too.

NOTES

For their comments on an earlier version of this chapter, I am grateful to Cynthia Chris, Darnell Moore, Judith Stacey, Urvashi Vaid, the gender group in the Department of Sociology at Rutgers, and audiences at conferences at Rutgers' Institute for Research on Women and at the School of Law in Newark, as well as Mary Bernstein, Verta Taylor, Nancy Whittier, and Peter Hennen.

1. Following Eng (2010), I am using the terms "queer" and "queering" broadly—including those who pose radical critiques of heteronormativity, as well as those who embrace and/or practice more normative (liberal, assimilationist) versions of homosexuality. His point, as I understand it, is that as LGBT couples and families have become increasingly assimilated, "queerness" has become a more generic category.

2. Interviews by Brekhus (2003) with suburban gay men found that degree of "urbanness" was more salient as a determinant of informants' worldviews than sexual orientation, and that urbanness, occupation, race, gender, and sexual orientation all intersected and shaped the self-identities and worldviews of these men. Brekhus differentiates among identity lifestylers, identity commuters, and identity integrators. Identity lifestylers select a particular identity and organize their lives, activities, auxiliary characteristics, and social networks around that identity as their central core essence. The identity commuter travels to identity-specific spaces to immerse him- or herself in an identity subculture, such as gay bars in New York. The identity integrator sees him- or herself as defined by a constellation of multiple dimensions. This last strategy best describes the lives of most queer parents in Maplewood.

3. Racial demographics are from City-Data.com, http://www.city-data.com/city/Maplewood-New-Jersey.html.

4. Income figures on Maplewood for 2009 are from City-Data.com, http://www.city-data.com/city/Maplewood-New-Jersey.html; Newark figures are from City-Data.com, http://www.city-data.com/city/Newark-New-Jersey.html.

5. In the late 1950s, several Newark neighborhoods were predominantly Jewish, and at least one was over 80 percent Jewish (Ortner 2003, 4).

6. Census figures are from City-Data.com, http://www.city-data.com/city/Newark-New-Jersey.html.

7. While no less committed to their children than their counterparts in Maplewood, lesbian mothers in Newark tend to employ parenting strategies that are quite different, reflecting what Annette Lareau (2003) calls "natural growth." While protecting their children's health and safety, they tend to defer to schools to diagnose and address problems that arise.

8. Closeted bisexual and homosexual men have at times been accused of importing AIDS into the black community and infecting women (Cohen 1997).

9. Surveys suggest that African Americans are supportive of gay civil rights even

though they also expressed more moral disapproval of homosexuality. Alan Yang, "From Wrongs to Rights," cited in Chauncey 2004, 55.

10. More recently, black women united (virtually) to proclaim "No Wedding, No Womb," targeting black men for refusing to marry the women they impregnate (Martin 2010).

11. Marriage data are from the Registrar of Maplewood Township, N.J., and the Office of the City Clerk, Newark, N.J., June 2011.

12. See, for example, *Jumping the Broom* (2005). Moore (2011), on the basis of interviews and participant observation in Los Angeles, presents a somewhat different perspective, arguing that same-sex marriage offers openings for queer people of color to educate and engage with their families around issues of homosexuality. While I do not disagree with this claim, it may be less descriptive of lower-income communities of color, as the recent experience of Newark suggests.

13. Personal communication, Darnell Moore, chair of the mayor's Lesbian, Gay, Bisexual, Transgender, and Questioning (LGBTQ) Advisory Commission, Newark, November 2010.

14. See also Duggan (2003) and Eng (2010). For a rare media acknowledgment of the diversity of gay and lesbian family life, see Tavernise (2011). Similarly, analyses of race and class that fail to consider the centrality of heteronormativity—the practices and institutions that legitimize and privilege heterosexuality and heterosexual relationships—are missing a crucial part of the story.

15. Gay men may be more apt to cross class boundaries intimately than heterosexuals or lesbians, according to research by Stacey (2011).

16. In 2009, Mayor Corey Booker appointed the Lesbian, Gay, Bisexual, Transgender, and Questioning (LGBTQ) Advisory Commission to advise him on matters of importance to the gay and lesbian community. In April 2011, the city announced the establishment of the Sakia Gunn High School for Civic Engagement, named after the young victim of a brutal homophobic hate crime. A brochure circulating to potential students and their families announced that the school is "committed to challenging students to understand the importance of advocacy at all levels of society: local, national, and global," and that it aims to empower "student-citizens."

17. For an elaboration of this argument, see Vaid (2010).

REFERENCES

Adam, Barry. 2003. "The Defense of Marriage Act and American Exceptionalism: The 'Gay Marriage' Panic in the United States." *Journal of the History of Sexuality* 12 (2): 259–76.

Alaya, Ana M. 2001. "Gay Pairs Find Comfort Zones." *Newark Star-Ledger*, August 15. http://www.nj.com/specialprojects/index.ssf?/specialprojects/census/gaycomfort .html.

Albelda, Randy, M. V. Lee Badgett, Alyssa Scheebaum, and Gary Gates. 2009. "Poverty in the GLB Community." Executive Summary, i–iv. Williams Institute, UCLA School of Law.

Badgett, M. V. Lee. 2009. *When Gay People Get Married: What Happens When Societies Legalize Same-Sex Marriage*. New York: New York University Press.

Blackwell, D. L., and D. T. Lichter. 2004. "Homogamy among Dating, Cohabiting, and Married Couples." *Sociological Quarterly* 45: 719–37.

Brekhus, Wayne H. 2003. *Peacocks, Chameleons, and Centaurs: Gay Surburbia and the Grammar of Social Identity*. Chicago: University of Chicago Press.

Bruck, Andrew. 2008. "Equality in the Garden State: Litigation and Social Activism in the Struggle for Marriage Equality." *Harvard Law & Policy Review* 2: 419–34.

Cahill, Steven. 2005. "Welfare Moms and the Two Grooms: The Concurrent Promotion and Restriction of Marriage in US Public Policy." *Sexualities* 8 (2): 169–87.

Cahn, Naomi, and June Carbone. 2010. *Red Families v. Blue Families: Legal Polarization and the Creation of Culture*. Oxford: Oxford University Press.

Calhoun, Cheshire. 2000. *Feminism, the Family, and the Politics of the Closet*. New York: Oxford University Press.

Canaday, Margot. 2009. *The Straight State: Sexuality and Citizenship in Twentieth-Century America*. Princeton, N.J.: Princeton University Press.

Capuzzo, Jill. 2007. "Yes, We're in Newark." *New York Times*, August 26. http://www.nytimes.com/2007/08/26/realestate/26living.html.

Carter, Prudence. 2011. "Straddling Racial Boundaries at School." In *Inside Social Life*, edited by Spencer Cahill and Kent Sandstrom, 366–82. New York and Oxford: Oxford University Press.

Castells, Manuel. 1983. *The City and the Grassroots: A Cross-Cultural Theory of Urban Social Movements*. Berkeley: University of California Press.

Chauncey, George. 2004. *Why Marriage? The History Shaping Today's Debate over Gay Equality*. New York: Basic Books.

Cherlin, Andrew. 2010. "For Many Americans, 'Marriage is an Economic Decision,' Sociologist Says." Interview with Melissa Block, *All Things Considered*, National Public Radio. September 29. http://www.npr.org/templates/transcript/transcript.php?storyId=130218357.

Choo, Hae Yeon, and Myra Marx Ferree. 2010. "Practicing Intersectionality in Sociological Research: A Critical Analysis of Inclusions, Interactions, and Institutions in the Study of Inequalities." *Sociological Theory* 28 (2): 129–49.

Cohen, Cathy J. 1997. "Punks, Bulldaggers, and Welfare Queens: The Radical Potential of Queer Politics?" *GLQ* 3: 437–65.

———. 1999. *The Boundaries of Blackness: AIDS and the Breakdown of Black Politics*. Chicago: University of Chicago Press.

Collins, Patricia Hill. 2004. *Black Sexual Politics: African Americans, Gender, and the New Racism*. New York: Routledge.

Decena, Carlos. 2011. *Tacit Subjects: Belonging and Same-Sex Desire among Dominican Men*. Durham, N.C.: Duke University Press.

Duggan, Lisa. 2003. *The Twilight of Equality? Neoliberalism, Cultural Politics, and the Attack on Democracy*. Boston: Beacon Press.

Edin, Kathryn, and Maria Kefalas. 2005. *Promises I Can Keep: Why Poor Women Put Motherhood before Marriage*. Berkeley: University of California Press.

Eng, David. 2010. *The Feeling of Kinship: Queer Liberalism and the Racialization of Intimacy*. Durham, N.C.: Duke University Press.

Epstein, Steven. 2009. "A Gross Unfairness: The Workings of the Straight State." *The Nation*, July 29.

Farrow, Kenyon. 2004. "Is Gay Marriage Anti-Black?" March 5. http://kenyonfarrow
.com/2005/06/14/is-gay-marriage-anti-black/.

Fitzgerald, Frances. 1987. *Cities on a Hill.* New York: Simon and Schuster.

Gardyn, Rebecca. 2002. "The Mating Game." *American Demographics* 24: 33–37.

Gates, Gary. 2007. "Geographic Trends among Same-Sex Couples in the US Census
and the American Community Survey." Williams Institute, UCLA School of Law.
November.

Ghaziani, Amin. 2010. "There Goes the Gayborhood?" *Contexts* 9 (3): 64–66.

———. 2011. "Post-Gay Collective Identity Construction." *Social Problems* 58 (1): 99–125.

Giddens, Anthony. 1991. *Modernity and Self-Identity: Self and Society in the Late Modern Age.* Stanford, Calif.: Stanford University Press.

Hays, Sharon. 1996. *The Cultural Contradictions of Motherhood.* New Haven, Conn.:
Yale University Press.

Hunter, Marcus Anthony. 2010. "All the Gays Are White and All the Blacks Are Straight:
Black Gay Men, Identity and Community." *Sexuality Research and Social Policy*
7: 81–92.

Joe.My.God. 2007. "Newark Gay Life: Bleak and Dangerous." December 3. http://joe
mygod.blogspot.com/2007/12/newark-gay-life-bleak-and-dangerous.html.

Jumping the Broom: A Black Perspective on Same-Gender Marriage. 2005. Silver Spring,
Md.: Equality Maryland Foundation and Washington, D.C.: National Black Justice Coalition.

Kalmijn, Matthijs. 1994. "Assortative Mating by Cultural and Economic Occupational
Status." *American Journal of Sociology* 100 (2): 422–52.

Klinenberg, Eric. 2010. "Going Solo: The Social Experiment of Living Alone." Sociology Department, Rutgers University, New Brunswick, N.J.

Lareau, Annette. 2003. *Unequal Childhoods: Class, Race, and Family Life.* Berkeley:
University of California Press.

Martin, Michel, host. 2010. "Activists Unite for 'No Wedding, No Womb.'" *Tell Me
More,* National Public Radio, September 22. http://www.npr.org/templates/story/
story.php?storyId=130047875.

McCall, Leslie. 2001. *Complex Inequality: Gender, Race, and Class in the New Economy.* New York: Routledge.

Moore, Mignon. 2010. "Articulating a Politics of (Multiple) Identities: LGBT Sexuality
and Inclusion in Black Community Life." *Du Bois Review: Social Science Research
on Race* 7: 315–34.

———. 2011. "The Changing Landscape of Sexual Politics." Paper presented at the
American Sociological Association, Las Vegas, Nev., August 20–23.

Mumford, Kevin. 2007. *Newark: A History of Race, Rights, and Riots in America.* New
York: New York University Press.

Ortner, Sherry. 2003. *New Jersey Dreaming: Capital, Culture, and the Class of '58.* Durham, N.C.: Duke University Press.

Roth, Philip. 1997. *American Pastoral.* New York: Houghton Mifflin.

Seidman, Steven, Chet Meeks, and Francie Traschen. 2002. "Beyond the Closet? The
Changing Social Meaning of Homosexuality in the United States." In *Sexuality
and Gender,* edited by Christine L. Williams and Arlene Stein, 427–45. Cambridge,
Mass.: Blackwell Publishing.

Stacey, Judith. 2011. *Unhitched: Love, Marriage, and Family Values from West Hollywood to Western China*. New York: New York University Press.

Stein, Arlene. 1997. *Sex and Sensibility: Stories of Lesbian Generation*. Berkeley: University of California Press.

———. 2008. "Feminism's Sexual Problem: Comment on Andersen." *Gender and Society* 22 (1): 115–19.

Stoddard, Thomas. [1989] 1998. "Why Gay People Should Seek the Right to Marry." In *Families in the U.S.: Kinship and Domestic Politics*, edited by Karen Hansen and Anita Ilta Garey, 475–79. Philadelphia: Temple University Press.

Tavernise, Sabrina. 2011. "Parenting by Gays More Common in the South, Census Shows." *New York Times*, January 18.

Taylor, Yvette. 2009. *Lesbian and Gay Parenting: Securing Social and Educational Capital*. Basingstoke, U.K.: Palgrave Macmillan.

Vaid, Urvashi. 2010. "Race, Sexuality and the Future of LGBT Politics." Paper presented at the annual Kessler Lecture, Center for Lesbian and Gay Studies, CUNY Graduate Center, New York, N.Y., November 18.

Warner, Michael. 1999. *The Trouble with Normal: Sex, Politics and the Ethics of Queer Life*. New York: Free Press.

Weston, Kath. 1995. "Get Thee to a Big City: Sexual Imaginary and the Great Gay Migration." *GLQ* 2 (3): 253–77.

2 Same-Sex Marriage and Constituent Perceptions of the LGBT Rights Movement

Kathleen E. Hull and Timothy A. Ortyl

M OST RESEARCH ON SOCIAL MOVEMENTS examines the words and actions of activists. Traditionally, when researchers turn their attention to a movement's nonactivist base, they do so to assess the effects of activists' choices on the constituents. For example, researchers often focus on how activists' tactical choices and framing of issues affect mobilization or the fostering of a collective identity among constituents. Very little research has addressed the more fundamental question of what a movement's constituency thinks of the job the movement is doing. Of course, there is every reason to assume that a causal relationship exists between constituents' views of a movement and their ability to be mobilized or the likelihood of their forming a sense of collective identity. Constituents who hold a highly negative view of a movement are not likely to support it with time, money, or other resources, and their sense of collective identity with activists and fellow constituents is likely to be low. Yet surprisingly little research has directly investigated constituents' views of movements.

This chapter seeks to correct this omission in the case of the lesbian, gay, bisexual, and transgender (LGBT) rights movement. We offer a detailed examination of how its everyday constituents view the LGBT rights movement, with particular attention to the movement's recent focus on same-sex marriage and its handling of marriage and family issues. On the marriage issue in particular, we have noticed that commentators (scholarly and otherwise) often make assumptions about what movement constituents think about the movement's goals and tactics. As described below, queer scholars and critics have been especially skeptical about whether the movement's pursuit of legal same-sex marriage represents the views and priorities of most constituents. By contrast, commentators supportive of the marriage focus assert that legal marriage is a desirable goal for constituents. These debates among scholars and activists about what constituents want or need occur in the broader context of long-running intracommunity debates about whether the pursuit of legal marriage represents a problematic bid for assimilation into the societal mainstream or a transformative redefinition of marriage and family (Eskridge 1996; Ettelbrick 1992; Hunter 1991; Polikoff 1993, 2008; Rauch 2004; Stoddard 1992; Sullivan 1996; Vaid 1995; Walters 2001; Warner 1999; Wolfson 1994, 2004).

Using data from individual and focus-group interviews with ordinary LGBT individuals, we address the following empirical questions: What do ordinary LGBT people think of the LGBT rights movement today? Do they feel represented by the movement? How do movement opinions and sense of representation vary among constituents? And, how do constituents view the movement's pursuit of the goal of legal same-sex marriage specifically, and greater recognition and protection for LGBT families more generally?

In examining these questions, we draw upon concepts from the social movements literature. Past work on how social movements evolve over time provides a backdrop for considering how well the LGBT rights movement represents the needs and interests of its constituents. Specifically, we use constituent perceptions of the movement to examine *secondary marginalization* within the LGBT rights movement. We find evidence of secondary marginalization among constituents, but we argue that the movement's focus on same-sex marriage contributes to such marginalization only in a limited way.

MOVEMENT EVOLUTION AND
SECONDARY MARGINALIZATION

Social movement scholars have long been interested in understanding how movements evolve over time and what implications those changes have for movement goals, priorities, and effectiveness. The work of classical theorists Max Weber and Robert Michels has been influential in shaping the understanding of social movement evolution. Weber predicted that the spread of formal rationality would push organizations toward formalization and bureaucratization, and the replacement of individual charismatic leaders by the routinization of charisma (Weber [1922] 1978). Michels's iron law of oligarchy asserted that formal organizations tend toward oligarchy, or rule by the few, even in cases where members desire more democratic forms of organization (Michels [1915] 1962). Applying these insights to social movements, resource mobilization scholars developed the Weber-Michels thesis, which posits that once social movement organizations (SMOs) attain a firm economic and social base, they move toward formalized bureaucratic structures and away from charismatic individual leaders in favor of a cadre of elite professional leadership (Zald and Ash 1966).

These tendencies enhance the long-term stability of SMOs, but at the price of increasing accommodation to dominant society; for most social-change-oriented SMOs, this translates into increasing conservatism in terms of goals and strategies (McCarthy and Zald 1977). Building on Selznick's (1949) seminal work on the co-optation of the Tennessee Valley Authority, a rich empirical literature has documented numerous examples of movements becoming more conservative and being co-opted (Coy and Hedeen 2005; W.A. Gamson [1975] 1990; Meyer and Tarrow 1998; Naples 2002; Piven and Cloward 1977; Staggenborg 1988).

One of the likely effects of movement formalization and conservatization is what political scientist Cathy Cohen calls secondary marginalization (Cohen 1999). According to Cohen, secondary marginalization occurs when the more privileged members of a marginalized social group attempt to manage the behavior, attitudes, and public image of the marginalized group in order to secure respect and resources from the dominant society (Cohen 1999, 70). The effect of secondary marginalization is to downplay the needs and priorities of less privileged members of the group. In some cases, more privileged group members make a bid for support from the dominant society by rendering less privileged group members invisible or defining them as outside the group's boundaries. Secondary marginalization intensifies existing inequalities within marginalized groups, as less advantaged group members are denied access not only to the material and symbolic resources of the dominant society, but to the more limited internal resources of their own group as well.

In the case of marginalized groups represented by formalized social movements, one likely outcome of secondary marginalization is that the needs of less privileged group members will receive less attention from movement organizations and leadership. Dara Strolovitch's recent research on national organizations advocating for marginalized groups confirms this effect. Using survey and interview data on 286 advocacy organizations representing women, racial/ethnic minorities, or low-income people, Strolovitch (2007) demonstrates that issues that primarily affect more disadvantaged members[1] of the marginalized group receive less attention and fewer resources than issues that affect the group as a whole or issues that mainly affect more advantaged members of the group. We suggest that secondary marginalization should be defined expansively enough to include not only the actions of movement organizations (i.e., giving less attention and resources to some issues), but also the perception by disadvantaged group members that the social movement is not doing a good job of representing their interests. In other words, there is a subjective component to secondary marginalization that is potentially independent of the actual behaviors of movement organizations and leadership.

Some recent work has specifically addressed the issue of secondary marginalization in the LGBT rights movement. In her comparative analysis of same-sex marriage litigation in Canada and the United States, Miriam Smith (2007) argues that the equal rights frame has prevailed in LGBT activism in both countries at the expense of a queer cultural frame that offers a more critical perspective on the institution of marriage. Smith notes that "[t]he rights frame has a powerful structuring influence on political discourse because of its fit with the legal legacies of human rights protections in constitutional law within both legal traditions and with the model of socio-legal mobilization provided by the African-American civil rights movement" (6). Smith points out that plaintiffs in key marriage cases in both countries were mostly white and middle class, and many were parents and had religious affiliations. Smith contends that the choice of such plaintiffs by marriage activists reflects a "policing of the gay image such that queer culture was rendered invisible" (18).

Amy Stone's research (2006, 2009) on campaigns to pass transgender-inclusive nondiscrimination ordinances in three Michigan cities highlights the secondary marginalization of transgender people in the LGBT rights movement. Stone argues that transgender people have often been subject to "implicit inclusion" (2006, 9) in the LGBT movement, meaning that while they are formally identified as part of the movement, their issues are not treated as important as or distinct from the issues of the dominant constituency (i.e., gay men and lesbians). Stone concludes that transgender marginalization is most likely to be overcome in situations where non-transgender movement activists are strongly committed to transgender inclusion and take an active role in getting transgender issues on the movement agenda.

Paralleling these scholarly investigations of secondary marginalization, there has been extensive debate within LGBT communities about the direction of the movement and the question of whether the movement adequately represents the concerns of its supposed constituencies. Queer scholars and activists have leveled harsh critiques against the movement's supposed tendency toward assimilationist goals and strategies, with the goal of legal same-sex marriage often singled out as a prime example of the broader tendency (e.g., Warner 1999). Such critics argue that the movement has betrayed its liberationist roots and turned its back on its most disadvantaged and stigmatized constituents in an effort to achieve social normalcy. In her book *Virtual Equality*, activist Urvashi Vaid (1995) argues that the movement's priorities increasingly reflect the interests of its most privileged members, those who are already most "mainstream" (i.e., white and upper middle class). Transgender activists have become more vocal about the movement's failure to address the needs of transgender people.

Several scholar-activists assert that the movement is using an overly narrow vision of family in formulating its policy goals and strategies. Rather than focusing intensively on legal marriage, these critics argue, the movement should be advocating for recognition and support for a wide diversity of family forms, such as single-parent households, polyamorous relationships, and close friends in nonsexual relationships who act as one another's primary support and/or caregiver (Duggan 2003; Polikoff 2008; see also BeyondMarriage.org 2006). Critics of the push for same-sex marriage frequently assert that marriage is a movement goal that is most compelling for, and most potentially beneficial to, the most privileged members of the LGBT movement constituency. However, this claim has received little empirical investigation to date.

By contrast, scholars and activists supportive of the movement's pursuit of same-sex marriage recognition challenge the argument that marriage will mainly benefit the movement's most advantaged constituents and that many constituents are not really that interested in marriage. One recent paper (Cahill 2009) uses U.S. Census data to argue that households headed by black and Latino/a same-sex couples actually have the most to gain from legal marriage rights, because they are most in need of the protections legal marriage provides. Specifically, these couples are more likely to be raising children and have lower household incomes than white same-sex couples.[2] Couples that include Latino/a partners are more likely to benefit from the immigration provisions of legal marriage. Concerning constituents' desire for access to marriage, activists such as Evan Wolfson assert that average movement constituents see marriage as an important movement objective, even if their enthusiasm for marriage is not always shared by movement elites. Citing data on gay men and lesbians' desire for marriage from polls conducted by gay publications, Wolfson asserts: "Even though equal marriage rights, until recently, seemed a dream, all available evidence suggests that the vast majority of gay and non-gay people alike share such sentiments" (1994, 583).

Our data on constituent perceptions of the LGBT rights movement provide the opportunity to assess in a systematic fashion the presence of secondary marginalization in the LGBT rights movement and the possible relationship between secondary marginalization of the most disadvantaged constituents of the movement and the movement's pursuit of legal marriage. What is the evidence for secondary marginalization by the LGBT rights movement, *based on perceptions of movement constituents?* And, if there is evidence of secondary marginalization, does it appear to be linked to the movement's pursuit of legal same-sex marriage, as queer critics of the movement contend?

RESEARCH METHODS

The findings we present are from a study of close relationships and conceptions of family among LGBT people. The study includes seventy-four individual in-depth interviews and seven focus-group interviews with thirty-one participants, for a total sample of 105 LGBT respondents. Interviews were conducted in 2007–2008. Topics covered in the individual and focus-group interviews included respondents' personal background and coming-out story, their current relationships (including their three closest adult relationships and broader social networks), their conceptions of family and marriage, and their views of the mainstream LGBT rights movement. Answers to the questions about the movement serve as the data for the analysis presented here. In this section of the interview, respondents were asked for their general opinion of the "mainstream LGBT rights movement" and whether they felt personally represented by the movement. If respondents requested clarification about the meaning of "mainstream LGBT rights movement," we gave examples of organizations that we consider part of the mainstream movement, such as the Human Rights Campaign, the National Gay and Lesbian Task Force, and Lambda Legal Defense and Education Fund at the national level and OutFront Minnesota at the local/state level. Respondents were also asked what they thought the current priorities of the movement are and what the movement's priorities should be, and they were asked their views of the movement's current focus on family issues such as same-sex marriage and gay/lesbian parenting. We collected background information on respondent characteristics through a demographic information sheet completed at the end of the interview.

The interview sample was drawn from people living in the Minneapolis–St. Paul metro area, rural areas within driving distance of the metro area, and the St. Cloud, Minnesota, area. We used a combination of methods to recruit people for the study. We rented a booth at the 2007 Twin Cities Pride Festival, a large two-day event held in a public park in Minneapolis in conjunction with the annual Pride parade. We staffed the booth for the entire event, distributing basic information about our study, answering questions about the research, and inviting interested parties to fill out a screening form to be considered for inclusion in the study. Just over one-third of the overall interview sample was recruited via the Pride Festival outreach. The rest of the sample was recruited through reaching out to a broad range of LGBT community organizations, posting flyers in public spaces frequented by LGBT people, advertising, and receiving unsolicited referrals from study participants. Potential participants were directed to a website where they could fill out a screening form and leave contact information. We paid respondents a $25 stipend for participating in the study.

In assembling the sample for this study, we made a special effort to correct for the weaknesses of some past studies of the LGBT population by giving priority to groups underrepresented in past research, especially bisexuals, transgender people, racial/ethnic minorities, working-class or poor people, and people living outside of large cities. This resulted in a sample that is probably more representative of the diversity of the LGBT population than many comparable studies, although our sample is likely more highly educated than the LGBT population as a whole.[3] Table 2.1 provides an overview of sample characteristics of the respondents.

All interviews were audio-recorded and transcribed verbatim. For the current analysis, we performed detailed coding of the section of the interviews covering respondents' views of the movement. We started with a basic set of codes (for example, whether the respondent expressed a positive, negative, or mixed opinion of the movement) and then used inductive analysis to develop more detailed subcodes. We analyzed the coded transcripts to identify patterns in the coding, particularly patterns related to respondent characteristics such as race/ethnicity, social class, sexual orientation, and gender identity. This step allowed us to assess the presence and degree of secondary marginalization among movement constituents.

CONSTITUENT PERCEPTIONS OF THE LGBT RIGHTS MOVEMENT

Our interview findings demonstrate how ordinary LGBT people perceive the LGBT movement.[4] We start with their general opinions of the movement, then describe respondents' sense of whether they are represented by the movement, their perceptions of what the movement's current priorities are and what its priorities should be, and their views of the movement's handling of marriage and family issues. We find that marriage and family issues are perceived to be among the movement's highest priorities, and most respondents express the view that this focus on marriage and family is appropriate. Although there is some evidence of secondary marginalization in the movement, we see only limited evidence that this marginalization is related to the movement's focus on marriage.

General Opinions of the Movement

A plurality of respondents who gave an opinion on the movement expressed a mixed opinion. Among those who had a clear positive or negative opinion, positive views were more common (see Figure 2.1). People who held a positive view of the movement mentioned several specific reasons for their assessment. Common perceptions included that the movement has made great strides recently; that the organizations who advocate on behalf of LGBT people are doing important work that the average LGBT person does not have the time or skill to do; that the movement's current approach of working within the political system is more effective than a more radical approach; and that the mainstream LGBT rights movement is holding its own against powerful, well-resourced enemies.

Table 2.1. Sample Characteristics

	Number	Percent
SEXUAL ORIENTATION		
Gay (male)	39	37%
Lesbian	22	21%
Bisexual	31	30%
Other/Questioning*	13	12%
GENDER IDENTITY		
Male	41	39%
Female	42	40%
Transgender or Genderqueer	22	21%
QUEER IDENTITY		
Queer†	38	36%
Non-queer	67	64%
RACE/ETHNICITY		
White (non-Latino)	70	67%
African-American or African	15	14%
Mixed race or Other‡	20	19%
POLITICAL AFFILIATION		
Democrat	63	60%
Republican	2	2%
Independent/Other	36	34%
Data missing	4	4%
SOCIAL CLASS		
Upper middle class	24	23%
Middle class	58	55%
Working class or Poor	23	22%
EDUCATION		
High school diploma or less	6	6%
Some college (no degree)	23	22%
Associate's or Bachelor's degree	41	39%
Graduate degree	29	28%
Data missing	6	6%

Table 2.1. *(continued)*

	Number	Percent
AGE		
18–29	19	18%
30–39	28	27%
40–49	26	25%
50–59	21	20%
60+	11	10%
PLACE OF RESIDENCE		
Minneapolis	55	52%
St. Paul	12	11%
Suburbs/Exurbs	32	30%
St. Cloud area	6	6%
RELIGIOUS AFFILIATION		
Christian	40	38%
Other	31	30%
None	34	32%

Note: Some percentages do not total to 100 percent because of rounding.

*Includes "queer," "omnisexual," "two-spirit," "questioning," and "no labels."

†Includes people who identified as "queer" or "genderqueer."

‡Includes Asian Americans, Latinos (any race), and American Indians.

Heather Weinhold,[5] a forty-three-year-old white middle-class lesbian, is an example of someone who expressed a positive opinion of the movement. She said:

> I think that we're doing a good job. I think we learned a lot from the civil rights movement and that we're taking a lot of those lessons, and that perseverance, and expressing our opinions. And we now have a vehicle. We can do that through HRC [Human Rights Campaign]. We can express our opinions not just as one person but as a group of people to representatives, to the com-

munities. I think Pride here, [the executive director] has done a great job with Pride. And showing the community of healthy individuals. That the majority of us aren't whacked. The media loves to pick up on the one or two people that are just bizarre in a crowd. "These are what gay people look like." And I think that this movement is really being smart about how we present ourselves to the world. Because we can present ourselves as a larger unit, I think it's harder to ignore us and to say, "Oh, it's just a few people." And it's not just a few people. It's your next-door neighbor.

Heather credits the movement with fighting off negative stereotypes and making "the world" see that LGBT people are not "whacked" or "bizarre." She also perceives that movement organizations have been successful in uniting the LGBT population as a viable political force.

People who express negative opinions of the movement do so for various reasons, with little consensus among them about the main shortcomings of the movement. While Heather perceived a unified movement, some argued that the movement is too fragmented. Others expressed concern that the movement has been co-opted and mainly

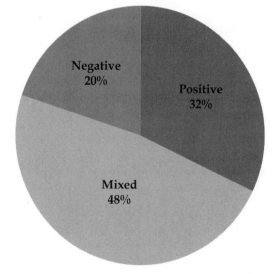

FIGURE 2.1. General opinion of the LGBT rights movement.

represents the needs of white middle-class gays and lesbians, imply-
ing that the movement is *too* unified around a narrow core of people
and interests. People sometimes critiqued movement strategies and
tactics, again for differing reasons. While some respondents argued
that the movement should take a more incremental or pragmatic approach to achieving its goals, others contended that the movement
should be bolder. Some observed that the movement has stagnated and
lacks energy, but others complained that it was trying to do too much
at once.

The concerns expressed by Lisa Chang were fairly typical of respondents who viewed the movement negatively. Lisa, a thirty-one-year-old
Asian-American middle-class lesbian, remarked:

> In general, no matter what they say or who they put in their
> pamphlets, I just believe them to be like, white men and women
> with a lot of money and weird agendas that I just, I don't find to
> be very queer. They're just, like, highly normative kind of things
> that they want to do. Like, I get that marriage is important to
> some people, I'm happy to be married, but it's not really like, if I
> were to choose a national campaign, it wouldn't be what I want
> to do. I understand that some lesbians want to go to some coun-
> try club to play with their kids or have their membership, I don't,
> it's like they don't get, they are not really interested in changing,
> in social change. I think they are really interested in kind of like,
> making us more like kind of heterosexual middle-class people,
> also white. And it's kind of like, well, why? Why would we want
> to do that? I mean, it's like, I understand for myself that I have
> kind of a low creativity in terms of, well, I don't really like this
> but I'm not quite sure what I would do differently, but they're a
> national movement. All they do is think about being gay, you
> know, you'd think they could come up with something that was,
> that changed people's lives in a positive way and wasn't just kind
> of more of the same garbage.

Even though Lisa is herself in a long-term relationship that she defines
as a marriage, she cites the movement's focus on same-sex marriage

as an example of the privilege and homonormativity that she believes characterize the mainstream movement. Lisa then went on to explain that she did not believe the current movement had much connection to the movement that began at Stonewall, with "trannies in a bar fighting about police brutality." In this observation, Lisa echoes the queer activists who fault the movement for straying from its roots in sexual and gender liberation.

Nearly half of all respondents expressed a mixed view of the movement. For example, Hector Campos, a twenty-six-year-old middle-class Latino gay man, expressed frustration with the lack of coalition-building between the LGBT rights movement and other social justice movements:

> I think we have a lot of capacity. . . . I think we could be more strategic, and [do] long-term thinking about how we get certain things achieved. Broader than that, I think we segment things too much. . . . We could be working on creating allegiances between different groups, you know, labor unions have been . . . folded in a little bit more . . . Like, why aren't there any LGBT organizations working with CLUES [Comunidades Latinas Unidas en Servicio, a local Latino nonprofit organization], for example. . . . We have like a huge Latino population here now, and you don't think that, you know, there's all these numbers of like LGBT Latinos? I mean, of course there are. You know, I mean there's so many, kind of, linkages to be made that people are not making.

Hector's observations reflect both a concern about the movement not effectively advocating for underrepresented populations, such as LGBT Latinos, and a perceived need to develop strategic alliances with groups with similar social justice concerns. His remarks echo a perennial critique leveled by some movement observers that the identity politics model, which emphasizes sexual orientation as a fixed characteristic and LGBT people as a discrete and stable social group, inevitably produces a "single-issue, zero-sum model of politics" (Epstein 1999, 75) that makes broader political alliances difficult.

Respondents who self-identified as transgender or bisexual appeared somewhat more likely than lesbian or gay respondents to express ambivalence about the LGBT movement. For example, Ryan Anderson, a forty-two-year-old white middle-class transgender man, expressed both gratitude for the movement's presence and frustration with its lack of full inclusion of transgender people and issues:

> Frankly, I'm grateful that [the movement is] there. I will be honest, though, and I will say that, and I can only speak for myself, but I do know that, in conversations within the trans community, there are a lot of people who say that the T has not caught up with the G, the L, or even the B. And that there's a lot of sadness around that. I think some of the most difficult conversations I had about my transition were with my gay and lesbian friends.

Such ambivalence toward the movement also appeared in the comments of some other transgender respondents. In fact, transgender and genderqueer[6] respondents tended to express more critical opinions of the movement than other respondents. Likewise, bisexual respondents were less likely to express a positive opinion of the movement than gay and lesbian respondents (although the difference was not as striking as the difference between transgender/genderqueer and non-transgender respondents).

There were no clear differences in overall opinion of the movement by race/ethnicity. In terms of social class, working-class and poor respondents were somewhat more likely to hold a positive view of the movement than middle-class and upper-middle-class respondents. At the same time, working-class/poor respondents were more likely to state they had no clear opinion of the movement, often owing to lack of knowledge of the movement's current activities.

Sense of Representation by the Movement

When asked whether they feel represented by the mainstream LGBT movement, only a third of the respondents answered affirmatively without qualifying their response. More commonly, respondents reported that they felt represented in some ways but not others, or they stated that they did not feel represented by the movement. Veronica Holloway, a forty-one-year-old middle-class African-American lesbian, is an example of someone who did not feel represented. She explained:

> I don't feel like I'm represented because I feel like some of the things that, for example, equal rights; equal rights to me as a black woman is completely different than someone that's just gay. Because I fight for equal rights every day because of the color of my skin. So my fight is harder. My fight is a lifetime. So you might get with the goals that you're reaching for. Could be marriage. But that's only one thing. Where my struggle still continues. So I feel like a lot of times that, no, their voice doesn't speak for me.

Veronica sees the movement's goals as possibly attainable, but not focused on her greatest challenges as an African-American woman living in a racist society. Indeed, many of the people who said the movement did not represent them, or did not fully represent them, pointed to identity factors, such as being a racial/ethnic minority, being bisexual or transgender, or not being part of the upper middle class. As a result, sense of representation by the movement was strongly patterned by social location (see Figure 2.2).

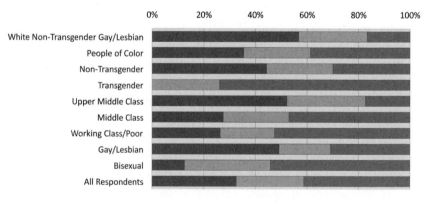

FIGURE 2.2. Whether respondent feels represented by movement.

Most glaring were differences along the lines of gender identity: None of the twenty-two transgender respondents in our sample reported feeling fully represented by the movement. For instance, Melanie Hughes, a twenty-five-year-old white working-class transgender woman (a self-described "tranny girl"), described feeling actively excluded by the mainstream LGBT rights movement:

> I see a big GL, sometimes B movement. And I see a trans movement but I can't say I've ever seen a GLBT movement. I mean it's kind of like I see people fighting for gay marriage and then I see people trying to get jobs. Or people doing mass anti-smoking campaigns for the GLBT movement. And I can't get healthcare honey! Fuck smoking! It's just basic, could we please get people to stop killing us legally? I'm really not concerned about who I'm going to be able to legally marry. I'd much rather have it be illegal to get stabbed in a bathroom. Just basic human rights. I feel like there's a trans movement working on getting people basic human rights. And then there's a GL sometimes B movement kind of just fighting for themselves and being, "Stay the fuck away from us. We're going to go get married and we're going to go get good jobs and we're going to focus on this and you guys are obviously screwed. So we're cutting you off."

For Melanie, the very idea of an "LGBT movement" is a fiction. She perceives the mainstream LGBT rights movement to be focused on gay and lesbian issues, coming from a place of relative privilege with a desire to create more privilege. Thus, she thinks that the most basic trans issues such as physical safety are completely marginalized.

Like transgender respondents, bisexual respondents were unlikely to state unequivocally that they felt represented by the movement. In explaining why they did not feel represented, bisexual respondents expressed concerns about experiencing biphobia within the movement, feeling misunderstood by lesbians and gay men, and feeling as though they were not treated as equal or legitimate participants in the movement. Other bisexual respondents said they did not feel represented because they simply do not need anything from the movement at this time, in some cases because they are currently in opposite-sex relationships and the movement is not working on issues that directly affect them.

Working-class and even middle-class respondents were less likely to say they felt represented than upper-middle-class respondents. Lillian Dominguez is a thirty-one-year-old Latina bisexual woman who considers herself middle class, yet the issue of class emerges as a reason she does not feel completely represented by the movement:

> Well, like when I went to the HRC dinner. Well, first of all the only way I could afford it is because [my partner] Jane got these comp tickets. She gets comp tickets for you name it. And she wanted me to feel welcome, and I dressed up and I talked with her people, and it was just totally inaccessible. It was all about money. Large money, and how can we raise more money. I do fund-raising, so I can understand that. But I just didn't see how it applies on an everyday level. There's a great little foundation here called The Rainbow Fund. I loved working with them. I was on their board and I helped; there's like this small communities-of-color fund, very small. We don't have a lot of money yet. That kind of work, I know, I see that money going to work every single day. But on the national level, I don't see any visibility [for people of color].

Lillian perceives large national organizations such as HRC to be focused on raising money, "large money," and "inaccessible" to people without a lot of money. She expresses more comfort working with a local organization in which she can see the impact of the money being spent. Lillian's comments also suggest a linkage between class-based and race-based feelings of nonrepresentation, as she quickly transitions from explaining her feelings of being an outsider based on class ("I dressed up" but the HRC event felt "totally inaccessible") to her concerns about lack of visibility for racial/ethnic minority issues among the large national movement organizations.

Patterns in feelings of representation by race/ethnicity are difficult to interpret because they appear to be influenced by the intersectionality of identity elements. In a direct comparison of white and nonwhite respondents, whites are a bit less likely to feel represented by the movement than nonwhites. But we suspect this racial difference is mostly attributable to the fact that the transgender and bisexual subsamples in our sample are disproportionately white,[7] and, as noted above, transgender and bisexual people often expressed frustration with the movement's indifference toward their concerns. As shown in Figure 2.2, when whites who are neither bisexual nor transgender are compared to other groups, they have a relatively high sense of representation by the movement, with more than half of white non-transgender gays and lesbians saying they feel represented by the movement.

Respondents who did feel represented by the movement usually pointed to the fact that the movement was working on issues that are important to them or that the movement was an effective advocate for LGBT people in general. Eddie Ferguson is a fifty-two-year-old white upper-middle-class gay man who works in health care. Asked if he feels represented, he replied:

> I think so. I'm going to have to say yeah. Even though it's, like, hard to trust. I'll trust them and their expertise, for them to work on it. There are fronts that, and likewise, that they would trust us on the medical front to like be doing things for the good of us all, on the other front. So, having that professional trust in each other, so yeah. I'm not going to judge what they do or, you know, and even if I didn't agree, it's like, I'm not sure who I would, who I would tell! [*laughs*] Other than getting involved with that front, you know. But yeah, I feel represented.

Drawing a comparison to his own work as a health professional, Eddie regards the movement's leaders as experts and professionals and states that he trusts their decisions about how to run the movement. Although only a minority of respondents gave such a positive response about their sense of representation, many of the people who gave mixed responses did acknowledge some ways in which the movement provides representation for themselves or for the broader community of LGBT people.

Perceived and Preferred Priorities of the Movement

We asked respondents to identify the actual priorities of the movement today, and later asked them what issues they would prefer to see the movement treat as priorities. We refer to the former as the *perceived priorities* of the movement, and the latter as respondents' *preferred priorities*. By far, marriage and family issues were most frequently mentioned as perceived priorities of the movement. More than half of the people in our sample said they thought marriage and family issues were a priority for the movement today. In fact, marriage and family issues were mentioned three times as often as any other perceived priority. The next most common perceived priority was the achievement of general equality for LGBT people. Other issues that were mentioned somewhat frequently included hate crimes legislation, nondiscrimination policies, and working on changing public perceptions of LGBT people.

The preferred priorities of respondents generally mirrored the perceived priorities, although respondents mentioned some issues they would like to see the movement address that were not seen as actual priorities of the current movement (see Figure 2.3). Marriage and family issues were identified as a preferred priority for the movement more than twice as often as any other issue, although the number of respondents who saw marriage and family issues as a current priority of the movement was somewhat higher than the number who said they thought it should be a priority. General equality, hate crimes legislation, employment discrimination, and working on changing public perceptions of LGBT people were also mentioned with some frequency. A few issues were mentioned more often as issues people would like to see the movement focus on than as issues the movement actually does focus on currently. Respondents identified the following specific issues as preferred priorities much more often than as perceived priorities: youth issues, transgender issues, visibility issues, and health care. Youth issues included the treatment of LGBT youth in schools and the handling of LGBT issues in school curricula, as well as the problem of youth homelessness. Health care was usually mentioned as an issue of access, although some also commented on the need to ensure that health-care providers are sensitive and informed on LGBT health concerns.

Number of Respondents Identifying Priority

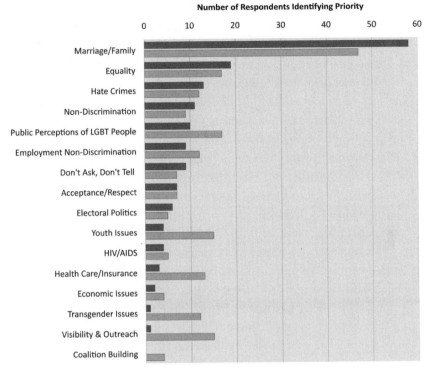

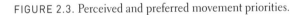

FIGURE 2.3. Perceived and preferred movement priorities.

When respondents identified marriage and family issues as a perceived or preferred priority, marriage was the specific issue mentioned most frequently. Thomas Holte is a fifty-six-year-old white middle-class gay man. Thomas's remarks reflect the views of respondents who identified marriage and family issues as one of the most important things for the movement to work on:

> Well, I think as far as the marriage thing, that's good because that's important. I think the most important thing is to have the benefits like health care, pension, social security. Those are important things for people my age, so that's what I kind of focus on, having had a problem with health care. It's very difficult for

> me to get it, even though the only thing I've had is carpal tunnel, and they won't touch me. So, yeah, I think that's a good thing to focus on. Equal benefits, and then with the marriage, even though I don't have a partner where I would get those from, it's still important, it really does make us equal.

So, even though Thomas would not directly benefit from legalized marriage in his current status as a single man, he views marriage as an important movement goal both for the material benefits it would bring ("health care, pension, social security") and for the way it would "make us equal." This idea that marriage or relationship rights would have broader equality effects was mentioned by a number of people who saw marriage and family issues as a priority for the movement.

Respondents also singled out several other specific family-related issues as priorities, including domestic partnership, adoption, and other parenting issues unrelated to adoption. Some respondents spoke vaguely about "marriage and family" or "family issues" without being specific. The only notable group differences that emerged on family issues were along gender-identity lines: only a handful of transgender respondents mentioned marriage and family issues as their preferred priorities for the movement. Overall, our findings suggest that respondents were generally sympathetic to the movement's focus on marriage and family issues, but some would prefer a broader framing of these issues.

Opinions of the Movement's Work on Family Issues

Because LGBT conceptions of family formed a major focus of our research, and because same-sex marriage has been such a visible issue for the LGBT rights movement over the last fifteen years, we specifically asked respondents for their views of the movement's work on marriage and family issues. We asked whether they felt the movement was focusing too much or too little on these issues, and whether they liked the way the movement approached these issues, or if they felt a different approach would be more effective. The majority of respondents who offered an opinion about the movement's handling of family issues had a positive view (see Figure 2.4). People who did not express an un-

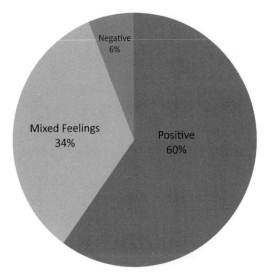

FIGURE 2.4. Opinions of movement's handling of marriage and family issues.

qualified positive opinion mostly offered a mixed opinion rather than a negative opinion. (Only five respondents expressed a strictly negative opinion about the movement's focus on marriage and family issues.)

Laura McIntosh, a twenty-nine-year-old mixed-race upper-middle-class lesbian, gave a response typical of people who had a positive opinion of the movement's handling of family issues:

> It should be the focus, because ultimately these are things that straight couples just do without a second thought. And the fact of the matter is that people want to have kids and they want to raise kids, and people want to get married and live their lives together. That we need to go through so many extra hoops just to do the same things other people do, for really no good reason. . . . Because kind of what it boils down to is, these are things that we can't just go about doing, just because we're gay. And that shouldn't be.

Laura, like many other respondents, thinks that LGBT people should have access to the same family rights as straight people as a matter of basic equality. Other people supportive of the movement's work on family issues noted that many children are waiting to be adopted and that a lot of LGBT people would love to be parents but face many barriers to achieving this goal.

We did not see any clear differences by race/ethnicity or social class in people's evaluation of the movement's handling of marriage and family issues. The fact that working-class/poor respondents and racial/ethnic minority respondents expressed as much support for the movement's work on family issues as other respondents contradicts the argument by queer commentators that marriage is an issue that is mainly desired by the most privileged segment of the LGBT population.

While respondents overall expressed a high level of support for the movement's focus on marriage and family issues, many did offer critiques of the way the movement is handling that focus. Three different sets of critiques appeared with some frequency. First, people expressed concern that other important issues do not receive enough attention when family issues are highlighted. Second, people critiqued the movement's strategy and tactics on family issues. Some respondents argued the movement should do more outreach in conservative areas, should take a more grassroots approach, should take a more incremental approach, should choose more obtainable goals, or should place more emphasis on education and changing basic attitudes toward LGBT people. Leslie Arnold, for example, is a thirty-five-year-old upper-middle-class white bisexual woman who believes the movement's tactics should be more grassroots. Leslie commented:

> I think they're addressing it in a good way. I mean, you have, like, the political stuff where they're pushing things through Congress and everything else, to get rights for certain things. But again, I think it needs to be kind of a ground-up process instead of jumping on top of it and shoving it in people's faces almost. I think there needs to be a little bit more coming in through the back door, so to speak, where you're almost sneak attacking them and educating them, even though they don't know they're being educated. You know what I mean? Instead of having the whole deal with people just waving their flags and flashing their

signs at political debates. It should be one of those things where there's like a grassroots thing, I guess. You almost need to have a grassroots base. And I think that would help quite a bit.

A third critique of the movement's handling of marriage and family issues was that the movement's approach to family was too narrow, either because the movement does not work on behalf of all family types or because it is too focused on the specific goal of marriage. Some respondents saw this narrowness as part of a larger problem of the movement trying too hard to assert the normalcy of LGBT people and families, echoing queer critiques of the movement's trend toward assimilation. Irene Bernhagen, for example, is a thirty-year-old middle-class mixed-race person who identifies as queer and genderqueer. Irene lives with a couple of men and is about to begin co-parenting with them. Expressing multiple concerns about the movement's family focus, Irene said:

I think the more we try to convince people . . . that we're just like everybody else, the more we limit ourselves in being able to . . . create space for all of the diversity in which we create families within our community. And I guess on a personal level I'm seeing that happen more and more as I think about going into a parenting relationship with two other people, where one of us is gonna not have legal rights to our kid because there's no way of doing that. Because oh my god that would look like polygamy, you know, and the next step down from that is marrying a goat. [laughter] You know, like I guess that's one of the things too. Like when I think about the argument, one of the things that I think is really dangerous, and I've been happy to see the advocates try to address this on some small level, is this idea that we need to fight the idea that queer people or gay people in particular asking for marriage rights means that we're asking for rights around polyamory or polyamorous relationships. I think that that's a slippery slope man, in terms [laughter] they're suggesting it's a slippery slope, but I also think it's a slippery slope in the other direction because don't start laying judgments on people's choices with regard to relationships. I don't believe that monogamous relationships are the only type of relationships that are valid and justified in this society, or should be. And so I think that we as a community need to be really careful about where we're laying our values or what we're assuming everyone's values are.

Like other respondents critical of the movement's family focus, Irene is concerned that putting forward a normative focus on the monogamous couple pushes less conventional families and relationships to the margins. Irene argues that the movement should be pushing to expand the types of families that are recognized by society and in policy rather than trying to fit LGBT people into current social and legal frameworks. A number of other respondents articulated principled concerns about the pursuit of legal marriage. Some rejected marriage as a patriarchal institution, others viewed it as a mechanism of social control, and a few noted that legal marriage would create further inequality within the LGBT population by rewarding those who conformed to dominant society's model of committed relationships.

Although we did not see clear differences in people's views on the movement's handling of family issues based on race or class, there were suggestive differences based on gender identity and self-identification as queer. Transgender people and people who self-identified as queer were somewhat more likely to express ambivalent views about the movement's work on family issues. Some transgender respondents pointed out that the marriage issue was not particularly important to their community. We found a few noteworthy differences in the critiques levied by queer- and non-queer-identified respondents. Non-queer respondents were more likely to offer tactical critiques of the movement's handling of marriage and family issues, whereas queer-identified respondents were more likely to offer substantive critiques. Substantive critiques include particular concerns that the movement's focus is not inclusive of all families; that the current focus affects only some segments of LGBT communities; or that there is too much focus on marriage.[8]

DISCUSSION

Our findings regarding constituent perceptions of the LGBT rights movement present a paradox. Only a minority of the respondents in our study feel unambiguously represented by the movement. Yet most respondents have a positive or mixed opinion of the movement rather than a predominantly negative view, and there is a fairly close alignment between the movement's current priorities (as perceived by respondents) and what respondents think the movement *should* be working on. A few issues (youth issues, transgender issues, LGBT visibility, and health care) are mentioned as desirable areas of focus but are rarely or never identified as actual current priorities of the movement. But marriage and family issues are most often identified as the movement's current focus *and* as a desirable focus for movement efforts. So why do most people in our sample feel the movement does not fully represent them, given that they both see the movement as doing a good job (or at least doing well in some areas) and perceive the movement to be focusing on the right issues?

This apparent paradox has a number of possible explanations. Our data indicate that even when people are supportive of the movement's broad goals, they can be quite critical of its specific strategies and tactics. For example, many respondents support the movement's focus on marriage and family concerns, but would rather see the movement approach these issues in a different way. Some respondents think the movement's focus on marriage is too narrow, and a better strategy would be to seek recognition and protection for a broader range of family forms. Others fault the movement's tactical choices: some respondents assert that the movement is moving too quickly on marriage, whereas others complain the approach is too incremental. We have the most detailed information on respondents' views of the movement's handling of marriage and family issues, but it is possible that people also have qualms about the way the movement is pursuing other desirable goals, such as reducing hate crimes or increasing nondiscrimination protections in the law. The sense of nonrepresentation may also reflect constituents' perceptions that the LGBT rights movement is a distant and inaccessible operation run by people who have little in common with the average constituent. Or, in some cases, the sense of nonrepresentation may simply reflect the fact that some constituents feel they do not need the movement's help at this time (as is the case for some bisexuals currently in heterosexual relationships).

Regardless of its source, this paradox complicates the task of assessing whether some constituents experience secondary marginalization by the organized movement, and whether such marginalization is in part the result of the movement's current focus on marriage, as queer critics contend. If we look narrowly at the question of whether the movement is working on the issues constituents care about, the answer appears to be mostly yes, with a few important exceptions. But if we define secondary marginalization broadly, to include constituents' own sense of being marginalized by the movement, our data suggest some clear patterns of marginalization. We found that people's sense of being represented by the mainstream LGBT movement was strongly patterned by social location, with transgender and genderqueer people, bisexual people, middle- or working-class people, and members of racial/ethnic minorities less likely to express an unambiguous sense of representation. Constituents' perceptions may be an imperfect gauge of the actual activities and priorities of a social movement, and in fact many of our respondents confessed somewhat sheepishly that they were not well-informed about the movement's current goals and strategies. But although it is theoretically possible that this subjective component of marginalization is unrelated to "actual" marginalization in terms of the movement's distribution of its symbolic and material resources, we suspect there is some relationship between the subjective experience of marginalization and the actual priorities of the movement. This is especially clear in the case of transgender constituents, because there have been several well-publicized rifts among activists and organizations regarding how to handle transgender concerns.[9]

We also sought to examine whether any secondary marginalization we observed in our data appeared to be linked to the movement's focus on marriage and family issues, and especially its pursuit of legal marriage. Recall that queer critics of the mainstream movement frequently allege that its approach to marriage and family is too narrow and assimilationist, and that it represents the needs and interests of the most privileged segment of its constituency. On this point, our evidence is somewhat mixed. On the one hand, our respondents expressed a high level of support for the general idea of focusing on marriage and family issues: it was the most frequently mentioned set of issues among respondents' preferred priorities for the movement, and only 5 of the 105 respondents expressed an unambiguously negative view of the movement's handling of these issues. Further, we saw no clear differences based on race/ethnicity or social class in the respondents' enthusiasm for the movement's marriage and family work, which calls into question the queer critics' assertion that marriage is a pet issue of the most privileged segment of the movement's constituency. On the other hand, transgender and genderqueer respondents, as well as queer-identified respondents, were more likely than other respondents to express ambivalence about the movement's handling of these issues by offering a mixed assessment rather than a mainly positive one. So, at least for the case of transgender, genderqueer, and queer-identified people, the subjective experience of marginalization may in part be linked to the movement's work on marriage and family issues, and the pursuit of legal marriage in particular. Transgender constituents do not see the movement working on the issues that have highest priority for them, and to the degree that they view movement efforts as a zero-sum proposition, they may view the focus of time and resources on marriage as part of the reason transgender issues are neglected. It bears repeating that many respondents who had positive or mixed views of the movement's work in this area offered critiques of the movement's approach; some of the specific choices the movement has made in goals and tactics could be contributing to some constituents' sense of marginalization or nonrepresentation, even when those constituents had a fairly positive take on the movement's focus in this area.

Our data have some obvious limitations. Like most research on the LGBT population, our study by necessity relies on a nonrandom sample of voluntary respondents, so we cannot claim that our findings are representative of the LGBT population as a whole. In particular, as noted above, our sample appears to be more highly educated than the broader LGBT population. Since education level is positively related to social and political liberalism, we can assume our sample is also more liberal than the overall LGBT population. In the case of LGBT people, more education probably also means more exposure to the queer intellectual perspective. If this is the case, and if marriage is viewed as a conservative or "non-queer" institution and movement goal, our findings may actually understate the level of constituent support for the movement's pursuit of legal marriage. In other words, a more representative sample of the LGBT population would probably express higher levels of support for the movement's marriage work.

Another limitation of our data is that our findings concerning the LGBT movement's ability to represent the full range of its constituents are based on constituent perceptions rather than "objective" data regarding the movement's choices and actions. In our view, this limitation is also a strength. Constituents may have inaccurate or incomplete perceptions of the movement's activities, but when it comes to questions of political representation, we would argue that perception is itself an important reality. Part of what social movements deliver for their constituents is a sense of belonging and a sense that their concerns are finding political expression. For groups that experience high levels of social exclusion, this intangible benefit of movement representation may be as important as some of the more concrete benefits the movement seeks to deliver. Constituents who do not feel represented by a movement that speaks in their name are likely to have low investment in the movement's success or failure, so their subjective experience of marginalization can have practical consequences for movement organizations, cohesion, and mobilization.

In summary, our findings are consistent with other research that has observed secondary marginalization in the LGBT rights movement, finding that transgender people, bisexuals, and people who articulate queer perspectives often feel marginalized by the mainstream LGBT rights movement (e.g., Smith 2007; Stone 2006, 2009; see also Phelan 2001). What we add to the past research is an explicit focus on marginalization from the perspective of movement constituents. In our view, this perceptual or subjective dimension of secondary marginalization has not received sufficient attention. We see evidence of subjective marginalization in the LGBT movement along dimensions of class, race/ethnicity, sexual orientation (i.e., bisexuality), and gender identity (transgender and genderqueer). Constituents' overall sense of representation by the mainstream LGBT movement is strongly patterned by social location. However, we found only limited evidence to support the idea that the movement's current focus on marriage and family issues (and particularly on marriage qua marriage) is a significant source of subjective marginalization in the movement. Respondents were generally supportive of the movement's focus on marriage and family issues, and there was little support for the idea that these issues were significantly more important to white, middle- or upper-middle-class constituents. However, the movement's work on marriage in particular may play a part in the subjective marginalization of queer, transgender, and genderqueer constituents.

Our analysis points to several promising areas for future research. More investigation is necessary to flesh out our understanding of why some constituents report that they do not feel represented by the LGBT rights movement, even though they have a fairly positive opinion of the movement and there is strong overlap between the movement's actual priorities and constituents' preferred priorities. Comparative studies could illuminate whether this paradox is unique to this particular movement or is a common phenomenon across different social movements. What are the specific features of institutionalized social movement organizations that produce constituent perceptions of representation, movement effectiveness, and aligned priorities? For example, past research has documented women's marginalization across a range of male-dominated movements (Brown 1992; Fonow 1998; J. Gamson 1997; McAdam 1992; Robnett 1997; Roth 1998; see Taylor 1999 for a discussion). Comparative analysis could address how much and in what ways the dynamics of gender marginalization in some movements resemble the secondary marginalization within the LGBT rights movement. Our research also raises the question of the influence of elite critiques of movements on constituents' perceptions. What are the mediating factors that explain when elite critiques, such as the critiques leveled by antiassimilationist queer commentators, penetrate ordinary constituents' consciousness?

More generally, how do constituent perceptions matter for movements? Can well-established movement organizations thrive indefinitely when they are providing a strong sense of representation for only the more advantaged members of their claimed constituency? What is the relationship between internal legitimacy (constituents' approval and sense of representation) and the external legitimacy and effectiveness of social movements? Answering such questions will require social movement scholars to widen their lens from the words and actions of social movement activists to include the concerns and perceptions of movement constituents.

NOTES

1. Strolovitch defines disadvantaged members as those who experience "intersectional marginalization," meaning they incur social disadvantage based on other social characteristics in addition to the identity of the marginalized group in question. For example, low-income women experience intersectional marginalization within the marginalized group defined by low income, and racial minority women experience intersectional marginalization within the group defined by gender.

2. Cahill observes: "Access to the 1,138 federal protections and benefits of marriage would clearly help Black and Hispanic same-sex couples provide for their children, save money, buy a house, or prepare for retirement. The federal benefits and protections of marriage that are currently only available to married opposite sex couples include filing their taxes jointly, Social Security survivor benefits, Medicaid spend-down protections and the ability to take time off from work to care for a sick or disabled partner under the Family and Medical Leave Act. Over a lifetime, the inability to marry means that all same-sex couples, regardless of race or ethnicity, often pay more in taxes but are unable to benefit from government policies designed to help maintain strong and healthy families" (2009, 243–44; notes omitted).

3. Data on lesbian, gay, and bisexual educational attainment are available from several sources, including the General Social Survey (GSS), the National Health and Social Life Survey (NHSLS), and the U.S. Census. (The census data include only members of cohabiting same-sex couples.) Badgett (2001) combined NHSLS data from 1992 and GSS data from 1989 to 1991, 1993, and 1994 to analyze earnings of lesbian/bisexual women and gay/bisexual men (defined as those who had had at least as many same-sex sexual partners as opposite-sex partners in their lifetime). In this combined sample, 43 percent of the lesbian/bisexual women and 49 percent of the gay/bisexual men had a high school diploma or less, compared to only 6 percent of respondents in our sample. Black et al. (2000) analyzed 1990 Census data for men and women in cohabiting same-sex relationships and computed the following percentages for those with a high school diploma or less: 21 percent of men age 25–34 and 14 percent of men age 35–44; 20 percent of women age 25–34 and 15 percent of women age 35–44. We are not aware of any good data on the educational attainment of transgender people.

4. Our sample includes very few people who could be considered LGBT movement activists, as opposed to movement constituents. Although we did some recruiting through LGBT organizations and at the annual Pride festival, the large majority of our respondents did not hold leadership positions in LGBT organizations or participate in movement activities on a regular basis. We also feel confident that our sample mainly represents ordinary constituents rather than activists on the basis of some of the comments respondents made in interviews and focus groups. For example, many respondents were hesitant to render judgments about the LGBT movement because they felt uninformed about its activities, and most respondents did not feel well represented by the movement, as we discuss below.

5. All names are pseudonyms.

6. "Genderqueer" (or "gender queer") is a fairly recent form of self-identification embraced by people who reject the male-female gender binary. The term can include, but is not limited to, transgender people. See Nestle, Howell, and Wilchins (2002) for a discussion.

7. Specifically, 77 percent of the transgender respondents are non-Latino whites, compared to 64 percent of the non-transgender respondents; and 84 percent of the bisexual respondents are non-Latino whites, compared to 59 percent of non-bisexual respondents.

8. Queer-identified respondents were disproportionately white and middle or upper middle class. Thus the overall lack of differences by race and class in support of the movement's work on family issues may mask some noteworthy intersectional dynamics. Being in the dominant social categories of white and middle class may in fact make one more likely to support the movement's work on family issues, but only if one does not self-identify as queer. Thus, ironically, the presence of queer respondents in the sample may make it more difficult to see the patterns predicted by queer critiques, namely that more socially privileged (white, middle-class) LGBT people will be more invested in the movement's work on marriage and family issues. It is difficult to disentangle the significance of whiteness and queer self-identification on views of the movement's marriage and family work, especially since very few nonwhites self-identified as queer.

9. For example, when the federal Employment Non-Discrimination Act was brought up for a vote in Congress in 2007, some politicians favored dropping the transgender protections from the bill to increase its chances of passage, and the Human Rights Campaign initially expressed openness to this possibility, but retreated in the face of an outcry from other movement organizations and from movement constituents.

REFERENCES

Badgett, M. V. Lee. 2001. *Money, Myths, and Change: The Economic Lives of Lesbians and Gay Men*. Chicago: University of Chicago Press.

BeyondMarriage.org. 2006. "Beyond Same-Sex Marriage: A New Strategic Vision for All Our Families and Relationships." http://www.beyondmarriage.org/full_statement.html.

Black, Dan, Gary Gates, Seth Sanders, and Lowell Taylor. 2000. "Demographics of the Gay and Lesbian Population in the United States: Evidence from Available Systematic Data Sources." *Demography* 37 (20): 139–54.

Brown, Elaine. 1992. *A Taste of Power: A Black Woman's Story.* New York: Pantheon.

Cahill, Sean. 2009. "The Disproportionate Impact of Antigay Family Policies on Black and Latino Same-Sex Couple Households." *Journal of African American Studies* 13: 219–50.

Cohen, Cathy J. 1999. *The Boundaries of Blackness: AIDS and the Breakdown of Black Politics.* Chicago: University of Chicago Press.

Coy, Patrick J., and Timothy Hedeen. 2005. "A Stage Model of Social Movement Co-Optation: Community Mediation in the United States." *Sociological Quarterly* 46: 405–35.

Duggan, Lisa. 2003. *The Twilight of Equality? Neoliberalism, Cultural Politics, and the Attack on Democracy.* Boston: Beacon Press.

Epstein, Steven. 1999. "Gay and Lesbian Movements in the United States: Dilemmas of Identity, Diversity, and Political Strategy." In *The Global Emergence of Gay and Lesbian Politics: National Imprints of a Worldwide Movement,* edited by Barry D. Adam, Jan Willem Duyvendak, and André Krouwel, 30–90. Philadelphia: Temple University Press.

Eskridge, William, Jr. 1996. *The Case for Same-Sex Marriage: From Sexual Liberty to Civilized Commitment.* New York: Free Press.

Ettelbrick, Paula. 1992. "Since When Is Marriage a Path to Liberation?" In *Lesbian and Gay Marriage: Private Commitments, Public Ceremonies,* edited by Suzanne Sherman, 20–26. Philadelphia: Temple University Press.

Fonow, Mary Margaret. 1998. "Protest Engendered: The Participation of Women Steelworkers in the Wheeling-Pittsburgh Steel Strike of 1985." *Gender and Society* 12: 710–28.

Gamson, Joshua. 1997. "Messages of Exclusion: Gender, Movements, and Symbolic Boundaries." *Gender and Society* 11: 178–99.

Gamson, William A. [1975] 1990. *The Strategy of Social Protest.* 2nd ed. Belmont, Calif.: Wadsworth.

Hunter, Nan. 1991. "Marriage, Law and Gender: A Feminist Inquiry." *Law and Sexuality* 9: 18–19.

McAdam, Doug. 1992. "Gender as a Mediator of the Activist Experience: The Case of Freedom Summer." *American Journal of Sociology* 97: 1211–49.

McCarthy, John D., and Mayer N. Zald. 1977. "Resource Mobilization and Social Movements: A Partial Theory." *American Journal of Sociology* 82: 1212–41.

Meyer, David S., and Sidney Tarrow. 1998. "A Movement Society: Contentious Politics for a New Century." In *The Social Movement Society: Contentious Politics for a New Century,* edited by David S. Meyer and Sidney Tarrow, 1–28. Lanham, Md.: Rowman and Littlefield.

Michels, Robert. [1915] 1962. *Political Parties: A Sociological Study of the Oligarchical Tendencies of Modern Democracy.* Reprint. New York: Free Press.

Naples, Nancy A. 2002. "Materialist Feminist Discourse Analysis and Social Movement Research: Mapping the Changing Context for 'Community Control.'" In *Social*

Movements: Identity, Culture and the State, edited by David S. Meyer, Nancy Whittier, and Belinda Robnett, 226–46. New York: Oxford University Press.

Nestle, Joan, Clare Howell, and Riki Wilchins. 2002. *GenderQueer: Voices from beyond the Sexual Binary*. Los Angeles: Alyson Books.

Phelan, Shane. 2001. *Sexual Strangers: Gays, Lesbians and Dilemmas of Citizenship*. Philadelphia: Temple University Press.

Piven, Frances Fox, and Richard A. Cloward. 1977. *Poor People's Movements: Why They Succeed, How They Fail*. New York: Pantheon.

Polikoff, Nancy D. 1993. "We Will Get What We Ask For: Why Legalizing Gay and Lesbian Marriage Will Not 'Dismantle the Legal Structure of Gender in Every Marriage.'" *Virginia Law Review* 79 (7): 1535–50.

———. 2008. *Beyond (Straight and Gay) Marriage: Valuing All Families under the Law*. Boston: Beacon Press.

Rauch, Jonathan. 2004. *Gay Marriage: Why It Is Good for Gays, Good for Straights, and Good for America*. New York: Times Books.

Robnett, Belinda. 1997. *How Long, How Long? African-American Women in the Struggle for Civil Rights*. New York: Oxford University Press.

Roth, Benita. 1998. "Feminist Boundaries in the Feminist-Friendly Organization: The Women's Caucus of ACT UP/LA." *Gender and Society* 12: 129–45.

Selznick, Phillip. 1949. *TVA and the Grassroots: A Study in the Sociology of Formal Organization*. Berkeley: University of California Press.

Smith, Miriam. 2007. "Framing Same-Sex Marriage in Canada and the United States: Goodridge, Halpern, and the National Boundaries of Political Discourse." *Social and Legal Studies* 16: 5–26.

Staggenborg, Suzanne. 1988. "The Consequences of Professionalization and Formalization in the Pro-Choice Movement." *American Sociological Review* 53: 585–606.

Stoddard, Thomas. 1992. "Why Gay People Should Seek the Right to Marry." In *Lesbian and Gay Marriage: Private Commitments, Public Ceremonies*, edited by Suzanne Sherman, 13–19. Philadelphia: Temple University Press.

Stone, Amy L. 2006. "More than Adding a T: Transgender Inclusion in Michigan Gay Rights Ordinances, 1992–2000." Ph.D. diss., University of Michigan.

———. 2009. "Like Sexual Orientation? Like Gender? Transgender Inclusion in Nondiscrimination Ordinances." In *Queer Mobilizations: LGBT Activists Confront the Law*, edited by Mary L. Bernstein, Anna-Maria Marshall, and Scott Barclay, 142–57. New York: New York University Press.

Strolovitch, Dara Z. 2007. *Affirmative Advocacy: Race, Class, and Gender in Interest Group Politics*. Chicago: University of Chicago Press.

Sullivan, Andrew. 1996. *Virtually Normal: An Argument about Homosexuality*. New York: Vintage Books.

Taylor, Verta. 1999. "Gender and Social Movements: Gender Processes in Women's Self-Help Movements." *Gender and Society* 13: 8–33.

Vaid, Urvashi. 1995. *Virtual Equality: The Mainstreaming of Gay and Lesbian Liberation*. New York: Anchor.

Walters, Suzanna Danuta. 2001. "The Marrying Kind? Take My Domestic Partner, Please: Gays and Marriage in the Era of the Visible." In *Queer Families, Queer*

Politics: Challenging Culture and the State, edited by Mary Bernstein and Renate Reimann, 338–57. New York: Columbia University Press.

Warner, Michael. 1999. *The Trouble with Normal: Sex, Politics, and the Ethics of Queer Life.* New York: Free Press.

Weber, Max. [1922] 1978. *Economy and Society: An Outline of Interpretive Sociology.* Edited by Guenther Roth and Claus Wittich. Reprint. Berkeley: University of California Press.

Wolfson, Evan. 1994. "Crossing the Threshold: Equal Marriage Rights for Lesbians and Gay Men and the Intra-Community Critique." *New York University Review of Law and Social Change* 21: 567–615.

———. 2004. *Why Marriage Matters: America, Equality, and Gay People's Right to Marry.* New York: Simon and Schuster.

Zald, Mayer N., and Roberta Ash. 1966. "Social Movement Organizations: Growth, Decay and Change." *Social Forces* 44: 327–41.

3 Beyond Queer vs. LGBT

Discursive Community and Marriage Mobilization in Massachusetts

Jeffrey Kosbie

O N NOVEMBER 18, 2003, the Massachusetts Supreme Judicial Court ruled in favor of same-sex marriage (*Goodridge v. Department of Public Health*). Over the next four years, activists mobilized on either side of proposed anti-same-sex marriage constitutional amendments. MassEquality mobilized activists to defend same-sex marriage, but activists fundamentally disagreed about the meaning of marriage and its relationship to a broader social movement. Focusing on post-*Goodridge* mobilization, this chapter asks how activists used discourse to overcome internal divisions. Mobilizing this diverse coalition depended on multiple framings of marriage that strategically connected multiple individual identities to an activist collective identity, while simultaneously minimizing critical discussion of identity differences between individuals.

While some lesbians and gays embrace same-sex marriage as an obvious movement goal, other activists and academics question or entirely reject marriage (Case 2010; Chauncey 2004; Conrad 2010; Polikoff 2008; Warner 1999).[1] This division is often characterized as one between the lesbian, gay, bisexual, and transgender (LGBT) and queer movements. In this description, LGBT is seen as a mainstream liberal reform movement, with marriage equality as a key goal. Queer is seen as a more radical, liberationist movement.

I reject this simple dichotomy. While debates and tensions over the meaning of marriage played out across the activist work at MassEquality, they did not follow a simple "LGBT" versus "queer" division. Some gay and lesbian activists participated in the movement precisely because they were married or intended to marry, but many others questioned the value of marriage. Queer activists criticized the focus on marriage as misplaced, suggesting that issues such as youth protection, job discrimination, or health care were more important. Yet these same activists were involved in the fight to protect marriage equality. Furthermore, about half of the activists involved were straight. None of these allies would directly benefit from same-sex marriage and some even questioned the social value of marriage (Myers 2008). All the activists agreed that *Goodridge* should be protected, but beyond that they differed on why protecting marriage was important and who should be involved in the work. Activists shared a collective identity as "marriage supporters," but their other identities informed their work and at times threatened shared goals.

Social movement scholarship has long identified internal dissent as a common feature of identity-based social movements (Cohen 1999; J. Gamson 1995, 1997; McCarthy and Zald 1987; Taylor and Whittier 1992). Recent scholarship increasingly suggests that this internal dissent may be productive (Bernstein and De la Cruz 2009; Ghaziani 2008; Halley 1994, 2000; Myers 2008; Roth 2004). If internal dissent over identity issues increasingly characterizes modern social movements (Taylor 2011), this dissent must be managed in order to be productive. This chapter examines the role of activist discourse in managing internal dissent over identity and framing. I treat MassEquality as a discursive community for the production of overlapping ideologies about same-sex marriage (Rochon 1998; Wuthnow 1989). By providing an institutional space for discourse, the organization allowed activists to connect the same work to different broader social identities and goals.

After a brief history of the same-sex marriage movement in Massachusetts, this chapter introduces the concept of shared identity discourse. I argue that multiple identities are managed through broad discussion of the meaning of marriage with only minimal, strategic discussion of identity itself. Shared identity discourse is an active project of building consensus on movement goals and managing tensions across multiple individual identities. My data illustrate how discourse about marriage draws in activists with otherwise competing identities. By illustrating how the content of the *Goodridge* decision shaped shared identity discourse at MassEquality, this chapter also contributes to the broader literature on the role of courts in social change (McCann 1994; Rosenberg [1991] 2008).

MULTIPLE IDENTITIES AND SHARED IDENTITY DISCOURSE

The Challenge of Multiple Identities

Scholars use the term *collective identity* to describe how activists share a common characteristic or status (Bernstein 2005; Hunt and Benford 2004; Klandermans 1994; Melucci 1996; Polletta and Jasper 2001; Taylor and Whittier 1992). Collective identity is often based on status categories, such as race or gender, but may also be constructed around common interests, such as environmentalism. I use a definition of collective identity based on group boundaries and shared goals (Hunt and Benford 2004; Taylor and Whittier 1992).[2] Boundaries define an "us" and a "them" through "members' common interests, experiences and solidarity" (Taylor and Whittier 1992, 105). By defining group boundaries, activists can identify shared grievances, goals, and strategies (Melucci 1995).

Collective-identity scholars frequently recognize internal movement disputes over identity that arise when activists either do not agree on movement goals or do not agree on how to define the "us" that benefits from the movement's goals (Einwohner, Reger, and Myers 2008; Klandermans 1994; McCarthy and Zald 1987; Taylor and Whittier 1992). While some scholarship suggests that multiple identities lead to movement infighting and eventual failure (McCarthy and Zald 1987), other scholarship focuses instead on dynamic changes in identity over a movement's life (Friedman and McAdam 1992; Ghaziani 2008; Klandermans 1994; Melucci 1995). Strategic uses of identity, intraorganizational boundaries, and "ally" identities can facilitate multiple identities within a movement (Bernstein 1997; Myers 2008; Reger 2002; Whittier 1995). Scholars of collective identity are increasingly concerned with understanding how activists bring multiple intersecting and competing identities into their work (Einwohner, Reger, and Myers 2008; Taylor 2011).

Scholarship on LGBT social movements has been particularly productive in studying dissent over movement identities (Armstrong 2002; Bernstein 1997; Epstein 1987; J. Gamson 1995; Ghaziani 2008; Halley 2000; Taylor and Whittier 1992). Amin Ghaziani identifies the central challenge as a debate within the LGBT community over whether lesbian and gay identity is fundamentally similar to or different from heteronormative identities (Ghaziani 2011). LGBT social movements have resolved this debate in different ways. Elizabeth Armstrong (2002) argues that the LGBT movement achieves "unity through diversity," making interest-group politics one expression of identity in a broader field. Paul Lichterman (1999) argues that when an organization values critical reflection on members' interests and other identities, the organization creates a "forum" for broad identity talk. The concepts of "unity through diversity" and "forum" both allow social movements to function without resolving internal divisions over the meaning of lesbian and gay identities. Similarly, Daniel Myers (2008) examines how an "ally" identity allows straight activists to work alongside LGBT movements without fully sharing the same identity as other activists. Ghaziani finds that some organizations may resolve this role of allies by redefining identity in terms of "us and them" instead of "us versus them" (Ghaziani 2011). Myers's and Ghaziani's efforts to blur the neat lines of group boundaries are useful for my consideration of how different identities interacted at MassEquality. In this study, I demonstrate that when allies are incorporated, identity conflicts are not always resolved. Activists at MassEquality prioritized the inclusion of diverse identities through a broad shared identity discourse on the meaning of marriage with minimal critical reflection on identity.

Frames as Shared Identity Discourse

Framing is the work of defining individual grievances as social problems that are properly addressed by collective action (W.A. Gamson [1975] 1990; Hunt, Benford, and Snow 1994; Snow et al. 1986). It involves a "process of people constructing and negotiating shared meaning" (W.A. Gamson 1992, 17). Successful framing defines a social problem in relation to an "us" and a "them" and brings a broader range of activists into a social movement (W. A. Gamson [1975] 1990). By defining grievances in particular ways, social movements seek to solidify a sense of collective identity in opposition to a perceived other (Morris 1992; Snow 2004).

Past scholarship has considered collective action frame disputes (Benford and Snow 2000) in relation to internal movement constituencies (Ghaziani 2008), countermovements (Fetner 2008), the public and the media (Benford and Hunt 2003; W. A. Gamson 1995, 2004), and the law (Pedriana 2009). I build on this work by illustrating how framing disputes can define the boundaries of a community, providing members with a safe space to disagree on the meaning of an issue. Instead of thinking of MassEquality as a coherent group in which every individual participates for the same reason, I treat the organization as a discursive community that serves as an institutional space for the production of multiple cultural meanings behind a single legal goal (Rochon 1998; Wuthnow 1989).[3] Framing disputes within a discursive community are not an attempt to define what is "right" or "proper" or who belongs in a social movement, but instead become a shared identity discourse that defines the relationship between a movement's goals and the different identities within the movement. In the process of debating marriage as a social movement goal, activists constructed an "us" that included all marriage supporters, even if they did not always agree on what it meant to be a marriage supporter.

I define *shared identity discourse* as the use of multiple frames of an issue to define a community with a common goal but with different identities and motivations for mobilization. By discourse, I stress the continuous negotiation of what it means to belong to the community of marriage supporters. If framing is typically understood to define an "us" that will mobilize around an issue, then shared identity discourse uses multiple frames to define a community that takes the place of a single "us." Through this process, a sort of activist identity is substantiated, but this does not supersede other individual identities. At MassEquality, this process played out as activists strategically emphasized and de-emphasized different meanings of marriage equality to construct shared boundaries defining the limits of who is a marriage

supporter. By focusing on building a community of marriage supporters (as opposed to a "them" of "haters"), MassEquality brought together
a broad group of activists at the cost of suppressing the consideration
of identity differences and the sometimes uncomfortable fit between
different meanings of marriage and broader goals for social change.

HISTORICAL BACKGROUND AND METHODS

In 1993, Freedom to Marry began the groundwork for a long-term campaign to secure marriage equality in Massachusetts. Early on, Freedom to Marry educated and lobbied legislators to allow same-sex parent
adoption rights and overturn sodomy laws. Anticipating backlash from
Vermont's same-sex marriage court decision in 1999 (*Baker v. State of
Vermont*), Freedom to Marry, the American Civil Liberties Union, the
National Gay and Lesbian Task Force, and other organizations began
working on a campaign to win public support for same-sex marriage
rights in Massachusetts. These groups formed MassEquality as an
umbrella organization for their efforts. Meanwhile, Gay and Lesbian
Advocates and Defenders filed the *Goodridge* lawsuit on April 11, 2001.
On November 18, 2003, the Supreme Judicial Court of Massachusetts
ruled in favor of same-sex marriage (*Goodridge*).[4] The court heavily
relied on the idea of marriage as a fundamental social institution in
reaching its conclusion (Kosbie 2011).

By the time *Goodridge* was decided, the Massachusetts legislature
had already convened for five constitutional conventions and rejected
one anti-same-sex marriage amendment proposed by conservative activists. In the wake of *Goodridge*, same-sex marriage activists anticipated
a protracted battle. MassEquality hired Marty Rouse as its first campaign director in early 2004 and began functioning as an independent
organization with its own staff and board of directors. While Mass-
Equality drew members from the different organizations represented
in the early same-sex marriage coalition, it functioned as a single organization in the three-and-a-half-year campaign to protect the right to
same-sex marriage in Massachusetts. Because I am interested in the post-
Goodridge period, I treat MassEquality as a single organization rather
than a coalition.[5] MassEquality mobilized against attempts to amend

the state constitution, using tactics that included door-to-door canvassing, electoral campaigning in support of pro-equality candidates, organizing constituent-legislator meetings, lobbying legislators, and rallying outside the State House. On June 14, 2007, the legislature rejected the final anti-same-sex marriage amendment by a vote of 151–45, concluding a campaign that included seventeen constitutional conventions to debate three separate amendments (Phillips and Estes 2007).

MassEquality publicly framed same-sex marriage mobilization with the themes of equality and rights, using the slogan "It's Wrong to Vote on Rights." But this abstract constitutional idea alone was not enough to mobilize a broad range of activists over several years. Instead, I argue that MassEquality employed frames as a shared identity discourse that tied multiple identities to its goals. By highlighting multiple legal and cultural understandings of *Goodridge*, activists at MassEquality could discuss same-sex marriage as a goal that is significant to more than just lesbians and gay men. MassEquality's campaign has served as a model: activists from MassEquality have shared their ideas and in many cases have gone on to work in and lead same-sex marriage campaigns in other states.[6]

Before beginning my research, I worked as a canvasser at Mass-Equality from 2005 to 2006. My experience with the organization helped identify key research concerns and potential interviewees. Following the final constitutional convention in 2007, I conducted sixteen semi-structured interviews that form the primary data for this research. Starting with personal contacts at MassEquality, I developed a theoretically informed convenience sample that included variations based on sexual orientation, age, gender, previous activist experience, and location in the organization. The interviews averaged forty-five minutes and focused on themes of identity, group interactions, framing of marriage, and mobilization. I recorded and transcribed interviews, allowing interviewees to review the transcripts. The initial review and coding of the transcripts focused on discovering the dominant themes in each transcript, with later coding guided by theoretical concerns pertaining to identity and framing. I use pseudonyms for most interviewees (identified by first name only) but use the real names of leaders (identified by full name and organizational role). In addition to interviews, I draw on limited participant observation in the MassEquality office and at protests and other public events. I also consulted organizational documents, newspaper accounts, and other publications to provide greater context for the discussion of framing.

MULTIPLE IDENTITIES AT MASSEQUALITY

As activists mobilized around marriage equality, they used shared identity discourse to define the boundaries of a community of marriage supporters. Matt explained that "there was a very strong sense of community. . . . I didn't feel weird or anything because I was straight." Similarly, Liz explained, "I think that there was cohesiveness because it's such a knowledge base." Liz's comment reflects how MassEquality functioned as a discursive community, with shared identity discourse producing knowledge about marriage and defining boundaries around the meaning of "marriage supporter." Frequent conversations between staff and volunteers reinforced the shared goal of protecting *Goodridge*, constructing a "them." Activists would use "haters" as shorthand for people against same-sex marriage. Similarly, after door-to-door interactions, canvassers rated people on a scale of one to five, with one being "strongly supports equal marriage rights/wants to be active" and five being "strongly against equal marriage rights." MassEquality, then, is composed of the "ones," those who are willing to mobilize in support of marriage equality. This construction of community was explicitly focused on the goal of defending *Goodridge*. Activists discussed how many legislators were planning to vote in support of same-sex marriage and in the canvass office a poster tracked how many postcards activists had delivered to legislators.

By discursively constructing a "marriage supporter" community, activists at MassEquality expanded "us" to include allies and others who were once part of "them" (Ghaziani 2011; Myers 2008). While Ghaziani's (2011) concept of "us and them" cannot capture the importance of "haters" in opposition to MassEquality, "us and them" helps explain how lesbians and gays emphasized solidarity with, instead of opposition to, straight allies. Unlike "us and them," this solidarity did not always equal cohesion. Activists continued to mobilize as gay and lesbian, progressive, religious, and radical. Being a "marriage supporter" meant activists participated in a particular discursive community and shared common goals, but not that they shared a clear movement identity (Jasper 1997). Despite a sense of community, there was underlying tension over who really stood to benefit from the organization's work. I argue that mobilizing this discursive community depended on strategic framing and de-emphasis of identity differences. Describing the multiple identities mobilized by the marriage-equality movement allows an examination of the underlying identity tensions in the marriage-supporter community.

Gay and Lesbian

Nine of my sixteen interviewees identified as gay or lesbian. Most of these activists directly related marriage to their personal identity. Julie Verratti, canvass director, explained, "I mean for personal reasons, it's an issue I feel close to in my heart or whatever, because I'm gay." Marc Solomon, campaign director of MassEquality, made this connection even more explicit: "I guess I feel like, you know . . . why should society treat gays and lesbians any differently, and to personalize it, why shouldn't I be able to get married?"

Some gay and lesbian activists identified directly with marriage as an institution, while others identified more directly with the movement as a whole. Among the latter, Eric talked about how his "own personal history is tied in so much with the history of . . . really kind of, of the movement in general." Focusing directly on the institution of marriage, Heather made identity central to her claims, saying, "I mean, it's a highly personal issue for me. I want to get married. . . . This is something that is going to impact every aspect of my life."

Activists did not agree on what it meant to identify as gay or lesbian. Charles explained, "They all have different ideas about what it means to be gay, or at least what it means to be gay and political." Many lesbian and gay activists defined these terms as an umbrella for anyone who was sexually attracted to persons of the same gender. Other activists stressed identification with a movement. One lesbian activist explained that "you can be homosexual and not be gay; gay is cultural." Another gay male activist said he disliked the term as a label, but admitted it was sometimes useful. Some gay and lesbian activists, including two of my interviewees, questioned the institution of marriage. For these activists, identifying as gay did not neatly explain their commitment to same-sex marriage. Moreover, a lesbian activist told me, "I don't understand why straight people [work with MassEquality]."

Progressive Political Identity

A progressive political identity motivated another large group of activists, including five of my sixteen interviewees who identified as straight.[7] These progressive activists not only described marriage equality as a progressive political position but also connected it to their personal identities. While many of these activists drew on a background in other progressive political movements, they stressed that marriage was a more intimate goal than their past political work. A straight male activist, James, emphasized the personal aspect of this movement: "And it's so personal. You know, it's a lot more personal than stopping the war, or fair trade coffee   when it's your best friend, you know, other people around you." Other activists more explicitly tried to bring their identity into the work. Rachel, a straight woman, told me, "For me it was never a question of well, this is not my issue. I never felt like this is not my issue. . . . I think that equal rights is everyone's issue." Amy Mello, the field director, explicitly brought up her sexuality: "The biggest thing about this for straight supporters is you really get to understand what it would be like to be in somebody else's shoes." Amy explained that while she felt welcomed into a community, she may not have understood marriage equality in the same way as gay and lesbian activists. Progressive activists were thus members of the marriage-supporter community, but did not share the same identity as others.

Religious Reformer

A small number of activists mobilized around marriage equality based on religious identities, including two of my interviewees. While these activists may have also mobilized based on lesbian and gay or progressive identities, they saw marriage equality as tied to their religious identities. Religious activists mobilized around marriage as an issue within their own religions and within the broader society. Anne Fowler, chair of the board of the Religious Coalition for the Freedom to Marry, explained that her work for marriage equality fit within her broader pastoral work to support her congregation. By mobilizing around same-sex marriage, Anne could make space for lesbian and gay members of her congregation. Similarly, George explained that he saw marriage equality as a broader issue of religious freedom. While he originally sought recognition of same-sex unions within his own religion, he became particularly interested in providing a religious counter-narrative to the Roman Catholic Church's opposition to same-sex marriage. By emphasizing religious freedom, George constructed an identity as a religious reformer.

Despite the prominent role that religion plays in mainstream discussion of same-sex marriage, religious activists felt marginalized at MassEquality. The Religious Coalition for the Freedom to Marry had an office within MassEquality's office space, but Anne explained to me that until the very end of the same-sex marriage campaign Mass-Equality did not fully value the contributions of religious activists. Maintaining a place for religious activists in the discursive community demanded that MassEquality make room for religion alongside a focus on marriage as a strictly civil institution.

Radical Political Orientation

While progressive activists are committed to mainstream liberal reform goals, radical activists are committed to more fundamental change in social structures. Radical and queer activists often entirely reject the institution of marriage (Conrad 2010), yet some of them work for marriage equality. One of my interviewees explicitly described himself as radical and queer, and another identified as queer.[8] In describing their political orientation, several other interviewees included some radical critiques of society. While they did not self-identify as radical, these activists explained that if they were not involved with MassEquality, they would be involved in more radical or queer political work.

Brian most clearly articulated a radical identity in describing his orientation:

Gay is men being attracted to other men. And has decreasingly so become its own unique culture, and has increasingly so become a culture that seeks to and is becoming assimilated into a heteronormative culture and society. . . . Queer is a broader statement of culture. . . . The culture that I am a part of and endeavor to continue to be a part of, and the community that I want to be a part of, is a non-assimilationist culture.

As seen here, radical critiques of social structures are part of how this subset of activists define themselves and their relation to mobilization efforts. They often expressed some hesitation about their personal involvement in same-sex marriage political work and whether it should be a goal of a lesbian and gay movement. While these activists were part of the marriage-supporter community, they expressed varying degrees of uneasiness over identifying with other activists. Despite these identity tensions, activists used shared identity discourse to maintain a community.

FRAMING MARRIAGE, BUILDING COMMUNITY

Activists at MassEquality used shared identity discourse not only to frame the meaning of marriage but also to define the limits of the activist community. Several activists directly referenced the idea of community in defining their personal commitment to marriage equality. For example, Brian did not personally support marriage but explained that "sometimes being a good community player is sucking it up and doing the work that is necessary." Framing serves this community function because it is part of the process of making meaning about politics (W. A. Gamson 1992). This shared identity discourse made marriage meaningful both as an institution and as a social movement goal. I derived four primary framing strategies from the interviews and other research: same-sex marriage as *constitutional equality*, marriage as a *cultural ritual*, marriage equality as *religious freedom*, and marriage as a *social movement battleground issue*. Some activists engaged in queer critiques of marriage, and I consider how this discourse on marriage was controlled so that activists could still participate in the movement.

Same-Sex Marriage as Constitutional Equality

Constitutional equality served as a master frame for the movement. As Marty Rouse explained, the campaign was to stop an amendment to the state constitution, not to convince people to support same-sex marriage. By talking about marriage equality as a constitutional goal, activists emphasized ideas about equality more than ideas about marriage itself. Anti-marriage activists often rallied around the slogan "Let the People Vote." Both of MassEquality's slogans, "No Discrimination in the Constitution" and "It's Wrong to Vote on Rights," responded by emphasizing marriage equality as a basic democratic right.

This discourse allowed lesbian and gay activists to emphasize solidarity with straight allies, expanding the definition of "us" (Ghaziani 2011). If marriage equality was understood as a goal of only lesbians and gay men, lesbians and gays might form an "us" opposed to a straight "them." Instead, when marriage equality was discussed in constitutional terms, "us" included all progressive activists opposed to "haters." A lesbian activist explained, "It's more that I think I should have the choice to get married, and I don't think anyone should take that choice from me." By emphasizing ideas of choice and equality, this activist transforms marriage from a lesbian and gay goal into a broader constitutional goal. Similarly, a straight activist told me, "I don't want to live in a state where we write discrimination into our constitution. I don't want to do that." Using a similar discursive strategy positions this progressive activist in the same "us and them" community with the lesbian activist. Constitutional constructions of marriage thus resonated with activists who were interested in broader issues of social equality.

Activists heavily drew on *Goodridge* and the law in framing marriage as a constitutional right. Amy Mello used *Goodridge* to create room for critics of marriage in the MassEquality community: "That the court had said equal and somebody had said oh, no, you're not. . . . So I understand the [queer marriage] critique and in a sense, I almost think that's not what this battle is about." Employing the law more broadly, Charles told me, "I guess I think of it mostly as civil marriage and access to the fourteen hundred benefits that you would be getting, state and federal. . . . If opposite-sex couples get it, then same-sex couples should get it too as a matter of civil rights, as a matter of being equal, under the law." In an even more direct reference to the constitution, Marc Solomon explained, "There were other arguments that were effective with legislators that would be less effective, I think, with the general public. Like about, you know the Massachusetts constitution is the oldest in history, and it's never been used as an agent of discrimination." Here we see how *Goodridge* specifically supported MassEquality's efforts to frame marriage in a way that created a broader understanding of "us."

By examining how constitutional equality was deployed against religious anti-marriage activists, the role of shared identity discourse in constructing community boundaries becomes clearer. Conservative religious activists relied on the argument that marriage is a traditional religious institution. In response, activists at MassEquality drew on the argument that marriage is a *civil* institution. Jenn explained that "I would in certain circumstances de-emphasize the religious aspect and focus more on marriage as a civil status. I recognize that the religious status has great meaning for people, but in my mind that is more related to personal aspirations." Even religious gay activists did not always try to directly argue on religious terms against conservative activists. George suggested, "This is more of a civil rights issue and this is about religious freedom." Jenn, like most other activists at MassEquality, recognized the legitimacy of religious marriage while at the same time minimizing religion's role in marriage equality. As discussed later, this discursive strategy marginalized activists who understood marriage primarily in religious terms. However, as seen in George's comments, this did create space for religious activists to argue that religious marriage and religious freedom are consistent with civil rights. This allowed religious activists to discursively join the marriage-supporter community by emphasizing religious freedom.

Marriage as a Cultural Ritual

Many activists discussed marriage in terms of the broad cultural and social acceptance that it represents. As Eric told me, "I think, because so many people understand marriage, we can use it as a jumping-off point." Marty Rouse echoed this point: "I would say personally, it's probably the community recognition, the cultural recognition of marriage. . . . Everyone knows what a marriage is." MassEquality used personal narratives to explain the cultural significance of same-sex marriage, emphasizing the intimate connections between the movement and the people it benefits. An ad campaign in the newspapers showed same-sex married couples, including a short snippet of their stories and why marriage mattered to them. In numerous press conferences, the organization invited married couples and their friends and families to talk about why marriage mattered to them personally. In some cases, canvassers highlighted their personal support for marriage equality during door-to-door interactions. Through these strategies, MassEquality and the activists involved attempted to construct marriage as a personal celebration, shared insofar as personal marriages drew upon a broader cultural schema.

By framing same-sex marriage as a cultural ritual, activists made dual claims that same-sex couples deserve equal access to the ritual of marriage and that state recognition of same-sex marriage confers social legitimacy on these relationships. This framing of marriage is perhaps most directly related to the idea of marriage equality as a lesbian and gay issue. Indeed, some lesbian and gay activists explained their own mobilization precisely in terms of marriage as a personal goal. For example, Heather explained it as being about "the societal recognition that this person standing next to me is my life partner in sickness and in health, and in whatever else." Another activist connected the institution more directly to individual identity: "I think we as individuals, in a fairly fundamental way, understand ourselves, identify ourselves as either married or single or divorced, or, you know, this is our sort of status in society, in a personal way."

By using personal stories in framing marriage as a cultural ritual, activists implicitly called attention to the lesbians and gays who would directly benefit from the movement. This emphasis suggested an "us" of gays and lesbians that did not include the "them" of allies. While allies might support the broader goal of social acceptance, they would not benefit in the same way as gays and lesbians (Myers 2008). However, the meaning of marriage as a cultural goal was constantly reformulated within the discursive community represented by MassEquality. While straight activists could not draw on personal stories in the same way, they could and did talk about marriage as a symbol of cultural acceptance. One straight male activist explained, "It's not about the marriage or the institution, it's about the people and their lives involved in it." James reformulated marriage equality as a cultural ritual to make room for progressive allies who understand themselves as directly supporting gay and lesbian friends. Marriage equality, according to this view, symbolizes a social commitment to recognizing lesbian and gay relationships as valid and equal. Lesbian and gay activists did not always use personal narratives in framing marriage as a cultural ritual. Jenn described marriage as "a series and a set of protections and recognitions for a family. It is a means to convey a level of social acceptance of a relationship."

The discursive work around marriage as a cultural ritual illustrates shared identity discourse in action. Marriage as a cultural ritual could be limited to lesbian and gay activists who had personal motivations for marrying. But other activists also participated in this discourse by emphasizing the broader cultural meaning of marriage. As seen in Jenn's comments, gay and lesbian activists responded by connecting their personal stories to the broader cultural themes. Discourse on marriage as a cultural ritual, however, still threatened to leave out activists who understood marriage in more religious terms as well as more radical activists who entirely questioned the institution of marriage.

Marriage Equality as Religious Freedom

Religious framing of same-sex marriage occupied a tenuous spot in creating community at MassEquality. For a small number of activists, religion was fundamental to how they discussed marriage. Anne Fowler explained that "it's civil marriage, but the religious communities are deeply implicated in this, partly I have to say because there is so much confusion about marriage." These activists defended the ability to see same-sex marriage within a religious tradition; as George explained, "marriage is a time-honored tradition." George's commitment to marriage equality was grounded in his religious understanding of marriage. For these activists, marriage's history in religion is crucial to their work.

Despite the importance of religion to this small subset of activists, most of my interviewees barely mentioned religion at all. This likely reflects traditional understandings of the Religious Right as part of the "them" opposed to lesbian and gay rights (Fetner 2008). In Massachusetts, anti-same-sex marriage activists described preservation of traditional marriage as a religious project. During many constitutional conventions, MassEquality and its allies occupied the sidewalks in front of the State House, with opponents across the street in front of Boston Commons. In one memorable instance, anti-same-sex marriage activists inflated a large "Jesus is Lord" balloon. Rather than respond with religious counter-arguments, most same-sex marriage activists focused on marriage as a civil institution. Their goal was to win support from religious people who were sympathetic to gay and lesbian equality. The focus on civil marriage, nevertheless, led to the marginalization of religious framings of marriage equality.

Nonetheless, closer examination of how most activists discussed marriage and religion reveals how they left open room for religious framings of same-sex marriage. While most activists stressed their commitment to defending *civil* marriage rights under *Goodridge*, they did not directly attack religion per se. When asked to define marriage in their own terms, many activists recognized religious definitions as legitimate while explaining that marriage was not a religious institution for them personally. For example, Charles, a gay male activist, told me that marriage "has a long history of being a contract, as well as being codified differently by the religions." Jenn similarly made room in the marriage-supporter community for religious activists, noting that "there are LGBT people . . . of every religion." Perhaps significantly, activists used "haters" instead of a religious term to signify their opponents. By describing anti-same-sex marriage activists in these more religiously neutral terms, activists left room in MassEquality for religious activists.

As Anne Fowler explained, religious activists worked to frame same-sex marriage in religious terms parallel to ideas about marriage as a civil institution. Anne inquired, "What is the business of religion? And it is often symbolic. And I think it really, just so much of what meant a lot to people was not what we said necessarily but that we were there saying it at all." This stress on symbolic work creates a space for religion that civil law cannot reach, but simultaneously reaffirms the core constitutional equality framing of MassEquality. At the final constitutional convention, a parade of religious leaders walked across Boston Commons to the State House steps, where other activists made room for them. All the activists joined the religious leaders in singing and chanting. Through continued discourse over the meaning of marriage, activists came to position religious meanings of marriage alongside other frames. Religious frames of marriage equality were not preexistent, but were instead constructed through shared identity discourse over the course of the campaign.

Marriage as a Social Movement Battleground Issue

Through shared identity discourse, activists produced meaning around marriage as a social movement goal, independent of what marriage means as an institution. Calling marriage equality the "cutting edge of . . . equality for gays and lesbians," Marc Solomon explained, "Once we hit, we were the one state where same-sex couples could marry, I think there was a strong sense that we're not going to let anybody take this away from us." Marty Rouse described May 17, 2004 (the day that marriage licenses were first issued[9]), as "a date in history that will always, you know, be there. And a very important marker in GLBT history and in America's history." Activists described the goal of defending *Goodridge* in the broader terms of defending turf against "haters," as expressed in a common chant from previous constitutional conventions: "Gay rights, under attack, what do we do? Stand up, fight back!" Drawing on this sense of defending something already earned, Heather told me, "This was the time and place where I could be most effective [in working for gay rights]."

Activists also described marriage equality as a battleground in a broader progressive movement. To Julie Verratti, marriage equality was "the civil rights issue of our generation. And . . . just a good issue to work on." Amy Mello considered marriage equality an "organizer's dream" because the general public was already thinking about it and "it was going to have such a big effect through the whole country." By situating Massachusetts as the precedent for the rest of the country, Amy made MassEquality's work into a broader campaign for equality. Brian also connected his work to a broader movement structure:

> And then there's an element of, the people who oppose same-sex marriage are the same people who oppose a woman's right to choose, are the same people who oppose, hate unions, hate sex-ed, hate communities of color, you know, it's all the same. So beating them, finding a way to win, I think is incredibly important in general for progressive and more left-leaning causes, organizations.

Here, marriage is not important as a goal on its own merits, but rather for its role in a broader structure.

The idea of defending *Goodridge* as a battleground issue was particularly important to mobilizing activists who otherwise questioned the institution of marriage. Brian particularly did not value marriage as an institution by itself, but he saw himself as part of a community that the movement was defending: "My motivation wasn't because I wanted to see happy gay couples, it was because I didn't want to see another ballot fight. . . . When marriage equality became a legal reality in Massachusetts, then it became time to protect it." Similarly, Liz told me, "The gay marriage debate is what is defined as the gay movement. And so, whether or not I like it, this is where the battleground for equality is. I mean, I don't plan on ever getting married. It couldn't happen to me. Pity the fools." Seen as a battleground, the campaign to protect marriage took on greater importance than the institution of marriage by itself. For activists who considered marriage a poor fit for lesbian and gay relationships, protecting marriage equality was more important for its role as a battleground issue. These activists' participation depended upon MassEquality's use of a "shared identity discourse" that left open multiple meanings of marriage, instead of a narrower framing of a lesbian and gay "us."

Queer Critiques of Marriage

Underscoring the heterogeneity of activists' understanding of marriage, some activists criticized it as a patriarchal or conservative institution. In fact, when asked directly about queer critiques of marriage, nearly all activists were at least familiar with the criticisms, even if they did not agree with them. These critiques ranged from questioning how marriage fit as a model for one's own relationship (without necessarily rejecting the institution) to radical rejection of the whole institution. Among the former, a straight activist told me, "That's kind of funny, because I've been with my partner for almost seven years and we're not married," and then explained that she did not think it was likely that she would get married. She did not necessarily reject the whole institution of marriage, but she did not think she would get married herself. Among the latter, Brian, who rejected the whole institution, told me:

> Marriage is too conservative and again it perpetuates a myth about what families should be and what families are. And some families are two gay parents and two lesbian parents, and sometimes they're interracial, and sometimes they're one parent, and sometimes they're three parents who are all in a relationship together.

It is important to note that Brian was unusual in the strength of his criticism of marriage as an institution. Many activists might have recognized such an argument in theory, but few agreed with it to the same extent. They questioned the legitimacy of marriage as the only relationship model in our society and often suggested they did not want marriage for themselves, but did not reject the institution in all cases. For example, Rachel emphasized how marriage was too narrow a model: "I just think the idea of the way we socially define a family is so limited . . . to be honest with you, I don't really care that much about it, you know. I just think that all couples deserve to have the same access to a commitment." Rachel thus recognized that marriage can be a good model for some relationships, but stressed how it is limiting to have only one dominant model.

While activists did not critique the institution of marriage in public, this concern was part of the internal shared identity discourse. In the ongoing project of assigning meaning to marriage as a movement goal, the queer critique of marriage was incorporated into other frames. Heather incorporated criticism of marriage in her reformulations of marriage as both an issue of constitutional equality and a battleground issue: "Personally, I don't think that this government, that the government of the United States, should be in the business of marrying people. I think that as long as the government is in the business of marrying people, I want access." The role of shared identity discourse in creating new meaning around marriage is illustrated in activists' changing understandings of marriage as a conservative institution. James explained that before joining MassEquality he had a negative view of marriage as a failing institution. After talking with activists and married couples about the positive benefits of marriage, he now explains that "if someone says marriage is too conservative, what they're actually saying is, my understanding of what marriage is, is too conservative. Marriage is a million different things to a million different people."

The prominence of a critique of marriage is striking within an organization working to support marriage rights. The fact that activists talked about queer critiques of marriage reinforces my argument that shared identity discourse brought together a community of activists who may not have supported marriage solely on the basis of individual interest and identity. By itself, a critique of marriage does not provide a basis for mobilization. However, when criticisms are inflected with recognition of marriage as a constitutional and a battleground issue, they can exist as part of a broader discourse encouraging mobilization. In fact, the willingness of activists to include criticism of marriage in the shared identity discourse was crucial to the participation of a number of activists.

Constructing Community through Shared Identity Discourse

Community was a central theme running across the interviews. Several activists stressed how important community formation was to their continued work at MassEquality. But this sense of being part of a community was not a simple result of collective identity. Activists never agreed on the meaning of marriage or on who benefited from the same-sex marriage movement. Instead, their ability to construct different and sometimes contradictory meanings of marriage against each other was crucial to the continued success of shared identity discourse. Activists used shared identity discourse to turn a framing dispute into a project of community boundary definition. By leaving the meaning of marriage unsettled, they constructed a community that included a broad range of identities. Here, I examine how discourse was used to build community across three key tensions.

The first and most obvious potential divide was between straight and lesbian or gay activists. The potential for division was apparent in comments by some lesbian and gay activists that they did not understand why straight people were so involved. Similarly, some straight activists questioned whether they could ever understand the issue in quite the same way as gays and lesbians. While serious tensions never arose over this divide, activists did at least some discursive work to build community over any potential tensions. Amy, a straight woman, said she "felt dumb at first [and] had to get used to coming out when [she] was meeting people." Critically, Amy never felt excluded after "coming out" as straight. Community was not built on the basis that everyone was the same. Instead, Amy might talk about marriage as a matter of equality while others talked about it as a deeply personal matter. By constantly sharing different identities and ideas about marriage, activists created space for straight and gay people to participate in the same movement.

Another tension around the religious meanings of marriage further illustrates how shared identity discourse constructed and expanded community boundaries. As previously discussed, religious activists often felt marginalized by the focus on marriage as a civil institution. Anne Fowler emphasized, "We have to keep convincing our side that we are with them. . . . Gay people have been so wounded and dissed by the Church that the instinctive feeling is that you are the enemy." She explained that as they kept talking about religious freedom, more activists *intellectually* understood the role of religion. Other activists continued to treat religion as *pragmatically* less important: civil marriage was the real concern and religion was a side argument. However, religious activists continued to participate in the discourse and insisted on being included in public events. Eventually, other activists paid greater respect to religious arguments. Civil marriage was still the primary concern, but religious freedom was an integral part of civil marriage. This new respect was dramatically illustrated when the religious leaders marched up the Boston Commons to occupy the center of the stairs in front of the State House.

Finally, tension around the inclusion of queer critiques of marriage is perhaps most interesting for an understanding of how shared identity discourse works. Queer critiques could have directly undermined MassEquality's work and sense of community. Heather told me that "the marriage movement is a lot of rich white gay men, frankly." Heather said she might want to get married, but she did not identify with others who she thought would benefit more directly from marriage. For Heather, protecting *Goodridge* was the most pragmatic way to address broader inequalities affecting the lesbian and gay movement. She did identify a limited sense of community with those "rich white gay men," insofar as they could share in the same discourse about marriage equality. As previously discussed, Brian and Liz similarly stressed community and the pragmatic importance of defending *Goodridge*. While I do not have data to compare Brian, Liz, and Heather to other queer activists who refuse to work on same-sex marriage, I can at least suggest that framing same-sex marriage as a battleground issue played a critical role in drawing some queer activists into the movement.

Perhaps most critically, queer activists did not have to hide their critiques of marriage. They did not share these criticisms outside of MassEquality, but in conversations with other activists they could express their reservations. These queer critiques thus had an impact on the discourse. Most activists still supported marriage, but they all understood the queer skepticism of marriage. Other activists began to think more critically about the role of marriage in the broader movement.

Activists thus did not share any single identity. Instead, they formed a community of marriage supporters with distinct identity claims and ideas justifying their common goal of achieving marriage equality.

CONCLUSION

The concept of shared identity discourse explains the complicated relationship between identity and mobilization in the same-sex marriage movement in Massachusetts. My findings are directly related to debates over the impact of court rulings on social change and activism (McCann 1994; Rosenberg [1991] 2008). Following the *Goodridge* opinion in 2003, activists conducted a three-and-a-half-year grassroots campaign to defend against attempts to amend the Massachusetts constitution. *Goodridge* impacted how activists framed same-sex marriage, allowing them to mobilize around defending the court's decision as a battleground issue. As others have argued, legal and cultural meanings of same-sex marriage shaped later collective action (Taylor et al. 2009).

The successful mobilization of MassEquality provides a good case for understanding the puzzle of successful collective action despite disagreement over identities and framings of marriage. I have described activists who identified as gay and lesbian, progressive, religious, and radical. Although all of these activist identities allowed participants to be marriage supporters, participants did not think of themselves as sharing the same identity, and identity was continuously negotiated and debated in the movement. This reflects a common tension over how to define identity across different internal groups in social movements (Einwohner, Reger, and Myers 2008). Disagreements between activists at MassEquality were even more pronounced with respect to how activists defined marriage equality as a movement goal. Marriage was variously framed as a cultural ritual, constitutional equal right, religious institution, movement battleground issue, or conservative institution. These different framings not only were distinct but at times were completely contradictory.

I introduce the concept of shared identity discourse to explain how activist framing strategies may define a social movement community that connects multiple identities to a single movement goal. Shared identity discourse provides additional leverage to explain a case where activists use multiple identities and frames. By de-emphasizing specific identities and allowing issue framing to remain unsettled, activists can use a framing dispute productively to create a movement community

(Ghaziani 2008 similarly argues that movement infighting may productively define a movement). My research is particularly relevant to past work on identity tensions within LGBT social movements (J. Gamson 1995, 1997; Ghaziani 2008; Taylor and Rupp 1993; Taylor and Whittier 1992). As LGBT movements try to incorporate allies or move toward an "us and them" community, they face the challenge of how to coordinate individuals with competing motivations (Ghaziani 2011; Myers 2008). While I agree that the lines between us and them are more blurred than past scholarship has recognized (Einwohner, Reger, and Myers 2008), my findings suggest that this blurring may be less about who "we" are and more about what "we" do. Unlike previous literature stressing the importance of clear protagonists and antagonists to successful framing (W. A. Gamson [1975] 1990), this approach suggests that framing strategies that leave identities fluid and unsettled may be successful precisely because they do so.

Important avenues for future research remain. Most important, I have not considered here how the focus on community may decrease the commitment of any single identity group. Previous scholarship has stressed the solidarity benefits of collective identity (Hunt and Benford 2004). Are these benefits diluted or lost as movements include broader communities instead of single identities? Shared identity discourse may allow lesbian and gay activists to stress commonality with others and build a common community, but this could come at the potential cost of less commitment by gays and lesbians themselves. Similarly, shared identity discourse may only work effectively in a single-issue movement. MassEquality has continued to work on other issues since 2007. While I have not conducted any follow-up research, I have heard the marriage campaign described as the height of activism at MassEquality. Future research could consider whether shared identity discourse might come into play in different stages of mobilization.

NOTES

1. Throughout this chapter, I use the labels "gay" or "gays and lesbians" for convenience, recognizing that these do not fit everyone involved. Some of my interviewees identified as "queer," but none identified as bisexual or transgender. Similarly, I use the label "straight," preferring it to "heterosexual" or other labels. I also primarily use the label "same-sex marriage" to reflect the usage of activists.

2. Polletta and Jasper (2001) offer an alternate definition that focuses on an individual's identification with a group.

3. My focus on marriage supporters as a discursive community offers an alternate understanding of the relationship between allies and movement identities (Jasper 1997, 86). For example, McAdam (1988) discusses the relationship to civil rights of white university students involved in Freedom Summer. I focus on how allies and other marriage supporters participate in a discursive community instead of sharing a movement identity.

4. This decision set an important legal precedent for later state decisions on same-sex marriage, many of which cite *Goodridge*. For a general discussion of same-sex marriage cases in other states, see Kosbie (2011).

5. Because of the historical limits of this study, I do not address important questions about the earlier role of coalitions in forming MassEquality (Van Dyke and McCammon 2010).

6. Key leaders from MassEquality were involved in mobilization efforts in other New England states and in California. For example, leading up to the 2012 election, several former leaders of MassEquality worked together at Equality Maine.

7. These activists did not necessarily self-identify as progressive. Instead they described their political commitments in varying personal terms. I have used the label *progressive* based on the association of marriage equality with progressive politics. Most of the activists I place in this group are straight. However, insofar as some gay and lesbian activists question the marriage model but support it as a progressive political issue, they may also fit this identity.

8. While "queer" is not necessarily equivalent to radical, it is typically understood to be a more radical and politicized identity than "gay." Of these two informants, one fundamentally rejected marriage as an institution while the other said he wants to get married someday.

9. The opinion in *Goodridge* was handed down on November 18, 2003, but with a six-month delay before it was effective.

REFERENCES

Armstrong, Elizabeth. 2002. *Forging Gay Identities: Organizing Sexuality in San Francisco, 1950–1994*. Chicago: University of Chicago Press.

Baker v. State of Vermont, 170 Vt. 194 (Supreme Court of Vermont 1999).

Benford, Robert D., and Scott A. Hunt. 2003. "Interactional Dynamics in Public Problems Marketplaces." In *Challenges and Choices: Constructionist Perspectives on Social Problems*, edited by James A. Holstein and Gale Miller, 153–86. New York: Aldine de Gruyter.

Benford, Robert D., and David A. Snow. 2000. "Framing Processes and Social Movements: An Overview and Assessment." *Annual Review of Sociology* 26: 611–39.

Bernstein, Mary. 1997. "Celebration and Suppression: The Strategic Uses of Identity by the Lesbian and Gay Movement." *American Journal of Sociology* 103 (3): 531–65.

———. 2005. "Identity Politics." *Annual Review of Sociology* 31: 47–74.

Bernstein, Mary, and Marcie De la Cruz. 2009. "What Are You? Explaining Identity as a Goal of the Multiracial Hapa Movement." *Social Problems* 56 (4): 722–45.

Case, Mary Anne. 2010. "What Feminists Have to Lose in Same-Sex Marriage Litigation." *UCLA Law Review* 57 (5): 1199–234.

Chauncey, George. 2004. *Why Marriage? The History Shaping Today's Debate over Gay Equality.* New York: Basic Books.

Cohen, Cathy J. 1999. *The Boundaries of Blackness: AIDS and the Breakdown of Black Politics.* Chicago: University of Chicago Press.

Conrad, Ryan, ed. 2010. *Against Equality: Queer Critiques of Marriage.* Lewiston, Maine: Against Equality.

Einwohner, Rachel L., Jo Reger, and Daniel J. Myers. 2008. "Introduction: Identity Work, Sameness, and Difference in Social Movements." In *Identity Work in Social Movements*, edited by Jo Reger, Daniel J. Myers, and Rachel L. Einwohner, 1–17. Minneapolis: University of Minnesota Press.

Epstein, Steven. 1987. "Gay Politics, Ethnic Identity: The Limits of Social Constructionism." *Socialist Review* 93–94: 9–56.

Fetner, Tina. 2008. *How the Religious Right Shaped Lesbian and Gay Activism.* Minneapolis: University of Minnesota Press.

Friedman, Debra, and Doug McAdam. 1992. "Collective Identity and Activism: Networks, Choices, and the Life of a Social Movement." In *Frontiers in Social Movement Theory*, edited by Aldon D. Morris and Carol McClurg Mueller, 156–73. New Haven, Conn.: Yale University Press.

Gamson, Joshua. 1995. "Must Identity Movements Self-Destruct? A Queer Dilemma." *Social Problems* 42 (3): 390–407.

———. 1997. "Messages of Exclusion: Gender, Movements, and Symbolic Boundaries." *Gender and Society* 11: 178–99.

Gamson, William A. [1975] 1990. *The Strategy of Social Protest.* 2nd ed. Belmont, Calif.: Wadsworth.

———. 1992. *Talking Politics.* Cambridge: Cambridge University Press.

———. 1995. "Constructing Social Protest." In *Social Movements and Culture*, edited by Hank Johnston and Bert Klandermans, 85–106. Minneapolis: University of Minnesota Press.

———. 2004. "Bystanders, Public Opinion, and the Media." In *The Blackwell Companion to Social Movements*, edited by David A. Snow, Sarah A. Soule, and Hanspeter Kriesi, 242–61. Malden, Mass., and Oxford: Blackwell Publishing.

Ghaziani, Amin. 2008. *The Dividends of Dissent: How Conflict and Culture Work in Lesbian and Gay Marches on Washington.* Chicago: University of Chicago Press.

———. 2011. "Post-Gay Collective Identity Construction." *Social Problems* 58 (1): 99–125.

Goodridge v. Department of Public Health, 440 Mass. 309 (Massachusetts Supreme Judicial Court 2003).

Halley, Janet E. 1994. "Sexual Orientation and the Politics of Biology: A Critique of the Argument from Immutability." *Stanford Law Review* 46: 503–68.

———. 2000. "'Like Race' Arguments." In *What's Left of Theory? New Work on the Politics of Literary Theory*, edited by Judith Butler, John Guillory, and Kendall Thomas, 40–74. New York: Routledge.

Hunt, Scott A., and Robert D. Benford. 2004. "Collective Identity, Solidarity, and Commitment." In *The Blackwell Companion to Social Movements*, edited by David A.

Snow, Sarah A. Soule, and Hanspeter Kriesi, 433–57. Malden, Mass., and Oxford: Blackwell Publishing.

Hunt, Scott A., Robert D. Benford, and David A. Snow. 1994. "Identity Fields: Framing Processes and the Social Construction of Movement Identities." In *New Social Movements: From Ideology to Identity*, edited by Enrique Laraña, Hank Johnston, and Joseph R. Gusfield, 185–208. Philadelphia: Temple University Press.

Jasper, James M. 1997. *The Art of Moral Protest: Culture, Biography, and Creativity in Social Movements*. Chicago: University of Chicago Press.

Klandermans, Bert. 1994. "Transient Identities? Membership Patterns in the Dutch Peace Movement." In *New Social Movements: From Ideology to Identity*, edited by Enrique Laraña, Hank Johnston, and Joseph R. Gusfield, 168–84. Philadelphia: Temple University Press.

Kosbie, Jeffrey. 2011. "Misconstructing Sexuality in Same-Sex Marriage Jurisprudence." *Northwestern Journal of Law and Social Policy* 6 (1): 238–78.

Lichterman, Paul. 1999. "Talking Identity in the Public Sphere: Broad Visions and Small Spaces in Sexual Identity Politics." *Theory and Society* 28: 101–41.

McAdam, Doug. 1988. *Freedom Summer*. Oxford: Oxford University Press.

McCann, Michael W. 1994. *Rights at Work: Pay Equity Reform and the Politics of Legal Mobilization*. Chicago: University of Chicago Press.

McCarthy, John D., and Mayer N. Zald. 1987. "The Trend of Social Movements in America: Professionalization and Resource Mobilization." In *Social Movements in an Organizational Society: Collected Essays*, edited by Mayer N. Zald and John D. McCarthy, 337–91. New Brunswick, N.J.: Transaction Books.

Melucci, Alberto. 1995. "The Process of Collective Identity." In *Social Movements and Culture*, edited by Hank Johnston and Bert Klandermans, 41–63. Minneapolis: University of Minnesota Press.

———. 1996. *Challenging Codes: Collective Action in the Information Age*. New York: Cambridge University Press.

Morris, Aldon D. 1992. "Political Consciousness and Collective Action." In *Frontiers in Social Movement Theory*, edited by Aldon D. Morris and Carol McClurg Mueller, 351–74. New Haven, Conn.: Yale University Press.

Myers, Daniel J. 2008. "Ally Identity: The Politically Gay." In *Identity Work in Social Movements*, edited by Jo Reger, Daniel J. Myers, and Rachel L. Einwohner, 167–87. Minneapolis: University of Minnesota Press.

Pedriana, Nicholas. 2009. "Intimate Equality: The Lesbian, Gay, Bisexual, and Transgender Movement's Legal Framing of Sodomy Laws in the *Lawrence v. Texas* Case." In *Queer Mobilizations: LGBT Activists Confront the Law*, edited by Scott Barclay, Mary Bernstein, and Anna-Maria Marshall, 52–75. New York and London: New York University Press.

Phillips, Frank, and Andrea Estes. 2007. "Right of Gays to Marry Set for Years to Come." *Boston Globe*, June 15.

Polikoff, Nancy D. 2008. *Beyond (Straight and Gay) Marriage: Valuing All Families under the Law*. Boston: Beacon Press.

Polletta, Francesca, and James Jasper. 2001. "Collective Identity and Social Movements." *Annual Review of Sociology* 27: 283–305.

Reger, Jo. 2002. "More Than One Feminism: Organizational Structure and the Construction of Collective Identity." In *Social Movements: Identity, Culture, and the State*, edited by David S. Meyer, Nancy Whittier, and Belinda Robnett, 171–84. New York: Oxford University Press.

Rochon, Thomas R. 1998. *Culture Moves: Ideas, Activism, and Changing Values.* Princeton, N.J.: Princeton University Press.

Rosenberg, Gerald N. [1991] 2008. *The Hollow Hope: Can Courts Bring about Social Change?* 2nd ed. Chicago: University of Chicago Press.

Roth, Benita. 2004. *Separate Roads to Feminism: Black, Chicana, and White Feminist Movements in America's Second Wave.* Cambridge: Cambridge University Press.

Snow, David A. 2004. "Framing Processes, Ideology, and Discursive Fields." In *The Blackwell Companion to Social Movements*, edited by David A. Snow, Sarah A. Soule, and Hanspeter Kriesi, 380–412. Malden, Mass., and Oxford: Blackwell Publishing.

Snow, David A., E. Burke Rochford, Jr., Steven K. Worden, and Robert D. Benford. 1986. "Frame Alignment Processes, Micromobilization, and Movement Participation." *American Sociological Review* 51 (4): 464–81.

Taylor, Verta. 2011. "Identity, Emotions, and Networks." Forthcoming in *Advances in Social Movement Research*, edited by Bert Klandermans, Connie Roggeband, and Jacqueline van Steckelenburg. Minneapolis: University of Minnesota Press.

Taylor, Verta, Katrina Kimport, Nella Van Dyke, and Ellen Ann Andersen. 2009. "Culture and Mobilization: Tactical Repertoires, Same-Sex Weddings, and the Impact on Gay Activism." *American Sociological Review* 74: 865–90.

Taylor, Verta, and Leila J. Rupp. 1993. "Women's Culture and Lesbian Feminist Activism: A Reconsideration of Cultural Feminism." *Signs* 19 (1): 32–61.

Taylor, Verta, and Nancy E. Whittier. 1992. "Collective Identity in Social Movement Communities: Lesbian Feminist Mobilization." In *Frontiers in Social Movement Theory*, edited by Aldon Morris and Carol McClurg Mueller, 104–30. New Haven, Conn.: Yale University Press.

Van Dyke, Nella, and Holly J. McCammon, eds. 2010. *Strategic Alliances: Coalition Building and Social Movements.* Minneapolis: University of Minnesota Press.

Warner, Michael. 1999. *The Trouble with Normal: Sex, Politics, and the Ethics of Queer Life.* New York: Free Press.

Whittier, Nancy. 1995. *Feminist Generations: The Persistence of the Radical Women's Movement.* Philadelphia: Temple University Press.

Wuthnow, Robert. 1989. *Communities of Discourse: Ideology and Social Structure in the Reformation, the Enlightenment, and European Socialism.* Cambridge, Mass., and London: Harvard University Press.

PART II Marriage-Equality Opposition

4 Winning for LGBT Rights Laws, Losing for Same-Sex Marriage

The LGBT Movement and Campaign Tactics

Amy L. Stone

I N 2000, OREGON LESBIAN, GAY, bisexual, and transgender (LGBT) activists successfully defeated yet another antigay ballot measure sponsored by the local Religious Right. This particular ballot measure, the latest in a series of statewide and local measures since 1988, would have eliminated any discussion of LGBT issues in public schools. By 2000 the Oregon LGBT community had become expert in ballot-box politics and was considered by many within the LGBT movement to have the strongest capacity to fight antigay ballot measures. Indeed, in the November 2004 election, as eleven states fought same-sex marriage bans across the country, a disproportionate amount of time, money, and volunteers flowed into the Oregon campaign in hope of a victory there. However, in Oregon, as in the other ten states, the marriage ban handily passed; same-sex marriage became outlawed in all eleven states. Why were Oregon LGBT activists able to defeat so many other ballot measures but not a same-sex marriage ban? What makes same-sex marriage bans difficult to defeat for even the most experienced activists?

From 1974 to 2012 the LGBT movement has faced 171 ballot measures on everything from local LGBT rights laws to same-sex marriage.[1] Ballot measures allow local voters to pass or reject laws through either an initiative or a referendum process, typically without going through the legislature. Occasionally the LGBT movement has put these LGBT rights on the ballot. However, the Religious Right proposes most of these ballot measures as an effective way to curtail the gains of the LGBT movement, particularly in the arena of local LGBT rights laws. The LGBT movement has overwhelmingly lost these ballot measures; 68 percent of measures proposed by the Religious Right have resulted in an anti-LGBT outcome. However, the LGBT movement has been more successful in some time periods than others. Between 1974 and 1996, *the period of local defeats*, the LGBT movement struggled to defeat ballot measures that disproportionately either targeted existing or tried to outlaw future LGBT rights laws. Between 1997 and 2003, *the winning streak*, the LGBT movement defeated a majority of antigay ballot measures for the first time, including almost all local referendums. Between 2004 and 2012, *the period of losing same-sex marriage*, the LGBT movement experienced a series of paralyzing defeats across the country in statewide ballot measures that introduced the prevention of same-sex marriage into state constitutions. It was not until November 2012 that the movement made progress in opposing same-sex marriage bans with the defeat of a same-sex marriage ban in Minnesota and the legalization of same-sex marriage in Maine, Maryland, and Washington.

Using historical evidence to compare the LGBT movement's earlier success with the difficulty of fighting same-sex marriage bans, this chapter examines why tactics developed to fight ballot measures during the LGBT movement's winning streak have not worked effectively against same-sex marriage bans. Existing accounts of marriage bans and other antigay ballot measures pay scant attention to the role of campaigns themselves in influencing outcomes, which is contrary to how many LGBT organizers and activists understand the importance of campaign tactics. This study examines both factors internal and external to the social movement that contribute to the success or failure of ballot-measure campaigns, including voter demographics, countermovement mobilization, and campaign tactics. Drawing on existing social movement theory about success, I demonstrate that both internal factors having to do with social movement organizing and external factors outside of the control of the movement can account for why same-sex marriage ballot measures have been so difficult to fight.

SOCIAL MOVEMENTS AND SUCCESS

Social movement success can be difficult to define, much less study. The definition of social movement success can include political, cultural, and mobilization outcomes (Bernstein 2003; Earl 2004; Staggenborg 1995). The significance of each type of success is subject to interpretation and disagreement by political actors within a social movement. Ballot measures are easier to study than many other social movement activities because a definitive outcome is demonstrated on election day as ballot measures pass or fail. In this study, I define ballot-measure success as the defeat of antigay ballot measures at the ballot box. Even with this narrow definition I acknowledge that many organizers within the LGBT movement may define success differently, including the success of movement building, the creation of social movement organizations, and coalition building, all of which are also outcomes of ballot-measure campaigns. Even social movement "failures" can have positive outcomes (Mansbridge 1986; Rupp and Taylor 1987). Organizers and activists may also define success as a better-than-expected outcome, such as a higher percentage of supportive voters than anticipated. Conversely, a ballot measure that is defeated at the ballot box may be described as a failure by organizers who lament the weakened or fractured community created by the campaign.

Explaining what makes a movement succeed is also causally complicated. Factors that may contribute to ballot-measure campaign success include such variables as the weather on or before election day, LGBT visibility in the local community, other issues on the ballot, other elections taking place, timing, and the virulence of the Religious Right countermovement. To explain social movement success, early social movement scholars focused either on factors related to the *internal* decision-making of the social movement (e.g., strategies, tactics, mobilization, collective identity) or on factors *external* to the movement (e.g., countermovement, political opportunities). For example, scholars William Gamson ([1975] 1990) and Jack Goldstone (1980) debated in early social movement literature about whether mobilization or the political environment had a more significant impact on social movement success. A re-examination of William Gamson's germinal study of movement success in *The Strategy of Social Protest* suggests that the answer is a combination of both internal and external factors (Frey, Dietz, and Kalof 1992).

Most studies of the LGBT movement and ballot-measure politics have examined votes on LGBT ballot measures from the perspective of factors external to the movement, typically voter demographics (see Camp 2008; McVeigh and Diaz 2009). While voter composition is significant, this scholarly emphasis suggests that campaigns are meaningless or insignificant. In order to understand the success or failure of ballot-measure campaigns we must examine ballot measures holistically, considering factors that are both external and internal to the LGBT movement. These factors are, of course, interrelated. Timing may be determined by the countermovement's proposal of a campaign. Campaign funding may be limited if many ballot measures occur simultaneously either within a state or among states. And a countermovement escalating its mobilization and altering its tactics may derail the agenda of the movement. All these factors play a role in understanding the disparity between the success of campaigns against different types of ballot measures in two time periods.

External factors such as countermovement mobilization and voter demographics clearly play a role in the success of ballot measures. Although most studies of external factors have focused on the role of political opportunity in explaining movement success, scholars have also demonstrated that the strength of a countermovement is particularly influential in shaping the tactics and institutionalization of a movement (Meyer and Staggenborg 1996) and ultimately affecting social movement success (Andrews 2004). These external factors have dramatic effects on the tactical choices of a movement, from the strategic deployment of movement identities (Bernstein 1997) to the development of a movement agenda (Fetner 2008).

However, external factors obviously do not solely account for social movement success. In her book on the temperance movement, Ann-Marie Szymanski (2003) suggests that selection of strategy, particularly the difference between moderate and radical strategic choices, is a significant factor in the success of the movement. Kenneth Andrews (2004) argues that movement leadership, organization, and resources affect strategies and tactics, which ultimately affect movement success.

Building on this literature on social movement success, I apply a holistic analysis of both internal and external factors to the study of campaigns to fight antigay ballot measures. By comparing successful and unsuccessful campaigns from multiple time periods, I demonstrate why the LGBT movement has become successful at defeating local referendums but not statewide same-sex marriage bans. These external factors include countermovement mobilization and voter support, along with other issues such as timing and location. Internal factors include movement resources for ballot-measure campaigns (e.g., funding, support from national organizations) and tactical developments (e.g., political messaging, training) within the movement.

STUDYING CAMPAIGNS

This chapter is part of a larger project on campaigns to fight antigay ballot measures that combines archival research, interviews, and participant observation. The data include antigay referendums and initiatives from the earliest referendum in Boulder, Colorado, in 1974 to campaigns around same-sex marriage in 2012. This research uses an expansive definition of antigay direct democracy, because it includes both referendums to rescind local gay rights ordinances or legislation and any initiative that directly or indirectly addresses LGBT rights.

Archival data on referendums and initiatives were collected at the Cornell University Human Sexuality Collection, the University of Michigan Labadie Collection, and the Gay and Lesbian Historical Society of Northern California. In addition, more than seventy-five newspaper sources were used to amass political messaging and historical details about individual referendums and initiatives. Between 2004 and 2012, I interviewed more than one hundred individuals involved in ballot-measure politics, including campaign leaders, professional consultants, field-workers in national organizations, and the occasional disgruntled community member, city clerk, or member of the Religious Right. Sixty-eight of these interviews were with LGBT organizers and community members in Michigan, the site of the largest winning

streak in the LGBT movement in 2001 and 2002. The remaining interviews were with national organization field-workers, professional consultants, and leaders of key ballot-measure campaigns, most of them
focused on the 2004–2009 time period. In addition to archival research
and interviews, I attended two National Gay and Lesbian Task Force
(Task Force) trainings, the 2002 "How to Win an Election" training
on referendums at the Task Force's annual meeting, Creating Change,
and the 2006 Midwest LGBT Power Summit training on same-sex
marriage initiatives. Prior studies of ballot-measure campaigns have
focused primarily on single communities or states (Dugan 2005; Stein
2001). This chapter overcomes the limitations of these studies by examining the outcomes of multiple campaigns that include both successful
and failed campaigns (see Kolb 2007, 10).

WINNING AND LOSING

Since the first contentious referendum on a newly passed gay rights
ordinance in Boulder, Colorado, in 1974, the LGBT movement has
fought against the escalating use of the ballot box by the Religious
Right. The Religious Right has used the ballot box to sponsor referendums, which typically retract an existing LGBT rights law in a city
or state, and to sponsor initiatives, which create a new antigay law. Initiatives can either be put on the ballot through petitions collected by
the Religious Right or referred by the legislature. At times the LGBT
movement has sponsored its own initiatives to create pro-LGBT laws,
but the majority of existing ballot measures that address LGBT rights
have been sponsored by the Religious Right. Indeed, in addition to the
over 155 antigay ballot measures sponsored by the Religious Right, at
least 85 additional attempted antigay ballot measures never made their
way to the ballot box (see Stone 2012). Most of these Religious-Right-
sponsored ballot measures were difficult to defeat in small towns, cities,
and states across the United States. The most challenging type of ballot
measures so far have been state-level same-sex marriage bans, which
deny recognition of same-sex marriage and frequently other forms of
relationship recognition as well.

The LGBT movement's success rate at defeating antigay ballot measures has a lot to do with when and where the ballot measure took place, along with the type of ballot measure. The LGBT movement has been dramatically more successful in certain time periods than others, as demonstrated in Figure 4.1. During the period of local defeats (1974–1996) and the period of losing same-sex marriage (2004–2012), the LGBT movement defeated less than a third of all antigay ballot measures. Between 1997 and 2003, the LGBT movement won the majority of direct legislation battles, including nine out of seventeen referendums and all four local legal restrictive initiatives. Although these ballot measures happened across the country, almost two-thirds of them were in seven battleground states: Oregon, California, Michigan, Florida, Washington, Maine, and Colorado. These states were disproportionately targeted because of the ease of their direct legislation requirements and strength of the Religious Right affiliates. In these battleground states LGBT rights were contested at the ballot box in surges of Religious Right opposition, particularly throughout the 1990s as the Religious Right began to target these states. However, beginning with the first same-sex marriage ballot measures in 1998 in Hawaii and Alaska, the Religious Right proposed same-sex marriage bans in new states, changing the terrain of ballot measures.[2] As I demonstrate, these battleground states were the sites of the most dramatic victories

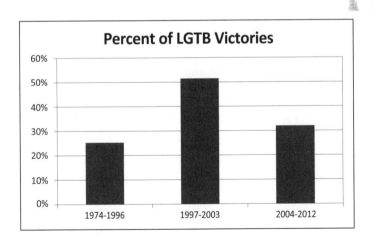

FIGURE 4.1. Percent of LGBT ballot-measure victories per time period.

and losses. The Religious Right is more successful at passing ballot measures in non-battleground states than battleground states (81 percent versus 60 percent) owing to the experience and strength of LGBT communities in battleground states. Most of these ballot measures (65 percent) are on the local level, in cities, towns, or counties, and the LGBT movement has a slightly higher success rate at defeating local ballot measures (34 percent) compared to statewide ballot measures (29 percent).

Different types of ballot measures were also used at different rates during different time periods. Table 4.1 shows the two most common types of ballot measures during each time period. Although the Religious Right has put everything from HIV/AIDS to the employment of lesbian and gay teachers on the ballot, three types of ballot measures are the most common: referenda on LGBT rights laws, legal restrictive initiatives (which eliminate government support of LGBT rights, including the passage of future LGBT rights laws), and ballot measures on relationship recognition (e.g., local domestic partnership laws, same-sex marriage bans). Legal restrictive initiatives were the most common ballot measure between 1974 and 1996, but their use on the statewide level was prohibited by the U.S. Supreme Court case *Romer v. Evans* in 1996. Although there were some local votes on domestic partnership laws in the 1990s, court cases in Hawaii and Alaska about same-sex marriage spurred the first small wave of same-sex marriage bans in 1998. However, it was the legalization of same-sex marriage in

Table 4.1. Most Common Kinds of Ballot Measures for Each Time Period

	1974–1996 N = 87	1997–2003 N = 32	2004–2012 N = 51
1.	Legal Restrictive initiatives (44.1%)	Referendum on Rights Law (46.9%)	Ballot Measure on Relationship Recognition (72.5%)
2.	Referendum on Rights Law (32.2%)	Ballot Measure on Relationship Recognition (34.4%)	Referendum on Rights Law (25.5%)

Massachusetts in 2003 that spurred a dramatic increase in same-sex marriage bans.

How and why each time period has such different success rates has to do with both external and internal factors. The external factors include countermovement mobilization and voter support, along with other issues such as timing and location. Internal factors include movement resources for ballot-measure campaigns (e.g., funding, support from national organizations) and tactical developments (e.g., political messaging, training) within the movement. In the early 1990s, LGBT leaders and organizers developed a set of successful tactics to defeat antigay ballot measures, tactics that included sophisticated messaging, field programs, and professional campaign staff. By the turn of the twentieth century, the LGBT movement was increasingly successful at fighting referendums to eliminate local LGBT rights laws and local legal restrictive initiatives that eliminate both current and future LGBT rights laws. However, these tactical developments did not result in the defeat of same-sex marriage bans.

THE PERIOD OF LOCAL DEFEATS

Between 1974 and 1996, the LGBT movement struggled at the ballot box. The agenda of the fledgling gay liberation movement in the 1970s did not include developing ways to fight for LGBT rights at the ballot box. By the start of the 1990s, however, the LGBT movement was pressed to divert resources to support ballot-measure campaigns, which is one way that the Religious Right has shaped the agenda of the LGBT movement (Fetner 2008). The defeats of this time period were triggered by external factors such as voter disapproval with LGBT rights and internal factors such as the limited resources of the LGBT movement.

External Factors

From 1974 to 1996 the antigay Religious Right grew dramatically as a movement. From fledgling grassroots organizations led by charismatic, short-lived leaders to large-scale national social movement organizations, the Religious Right developed into a large and powerful social movement during this time period. The antigay Religious Right grew out of small, localized social networks that ran through conservative Christian churches, radio, and television shows (Hardisty 1999). However, by the late 1980s, an organized antigay Religious Right existed, a national movement connected through networks between local and statewide organizations. The 1992 Republican National Convention and the election of Bill Clinton to the presidency and his early support of banning discrimination against gays in the military sparked a culture war that led to accelerated antigay activity across the country. In 1992 and 1993 dozens of antigay ballot measures were sponsored, particularly in Oregon (Fetner 2008). The most infamous antigay ballot measures at this time were Colorado Amendment 2 and Oregon Ballot Measure 9, legal restrictive initiatives that both eliminated existing and future LGBT rights laws and prohibited government support of LGBT rights.

Religious Right campaigns, however, varied in their size and capacity. Some Religious Right campaigns were highly organized professional affairs; however, many were volunteer led, poorly funded, and relied heavily on existing homophobic attitudes to mobilize voters. One of the most influential developments during this time period of Religious Right victories was political messaging about "special rights." Political messaging is the use of sound bites to educate or persuade the public, in this case, voters. They are one of the major ways social movement activists frame their issue to the non-movement public. By crafting political messaging that described LGBT rights as "special rights," the Religious Right used secular, legal language that appealed to moderate and racial minority voters. Special rights messaging framed gays as counterfeit minorities, usurping civil rights from "deserving minorities" like African Americans (see Bates 1995; Dugan 2005; Hardisty 1999; Stein 2001; Stone and Ward 2011). This special rights messaging was used across the country from the early 1990s onwards.

This messaging easily harnessed voter ambivalence about gay rights. Voter attitudes were extremely inconsistent. A majority of Americans reported not knowing someone who was gay or lesbian in the late 1970s (Yang 1997), and more than 70 percent of the nation believed that homosexuality was always wrong (Wilcox and Wolpert 2000). In the early 1990s there was a sudden and dramatic increase in support for

LGBT rights (Loftus 2001). These attitudes had tremendous regional variation. Even in the 1970s, campaign polls in more liberal cities such as Seattle and San Francisco showed greater voter support of lesbian and gay rights. For example, when the Seattle Religious Right tried to repeal a nondiscrimination ordinance that included sexual orientation, campaign polling in 1978 showed that 66 percent of voters did not want to repeal the ordinance (Citizens to Retain Fair Employment 1978).

Internal Factors

In the first antigay ballot measure in 1974, the gay and lesbian movement was dramatically unprepared for ballot-box politics. A fledgling movement with few resources and few social movement organizations, the movement had neither the resources nor the manpower to fight many of the first referendums and initiatives. A few early victories included the defeat of initiatives in Seattle, California, and Austin. However, many local communities floundered, with limited resources and little idea of how to run a campaign. It was not until a wave of Religious Right activism in 1992 that national LGBT organizations like the Task Force, the Gay and Lesbian Victory Fund (GLVF), and the Human Rights Campaign (HRC) began to coordinate efforts across the country and develop organized programs to defeat these initiatives. Programs like the Task Force's Fight the Right program used "No on 9," the campaign to defeat Ballot Measure 9, as an exemplar to spread tactics to defeat these ballot measures across the country.

Ballot-measure campaigns became increasingly sophisticated turn-out campaigns, in which activists systematically identified supportive voters and reminded them to vote. Campaigns across the country also gradually became more sophisticated in their use of political messaging. Although polling to develop messaging occurred in some early campaigns, many campaigns spent time reiterating the opposition's messaging or trying to frame the issue as something other than gay rights. The Religious Right messaging around special rights was particularly damaging to the success of campaigns. According to one campaign organizer, "there is no one good phrase or slogan to counter 'special rights.' It takes fifteen minutes of real discussion to undo the damage that phrase does" (Gerstmann 1999, 105).

Thus in the period of local defeats, the LGBT movement struggled to defeat both referendums on LGBT rights laws and legal restrictive initiatives. These struggles were a complex combination of growing Religious Right strength, effective special rights messaging, voter disapproval, and the limitations of the LGBT movement's resources. However, at the end of this period of local defeats, a consensus had grown within the LGBT movement over which tactics were most effective in fighting antigay ballot measures (Stone 2012), and more movement resources were diverted to supporting campaigns to defeat these ballot measures.

THE WINNING STREAK

On the heels of the *Romer v. Evans* Supreme Court victory in 1996, which invalidated the statewide legal restrictive initiative Colorado Amendment 2, the LGBT movement entered into a winning streak at the ballot box. These victories included the retention of a gay rights ordinance in Miami-Dade County in 2002, which was both a symbolic victory and evidence of the LGBT movement's growing potency. LGBT organizers also defeated local legal restrictive initiatives and a wave of antigay direct legislation in Michigan. These wins were a turning point for the defeat of local referendums, one of the most common types of ballot measures up to this time. This success extended through the period of losing at same-sex marriage, although referendums became far less common after 2003. From 1974 to 1996, on average 39.4 percent of voters affirmed local LGBT laws in referendum campaigns; however, from 1997 to 2012, on average 50.6 percent of voters affirmed these local LGBT laws. Indeed, since 1997 the LGBT movement has won the majority of referendums sponsored by the Religious Right (sixteen out of twenty-six).[3]

These victories were significant after a long history of losing. Most of the victories during the winning streak were from battleground states such as Michigan, Maine, and Florida, which the Religious Right targeted with continuous ballot measures. Some important defeats took place in battleground states as well. Three of the most significant were statewide losses for a ballot measure on Maine nondiscrimination legislation (in 1998 and 2000) and the passage of the Knight Initiative in California in 2000, which banned same-sex marriage.

These gains occurred despite the growing strength of the Religious Right and only slightly more supportive voters. However, internal factors such as increased campaign trainings, tactical development and dissemination, and better political messaging improved the rate of success.

External Factors

After the prohibition of statewide legal restrictive initiatives in 1996 with the Supreme Court case *Romer v. Evans*, the Religious Right shifted its focus to a range of different referendums and initiatives. The Religious Right grew in size and strength through the development of a strong marriage movement in response to same-sex marriage gains in Hawaii and Alaska; it was also buoyed by the 1996 welfare reforms, which transformed both the funding of welfare recipients and support for abstinence-only sex-education and marriage-promotion programs. Government-sponsored marriage-promotion programs that disproportionately targeted white, middle-class conservative Christian families put money into the coffers of the marriage movement (Heath 2009). Both the marriage movement and traditionally antigay organizations such as Focus on the Family became more closely allied with ex-gay organizations (Green 2000). In 2003, the marriage movement grew exponentially in response to the legalization of same-sex marriage in Massachusetts.

In contrast to increasing Religious Right strength, which did not bode well for success, voters were becoming increasingly sympathetic toward lesbian and gay rights, particularly employment nondiscrimination rights (see Mucciaroni 2008). However, this surge in voter sympathy alone may not have been enough to account for the dramatic shift in LGBT campaign victories, as some cities with strong LGBT communities and LGBT-supportive voters lost campaigns.

Internal Factors

The biggest changes in the late 1990s were the tactics deployed and supportive movement infrastructure that was developed to fight antigay ballot measures. According to campaign trainer Dave Fleischer, described by many LGBT activists as the father of ballot-measure campaign tactics, "the reason we started winning at the local level on these nondiscrimination ballot measures is that we finally started campaigning. . . . The single biggest difference, more than techniques, is whether you're campaigning at all. And whether you're doing it on a scale where you can get the results you need."[4] In the campaigns of this time period, an infrastructure grew to support both campaigns and the spread of campaign tactics. In this growing infrastructure, national organizations developed trainings and field programs, field-workers from national organizations learned to work with local activists, and statewide organizations grew larger and more stable. Amin Ghaziani (2008, 226–27) suggests that before the turn of the twenty-first century the LGBT movement shifted from being a movement in which organizations played an occasional role to being a movement run by heavily institutionalized, politically mainstream organizations. This "organizational movement" style was contested, particularly during the controversial 2000 Millennium March on Washington, when many activists argued that the movement was too hierarchical and commercial. Despite these charges, both major national organizations, HRC and the Task Force, experienced growth spurts during this time.

As national organizations grew, field-workers developed better training programs to teach local activists how to run campaigns. The Task Force remained heavily involved in local campaigns, building a strong field program from 1999 to 2003 as it recruited Dave Fleischer from the GLVF. The fieldwork support staff in the Task Force eventually grew from a small team to eleven paid field-workers under the supervision of Fleischer. From 1997 to 2001, Fleischer and his team offered small-scale campaign trainings, first through GLVF and then through the Task Force. In these trainings, activists learned about how to raise funds, develop campaign messages, conduct voter identification through phone banks and door-to-door canvassing, and engage in coalition building. This training was developed into the Power Summit, launched by the Task Force team in 2001. The Power Summit training usually took place in an easily accessible city in a contested state where both local activists and activists from nearby states could be trained. In 2003 alone, the Power Summit team held trainings in California, Oregon, the Ohio Valley, and New Mexico, mobilizing at least two hundred local activists who would go on to become campaign managers and leaders. Power Summit trainings became increasingly hands-on, practicing techniques such as door-to-door canvassing and fund-raising. The training expanded, becoming not just a way of training activists but a way of launching and mobilizing campaigns. For example, when New Mexico was threatened by an attempted referendum that did not make it to the ballot, the August 2003 New Mexico Power Summit raised $46,000 for the campaign in one afternoon through the efforts of thirty-five training volunteers.[5] Many activists interviewed attributed victories during this time period to the Power Summit trainings and the tactics learned there.

National organizations not only became involved in training activists but also contributed staff support and money to local and statewide campaigns. Both HRC and the Task Force became more financially supportive of campaigns, particularly by providing "early money" to fund the hiring of a campaign manager or polling for message development. One of the most significant resources that the national organizations provided to state and local campaigns was manpower, specifically full-time staff members who could support existing campaign workers. More financial support and manpower went to symbolically significant campaigns. When LGBT residents of Miami-Dade County, Florida, defended their local nondiscrimination ordinance in a referendum in 2002, national support poured into the campaign. The Task Force and HRC collectively donated $60,000 of early money to the campaign to get it running, and the Task Force sent its entire field staff team to Miami-Dade in the final three weeks of the campaign, along with recruiting volunteers nationally. Statewide organizations also grew in numbers and strength in the late 1990s; several statewide organizations, such as Basic Rights Oregon and Michigan Equality, were instrumental in helping local campaigns.

Improved organization and the wide dissemination of tactics also enhanced the political messaging used in local campaigns. Referendum campaigns increasingly used language that focused on "saying no to discrimination against gays." Using selected phrases like "discrimination" and what one campaign activist referred to as "the g word" was an effective, narrow sound bite that appealed to voters' sense of fairness and acknowledged that LGBT rights were up for vote. There was controversy about the use of the word "gay" from both sides of the political spectrum: some activists were afraid that its use would make them targets for increasing homophobia, and others believed that it ignored the complexity of the larger LGBT community (see Stone 2012).

During the LGBT movement's winning streak in 2001 and 2002, it was clear that the movement had learned a lot about ballot-measure campaigns. Even in the face of increasing Religious Right mobilization, key shifts in campaign tactics and growth of the movement infrastructure to support campaigns influenced social movement success at the ballot box. An examination of the time period just from 1997 to 2003 would lead to the conclusion that internal factors predominantly account for social movement success. However, this explanation of ballot-measure success becomes more complex as one considers same-sex marriage bans, where the LGBT movement experienced defeat after defeat. Although the same movement infrastructure and politically savvy tactics were used in many campaigns to fight marriage bans, the movement has been overwhelmingly unsuccessful.

LOSING SAME-SEX MARRIAGE

This winning streak did not continue after 2003. Indeed, in the 2000 and 2002 elections it was evident that same-sex marriage bans would be difficult for the LGBT movement to fight. The movement did not just start losing ballot measures, but started being defeated by large margins that resembled the earliest referendum battles in the late 1970s. Most of these initiatives were same-sex marriage bans that passed as constitutional amendments in states with no history of antigay ballot measures. These initiatives were statewide, difficult to revoke without revisiting the ballot box, and passed by a large margin. Many of them were super–Defense of Marriage Acts (DOMAs), which extend restrictions on same-sex marriage to domestic partnerships or anything "like marriage." The biggest defeat came on the heels of the winning streak, in the November 2004 election, when twelve states voted on marriage-ban constitutional amendments, nine of which were super-DOMAs. Indeed, until 2012 the LGBT movement had won only two statewide votes on same-sex marriage or domestic partnerships: it defeated a 2006 super-DOMA marriage ban in Arizona and won a 2009 referendum to retain domestic partnership benefits that conferred all the rights of marriage in Washington State. However, in November 2012, the LGBT movement won four major statewide ballot measures on same-sex marriage, including the defeat of a same-sex marriage ban in Minnesota. Voters in Maryland and Washington State affirmed the legalization of same-sex marriage by their state legislatures through referendums. In this historic election, same-sex marriage was legalized for the first time through a ballot measure sponsored by the LGBT movement in Maine.

The success from the earlier time period did not persist for reasons both internal and external to the movement, including external issues like increasing Religious Right professionalism and lack of voter support, and internal issues like messaging problems that arose once the dominant type of ballot measure shifted from referendums to same-sex marriage bans. The confluence of uneven LGBT organization in different states and the Religious Right's focus on non-battleground states also contributed to many losses. However, like the winning streak on referendum campaigns, the combination of increasing voter support for same-sex marriage and increasingly savvy LGBT movement tactics led to the 2012 victory.

The Right's Growing Sophistication

Between 2004 and 2012, the Religious Right became more professional, organized, and politically sophisticated in its largest ballot-measure campaigns. During this time period the Religious Right escalated its use of ballot measures and organized in many new states, creating professional, well-funded campaigns.

The Religious Right became more sophisticated in running ballot-measure campaigns, using professional consulting agencies and statewide media campaigns to fight LGBT rights in a way they never had previously. The two most significant victories by the Right at this time were California Proposition 8 in 2008 and Maine Question 1 in 2009, both of which overturned legal same-sex marriage granted by either

the courts or the legislature. The most publicly visible of these constitutional amendments was California Proposition 8 in 2008, which
countered a 2008 decision by the California Supreme Court to allow
same-sex marriage (see Oliviero, chapter 5 herein). Political Research
Associates analyst Surina Khan (2009, 3) describes the Proposition 8
campaign as a "shrewd, media-savvy, well-funded and well-organized
grassroots movement that understood California's complex geographic
and political landscape." With record-breaking fund-raising of over
$40 million from across the country, it created a "well-funded operation
that rivaled any major electoral campaign in its scope and complexity"
(Khan 2009, 3). According to Frank Schubert, political operative and
campaign manager for the Yes on 8 campaign, the campaign set "ambi-
tious goals":

> Our ability to organize a massive volunteer effort through reli-
> gious denominations gave us a huge advantage, and we set am-
> bitious goals: to conduct a statewide Voter ID canvass of every
> voter; to distribute 1.25 million yard signs and an equal number
> of bumper strips; to have our volunteers re-contact every unde-
> cided, soft yes and soft no voter; and to have 100,000 volunteers,
> five per voting precinct, working on Election Day to make sure
> every identified Yes on 8 voter would vote. All of these goals, and
> more, were achieved. (Schubert and Flint 2009)

Yes on 8 grew into the largest antigay campaign thus far in history. Part
of its power was the coordination of Mormon, Catholic, and Protes-
tant opposition to same-sex marriage in the California, Arizona, and
Florida campaigns, which relied heavily on the coordinating efforts
of antigay pastors across the country.[6] The methods used in California
were emulated by Schubert in Maine in 2009 and all four victory states
in 2012, as similar political messaging and strategies were used in all
six states.

In addition to these large-scale professional campaigns, the antigay
Right has developed sophisticated messaging about same-sex marriage
that challenges the LGBT movement. In a survey of newspaper accounts on the subject, the most common arguments against same-sex

marriage include the protection of marriage as an institution, morality, public opposition to same-sex marriage, and the importance of heterosexual marriage for raising children (Fisher 2009). These arguments are often coupled with the depiction of courts and judges as antidemocratic "activists." In more liberal states these messages included using gay male spokespeople to assure voters that same-sex couples did not need the rights and benefits of marriage or that they could access those rights and benefits through domestic partnership benefits (Pinello 2006, 124). This messaging often weakened moderate and liberal voters' support for same-sex marriage by suggesting that the Right was supportive of civil unions but not of marriage for same-sex couples (Oliviero, chapter 5 herein). For example, a political ad on the Yes on 8 website depicted a heterosexual family who were close friends with their gay neighbors but who opposed extending the benefits of marriage to them. The ad described how the parents, Jan and Tom, were relieved to discover that their neighbors would get the same benefits of marriage with a domestic partnership, and thus they felt comfortable voting for Proposition 8.

The most common and lasting messages pertained to the sanctity of marriage as an institution and the ways that giving same-sex couples access to marriage would radically alter and/or diminish the institution. However, Right political organizers found that in more liberal states, weak supporters of same-sex marriage are easily persuaded by messaging about children and the unanticipated consequences of allowing the legalization of same-sex marriage. Indeed, in early polling for the Yes on 8 campaign by the opinion-polling firm Lawrence Research, over 60 percent of "No" supporters polled changed their minds when confronted with information about how health education teachers would have to teach children about same-sex marriage (People for the American Way 2008). The danger of LGBT rights to children is a longstanding political message that can be traced back to the early Dade County referendum in 1977. Some of the most popular and effective messaging during marriage-ban campaigns was using pro-LGBT children's literature to demonstrate the perils of same-sex marriage. Most notoriously, the book *King and King* was used in a widely aired Yes on 8 commercial in which a young girl comes home to her mother after reading the book in school; this ad was repurposed in several states in 2012. Other commercials, such as for Oregon Ballot Measure 36 in 2004 and Maine Question 1 in 2009, suggested that the consequences of same-sex marriage include children learning about gay sex in kindergarten and being forced to attend their teacher's lesbian wedding. One of the organizers of the Yes on 8 campaign suggested that this messaging was a strategic way of making Religious Right campaigns appear less homophobic and focusing on the "consequences" of same-sex marriage for children rather than criticizing same-sex couples who wanted to get married (Schubert and Flint 2009). One Task Force field-worker stated: "I think voters are afraid their kids will become gay. . . . It's not a fear of gay people, it's that they believe being straight is better." This messaging was more heterosexist than homophobic, inspired less by the fear of actual LGBT individuals than by concerns that children would grow up to be LGBT.

The combination of large-scale professional campaigns and effective messaging made the Religious Right a daunting force in this time period.

Voters

Perhaps the biggest issue in many states with same-sex marriage bans was that voters overwhelmingly supported same-sex marriage bans from the beginning and in such large numbers that even the most professional campaign might be ineffective. The largest and most significant external factor in all ballot-measure campaigns is that voters have not been supportive of same-sex marriage until recently. Of all the civil rights issues pressed by the LGBT movement, "the most threatening issue . . . is marriage. No issue prompts such widespread perceptions of an institution under siege by a sinister force. No other provokes calls for laws and constitutional amendments to 'defend' it from 'attack'" (Mucciaroni 2008, 21). Many studies have demonstrated that fewer voters support same-sex marriage than broader LGBT rights, such as employment discrimination protections (Yang 1997; Egan and Sherrill 2006). Indeed, domestic partnerships and civil unions are far more popular with the general public than same-sex marriage (Yang 1997). Yet these trends are changing: in 2011 for the first time a higher percentage of American adults supported same-sex marriage than opposed it (PEW Research Center 2012). These trends are evident at the ballot box. Since 1992, voters on average more consistently vote pro-gay for referendums on employment discrimination protections (49 percent on average) or domestic partnerships (53.3 percent on average) than for ballot measures on same-sex marriage (35.3 percent on average).

In studies of actual voters in California after Proposition 8, political ideology was most influential in affecting the vote, followed by religion (David Binder Research 2008). Changes in these attitudes would require demographic and cultural ideological changes (Loftus 2001, 778). As Table 4.2 demonstrates, these demographic and ideological changes may be in progress, as voters have become increasingly opposed to marriage bans and report increasing support for same-sex marriage in polling data.

As with many ballot measures, where the measure takes effect heavily influences the level of existing support for same-sex marriage. The Religious Right's focus on heartland states was a particularly strategic choice. A national study of marriage bans examining county-level data found that areas with predominantly traditional gender roles and family structures, along with weak community cohesion, were more likely to support a marriage ban (McVeigh and Diaz 2009). There are also strong regional differences in the acceptance of gays and lesbians

Table 4.2. Average Percent Voting to Oppose Marriage Bans or Approve Domestic Partnerships/Same-Sex Marriage (statewide votes only), 1998–2012

TIME PERIOD	N	MEAN	STANDARD DEVIATION	LOWEST PERCENT	HIGHEST PERCENT
1998–2002	7	31%	4.3	25% (Arkansas)	39% (California)
2004–2005	14	29.1%	7.9	14% (Mississippi)	43% (Oregon)
2006–2007	10	37.2%	12.5	19% (Alabama)	51.8% (Arizona)
2008–2009	5	46%	5.6	37.9% (Florida)	53.15% (Washington)
2012	5	49.9%	6.2	38.9% (North Carolina)	53.7% (Washington)

in public opinion, with less support in Southern and Central states (Loftus 2001). This trend persists with opinions on same-sex marriage; in 2012 a majority of American adults in New England, the Pacific Coast, and Mid-Atlantic and Mountain West states supported same-sex marriage, whereas only one-third of adults in Southern states did (PEW Research Center 2012). However, support is growing across all regions and demographics. A study of marriage-ban votes over time suggests that "while the vote on the marriage initiatives is best explained by partisan and ideological variables, declining support for marriage bans can also be explained somewhat by the measures' diminishing appeal in states with fewer voters identifying as 'born-again' or evangelical Christians" (Egan and Sherrill 2006, 1). As demonstrated by Table 4.2, voters have gone from an average of 31 percent to 49.9 percent in opposition to marriage bans or support of legal same-sex marriage. Much of the deviation within each time period, however, was due to the disparity between more liberal states such as Washington or Oregon and conservative states like Arkansas and Alabama.

Campaigns in Unusual Places

LGBT political actors in states like Nebraska and Alabama faced statewide votes on same-sex marriage with no ballot-measure campaign experience and a voting public unaccustomed to addressing LGBT issues at the ballot box. Of the thirty-four states with marriage-ban ballot measures (excluding Washington), there had never been a statewide antigay ballot measure in twenty-six of those states. Indeed, in most of the states, such as South Dakota and Virginia, there had never been a local antigay ballot measure. There was no cadre of experienced ballot-measure campaign organizers to call upon, although there were campaign professionals aplenty to hire.

This difference in experience mattered. LGBT communities with past ballot-measure experience fared better than communities without such experience. Before 2012, states with ballot-measure experience (either a different type of ballot measure or a previous marriage-ban vote) on average had 43 percent of voters opposing the ban, whereas states without ballot-measure experience had 30 percent of voters rejecting the ban.[7] Five states had attempted ballot measures in the past that never made it to the ballot box but may have resulted in preemptive LGBT organizing. Campaigns in these states with previously attempted initiatives fared better than states with no experience at all. An examination of these campaigns in the heartland of America shows a dramatic disparity in the amount of available resources, organizational support, and public opinion available to fight these ballot measures. A few LGBT communities—for example, in Mississippi—did not mount a campaign at all. Campaigns in states like North Dakota and Montana worked with a shoestring budget of less than $150,000. Many of these communities ran a campaign in states with weak movement infrastructure, with few LGBT organizations generally, and no statewide political organization. However, LGBT communities in Arizona, Virginia, and Wisconsin mobilized local resources to raise millions of dollars and ran large-scale campaigns. These fund-raising differences were exacerbated in crowded election cycles in 2004 and 2008, when many ballot measures were on the ballot at the same time. During these election cycles, LGBT donors and national organizations, which often gave critical early money to campaigns, had to make decisions about which campaigns were the most important and most likely to succeed. In 2004, most movement resources went to the campaign to fight Oregon's Ballot Measure 36 because of the long history of successful LGBT ballot-measure campaigns in Oregon. The competition for financial resources was even more intense in 2008, when the California "No on 8" campaign got the lion's share of attention and resources, because it was the first ballot measure aimed at invalidating existing same-sex marriages. Campaign leaders in Florida, Arizona, and Arkansas described how difficult it was to raise funds for their respective campaigns. One Arizona campaign worker described how even state residents were donating to the "No on 8" campaign in California rather than supporting the campaign in their home state.

In addition to disparities in financial resources, heartland campaigns lacked experience and, frequently, enthusiasm. Doug Gray, a campaign consultant, commented that when he was working on the Missouri campaign in 2004, marriage as an issue "was thrown upon us. . . . We weren't asking for marriage [in Missouri] . . . this isn't a fight in a battle that we brought on" (see Heath, chapter 7 herein).

Other activists commented that it was difficult to build enthusiasm in a campaign that "no one thought had a chance" of winning. Indeed, in many of these states, early polling of voters demonstrated the resounding lack of support for same-sex marriage in that state, making running campaigns even more difficult.

For heartland campaigns, the lack of LGBT organization and enthusiasm for same-sex marriage as an issue was coupled with the Religious Right's tactical brilliance in selecting non-battleground states to result in a series of same-sex marriage bans that passed. This confluence of internal and external factors was the most significant factor in the lack of LGBT success during this time period. Most of the media attention has focused on campaigns in states like Maine and California, battleground states where the LGBT movement will likely launch proactive initiatives to regain same-sex marriage rights. It is worth noting, however, that the majority of marriage bans have passed in non-battleground states.

Challenging Existing Campaign Tactics

These external factors, particularly voters' attitudes, have dramatically challenged the tactics used by the LGBT movement to fight antigay ballot measures. The lack of support for same-sex marriage among voters raised questions about the two dominant tactics that had previously been used effectively by activists: voter identification and disciplined messaging. Both of these tactics as they were developed by earlier LGBT campaigns assumed that a pool of supportive voters existed who simply needed to be informed about the referendum or initiative and then reminded to vote on election day. These "turnout" campaigns rarely focused on persuading voters to change their minds. However, public education and grassroots canvassing focusing on persuasion, along with messaging that was open and visible about same-sex relationships, contributed to the 2012 victories.

Because of the low support for same-sex marriage, LGBT campaigns were suddenly forced into the position of having to run persuasion campaigns, which focus on persuading voters to reconsider their opinions on an issue. The targets of persuasion campaigns are typically undecided and "soft opponents," people who could potentially be persuaded. In existing marriage-ban campaigns the power of the opposition's messaging made almost all undecided voters eventually vote against same-sex marriage. Developing persuasive messaging and ways of delivering that messaging has been a challenge for the LGBT movement. First, the clear, concise messaging developed for referendums about the perils of discrimination against gays cannot easily be applied to marriage-ban campaigns because many voters do not view lack of access to marriage as a form of discrimination. In addition, the messaging most commonly used by LGBT opponents of marriage bans is evasive messaging that focuses on the threat to the state constitution and the effects on heterosexual allies. This messaging did not address the Religious Right's scare tactics around teaching same-sex marriage in schools to children, which persuaded many undecided voters to vote in favor of Proposition 8 in California. In a confidential interview, a Task Force field-worker suggested that the biggest lesson from Proposition 8 is that "We haven't found a way to really combat the opposition's messaging." According to one HRC staff member, the biggest lesson from the California and Maine campaigns was that "we have to stop pretending that kids don't exist and kids aren't going to hear about same-sex marriage. We try to avoid children like the plague but we need to be proactive about bringing up kids."

To create this new messaging, since the dramatic defeats in 2004 both national and statewide LGBT organizations have engaged in extensive research on effective, persuasive political messaging for same-sex marriage initiatives. Using a combination of polling and focus groups, LGBT activists have been working to find messaging that "changes hearts and minds." This work to develop persuasive messages has included extra-campaign field experiments to gather systematic evidence on whether or not persuasive messaging can work. These experiments have included an experiment by Basic Rights Oregon in 2009 to test whether or not direct mail or door-to-door canvassing is the best vehicle to persuade voters. In addition, since 2009, the Vote for Equality project in the Los Angeles Gay and Lesbian Center has engaged in the most extensive persuasion experiment to date by altering door-to-door canvassing scripts through interactions with voters. Engaging in thousands of conversations, the canvassing experiment has worked to develop new ways of having conversations with voters about same-sex marriage; rather than using one sound bite, this canvassing model poses a series of questions to voters about their attitudes about marriage. The canvassing models developed have been effective in persuasion and are used all across the state by other organizations, where it has been called "the most sophisticated canvassing model with which we have ever worked" (Equality California 2009, 17) owing to its adaptability, length, and the way it encourages volunteer interaction with voters.

Even with all of this work, some activists are skeptical that genuine persuasion on a complex issue like same-sex marriage can happen during the intensity of a campaign. According to one analysis of persuasion of California voters, "Moving people on the issue of same-sex marriage is a cultural endeavor much more than a political endeavor. The meaning of marriage runs deep in people's psyches" (Equality California 2009, 14). In response to concerns about persuasion, there has been a push to start a "campaign before the campaign," preempting campaign work with years of persuasive public education with large media buys and one-on-one discussions. The Equality California (EQCA) campaign, Let Freedom Ring, is an excellent example of this type of public education. Two years before same-sex marriage was on the ballot in California, EQCA launched a campaign in Santa Barbara County in the summer of 2006 and made a slight shift in public opinion at that time. Many activists point to the rejection of Proposition 8 in Santa Barbara County as evidence that the campaign was successful. Other efforts since then have included the national Why Marriage Matters campaign spearheaded by the national organization Freedom to Marry and grassroots education in Maine between 2009 and 2012. In Maine, according to campaign organizers, the 2009 campaign continued until organizers were confident that a majority of Mainers supported same-sex marriage in 2012.

This work on messaging and public education ultimately paid off. Campaigns in 2012 developed messages about same-sex marriage that were more direct; they featured gay and lesbian spokespeople, showed same-sex individuals and relationships, and openly addressed the issue of same-sex marriage being taught in school. For example, in one political ad for the Yes on 1 campaign in Maine, parents Amy and Rob stress that "what we do in a school is no substitute for what happens at home" and "no law is going to change the core values we teach our kids." In Minnesota, political ads included multiple lesbian couples talking about love and commitment and the child of two lesbian mothers. Campaigns also used more advanced canvassing models developed in other states.

The four ballot-measure victories in 2012 came at the end of a series of continuous defeats at the ballot box. These continuous defeats were a product of external factors—a stronger Religious Right, campaigns in new states, and unsupportive voters—that challenged the way of running campaigns that worked so effectively for the LGBT movement during its winning streak before 2004.

ANALYSIS AND CONCLUSION

Campaigns and movements influence each other in complex ways. Campaigns may create networks and collective identities to strengthen movements, link the public and the movement, and alter the existing political opportunities for the movement (Staggenborg and Lecomte 2009; Tilly 2004). I argue that we cannot understand the success or defeat of antigay ballot measures without examining both factors external and internal to the LGBT movement. During the earliest time period of antigay ballot measures, from 1974 to 1996, the LGBT movement was stymied by lack of LGBT resources, along with lack of voter support for LGBT rights. Although some tactics were developed by the LGBT movement to fight these ballot measures, the Religious Right won the majority of antigay ballot measures. From 1997 to 2003, the LGBT movement experienced a winning streak that was a confluence of rising voter support for nondiscrimination protections and increasing movement organization and training to support ballot-measure campaigns.

Although the LGBT movement had a winning streak from 1997 to 2003, it was quickly followed by a losing streak as same-sex marriage bans proved to be devastating at the ballot box. This dramatic series of victories followed by a series of defeats raises questions about why LGBT movement tactics developed to fight antigay referendums and legal restrictive initiatives were not effective in fighting same-sex marriage bans.

The answer lies in many factors beyond the control of the LGBT movement. First, the Religious Right developed larger and more professional campaigns to support same-sex marriage bans, particularly in states like California, Maine, and Arizona. These professional campaigns used politically savvy messaging that appealed to liberal and undecided voters; identified and mobilized voters through both churches and voter identification programs; and engaged in strong coalition building across religious faiths. Second, the Religious Right was able to run campaigns in states outside of the typical battleground states that it had been fighting in for the previous thirty years. In these heartland states, like South Dakota and Alabama, the Religious Right could easily fight an LGBT campaign that was inexperienced in running ballot-measure campaigns and harness the sentiments of voters who opposed same-sex marriage. Although these factors were external to the LGBT movement, they have led to the alteration of LGBT campaign tactics, as LGBT organizers and leaders search for new ways of messaging about same-sex marriage.

From a social movement theory perspective, these data demonstrate the interplay between internal and external factors in understanding social movement success. Although examining success at the ballot box before 2004 suggests that changes in movement tactics can account for a winning streak, these tactics simply could not remain effective in the face of changing external circumstances, especially the strong voter opposition to same-sex marriage and the growing strength of the Religious Right. Theoretically, this study demonstrates the need for a holistic understanding of social movement success and for the need to bring the study of campaigns squarely into the literature that seeks to understand the outcomes of antigay ballot measures.

NOTES

1. These LGBT rights laws typically outlaw discrimination in public accommodations, housing, and employment. Same-sex marriage rights are also a form of LGBT rights. However, in this chapter the term "LGBT rights laws" exclusively refers to nondiscrimination laws.

2. I am including in this analysis legislatively referred initiatives as sponsored by the

Religious Right. In all cases, the Religious Right provided the pressure to get marriage bans on the legislative agenda and ran the campaign to pass the marriage ban.

3. This difference was even more dramatic for legal restrictive initiatives, which were 43 percent before 1997 and 56.9 percent afterward.

4. Dave Fleischer, interview with the author, July 3, 2009.

5. Information from the National Gay and Lesbian Task Force, www.thetaskforce.org.

6. This coordination included a series of seven conference calls with antigay pastors in an estimated 170–180 locations in Arizona, California, and Florida throughout the summer and fall of 2009. People for the American Way, www.pfaw.org.

7. This difference is statistically significant at the $p < .001$ level ($t = 4.11$, df = 34). Even the states that had experienced an attempted initiative (37.9 percent) did better than states with no initiative experience (29 percent).

REFERENCES

Andrews, Kenneth T. 2004. *Freedom Is a Constant Struggle: The Mississippi Civil Rights Movement and Its Legacy*. Chicago: University of Chicago Press.

Bates, Vernon L. 1995. "Rhetorical Pluralism and Secularization in the New Christian Right: The Oregon Citizens Alliance." *Review of Religious Research* 37 (1): 46–64.

Bernstein, Mary. 1997. "Celebration and Suppression: The Strategic Uses of Identity by the Lesbian and Gay Movement." *American Journal of Sociology* 103 (3): 531–65.

———. 2003. "Nothing Ventured, Nothing Gained? Conceptualizing Social Movement 'Success' in the Lesbian and Gay Movement." *Sociological Perspectives* 46 (3): 353–79.

Camp, Bayliss. 2008. "Mobilizing the Base and Embarrassing the Opposition: Defense of Marriage Referenda and Cross-Cutting Electoral Cleavages." *Sociological Perspectives* 51 (4): 713–34.

Citizens to Retain Fair Employment. 1978. "Chronicle of Key Events in the Campaign against Initiative 13." Box 4, Human Rights Campaign Fund records, #7712. Division of Rare and Manuscript Collections, Cornell University Library.

David Binder Research. 2008. "Proposition 8: Post-Election California Voter Survey." http://www.eqca.org.

Dugan, Kimberly B. 2005. *The Struggle over Gay, Lesbian, and Bisexual Rights: Facing Off in Cincinnati*. New York: Routledge.

Earl, Jennifer. 2004. "The Cultural Consequences of Social Movements." In *The Blackwell Companion to Social Movements*, edited by David A. Snow, Sarah A. Soule, and Hanspeter Kriesi, 508–30. Malden, Mass., and Oxford: Blackwell Publishing.

Egan, Patrick J., and Kenneth Sherrill. 2006. "Same-Sex Marriage Initiatives and Lesbian, Gay and Bisexual Voters in the 2006 Elections." National Gay and Lesbian Task Force. http://www.thetaskforce.org.

Equality California. 2009. "Winning Back Marriage Equality in California: Analysis and Plan." http://www.eqca.org.

Fetner, Tina. 2008. *How the Religious Right Shaped Lesbian and Gay Activism*. Minneapolis: University of Minnesota Press.

Fisher, Shauna. 2009. "It Takes (at Least) Two to Tango: Fighting with Words in the Conflict over Same-Sex Marriage." In *Queer Mobilizations: LGBT Activists*

Confront the Law, edited by Scott Barclay, Mary Bernstein, and Anna-Maria Marshall, 207–30. New York: New York University Press.

Frey, Scott R., Thomas Dietz, and Linda Kalof. 1992. "Characteristics of Successful American Protest Groups: Another Look at Gamson's *Strategy of Social Protest*." *American Journal of Sociology* 98: 36–87.

Gamson, William A. [1975] 1990. *The Strategy of Social Protest*. 2nd ed. Belmont, Calif.: Wadsworth.

Gerstmann, Evan. 1999. *The Constitutional Underclass: Gays, Lesbians, and the Failure of Class-Based Equal Protection*. Chicago: University of Chicago Press.

Ghaziani, Amin. 2008. *The Dividends of Dissent: How Conflict and Culture Work in Lesbian and Gay Marches on Washington*. Chicago: University of Chicago Press.

Goldstone, Jack. 1980. "The Weakness of Organization: A New Look at Gamson's *The Strategy of Social Protest*." *American Journal of Sociology* 85: 1017–42.

Green, John C. 2000. "Antigay: Varieties of Opposition to Gay Rights." In *The Politics of Gay Rights*, edited by Craig Rimmerman, Kenneth D. Wald, and Clyde Wilcox, 121–38. Chicago: University of Chicago Press.

Hardisty, Jean V. 1999. *Mobilizing Resentment: Conservative Resurgence from the John Birch Society to the Promise Keepers*. Boston: Beacon Press.

Heath, Melanie. 2009. "State of Our Unions: Marriage Promotion and the Contested Power of Heterosexuality." *Gender and Society* 23 (1): 27–48.

Khan, Surina. 2009. "Tying the Not: How the Right Succeeded in Passing Proposition 8." *Public Eye* 24 (1): 1–9.

Kolb, Felix. 2007. *Protest and Opportunities: The Political Outcomes of Social Movements*. Frankfurt: Campus Verlag.

Loftus, Jeni. 2001. "America's Liberalization in Attitudes toward Homosexuality, 1973 to 1998." *American Sociological Review* 66 (5): 762–82.

Mansbridge, Jane. 1986. *Why We Lost the ERA*. Chicago: University of Chicago Press.

McVeigh, Rory, and Maria-Elena D. Diaz. 2009. "Voting to Ban Same-Sex Marriage." *American Sociological Review* 74 (6): 891–915.

Meyer, David S., and Suzanne Staggenborg. 1996. "Movements, Countermovements, and Political Opportunity." *American Journal of Sociology* 101 (6): 1628–60.

Mucciaroni, Gary. 2008. *Same Sex, Different Politics: Success and Failure in the Struggles over Gay Rights*. Chicago: University of Chicago Press.

People for the American Way. 2008. "Gearing Up for a Fight." http://www.pfaw.org.

PEW Research Center. 2012. "Behind Gay Marriage Momentum, Regional Gaps Persist." November 9. http://www.people-press.org/2012/11/09/behind-gay-marriage-momentum-regional-gaps-persist/.

Pinello, Daniel R. 2006. *America's Struggle for Same-Sex Marriage*. Cambridge: Cambridge University Press.

Rupp, Leila, and Verta Taylor. 1987. *Survival in the Doldrums: The American Women's Rights Movement, 1945 to the Present*. New York: Oxford University Press.

Schubert, Frank, and Jeff Flint. 2009. "Passing Proposition 8." *Politics* 30 (2): 44–47.

Staggenborg, Suzanne. 1995. "Can Feminist Organizations Be Effective?" In *Feminist Organizations: Harvest of the New Women's Movement*, edited by Myra Marx Ferree and Patricia Yancey Martin, 339–55. Philadelphia: Temple University Press.

Staggenborg, Suzanne, and Josee Lecomte. 2009. "Social Movement Campaigns: Mobilization and Outcomes in the Montreal Women's Movement Community." *Mobilization* 14: 405–27.

Stein, Arlene. 2001. *The Stranger Next Door: The Story of a Small Community's Battle over Sex, Faith, and Civil Rights*. Boston: Beacon Press.

Stone, Amy L. 2012. *Gay Rights at the Ballot Box*. Minneapolis: University of Minnesota Press.

Stone, Amy L., and Jane Ward. 2011. "From 'Black People Are Not a Homosexual Act' to 'Gay Is the New Black': Mapping White Uses of Blackness in Modern Gay Rights Campaigns in the United States." *Social Identities* 17, no. 5: 605–624.

Szymanski, Ann-Marie E. 2003. *Pathways to Prohibition: Radicals, Moderates, and Social Movement Outcomes*. Durham, N.C.: Duke University Press.

Tilly, Charles. 2004. *Social Movements, 1768–2004*. Boulder, Colo.: Paradigm.

Wilcox, Clyde, and Robin Wolpert. 2000. "Gay Rights in the Public Sphere: Public Opinion on Gay and Lesbian Equality." In *The Politics of Gay Rights*, edited by Craig A. Rimmerman, Kenneth D. Wald, and Clyde Wilcox, 409–32. Chicago: University of Chicago Press.

Yang, Alan S. 1997. "Attitudes toward Homosexuality." *Public Opinion Quarterly* 61: 477–502.

5 Yes on Proposition 8

The Conservative Opposition to Same-Sex Marriage

Katie Oliviero

> *In a real sense, there are three partners to every civil marriage: two willing partners and an approving state.*
> —*Goodridge v. Department of Public Health,*
> Massachusetts Supreme Judicial Court, 2003

ORMAN ROCKWELL'S JUNE 11, 1955, *Saturday Evening Post* cover featured a young white woman in a yellow dress and white heels snuggling under the shoulder of her fiancé as she signs their marriage license. The state, represented by a marriage license clerk, enlists the spectator with a wry glance to witness this performative act of civil marriage where woman becomes wife, all under the sheltering arm of her boyfriend-turning-husband. The clerk's skepticism suggests how the mythologization of marriage as a primarily emotional and private relationship conceals its public, regulatory purposes (Cott 2000; Stevens 1999; Warner 1999). Absorbed by each other while filling out the license, the couple seems blissfully distanced from the legal significance of marriage.

Half a century later, Richard Williams (2004) parodied this Rockwellian scene on the heels of the 2003 Massachusetts Supreme Court's decision *Goodridge v. Department of Public Health*, which legalized same-sex marriage. Published in *MAD Magazine*, the satirical image anticipated the rogue 2004 granting of marriage licenses to same-sex couples by San Francisco county clerks and California's subsequent battles over gay nuptials. Garnering national attention (see Taylor et al., chapter 6 herein), this lesbian, gay, bisexual, transgender, and queer (LGBTQ) civil disobedience led to the 2008 California Supreme Court decision *Re: Marriage Cases* legalizing same-sex marriage, which was in turn challenged by the notorious state ballot initiative opposing equal civil recognition for same-sex couples, Proposition 8. "If," Williams queries in the illustration title, "Norman Rockwell Depicted the 21st Century" he'd stage a scene that was unremarkably the same—but for a photocopier in lieu of a potbellied stove, a spittoon transubstantiated into a trashcan, and a gay male couple. Wearing short-shorts and sleeveless T-shirts reminiscent of mid-1980s Fire Island cruising outfits, the couple camp their 1955 counterparts to highlight both the ultimate unremarkability of petitioning for inclusion in civil marriage, as well as the potentially transformative and subversive impact on that institution. The mustached fellow's yellow shirt references the mid-century bride's lemon-yellow New Look dress, a framing method that draws parallels with that nostalgic scene to critically highlight crucial gendered, sexual, and state differences. On the left side in the Williams illustration, the "marriage license" sign engraved upon a door opening into the clerk's office is freighted with new significance that was unremarkable to the couple in that everyday mid-century image. On the right, the red-and-white-striped United States flag clumped on top of the bookcase is now magnified as the previously inconspicuous presence of state-sponsored marital and sexual regulations. Through the continued denial of marriage licenses by most states, both the sign and the flag signal the authority of government to shun this relationship despite its increased, though still uneven, cultural visibility and greater legal legibility in the form of state-based same-sex marriage and domestic partner legislation.

The Williams illustration underscores the symbolic meaning of key objects in the iconic Rockwell image in order to reframe the political and social meanings surrounding both straight and gay marriage. Social movement theorists understand framing as a process of drawing upon existing social symbols, beliefs, practices, and identities to make sense of a situation and communicate a grievance (Gamson and Meyer 1996; McAdam 1996; Snow and Benford 1992). Certain master frames, such as the presumed stability of heterosexual marriage, may resonate across historical and geographical differences, but their meanings are fundamentally site-specific (Zald 1996, 271). Consequently, successful frames are inherently modular (Tarrow 1996) and appropriated by diverse actors who reassign the meaning of symbols by putting them into another political context to highlight different grievances and claims (Meyer 2007; Tilly and Tarrow 2007; Snow and Benford 1992; Taylor et al., chapter 6 herein). Symbols and rhetoric can be borrowed between movements and countermovements engaged in collective action to generate competing frames of contention about the same controversy. Framing techniques can also spill over between movements with similar ideological commitments but different objectives (Tarrow 1998). Juxtaposed against Rockwell's image, Williams's illustration emphasizes competing frameworks over civil marriage's public and private meanings, pointing to how matrimony's significance grows from their entangled contradictions. What ideals and behaviors marriage does and should transmit are at the heart of clashes between marriage-equality activists who support same-sex marriage and marriage "protection" proponents who oppose it. Among progressive and queer scholars concerned with sexual diversity, these conflicts also animate controversies over gay marriage's relationship to government-sponsored sexual regulation and neoliberalism. The latter is understood here as the processes of economic privatization by which the state divests itself of responsibility for collective welfare, displacing it onto private nongovernmental entities such as the marital dyad, corporations, and charities.

It is both gay marriage's resemblance to, and queering of, its heterosexual counterpart that makes it such an emotionally laden and threatening topic among conservative and queer activists alike. Viewed as homonormative by queer theorists for assimilating the diversity of nonnormative sexual desire into a rigid matrimonial form mimicking heterosexual conventions (Duggan 2002; Warner 1999), it is seen as a symptom of moral degeneracy for the Right. So it is unsurprising that queerness in all forms—which in the homophobic mind is equated with same-sex marriage as well as with other nonnormative sexual behaviors—is targeted by conservative movements as the central cause and symptom of the decline of marriage, as well as broader ideals of the intimate nuclear family.

This chapter argues that the Protect Marriage Coalition (PMC), an umbrella organization that spearheaded the 2008 "Yes on Proposition

8" campaign to overturn same-sex civil marriage recognition in California, shares queer theorists' framing of marriage as a public, not private, institution. The PMC advances marriage as an exceptional relationship endowed with special governmental rights to promote conservative social responsibilities and public morals. By disciplining diverse kinship and reproductive behaviors into a narrow understanding of the heterosexual family, the state regulates sexual behavior through marriage. Normative matrimony's heterosexual form and reproductive function is supposed to communicate narrow cultural and economic morals that are understood as public, not private. Both the traditional marriage movement and queer countermovement share this frame of contention: mirroring the wry skepticism of Rockwell's county clerk, scholars such as Nancy Cott, Lisa Duggan, Mae Ngai, Jacqueline Stevens, and Michael Warner have long pointed out that distinctly modern formulations equating marriage with romantic love and private emotions conceal its very public role as an institution through which the state reproduces normative ideals of moral citizenship and cultural belonging. Not only do formal rights of national citizenship flow through marriage, but matrimony is also a key mechanism through which the government invests its participants with key benefits—privacy protections, inheritance, social security, economic incentives, and so on—essential to broader notions of participatory citizenship that are denied to unmarried persons. Queer theorists and historians demystify marriage, observing how a rhetoric of love and private intimacy conceals state disciplinary forces (Cott 2000; Warner 1999). They define civil marriage primarily as a public intimacy generated through governmental processes of regulation and exclusion that endows different-sex relationships—or those that resemble them—with special, exceptional rights.

This chapter examines how gay rights opponents adopt facets of the queer critique of marriage, reworking its progressive and even subversive critiques of heteronormativity to influence cultural beliefs and public policies in distinctly reactionary directions. By juxtaposing conservative and queer frameworks of marriage and public intimacy, I argue that both movements deconstruct the relationship between civil matrimony, state regulation, private emotions, and public values in similar but distinct ways to generate competing frames of contention.

The analysis focuses on the political rhetoric and tactics of the "Yes on Proposition 8" campaign to ban same-sex marriage as articulated in their website materials, advertisements, and protest actions. I examine how this conservative marriage movement's performative tactics (McAdam 1996; Taylor and Van Dyke 2004; Taylor et al., chapter 6 herein) and visual framing draw upon dominant conceptions of heterosexuality to reinforce normative conceptions of marriage as a public institution. In the guise of merely protecting traditional marriage culture, they also generate new restrictive legal formulations of it.

After introducing the public policy history surrounding the ballot initiative, the first section interprets a performative Yes on 8 activist protest to unpack the broader anti-same-sex marriage movement's understanding of the relationship between state-endowed special rights, exclusion, sexuality, civil matrimony, and social vulnerability. I argue that the tactical repertoires of the antigay marriage movement reinforce through public and theatrical forms of protest the PMC's understanding of matrimony as an exclusionary institution communicating narrow public values and conferring special rights on different-sex couples. Such tactics forge collective solidarity and a public heterosexual identity within the movement, as well as mobilize public opinion and voters to oppose legislation supporting same-sex nuptials.

Interweaving analysis of the conservative marriage movement's position papers with "Yes on Proposition 8" political advertisements and cyber campaigns, the second and third sections examine how the PMC uses visual and rhetorical framing techniques to claim that gay matrimony and queer sexuality threaten family and children. A recognizable symbol, that of the vulnerable child of color, operates as a placeholder through which arguments against same-sex marriage, such as the danger of the gay pedophile, can be tacitly articulated. Covert analogies between *hetero*sexuality and racial identity inhibit intersectional alliances between LGBTQ and race-based civil rights. These sections reinforce how the modularity of social movement frames derive from borrowing symbols from multiple social change arenas (here, family unity, racial uplift, and antipoverty measures), combining them in a different ideological context (traditional marriage) to craft claims on the state.

The conclusion discusses how the PMC's framing and tactical

repertoires expose similarities between queer and conservative visions of public intimacy. Unlike their progressive counterparts, however, conservative movements revel in the exceptionality of heteronormative public intimacy. In contrast, the tactical repertoires used by marriage-equality countermovements to challenge Proposition 8 highlight the exclusionary nature of heteronormative marriage, while also generating expanded and queerer visions of state-sanctioned public intimacies. Reflecting the contested status of gay marriage within LGBTQ communities, I conclude that queer critiques of same-sex marriage overlook the fact that broadening the scope of civil recognition is necessary to satisfy the distinctly queer goals of supporting and celebrating a diverse array of sexual, caretaking, and living arrangements.

PROPOSITION 8

In May 2008 the California Supreme Court joined what was then only the state of Massachusetts and briefly legalized same-sex marriage.[1] In this landmark decision, *Re: Marriage Cases*, the court struck down a family law—a statutory Defense of Marriage Act or "mini-DOMA"—passed by voter ballot initiative in the year 2000 that limited marriage in California to different-sex couples.[2] The decision also endowed sexual orientation with the same antidiscrimination protections—"strict scrutiny"—extended to race, religion, and national origin in the Golden State, an unprecedented advance in equal protections jurisprudence that gay rights advocates had been working toward for decades. California's domestic partnership formulation was established in 1999 and expanded through subsequent legislation to become the most comprehensive in the nation, bestowing the same state-level rights and responsibilities of marriage in all but name. Nonetheless, the *Re: Marriage Cases* decision argued that domestic partnership neither provides equal legal standing nor social recognition for gay couples.

Anticipating the ruling of this landmark case or another like it in California, a coalition of conservative public policy groups and religious organizations that included the Family Research Council, the National Organization for Marriage, the Knights of Columbus, and the Church of Jesus Christ of Latter Day Saints (LDS) established the organizational and financial groundwork to create a ballot initiative overturning any potential judicial ruling. After the May 2008 decision recognizing same-sex matrimony, supporters of "traditional" marriage gathered almost 1.2 million signatures to put a referendum on the November 2008 ballot—Proposition 8. If passed, the voter initiative would bolster the existing statutory DOMA, this time amending the state constitution to declare that "only marriage between a man and a woman is valid or recognized in California." Like other mini-DOMAs amending state constitutions, this heteronormative codification would be much more difficult for gay marriage advocates to repeal. A yes vote supporting Proposition 8 banned same-sex marriage, while a no vote upheld it, a negative formulation that confused voters and has been replicated in other states, such as Maine in 2009. If passed, Proposition 8 would invalidate the first part of the *Re: Marriage Cases* decision recognizing same-sex marriage, but it would leave the heightened antidiscrimination protections intact.

Through umbrella groups such as the PMC, "Yes on 8" proponents initiated an intensive media and volunteer campaign, raising almost $40 million—$22 million of which is estimated to have been raised by the LDS Church (Cowan 2010). After a lethally sluggish start in the summer of 2008, marriage-equality groups—"No on 8"—raised over $43 million, the majority of which was donated that fall (Egan and Sherrill 2009; Khan 2009; Kim 2008). A national record was set for social policy fund-raising, and was second only to the presidential fund-raising campaigns (Kaye 2009).

In November 2008, California residents voted by a 4 percent margin (52 percent to 48 percent) to support the proposition and thus California once again denied marriage rights to same-sex couples, this time by amending its constitution.[3] Highly publicized demonstrations ensued in Los Angeles, San Francisco, and other California cities, with the mostly peaceful and emotional crowds declaring "Stop H8" and marching on the Santa Monica LDS Church, the Sacramento Capitol Building, and the LGBTQ neighborhoods of West Hollywood and the Castro.

Proposition 8 was appealed by a coalition of gay and civil rights groups, initially on procedural grounds. They argued that because gay marriage was an existing civil right established by the May 2008 California Supreme Court ruling, Proposition 8 was a revision of the state constitution rather than an amendment to it.[4] To prevent a majority from infringing upon the rights of a minority, California law requires two-thirds of the legislature to support a constitutional revision before it can be placed on the ballot. In contrast, amendments can be passed by referendum through a raw majority of electoral votes, which Proposition 8 garnered. While the California Supreme Court later upheld the initiative's procedural approach in May 2009, it also retained the validity of the eighteen thousand same-sex marriages performed between June and November 2008. A federal suit was filed in a San Francisco district court, and in August 2010 the judge ruled that Proposition 8 denied same-sex couples the fundamental right to marry, violating the right to due process and equal protections guaranteed by the 14th Amendment (*Perry v. Schwarzenegger*). The ruling was appealed to the United States 9th Circuit Court by the supporters of the ballot measure, ProtectMarriage.com, who in the fall of 2011 were granted standing by the California Supreme Court to defend Proposition 8 because the state governor and attorney general declined to do so. In February 2012, the 9th Circuit Court ruled that Proposition 8 violated equal protection guarantees by stripping same-sex couples of the previously established right to describe their relationship as marriage, reclassifying their relationships and families as inferior, and therefore unfairly denying gays and lesbians dignity and status (*Perry v. Brown* 2012, 5). The 2–1 decision, however, was narrowly construed and stayed pending appeal. It declined to address same-sex couples' fundamental constitutional right to marry, and only prohibited California and other states with preexisting marriage rights from unfairly singling out gays by stripping them of established protections and designations. In December 2012, the United States Supreme Court granted review of the Proposition 8 case as well as a challenge to the Federal Defense of Marriage Act (*Hollingsworth v. Perry* 2012; *United States v. Windsor* 2012). Anticipated by the summer of 2013, the decision will be among the landmark cases defining future marriage and equal protection laws.

PERFORMING AND REPRESENTING
MARRIAGE AS PUBLIC

Set against the white-frosted tiers of the Los Angeles City Hall and rallied on by celebratory cheers, a young Chinese-American couple exchanged vows that pledged to make marriage safe for heterosexuals, children, and the larger society (Dickenson 2008). But for the activists waving protest placards reading "Protect Children, Protect Speech, Protect Traditional Marriage—Yes on 8," this might have been the city-hall marriage of many modern couples. But by exchanging their vows at an architectural marker of state power, and having them authorized and acknowledged by a pastor and a crowd of witnesses expressly opposed to gay marriage, this couple used a tactic that combined the familiarity of marriage symbols with the publicity and interactivity of a protest to emphasize conservative matrimonial ideals. Their performance activism highlights how marriage is a social and governmental institution relying upon an exclusionary politics of public intimacy to invest some participants with cultural legitimacy by denying others. Exclusion is necessary to protect against what Mike Huckabee termed a "marital state of emergency" (Goldberg 2007, 68) where, as one Proposition 8 supporter declared, "homo-sex is a threat to national security" (LaGanga 2009). Expanding the definition of civil marriage to include same-sex couples makes it vulnerable in the eyes of PMC activists, counterfeiting it into what a former Miss California notoriously called "opposite" marriage, cheapening the real thing.

As a subset of "repertoires of contention" that include framing practices, tactical repertoires are intentional forms of claim making in which recognizable cultural symbols, behaviors, and rituals are strategically deployed to publicly contest authority and dominant power relations (Taylor and Van Dyke 2004; Taylor et al., chapter 6 herein; Tilly and Tarrow 2007). Echoing its counterpart in theater and performance studies, "repertoire" references both the defined and often predictable set of techniques used by collective actors as well as their interaction with the intended audience and their impact on public opinion. Combining Verta Taylor and Nella Van Dyke's approach (2004) with a

performance studies lens emphasizes how the embodied and theatrical nature of tactical repertoires generates "interactive episodes that
link social movement actors to each other as well as to opponents and
authorities for the intended purpose of challenging or resisting change
in groups, organizations, or societies" (2004, 266). Like frames, tactical
repertoires are modular (Tarrow 1993), borrowed between movements
to contest forms of authority ranging from political ideology to the state
by resituating established cultural symbols in different contexts. By performing wedding ceremonies as part of a Yes on 8 protest, the PMC
combined the familiar trappings of a marriage ceremony (vows, rings,
witnesses, pastor) with a new context (public activism contesting same-
sex marriage). This tactical repertoire highlighted marriage's role as
an exclusionary institution promoting particular public morals endowing heterosexual couples with special rights. Activist repertoires have
both external and internal effects: they make claims upon the state and
mobilize resources, and also generate an oppositional consciousness
and collective identity among participants who may influence future
actions. The PMC's wedding protests choreograph a sense of public
moral responsibility among its supporters that elevates heterosexual
identity from an unstated presumption to a self-aware oppositional consciousness that promotes future activism.

The tactical repertoire of the Yes on 8 campaign frames same-sex
marriage as threatening because it promotes the delusion that marriage
should primarily nourish the personal emotions and intimate desires
of individual adults, thus neglecting the larger social and moral good.
At best, gay couples can feel and express private love, a romantic sentiment that is inferior to the socially regulatory role of public intimacy.
Maggie Gallagher, the president of the Institute for Marriage and
Public Policy and the National Organization for Marriage, both PMC
organizations, explains: "if marriage is primarily emotional, personal,
private and expressive, the state has no reason, nor right, to interfere
by preferring any form of marriage to no marriage" (Gallagher 2004b,
231). In light of the privacy protections already tolerantly extended via
formal domestic partnership legislation and the informal right to love
and have sex with one's chosen adult partner, the PMC's view is that
gays are already endowed with the proper amount of state recognition

to safeguard these private expressions. Yes on 8 campaign advertisements repeatedly reference California's domestic partnership legislation, which ensures same-sex couples the "same rights, protections, and benefits . . . responsibilities, obligations and duties . . . as are granted to and imposed upon spouses."[5] In the stick-figure aesthetics through which campaign videos such as "Proposition 8 Made Simple" are narrated (ProtectMarriage.com 2008c), domestic partnership is advanced as providing the proper minimal degree of state intervention and regulation to recognize these private expressions without infringing on the more robust heteronormative family values fleshed out through civil marriage. Available in both short and long formats, these online advertisements highlight the overlap between a movement's framing processes and tactical repertoires: they provide accessible answers to common questions about same-sex marriage to convince unsure voters, as well as provide a persuasive script for proponents of Yes on 8.

The PMC's framing obscures the political battles that led up to civil unions and other same-sex protections established in *Baker v. State of Vermont* and *Lawrence v. Texas*, while concealing the continued neglect of basic formal antidiscrimination and, until recently, antiviolence protections.[6] Cries of "special rights" give license to outrage over gay marriage, a timeworn master frame of civil rights opponents (see Dugan 2005; Herman 1997; and see chapter 4). The special rights frame reactivates stereotypes of the "homosexual agenda," in which queers are ungrateful and ultimately deviant imposters trying to cheat honest heterosexual persons and institutions from their earned public protections. As Didi Herman (1997) and Kimberly Dugan (2005) observe, these configurations depend upon misrepresenting gays as a disproportionately powerful, overprivileged minority endowed with almost mythic wealth and political capital incongruent with their moral perversity and marginal population.[7] Both discourses of benevolence and special rights become emotionally potent, encouraging feelings of resentment, alienation, disgust, and ultimately backlash in response to a wealthy gay elite conspiring to oppress ordinary—that is, straight—people. Thus, the limited privacy protections enumerated in domestic partnership legislation provide a circumscribed site of tolerance (Brown 2006) for private intimacy that the PMC poses as an alternative to public equality, recirculating homophobia under the sign of flexible alternatives to marriage.

Misunderstanding marriage as a private emotional institution detracts from its social obligation, what the Family Research Council dubs the "natural, morally valuable opportunities for human flourishing" that heterosexual matrimony keeps "alive, intact and available for subsequent generations" (Family Research Council 2004). Mere "love" and "mutual commitment" can unite anyone, the PMC claims, but these personal freedoms of intimacy are ranked lower than the public imperative of marriage to embody and reproduce normative familial relationships. For heterosexual matrimony is an indicator of and producer of normativity,[8] which conservative movements contend protects vulnerable children, women, and society from the precariousness of sexual and familial diversity that is morally confusing and can lead to depression and even criminality. In renewing their vows as part of a Yes on 8 protest, the Chinese-American couple's wedding performance at Los Angeles City Hall asserted this institution's association with public, heterosexual morality. By staging what is usually a private extralegal ceremony in the public square, they underscored the relationship between heterosexual matrimony and conservative social values.

Although they claim to merely revitalize traditional matrimonial ideals, Proposition 8 and other anti-equality campaigns conceal how they are using the law to redefine the meanings of the institution of marriage. Marriage itself was transformed when in 1977 the California Family Code first reconfigured civil nuptials as a contract between a man and a woman rather than "unmarried person[s]." This definition was reinscribed by first the 2000 and then the 2008 Defense of Marriage Acts, which declared only heterosexual matrimony to "be valid or recognized" in the state of California. These narrowly tailored definitions are purportedly only making explicit the self-evident reproductive and heteronormative function of civil marriage (Gallagher 2004a, 52). But their codification has significant consequences beyond marriage, negatively impacting the recognition of out-of-state marriages, employment benefits, inheritance rights, parenting responsibilities, health care, and immigration. The PMC conceals this transformation of civil law by co-opting classically liberal calls for minimal governmental interference. The state is purportedly supposed to step into family law only in situations such as adoption to "give children other parents to do what their own original parents have failed to do" (Gallagher 2004a, 65). The government is framed as a surrogate parent, a second line of defense against irresponsible childbearing. But its proper role is not merely to provide a safety net for needy children, but to act as a *guardian ad litem* endowed with significant governmental powers to protect conservative social values even more so than people. "Super" DOMAs are a case in point, such as the recently overturned 2008 Arkansas amendment forbidding not only gay nuptials, but also any unmarried "sexual partners" from fostering or adopting children.[9] Hence, if it legalizes same-sex marriage, the state will be overreaching its compensatory status as a surrogate parent, violating these traditional marital rights, and exposing the larger society to uncertainty and confusion. If marriage is supposed to promote normativity and any same-sex relationship categorically deviates from this frame, then civil marriage equality can only threaten heterosexual primacy and the government has overreached its prescribed boundaries. DOMAs are required to guard against that overreach and reinforce traditional understandings of heterosexual marriage.

In the name of merely preserving past understandings by inscribing them into the law, these protectionist public policies are actually rewriting the legal and cultural meanings of matrimony and demanding greater degrees of state intervention. Historians highlight how contemporary understandings of both sexual identity and romantic marriage are modern inventions that would be largely unrecognizable prior to the nineteenth century (Cott 2000; D'Emilio 1993; Rupp 2001). The *Goodridge* and *Re: Marriage Cases* decisions cited these historical processes as justifications for legalizing same-sex marriage in Massachusetts and California. By emphasizing how the social meanings of behaviors shift over time, this jurisprudence queers legal understandings of identity and history (Chauncey 2004, 2008) even as those understandings "domesticate" queer plurality into narrower and normative private marital intimacy (Franke 2004; Ruskola 2005). The PMC adapts such queer methodologies and LGBTQ countermovement tactics, drawing upon the mutability of legal and cultural forms to rewrite relatively recent heteronormative understandings of marriage as a tradition standing outside history and the law. By creating new legal and social meanings in the name of protecting old ones, the PMC is appropriating queer theory's approach to history and marriage to promote conservative visions of them. Rather than highlighting the transformative processes of history, however, the conservative marriage movement's tactics are creating ahistorical and increasingly restrictive definitions of matrimony, family, and heterosexuality. The PMC nonetheless epitomizes the modularity of tactical repertoires by claiming something old—namely, the historically public role of civil marriage—as something new to challenge the recent association of marriage with private romantic love.

FRAMING SAME-SEX MARRIAGE
AS A THREAT TO THE FAMILY

The Yes on Proposition 8 campaign generalized the threat beyond heterosexuality to the family itself. Reflecting the modularity of framing tactics, it combined rhetorical and visual tactics of clarity with the icon of the vulnerable child to claim that childhood innocence and parenthood are endangered by gay marriage. Linda Kintz (1998) observes that frameworks of clarity resolve contradictory or unstable positions: here, the celebration of marriage culture and children's need for two-parent homes is rendered consistent with opposition to same-sex marriage and procreation. Clarity combines the emotions that accompany commonsense phenomena such as the powerlessness of children or heterosexual procreation with normative ideals such as the married family. Such simplified frameworks activate naturalized notions of biological reproduction and family stability whose diversification can easily be reframed as peril. The protect marriage movement contends that same-sex marriage threatens the protective forces and moral effects of heterosexual marriage by composing first children, then women, and finally fathers as vulnerable.

One Proposition 8 campaign commercial depicted the confusion that ensues when a young, blonde girl asks her fathers where babies come from. She glances uncertainly between her dads when she finds out they "come from mommies, dear," an answer that contradicts her friend who said that both men and women are required (ProtectMarriage .com 2008b). One of the men shifts uncomfortably away from her at this reference to heterosexual reproduction and suggests to his partner that she shouldn't play with that particular friend. She peeks over at this dad, who has now almost turned his back on her to focus his attention on his husband, and cautiously asks, "Then what is marriage for?"

The campaign frameworks depend upon clarity, contrasting a child's presumably inevitable questions about reproduction and gender with queer diversifications of parenting. They pose gays' reorganization of biological reproduction and parenting as a deceitful misrepresentation of a reproductive truth that confuses and alienates children. The little girl uncertainly compares her friend's understanding of heterosexual reproduction against the maleness of both her parents' bodies. This glance performs normative assumptions of heterosexual social relations. The commercial implies that unless the child is isolated from friends and the public world, the everyday reality of heterosexual gender difference will make these usually simple questions unavoidable and morally confusing. To explain the details of how two men can become two daddies would require a bewildering exposure to sexual complexities that would further corrupt the child's innocence—a purity reinforced by her femininity, age, and whiteness. Unsurprisingly, frameworks of heteronormativity and reproductive essentialism are sharpened by discourses of clarity and vulnerability that focus on the the purported exploitation and bewilderment of children. Focus-group testing showed that this framing slippage reinforced the ambivalence of some voters who were undecided about same-sex marriage (Schubert and Flint 2009; and see chapter 4). Such framing techniques sharpen any uncertainties among these voters about what it is exactly that queers do, whether in bed, at home, or in the public square.

When the child in the commercial calls out "Daddy?" to ask her question, the fact that there are two fathers creates more uncertainty and suggests a double neglect of this child. The more defensive father focuses his attention on his husband in a way that codes him as the nonbiological parent and signifies that this child is secondary to their intimacy. Consequently, the child is doubly abandoned. She is taught that mothers don't matter beyond the biological material of an egg and womb and that she is linked to her second parent only by the mercurial bonds of law and emotion. Without the genetic connection, when her second dad dislikes or is made uncomfortable by her questions, he can easily marginalize her to focus on what anti-equality advocates contend is the primary center of gay marriage—the adult intimacies and bond that will inevitably neglect the child. Gay marriage, this framing strategy implies, threatens children less by absenting fathers through lesbianism, but by doubling them—generating a kind of masculine grotesque (Russo 1995) in excess of gendered and heterosexual norms.

If marriage equality framing normalizes same-sex relationships by associating them with the family and parenting, then the bewildered tone of this ad contrasts clarity with neglect to shatter that comfortable affiliation. *Parent* is recast as antithetical to *queer*; *gay* becomes synonymous with *childlessness*. As scholars of social movements have suggested, seemingly commonsense and simple ideals convey more complicated emotional values that the PMC strategically invoke (Goodwin, Jasper, and Polletta 2001, 2004; Taylor 1995, 2000; Taylor and Rupp 2002; Whittier 2001). Clarity generates what social movement theorists term "reflex" and "moral" emotions (Goodwin, Jasper, and Polletta 2004, 416, 422). Through veneers of straightforwardness and rationality, it operates beyond critical analysis to call upon more involuntary reflex feelings that in this case strive for an uncomplicated understanding of family and reproduction that is normatively conflated with heterosexuality. Drawing from commonsense biological and heteronormative frameworks, discourses of clarity interweave dominant cultural and ethical values to generate complex moral responses, such as the protective feeling toward vulnerable children that is evoked here. By combining the soothing effects of simplicity with the commonsense protection of innocent children, clarity creates a reflexive and moral emotional regime that short-circuits our ability to capture purported ambiguities (see Kintz 1997, 1998) such as recognizing that same-sex marriage actually reinforces social and legal support for matrimony. Despite aspirations to truthfulness, clarity forecloses the audience's ability to absorb fact-based information that challenges its commonsense presumptions, such as empirical evidence testifying to the comparative emotional health of children in same-sex households (Averett, Nalavany, and Ryan 2009). Consequently, the PMC testifies to how regimes of clarity are highly selective and uneven about which vulnerabilities matter more than others. The developmental vulnerability of presumably heterosexual children is emphasized, while the exposure of gay youth and adults to physical violence is not, as the broader movement's opposition to a federal Equal Non-Discrimination Act and anti-bullying legislation demonstrates.[10] The framing strategy of this particular advertisement demonstrates how a discourse of simplicity equates heterosexuality with childbearing, welding this reproductive essentialism to marriage and proper parenting. Attempts to diversify or decenter these ontologies are charged with threatening these commonsense truths. Gay parenting becomes a contradiction in terms, or, as Gallagher testified in favor of a Federal Marriage Protection Amendment, gays "merely tolerat[e]" children rather than nurture them (U.S. Congress 2003, 32).

Consequently, the challenge of gay marriage to heteronormativity is easily reframed as a threat to parental rights, children's education, and children themselves. In focus-group testing, PMC marketing consultants found that Californians were unlikely to oppose gay marriage qua gay marriage, but would ban the unions if they were linked to harming children (Schubert and Flint 2009). The National Organization for Marriage (NOM), a PMC member, subsequently exported these strategies to other state and federal battles: litigation around Maine's 2009 ballot initiative overturning LGBTQ nuptials led to the release of an internal memo directing NOM organizers to "develop side issues to weaken pro-gay marriage political leaders and parties" by raising "such issues as pornography [and] protection of children" (National Organization for Marriage 2009b, 12). My analysis of the PMC shows that this strategy is particularly effective if the bodily and emotional vulnerability of children is grafted onto much larger ideals, such as the reproductive future of the nation and the imperiled status of fatherhood itself. As the following sections argue, Proposition 8 campaign commercials warning that same-sex marriage will lead to a loss of control over sexual values taught in school and at home depend upon the placeholders of childhood vulnerability as well as parental rights.

On the eve of the granting of the first marriage licenses to same-sex California couples, the Family Research Council published an advertisement in the *Wall Street Journal*:

> On Monday, Judges are removing the word husbands from California marriage certificates. The next step will be to remove father from birth certificates. Enjoy this Father's Day . . . It might be your last. (Family Research Council 2008)

In this warning, the legal redefinition of marriage is linked to the disenfranchisement of fathers. They will be rendered obsolete: biologically by artificial insemination among lesbians; socially by the masculine grotesque of male couples or lesbians; legally in the eyes of the state on birth and marriage certificates; and nationally in the eradication of Father's Day. This four-fold construction of paternal precariousness delineates a very narrow vision of what a father is; biology is once again wedded to the legal recognition of fatherhood that trumps more affective and intersocial paternal roles.

By connecting same-sex matrimony with threats to fatherhood, marriage is betrayed not only as a socially moralizing institution, but also as a legal mechanism to discipline men into the responsibilities and roles of fatherhood. "Good fathers are made, not born," Gallagher notes, riffing off of Simone de Beauvoir. "Far more than mothers, reliable fathers are cultural creations, products of specific ideals, norms, rituals, mating and parenting practices" (Gallagher 2002, 7–8). Marriage becomes a civilizing tool, channeling men's presumed promiscuity into more proper channels of fidelity, reproduction, and economic responsibility. Civil marriage ostensibly signals a consent to paternity that mere cohabitation and reproduction between unmarried couples does not, and marriage also demands social recognition and enforcement of paternity. Paralleling the wedding ceremony's linguistic and legal transformation of gendered individuals into spouses, marriage becomes the performative institution through which men can signal their consent and commitment to fatherhood, which in turn acculturates them into normative heterosexual paternal values. Conservative frameworks thus argue that same-sex civil marriage would condone the shirking of paternal responsibilities. It would weaken families and society, making fathers obsolete by doubling them or absenting them through sperm donation. Men can fight against this legal and technological obsolescence by opposing same-sex marriage.

The PMC's framing and tactical repertoires generate a vocabulary through which new legal claims are made on the state. Marriage is presumably the key to integrating men into family life and to reproducing not only children, but also the family system itself (Gallagher 2004b, 233). But the marriage contract is notoriously unclear: it is vague about the precise responsibilities and norms of marriage, which are primarily specified through divorce decisions that detail the role of gendered parenting, custody, alimony, cohabitation, and caretaking. By legally codifying who can participate in marriage and limiting it to a man and a woman, however, the marriage protection movement is paving the way for the formalization and state regulation of the requirements and processes of matrimony. Gallagher advocates for fleshing out the marriage contract from—at best—a vague legal articulation of minimal parental and economic responsibilities, to codifying detailed social and parental obligations in marriage law statutes. These include further reinforcing the special rights of heteronormative matrimony by preferring married couples within adoption, refusing "legal fatherlessness" via anonymous sperm donation, reviving common-law provisions for child support cases, and requiring "due diligence"—usually a waiting period and counseling—prior to divorce (Gallagher 2004b, 240).

Even proper modes of communication are legislated in the legally recognized framework of Covenant Marriage developed by Tony Perkins of the Family Research Council and available in three states. When Arkansas, Arizona, or Louisiana couples choose this nostalgic form of marriage, they agree to undergo premarital and pre-divorce counseling, usually with a clergy member, and sign a "Declaration of Intent" that they have disclosed all information that might threaten this lifelong commitment (Nock, Sanchez, and Wright 2008). Participants also agree that the dissolution of their union will be determined by the more stringent fault-based divorce grounds of abandonment, abuse, incarceration, or death that were replaced by no-fault approaches in the 1960s and 1970s. Within this legal alternative to conventional marriage, we again see a conservative transformation of marriage ideals disguised as merely clarifying and protecting traditional obligations. By protesting anonymous sperm donation and other contemporary family law formulations such as divorce, these formulas are trying to restore a mythic time, in this case a commonsense parenthood regime where there is a strict linearity between gametes, reproductive anatomy, society, morality, and the law.

Feminist scholars point out that the presumption that two equal individuals freely consent to marriage combines with the vagueness of the marriage contract to conceal gendered power inequalities that systematically disenfranchise women and noncitizens (Fineman 1991; Pateman 1988; J. Williams 2009).[11] But if the marriage contract masks and defers these gendered and ethnic presumptions, then Covenant Marriage and the proposed legal codifications of marital responsibilities expose the state's investment in heteronormativity—another mechanism by which conservative movements transform matrimony in the name of preserving it. These redefinitions of marriage try to fortify overstated, naturalized ties between biological procreation, heterosexuality, and matrimony. Such conflations depend, of course, upon abjecting queers, same-sex marriage, and new reproductive technologies such as in vitro fertilization, on the grounds that they threaten children and heteronormativity. When combined with the PMC's framing techniques, the call to legally mandate currently amorphous marital responsibilities demonstrates the movement's ability to transform sociolegal notions of matrimony, heightening their heteronormative dimensions in the name of preserving them.

Curiously, even as it valorizes heterosexual parenthood, this nostalgic family framework marginalizes women. Motherhood is naturalized and reduced to the embodied experience of conception, gestation, and birth. Through this biological essentialism, women's everyday parental activities after birth are sidelined and the significance of the maternal-child bond is decentered to emphasize the father. By shrinking women's parental labor to the bare bodily activities of maternal reproduction, women are erased, ghosted. Marginalizing women can function as a compulsive attempt to defer uncertainty about men's relationship to the reproductive dyad and the decline of patriarchal authority within feminist and LGBTQ social movements. Indeed, when gay marriage is invoked as a threat to women, it is based on outdated family breadwinner models and presumptions that women seek monogamous sexual security as opposed to men's innate promiscuity. This reasoning appropriates first- and second-wave feminist critiques of patriarchal marriage (e.g., Firestone 1970) to argue that marriage arose for women and children from historical circumstances of gendered divisions of labor and reproductive roles. Matrimony is framed as protective, "stem[ming] from deep economic vulnerabilities imposed on women by pregnancy and childbearing" that are still evident in wage gaps and other workplace "mommy penalties" (Gallagher 2004a, 55). But unlike the feminist movements' critiques of marriage and androcentric labor norms, PMC framing strategies embrace and naturalize gender roles: women exchange sexual exclusivity for their husband's assumption of the "risks of paternity" (Gallagher 2004a, 56), which include taking economic responsibility for women and their children as well as repudiating promiscuity. Narratives of exchanged risk obscure key structural and cultural differences between the vulnerability of children and women. In conflating women and children's vulnerability, the protect marriage movement infantilizes women, marginalizing their parental role even as their biological tie to parenthood naturalizes it. By revitalizing the language of protectionism to frame marriage as the neoliberal antidote to feminized poverty, the PMC overlooks and condones the structural gendered divisions of labor and wage gaps that make many women economically precarious.[12] Gendered and age-based protectionism become placeholders to divert attention away from institutional remedies for socioeconomic vulnerabilities.

Reading against the grain of PMC frameworks, men's presumably voracious sexuality and tenuous connection to parenthood and women emerge as sites of anxiety that require the firmer legal tie of civil marriage. By disciplining men into the responsibilities of fatherhood and husbandhood, marriage channels presumably hardwired "erotic energies" and nonmonogamous propensities to "a relatively narrow, but highly fruitful channel—to give every child the father his or her heart desires" (Gallagher 2002, 9). Gallagher routinely emphasizes the mental health and emotional benefits marriage confers primarily upon men. When combined with the PMC's conflation of homosexuality with gay men and subsequent erasure of lesbian women,[13] we start to see how resistance to gay marriage becomes an ultimately futile attempt to recover a time when the sociolegal status of heterosexual men was more dominant. The return to patriarchal authority is confused with a purportedly more faithful relationship to children and wives. Thus homophobic marriage initiatives function as proxies through which to shore up uncertainty about men's dominant family role.

A significant PMC frame focuses on how same-sex marriage challenges more transcendental ideals of parental and religious rights. With a grainy aesthetic reminiscent of a videotape dubbed over one too many times, a prominently circulated campaign advertisement, "It's Already Happened," featured a young girl exclaiming that she learned in school today that "a prince married a prince and I can marry a princess" as she hands her mother the book *King and King* (ProtectMarriage.com 2008e). Her mother's widened eyes and grimace cue a worried horror that is reinforced by the overlaid narration of a law professor. He warns that state laws mandating the teaching of respect for marriage in schools ensure that homosexuality, too, will be taught—as it was in post-*Goodridge* Massachusetts, where second graders learned that boys can marry each other after a court permitted the teaching of *King and King* in schools. A case number, law book, and California family code citation flash across the screen to gesture to the presumably irrevocable force of state authority. When combined with the gritty, on-the-cheap video aesthetic reminiscent of early personal injury lawyer advertisements, these tactics emphasize that parental rights and childhood innocence are being abused by the state. The dubbed, blurry videography references the form and impact of gay marriage itself, declaring it to be a vulgar copy of legitimate marriage. Backed up by the force of law, same-sex marriage will degrade the institution's overall quality and injure its social values and legal exceptionality, here framed as parental rights as well as childhood innocence.

An interview with the aggrieved Massachusetts parents who lost their suit over the teaching of *King and King* fleshes out the personal impact of these abstracted consequences. The Wirthlins argue that the court's decision against them infringes upon parents' rights to object to curricula promoting homosexuality. Children are too young to understand the concept of gay marriage, they argue, and neutral references to same-sex marriage or sexual diversity in schools will infringe upon children's freedom of independent thought. For "the state must teach these things to children before they've had a chance to make up their own mind" (ProtectMarriage.com 2008d). Marriage equality would lead to a fall from grace, where the mandatory teaching of this knowledge will mar childhood innocence. But because they are children whose ignorance is compounded by a trusting nature, the transgression is doubly egregious here, for these are children without any choice, their wide-eyed purity trampled by the systematic mandates of state education.

These campaign frameworks argue that should same-sex marriage be legalized, putatively neutral state education requirements will mandate positive representations of gay sexuality in schools. This framing tactic overlooks how, prior to the 2008 *Re: Marriage Cases* decision, states such as California already required that sexuality education curricula discuss marriage in a manner appropriate for students of all "races, genders, sexual orientations, ethnic and cultural backgrounds, and pupils with disabilities."[14] Rather than directly challenge established law, however, the PMC argues that same-sex marriage, and not the current educational frameworks, will introduce children to the concept of homosexuality and sexuality at developmentally inappropriate times. At the very least this will confuse children, and, more insidiously, this inappropriate knowledge will trammel their innocence. By depicting gay nuptials as the blatant elevation of private adult desires over the larger social needs of children, gay marriage and queer sexuality are recast in a child molestation narrative where adult sexual desire is indulged at the cost of childhood sexual innocence and agency. Backed by the power of the state in the form of civil marriage recognition as well as education requirements to teach respect for marriage, LGBTQ couples are once again cast in a special rights narrative (Dugan 2005; Herman 1997; and see chapter 4) where their disproportionate rights victimize a helpless public. It is not surprising that PMC discourses resonate with latent conflations of pedophilia and homosexuality: their tactics and framing strategies resemble those of the 1978 Briggs initiative that attempted to bar gays and LGBTQ rights supporters from teaching in

California schools.[15] The twenty-first-century courts are positioned as perpetuating and condoning similar assaults against the futile protests of parents trying to protect their children from perverse, developmentally inappropriate knowledge. Instead of serving *in loco parenti*, the school and the state are supplanting parental authority by assaulting the innocent child and, with it, the reproductive future of the nation itself.

Proposition 8 commercials focused on education are effective because they revitalize the emotional specter of gay pedophiles lurking in the schools and tap into the association of queerness with an imperiled national future. A more ominous campaign commercial makes these hazards explicit. Against a background of children's finger paintings and the tinkling of a music box, "California Proposition 8—To Protect Children" argues that "5 year olds don't know what transgender and bisexuality are" in printed block letters that contrast with a child's shaky signature, "Ronald," on a Gay, Lesbian and Straight Education Network (GLSEN) ally pledge in the next frame. Tolerance, the advertisement intones, is taught through "kindness to everyone, not confusing them when they are just learning to make their letters" (Protect Marriage.com 2008a).[16] Given that gays and lesbians are already endowed with equal rights, the supertitles state, it is the children who must be protected from activist agendas through supporting Proposition 8. With the child represented only by his wobbly handwriting and the tinkling background music of the music box he opened a moment before, he is a ghost in this campaign advertisement.[17] But this ghost becomes a warning where the special rights of gay couples erase those of the innocent child. In this tactic, civil recognition of same-sex marriage disregards children's unique cognitive and developmental immaturity, emblemized by an uneven signature and the absence of Ronald himself. Thus the GLSEN pledge is akin to a forced confession, a coercive act that once again invokes the specter of pedophilia.

This commercial mobilizes confusion and coercion as the inherent dysfunction of the queer family itself. As the Family Research Council reminds us, representations of lesbians and gays that "resembl[e] the stereotypical ideal of a married couple" are a deception of the homosexual agenda contradicting social science research finding that "such idealized 'families' are utterly atypical among homosexuals" (2004). Kindness to all, the PMC commercial intones, is also the freedom from this malfunction that gay marriage and teaching gay tolerance implies. Directed now toward kids, once again kindness and clarity are mobilized in the name of denying LGBTQ intimacy and antidiscrimination rights. The PMC argues that a politically correct conspiracy and gay activists' calls for acceptance have trumped commonsense concerns over children's developmental needs. In the name of protecting innocent and vulnerable children, the PMC is able to publicly articulate and then conceal a moral disgust toward, and pernicious stereotypes of, queers.

MOBILIZING RACE TO FIGHT SAME-SEX MARRIAGE

Proposition 8 combines confusion with homophobic associations between queerness and pedophilia to claim that same-sex marriage increases children's vulnerability and threatens the moral and biological future of the nation. Lee Edelman notes that because the child epitomizes the promise of the future in heteronormative worldviews, the nonprocreative orientation of queer sex therefore emblemizes "social death." Queerness, Edelman argues (and celebrates), has "no future," and the peril it poses to heteronormative futures is embodied in the figure of the vulnerable child endangered by the predatory homosexual (2004). Reinforcing how symbolic frameworks are modular and borrowed between movements and countermovements, the PMC combines childhood vulnerability and queer social death with racialized discourses of sexual immorality. Its youth-focused cyber campaign, iprotectmarriage.com,[18] features an image of a scraped, graffitied skateboard that frames the almond eyes and skin of a solitary boy staring solemnly into the camera, asking "Which Parent Doesn't Matter, a Mom or a Dad?" (iprotectmarriage.com 2008b). By depicting this child as radically alone in a turbulent world referenced by the graffiti, this visual framing claims that in denying the need for different-sexed parents, gay marriage implies that none are required at all. It effectively orphans kids and leaves them unprotected and exposed to violence.

Walls marked with tagging signal urban blight in the popular imagination. Thus, through the "cultural borrowing" essential to framing techniques (Taylor et al., chapter 6 herein), this image aligns the diversification of parenting through same-sex marriage with its weakening through teenage motherhood and paternal irresponsibility that is presumed to plague those city centers. Its vaguely nonwhite signifiers of race testify to how Proposition 8 tacitly racialized queerness via the specter of sexual immorality. For not only homosexuality, but also premarital sex, teenage pregnancy, absent fathers, and neglectful mothers are associated with the deviancy and presumed criminality of communities of color (Collins 2005; Roberts 1997). This racialization is both ironic and politically potent given the grassroots organizing for Proposition 8 within communities of color (Dickenson 2008) and the interconnected struggles against racism and homophobia within them (Foster 2010; Moore 2010). Historic and new racisms disparage people of color by denigrating their sexuality as excessive, claiming that it threatens the health and purity of the body politic, whether represented by white women, teenage chastity, HIV-negative status, or the viability of the social welfare system (Collins 2005). Because queerness is always in excess of heteronormative sexual morals, it is also a paragon of hypersexuality that the PMC reattaches to these revitalized, racialized narratives of sexual immorality to recruit conservative and poor voters of color.

Voting Yes on 8, campaign frameworks imply, can publicly repudiate the association of these communities with sexual excess. The PMC therefore appeals to conservative discourses of dignity generated by the conjunction of racialized and homophobic sexual values. Heterosexism within different communities of color is forged in part through the confluence of sexual excess and race in white dominance narratives (Foster 2010; Moore 2011). The marginalization of LGBTQ people functions as much to guard against these racialized charges of sexual excess and hyper-reproductivity toward people of color as it does to shore up the primacy of heterosexuality within them—doubling the deviance of queers of color in the process (Ferguson 2004). Consequently, this Yes on 8 image revitalizes more general racialized frames of hypersexuality and parental irresponsibility and cements them to these homophobic legacies of white supremacy and colonialism.

Indeed, the postelection focus on Proposition 8 support within Latino and black communities masks its stronger backing by older and more religious subgroups—obscuring for both sides how race and ethnicity are not the most relevant categories through which to evaluate the initiative's success. A widely publicized exit poll found that 70 percent of African American voters supported Proposition 8.[19] In the leftist public imagination, this ultimately inaccurate statistic wedded blackness to homophobia, obscuring how even in this unrepresentative poll the majority of racial subgroups supported the measure, joined by 49 percent of whites. When more accurate surveys with larger sample sizes revised African American support to approximately 58 percent, charges of hypocrisy and reverse discrimination remained rampant, primarily targeting first the black and then the Latino community, which supported the referendum by 59 percent as opposed to 48 percent of Asians (Egan and Sherrill 2009, 1). The progressive media's quick condemnation of African American Proposition 8 supporters as hypocritical overlooked the fact that in terms of raw numbers almost five times more people identifying as white voted for the measure. It also muted how subgroups affiliated by religious attendance, party, ideology, and age were most influential (Egan and Sherrill 2009, 3). Seventy percent of supporters identified as Republican, conservative, or religious. Controlling for religiosity, African Americans were not significantly different from other supporting groups. Sixty-seven percent of voters over the age of sixty-five carried the measure, while 74 percent of youth under twenty-nine opposed, roughly equaling the voting pattern of those with college educations (Guerra, Magnabosco, et al. 2008, 3).

Prominent media narratives decrying the hypocrisy of racial minorities failed to capture this electoral complexity. Nor could they contextualize how opposition toward same-sex matrimony within some communities of color goes beyond homophobia to responses to white supremacy. As part of the cultural repertoire of respectability, heterosexual marriage provides a sexual propriety denied to African Americans first by chattel slavery and subsequently by pervasive stereotypes such as the welfare queen (Moore 2010, 2011), which shaped regulations denying low-income married and cohabiting women access to public benefits until the late twentieth century (Smith 2007). Quick condemnation of African American and Latino support for

Proposition 8 implicitly conflates the appeal to sexual dignity with both assimilation and homophobia, concealing how new forms of racism and sexual deviance in a compulsory heterosexual culture may compel skepticism about gay marriage in conservative and religious communities of color (Foster 2010; Moore 2011). It also obscures how the conjunction of racial or ethnic identity with queerness requires an intersectional approach to same-sex marriage, where recognition of LGBTQ rights is embedded within antiracist struggles for communities of color (Moore 2010, 327).

Some marriage-equality frameworks uncritically associate gay rights with civil rights, particularly through analogies between barriers to same-sex marriage and race-based segregation or antimiscegenation laws. These uncritical analogies have generated a discourse where African American support for Proposition 8 is a perplexing, hypocritical betrayal of their own history. Charges of hypocrisy among some marriage-equality supporters overlook a history of African American support for gay rights that is evident in the endorsement by the National Association for the Advancement of Colored People (2012; Barbaro 2012) of the procedural challenge to Proposition 8 and black opposition to the failed 1978 Brigg's initiative forbidding lesbians and gays from teaching in public schools. They obscure how socially appropriate recognition of LGBTQ relationships within some black communities complicates presumptions that visibility, assimilation, and individualism are the indicators of sexual acceptance (Moore 2010, 2011). Uncritical analogies between racialized and sexualized discrimination also unwittingly reinforce broader conservative attempts to undermine antiracist justice efforts. Rather than shining light on the government's investment in using marriage as an antidote for poverty among people of color in lieu of social welfare provisions (Roberts 1997; Smith 2007), the framing strategies of the PMC shift focus from the neoliberal state to an already marginalized social group. Similarly, leftist claims that African American Proposition 8 supporters are hypocritical actually minimize the sexual intolerance and fear held by white, conservative, and religious Proposition 8 supporters, by championing their ideological opposition to gay marriage as morally consistent. This stance simultaneously condemns any black opposition toward same-sex marriage or different notions of the intersections between race and sexuality as another form of sexual deviance.

The framing strategies of both the PMC and those on the left decrying African American hypocrisy obscure how the same sexual moralizations applied to queers are also used to justify increased state regulation of poorer persons and people of color in respect to kinship formation and reproductive health and sexual choices via the allocation of Temporary Assistance for Needy Families (TANF) funding for marriage promotion. Oft-cited fears of welfare recipients' reproductive excess have led to the implementation of family caps within some state TANF programs, where the already paltry per-child stipend is often denied for offspring born while their mothers are accessing state assistance (Smith 2007). Discourses of parental irresponsibility lead to the surveillance of recipients' sexual and marital choices (Roberts 1997). In many states, women's TANF benefits are docked unless they identify their children's fathers, effectively creating government-mandated relationships that the parents would not have otherwise chosen and which can exacerbate domestic violence (Smith 2007).

Racialized narratives of sexual immorality and parental irresponsibility, however, are more easily assimilated into the larger governmental marriage movement and consequently the homophobic marriage lobby. Three out of four of the 1996 welfare reform objectives highlighted marriage as a means of ending dependence on government assistance.[20] In addition to hitching economic assistance to work requirements ("workfare"), "marriagefare" purportedly promotes personal responsibility by encouraging two-parent families and reducing out-of-wedlock births for welfare recipients. In 2000, the George W. Bush administration launched the Healthy Families Initiative to assess and strengthen the late 1990 marriage promotion programs. The Deficit Reduction Act of 2005 allocated $150 million each year until 2010 for marriage and fatherhood promotion, funding that was extended to 2014.[21] Nine states explicitly provide financial marriage incentives that include $100 monthly bonuses and back child-support releases upon remarrying (Smith 2007, 174–77).

The intertwining of "marriagefare" with "workfare" in state public assistance programs reflects conservative frameworks aligning matrimony with white, middle-class, and heterosexual norms, reinforcing them in the process. Promoting marriage as an antidote to poverty presumes an outmoded and highly gendered breadwinner model where the husband is assumed to be able to earn a family wage that in a service-based economy is largely unavailable to the middle as well as the poorer classes. The cumulative effects of structural racism, particularly unequal educational opportunities and reduced wages, make the breadwinner ideal disproportionately unavailable to communities of color. The majority of marriage promotion programs are open to the public, and one Oklahoma case study found that primarily middle-class couples accessed these resources, effectively redirecting state assistance designated for more economically needy persons to those who require it less (Heath 2006, 2012). Marriagefare also targets gender differences as the central source of relationship conflicts, overlooking structural dynamics such as poverty and racism that create stress and make couples vulnerable to domestic violence and divorce. The Yes on 8 frameworks thus revitalize historical sexual stigmatizations of poverty and call upon their latent racial associations to once again rebrand homosexuality as the embodiment of deviant sexual excess par excellence. Consequently, like heterosexual marriage promotion initiatives, the PMC campaign performs an effective sleight of hand to reanimate the queer body as the paragon of deviance, while both drawing from and concealing the racialized and classist discourses of sexual immorality.

This strategy of making racialized and gendered bodily meaning both present and absent abounds throughout the PMC's tactics, particularly for the Chinese-American couple discussed above who renewed their vows as part of a multicultural Yes on 8 rally. By taking a performative pledge to make marriage safe by highlighting their heterosexual, reproductive difference, this couple also obscured more ominous historical parallels. Until changes were made to the quota system and family reunification procedures of the mid-nineteenth century, Chinese Americans were effectively forbidden to marry through the combined effects of antimiscegenation statutes and U.S. immigration policy that restricted Asian immigration in general, and that of Asian women in particular (Ngai 2004). To use Chela Sandoval's term (2000, 119–20), this couple "inoculates" the PMC campaign against charges that it is revitalizing racist discourses of sexual immorality under the sign of protecting heterosexuality. They publicly display a small dose of visible, corporeal difference to serve as an alibi (Lee 2000) against critiques that the PMC is reasserting nativist and white supremacist moral logics. The presumed innocence and generalizability of an idea—such as marriage's inherent good and its reproductive necessity—obscures how racialized discourses of sexuality and morality are updated for contemporary kinship and state relations. The PMC reinforces how the modularity of framing tactics derives from using mainstream cultural symbols such as the heterosexual family to covertly articulate taboo but ideologically persistent stereotypes such as racialized sexual excess.

Yes on 8 consistently used the alibi of their nonwhite supporters to neutralize marriage-equality advocates' analogies between race and sexual orientation, as well as to challenge the extension of antidiscrimination guarantees to sexual identity. In a cyber-quiz for young people presenting various anti-same-sex marriage arguments, one African American woman takes offense at the comparison between same-sex and interracial marriage prohibitions, arguing that her race is not a choice and cannot be changed, while people are counseled out of their homosexuality all the time because it is a choice and lifestyle (iprotect marriage.com 2008a).[22] The actress references her own skin as a bodily signifier of both nongay identity and the legacy of racism, using it to license a personal account of discrimination that undermines LGBTQ calls to recognize historical legacies of homophobic violence and marginalization. In light of the opposition of several PMC member organizations to hate-crimes legislation and affirmative action, this tactic conjures race as an alibi. Structural discrimination is positioned as a site of collective memory through which people of color derive authenticity and an exclusive voice that other identity groups may not claim, no matter how careful LGBTQ equality advocates are to distinguish between different histories and effects of systematic prejudice. But even as the young actress makes racism present, she calls upon more color-blind solutions: the structural racism her skin evokes can only be wielded as an alibi to dispel those inauthentic, and presumably opportunistic, claims of discrimination by gays to invalidate them. As the organization's opposition to hate-crimes bills attests, race-based animus is firmly relegated to the past and erased in the present. Within these narratives, the only political meanings that can be culled from racial differences are exclusive understandings of structural violence that primarily function to *neutralize* charges of discrimination and undermine equal protections for gays *and* people of color, not to expand them.

Such divisive frames of contention capitalize upon the controversy on the left surrounding the analogy between prohibitions against interracial and gay marriage. These comparisons may be deservedly critiqued for flattening the significant differences between structural racism and homophobia and equating very different historical anatomies of prejudice. Easy analogies conceal some inattention to structural racism and other inequalities on the part of LGBTQ activism. They also tacitly reinforce postracial narratives in which racism is located firmly in the past. Too often, race is mentioned in the present only within national progress narratives that at best mark off how far we have come and at worst undermine attention to contemporary racisms and inequality. Consequently, these easy comparisons obscure more complicated understandings of how racism and homophobia can act in concert to amplify deviancy and rank different kinds of oppression. This inattention to difference structured the quick condemnation of African American support for Proposition 8 as hypocritical, scapegoating the black—and, to a lesser degree, Latino—community and overlooking other significant subgroup backing, as discussed earlier.

But the dismissal of any comparison between antimiscegenation and homophobic legislation can ignore the modular nature of social movement frameworks and their impact on public policy. Tactics are borrowed between movements and countermovements, as well as among organizations that share similar social justice commitments but make distinct racial or sexual equality claims. Analogies between different forms of grievance are essential to public policy procedures, and prohibiting them stalemates powerful legal arguments. These include calling upon landmark Supreme Court decisions like *Loving v. Virginia* (1967) that struck down interracial marriage bans as judicial precedents for cases such as the 2008 California *Re: Marriage Cases* that Proposition 8 sought to overturn, all of which are instrumental in expanding legal definitions for understandings of family within and beyond marriage. Establishing legal precedent is a crucial tool in creating legal change. Borrowing past judicial reasoning and applying it to contemporary concerns is how our common law system functions. Certainly, the tendency of the common law to treat "likes alike" can erase crucial differences, such as the distinction between homophobia and racism, or obscure vital similarities, evident in the 1984 *Bowers v. Hardwick* decision, which denied privacy rights to gays. Repudiating any parallels between homophobia and racism also prepares the cultural groundwork to invalidate the second significant finding of the May 2008 California Supreme Court decision, which endowed sexual orientation with the same robust civil rights extended to race. Opponents of gay marriage and antidiscrimination protections for gender identity and sexual orientation use the alibi of their nonwhite supporters to dispel both the analogy of race with sexual orientation and the extension of similar levels of equal protection guarantees to gays and lesbians. In fact, these heightened antidiscrimination protections hold more promise than marriage for challenging the employment, housing, custody, and socioeconomic disparities affecting queer lives. Indeed, schisms between queer and lesbian and gay social justice movements in part derive from the perception that the latter have prioritized civil marriage equality over antidiscrimination initiatives.

The PMC capitalizes upon these controversies to exacerbate tensions between race and queerness and further inhibit intersectional critiques. Conservative opponents of same-sex marriage market themselves as paragons of multiculturalism. They claim to be a diverse coalition unified by the universal commitment to protect normative marriage, which is supposed to counter critiques of homogeneity and construct same-sex couples and their supporters as wealthy, white elites. The Proposition 8 website and campaign images feature multichromatic arrays of skin tones and facial features. Multiracial frameworks were acutely deployed in the well-publicized (and parodied [Colbert Report 2009]) "Gathering Storm" advertisement that NOM broadcast after the Iowa Supreme Court recognized same-sex marriage in May 2009. In a twist upon gay liberation iconography, NOM recruited a "rainbow coalition of people of every creed and color" to come "together in love to protect marriage" and religious liberties (National Organization for Marriage 2009a). A background of black storm clouds envelops the actors' limbs and torsos, prefiguring how same-sex marriage is on the edge of trampling an unspecified set of rights. One Asian-American woman warns of how "my freedom will be taken away" while another laments that "same-sex marriage proponents are not content with same-sex couples living as they wish." The ad then jump-cuts to a white woman commenting that "they want to change how I live." Multiculturalism is marketed as a campaign tool to legitimate the exclusion of queers. The ethnic vagueness of the nonwhite characters embodies how people of color are grouped together as an alibi to mark off how this "nation for marriage" has already redressed discrimination, narrowly understood here as white homogeneity and legal forms of discrimination struck down by *Brown v. Board of Education* and the 1964 Civil Rights Act. The nation has atoned, and nonwhites have been recruited into a multicultural solidarity with whites, who now must battle against religious and cultural discrimination from the same-sex marriage movement. As a sunrise cracks over the storm clouds, a man of color calls upon the hope embodied by this rainbow coalition coming together in love to protect marriage, the celestial iconography pointing to a religiosity that proclaims itself to be so universally broad as to embrace ethnic diversity—but not sexuality—within its ranks. Through a tokenized identity politics, these framing methods segregate sexual recognition and nondiscrimination from religion and race, attempting to fragment coalitional possibilities. They reflect NOM's stated campaign strategies to "fa[n] the hostility raised in the wake of Prop 8" and "drive a wedge between gays and blacks" by developing media around African American spokespeople's objections to equating gay marriage with civil rights, as well as making marriage a "badge of Latino identity" (National Organization for Marriage 2009b, 13).

CONCLUSION

This analysis of the "Yes on Proposition 8" campaign demonstrates how opponents of same-sex marriage both adapt and echo the queer countermovement's critique of marriage and normative public intimacy. Just as the MAD Magazine cartoon parodies the Norman Rockwell image of marriage, the homophobic marriage campaign argues that civil matrimony is more than a private romantic relationship. By declaring that gay nuptials threaten children and parenthood, and challenging analogies between gay rights and antiracist struggles, the PMC's tactical repertoire and framing strategies attempt to claim that heterosexuality, traditional masculinity, and the national future are at stake. Heterosexuality stands in for the normative values of gendered obedience, cultural assimilation, and familial economic independence. The state must actively encourage these public intimacies through processes of exclusion, endowing heterosexuality and heterosexual marriage with special rights.

The PMC's framing of marriage imitates in a conservative register the observations of the feminist and queer countermovements that marriage reinforces archaic gender norms that primarily benefit white, middle-class men. Theorists such as Katherine Franke and Michael Warner critique same-sex marriage for advancing a singular notion of familial stability and sexual normativity that disciplines the diversity of queer behaviors into a narrow institutional form that creates good gays by castigating bad, nonmarital gay sex. Their claims have some merit. Legal decisions recognizing same-sex marriage argue that matrimony provides an essential public good and promotes social stability and the optimal environment for raising children (see particularly *Varnum v. Brien*, Iowa 2009). Equating marriage with family stability persists despite demographic evidence that cohabitation outstrips marriage, with wedded couples comprising 45 percent of households (Economist 2011). Only about 20 percent of children are raised in an idealized family framework, while 24 percent are born to cohabitating households and 40 percent live in them throughout childhood (National Marriage Project 2011, 1). Thus the state investment in marriage, gay or straight, can most generously be interpreted as an attempt to encourage a relatively narrow set of public values centered on familial stability that is incongruent with actual living arrangements.

As my earlier discussion of marriagefare demonstrates, idealized frameworks of nuclear familial stability also operate in tandem with the neoliberal "withdrawal" (Fineman 2004, 2008) of state responsibility for public social and economic welfare. Crucial caretaking and financial responsibilities are displaced onto the private family, which is increasingly unable to bear such burdens because of precarious employment, social welfare cuts, costly health care, and wage stagnation (see Fineman 1995, 2004, 2008; Smith 2007). Consequently, there is merit in queer and feminist critiques that expanding marriage to include same-sex couples inhibits what Martha Fineman terms a more "responsive" state (2008). Both the PMC's celebration of marriage's heterosexual public values and same-sex marriage jurisprudence conflating matrimony with social stability encourage the continued withdrawal of the government from its public socioeconomic responsibilities. As the *Goodridge* court recognizing gay nuptials in 2003 observed, marriage "conserv[es] scarce State and private financial resources" and therefore should be extended to same-sex couples precisely because of the dependent children and aged parents in their care (336–37). Marriage, gay or straight, promotes a public *social* intimacy that works in tandem with neoliberal *economic* processes of privatization.

Unlike their marriage-equality counterparts, however, the PMC's conservative approach to public intimacy depends upon a tokenized identity politics that appropriates children and people of color as vulnerable populations, hijacking progressive notions of structural discrimination and social justice for reactionary ends. Gay marriage is consequently framed as a mutilation of "traditional" marriage, a dismemberment that DOMAs such as Proposition 8 and the heteronormative marriage protests described here guard against. In turn, phenomena such as covenant marriage or DOMAs that go beyond marriage to roll back any existing legal recognition for diverse kinship relationships (e.g., Arkansas) are not just protecting heterosexual marriage, but creating new homophobic sociolegal meanings for it.

I conclude by briefly addressing tactical repertoires that may be useful for both queer and marriage-equality movements, where tactics are understood as temporary strategies that respond to and work within specific power arrangements and adapt to shifting political and legislative landscapes (de Certeau 1984; Taylor and Van Dyke 2004). Since 1998, the Lambda Defense and Education Fund has encouraged its constituents to stage "Strolling Wedding Parties" where the symbols, attire, and rituals of the wedding are used as theatrical props to contest institutional inequality and homophobia. In a 2004 South Carolina action, one lesbian and one gay male couple demanded marriage licenses from the county clerk, and then—after their inevitable denial—marched down Main Street bedecked in wedding attire to draw attention to gay marriage and critique the grounds upon which it is denied. When gay couples, their supporters, friends, and family wield wedding props to protest the denial of marriage-equality rights, the combination of familiarity and spectacle references the dailiness, and therefore unremarkability, of their demands. Like the aesthetic similarities between the Rockwell and Williams pieces described at the beginning of this chapter, such repertoires performatively claim "what is the big deal about marriage"—straight or gay. But in a legal environment that purports to condemn discrimination, and goes so far as to promote marriage through abstinence-only education initiatives and social welfare incentives, the familiarity of these wedding symbols conflicts with the denial of same-sex marriage rights, highlighting the exclusionary nature of state understandings of public intimacy.

Just after the passage of Proposition 8, two of the plaintiffs for *Re: Marriage Cases* renewed their marriage vows on the steps of the Beverly Hills courthouse where they had signed their license the summer before during the five months between the court decision recognizing same-sex unions and passage of Proposition 8 barring them. Shortly afterward, another same-sex couple attempted to get a license from the county clerk who had married the plaintiffs a few months before. The predictable rejection that ensued was choreographed to highlight the exclusionary nature of state heteronormative marriage laws—an exceptionalism reinforced by an unwitting different-sex couple that was simultaneously granted a license to the strobe of camera flashes.[23] Paralleling San Francisco Mayor Gavin Newsom's rogue 2004 directive allowing county clerks to grant marriage licenses (see Taylor et al., chapter 6 herein), both the media spectacle of this tactical repertoire and the ensuing voiding of these licenses forge public sympathy. By performatively demanding recognition that is denied, these activists succinctly communicate their grievances and live out their desired vision of same-sex public intimacy (Taylor et al., chapter 6 herein).

The tactical repertoires of both the PMC and the marriage-equality movement deploy the familiarity of marriage rituals to generate competing claims about the benefits or harms of exclusionary institutions generating public intimacy. Social movement theorists argue that the success of competing frameworks is influenced by groups' access to political opportunity, resources, cultural legibility, and the impact of macrohistorical forces (for an overview, see Taylor, Rupp, and Gamson 2004; Snow 2004). The impact of cultural frameworks is both internal, generating oppositional identities primed for future activism, and external, shaping political opinion, voters, and legislative decisions (Stone, chapter 4 herein; Taylor et al., chapter 6 herein). When couples renew their wedding vows and pledge to protect marriage, they performatively generate a collective sense of heterosexual identity committed to conservative public morals. Strolling wedding parties and marriage license disobedience on the part of same-sex couples create an oppositional consciousness that intentionally challenges state-sponsored homophobia and exclusion. Both Yes on 8 and the marriage-equality movements demonstrate how the internal cultivation and politicization of collective identity has the potential to shape the external impact of movements (see J. Gamson 1997; Taylor and Rupp 1993; Taylor, Rupp, and Gamson 2004; Taylor and Van Dyke 2004). The exclusionary frameworks of the Yes on 8 campaign effectively elevated heterosexuality from an unstated presumption to a self-conscious collective identity galvanizing future activism among opponents of same-sex marriage.

In the four years following Proposition 8, however, eight additional states and the District of Columbia have recognized same-sex marriage, reflecting the success of the marriage-equality movement's challenges to the PMC's celebration of exclusionary public intimacies and heterosexual identity. Political opportunity theorists observe that state-focused social change operates conservatively, adapting more radical claims into established institutional forms (Meyer 2007). In that light, the relative success that marriage-equality activists have enjoyed at the state level can in part be attributed to their savvy engagement with, and expansion of, some of the more conservative associations of marriage with family stability and children. The marriage-equality movement's tactical repertoires throw into relief the injustice of the PMC's sexuality-based exclusionary public rights framework. Same-sex marriage advocates effectively highlight how identity-based exclusion is at odds with powerful American democratic ideologies of inclusion, even if exclusion persists on a daily level.

By putting old symbols into new contexts, the marriage-equality movement's performance repertoires hold open the possibility of communicating alternative meanings about the public values and behaviors of marital intimacy, as well as what kinds of kinship relations the state should recognize. Both queer theorists and the PMC emphasize how marriage's romantic association with private emotions and love— a cultural by-product of nineteenth-century industrial capitalism— conceals its primary role as a state institution, conveying significant rights and responsibilities. Bolstered by the research findings of think tanks such as the Williams Institute, the same-sex marriage movement draws attention to these rights and responsibilities—particularly the economic, health, medical, and social-security entitlements—and the harm generated by their denial. Marriage-equality movement tactics such as marriage license civil disobedience highlight the neoliberal state's withdrawal from public welfare responsibilities such as health care and retirement pensions, entitlements that are currently distributed through privatized entities such as marriage and the corporation, if at all.

Postelection critiques of the "No on Proposition 8" campaign strategies, however, primarily focused on how campaign materials relied on abstract discourse about civil rights rather than explicit references to gays' personal or civil investment in marriage. Indeed, queer people were conspicuously absent in advertisements, flouting strong social science data demonstrating that personal knowledge of one LGBTQ person significantly shifts support for rights and recognitions. Although the subject is beyond the scope of this chapter, visibility politics has its limits, particularly for those whose gender identities, practices, and affinities complicate straight/gay binaries (Bernstein 1997). But visibility politics and performative tactics are relevant in this analysis. They have the ability to draw needed attention through the same-sex marriage debate to progressive social justice efforts that strive to democratize access to core social accommodations such as health-care and

206 • Katie Oliviero

retirement benefits. Access to these basic public goods are currently allocated along boundaries of marriage and class but need to be more broadly available across economic, educational, age, racial, gendered, and sexual differences. Same-sex marriage enables these broader social justice possibilities through the use of countermovement tactics that expose the state regulation of matrimony and unequal distribution of material resources. Beyond rights and recognition, some queer people want to be involved in this regulatory institution that reinforces rigid gay/straight binaries because it enables access to material benefits that the government fails to deliver. By decentering the heterosexual nature of matrimony, *same-sex* marriage is one step toward a broader social justice vision that democratizes access to key resources such as health care and social security beyond (gay or straight) nuptials (Beyondmarriage .org 2006; Fineman 1995, 2004; Polikoff 2008).

The *Re: Marriage Cases* decision recognizing same-sex marriage in California and challenged by Proposition 8 declined to ponder if "the name 'marriage' is *invariably* a core element of the state constitutional right to marry." But this deferral opened up for legal audiences whether or not "this civil institution is distinct from the religious institution of marriage." The California Supreme Court provocatively hinted at a future sociolegal context in which "the state [could] assign a name other than marriage as the official designation of the formal family relationship for *all* couples," distinguishing between civil and social meanings of matrimony (434, emphasis in original). Social movement scholars and feminist legal theorists observe that political change is incremental, at best assimilating more expansive claims into established institutional forms, nudging progress along while simultaneously generating backlash and new forms of restrictions. Echoing this perspective, it is my contention that creating expanded legal and social recognitions for a variety of interdependent kinship and caretaking relationships beyond civil matrimony requires federal recognition of same-sex nuptials, as well as the legal bifurcation between the social and civil meanings invested in the word *marriage*. In December 2012, the United States Supreme Court granted review of two cases challenging the constitutionality of the federal DOMA and its state counterparts like Proposition 8. Decisions are anticipated in June of 2013. Irrespective of the outcomes of these cases, cultural and legal recognitions of relationships outside the heteronormative model are crucial tools to broaden our notion of intimacy beyond marriage and sexual notions of the family (Beyond-marriage.org 2006; Fineman 1995, 2004; Polikoff 2008). Striking down the federal DOMA and creating both state-level same-sex marriage recognition and federal civil partnership legislation prepares the cultural and legal framework for future national conversations differentiating between governmental and extralegal nuptials. Alternatives to heterosexual marriage therefore are crucial sociolegal paradigms where the social and religious meanings attached to marriage can flourish, albeit distinct from formal legal recognition of interdependent and caretaking relationships that extend beyond the limited institution of matrimony and its name.

NOTES

Special thanks to the anonymous reviewers as well as Leila Rupp, Verta Taylor, and Mary Bernstein for their rigorous editorial eye in revising what began as a humble conference paper. And *grazie mille* to Leila for her mentorship, red pen, and tireless support of my work among cross-disciplinary spaces. Juliet Williams's interdisciplinary approach to popular culture and politics, as well as her conferences on marriage, were formative in encouraging and shaping this research topic. Martha Albertson Fineman's research on caretaking helped forge my interests in public intimacy and the responsive state long before I had the language to articulate them, and Jennifer Musto asked rigorous, thoughtful questions over the years. Needed time and research funds were provided by the University of California, Los Angeles, Center for the Study of Women, particularly the Jean Stone Dissertation Research Fellowship, as well as the University of California, Los Angeles's Lesbian, Gay, Bisexual, and Transgender Studies Teaching Fellowship. And many thanks to Martha Fineman and the Feminism and Legal Theory Project at Emory University School of Law, which sponsored my Postdoctoral Fellowship with the Vulnerability Human Condition Initiative and allowed me to complete this chapter.

 1. See *Goodridge v. Department of Public Health*, 798 N.E.2d 941 (Mass. 2003). As of November 2012, nine states and the District of Columbia recognize same-sex marriage: Massachusetts (2004); Connecticut (November 2008); Iowa (April 2009); Vermont (September 2009); New Hampshire (January 2010); Washington, D.C. (February 2010); and New York (June 2011). Until 2012, marriage-equality measures worldwide were approved by the courts or legislatures and uniformly rejected at the ballot box. Making electoral history, Maine, Maryland, and Washington voters approved same-sex marriage referendums during the November 2012 election. Internationally, these states join the Netherlands (2001), Belgium (2003), Spain (2005), Canada (2005), South Africa (2005), Norway (2008), Sweden (2009), Portugal (2010), Iceland (2010), Argentina (2010), and Spain (2005/2012). Though they

can only be performed in Mexico City (2010), gay nuptials are recognized countrywide. These countries join a bricolage of civil unions, Pacte Civil de Solidarité (PAC), and domestic partnership legislation in countries such as France, England, Brazil, Australia, Colombia, Finland, Germany, and Greenland, many of which are considering civil marriage laws (Economist 2012).

2. For the statutory DOMA, see California Family Code, section 308.5.

3. California Constitution, article I, section 7.5.

4. *Strauss v. Horton*, 46 Cal.4th 364 (2009).

5. See the California Domestic Partner Rights and Responsibility Act of 2005, Family Code Section 297.5.

6. See the 2009 Matthew Shepard and James Byrd Jr. Hate Crimes Prevention Act, 111th Congress, 2647.

7. Social science data demonstrate that LGBTQ people tend to be poorer, with less political and cultural capital (Albelda et al. 2009; Badgett 2001).

8. As Gallagher states: "The purpose of marriage law is inherently normative, to create and force others to recognize a certain kind of union: permanent, faithful, co-residential and sexual couplings" (Gallagher 2004a, 43).

9. See the Arkansas Adoption and Foster Care Act (Proposed Initiative 1), approved by the voters during the November 2008 election, and deemed unconstitutional by the Arkansas Supreme Court in April 2011. *Arkansas Department of Human Services v. Cole*, Ark., No. 10-840, April 7, 2011 (affirming 36 FLR 12841284).

10. Brian Brown, the National Organization for Marriage's executive director, mobilized opposition to North Carolina's School Violence Prevention Act, which defined bullying and harassing behavior to include acts motivated by actual or perceived sexual orientation and gender identity. See Brian Brown, "Return America Bulletin," June 3, 2009, e-mail on file with author.

11. These gendered and nationalistic deferrals are evident in sexual assault laws that until the early 1990s exempted spouses from prosecution (Pateman 1988) and still apply disparate standards of evidence. They are also reflected in equal treatment divorce principles that in practice socioeconomically disadvantage women (Fineman 1991). This vagueness conceals tacit ethnic and nationalist presumptions that are exposed by a heightened scrutiny of the relationships of binational spouses in green card applications (J. Williams 2009).

12. Social science research indicates that women's poverty neither stems from nor results in marital status. Because individuals still tend to marry within their socioeconomic and educational classes, and poorer people have a tendency to be underemployed, unstably employed, and paid minimal wages, marriage on its own isn't likely to mediate poverty. And because joint income is taxed at a higher level, when a woman makes significantly less than her partner, her individual take-home salary may actually be harmed by marriage in a way that can offset the benefits of sharing living expenses (Roberts 1997; Smith 2007).

13. Social conservatives' support for normative gender relations makes gay women ambivalent figures for opponents of gay rights (Herman 1997). Lesbian mothers embody normative understandings of feminine maternity that lesbianism itself decenters. Gay rights opponents manage this paradox by stereotyping and pathologiz-

ing lesbians' gender presentation as a form of sexual deviance—another valence of the masculine grotesque.

14. California Comprehensive Sexual Health and HIV/AIDS Prevention Act, Education Code 51933(4).

15. In ruling that Proposition 8 infringes on the constitutional right of same-sex couples to marry, the 2010 *Perry v. Schwarzenegger* decision cited historian George Chauncey's trial testimony that these campaign ads drew from cultural stereotypes conflating homosexuals with child predators that were common in 1970s ballot initiatives restricting the employment opportunities of gays (*Perry v. Schwarzenegger* 2010, 20–21). While I concur, my research points to the fact that these stereotypes are overt and explicit, whereas both Chauncey and Justice Walker argued that these threats were latent (134).

16. This video was made private as of February 2012. A copy is on file with the author.

17. The child's signature reads "Ronald," a gendering that is significant given the more prevalent representation of girls' threatened innocence in campaign videos. The latter emphasis reflects normative associations between femininity, innocence, and its converse—moral risk. But this advertisement reveals that threats to boys' heterosexuality haunts this rhetoric of developmentally and morally inappropriate education—a risk that is hinted at through veiled allusions to pedophilia in lieu of direct visual references to boys, who are here represented only by the signature.

18. As of November 2012 this website is no longer available. The referenced images, videos, and text are on file with the author and the website is digitally archived at http://web.archive.org/web/20080828230657/http://iprotectmarriage.com/.

19. This ultimately inaccurate poll found that Proposition 8 was supported by 49 percent of whites, 70 percent African Americans, 53 percent Latinos, 49 percent Asians, and 51 percent Others. See http://www.cnn.com/ELECTION/2008/results/polls/#val=CAI01p1.

20. See the Personal Responsibility and Work Opportunity Reconciliation Act of 1996, Public Law 104–193, 110 Stat. 2105.

21. Deficit Reduction Act of 2005, Public Law 109–171, 120 Stat. 4; Claims Resolution Act of 2010, Public Law 111–291, 124 Stat. 3064.

22. The video is no longer available and is on file with the author.

23. Author's field notes, February 13, 2009.

REFERENCES

Albelda, Randy, M. V. Lee Badgett, Alyssa Schneebaum, and Gary Gates. 2009. *Poverty in the Lesbian, Gay, and Bisexual Community*. Los Angeles: Williams Institute, UCLA School of Law. http://williamsinstitute.law.ucla.edu/wp-content/uploads/Albelda-Badgett-Schneebaum-Gates-LGB-Poverty-Report-March-2009.pdf.

Averett, Paige, Blake Nalavany, and Scott Ryan. 2009. "An Evaluation of Gay/Lesbian and Heterosexual Adoption." *Adoption Quarterly* 12 (3): 129–51.

Badgett, M. V. Lee. 2001. *Money, Myths, and Change: The Economic Lives of Lesbians and Gay Men*. Chicago: University of Chicago Press.

Baker v. State of Vermont, 744 A.2d 864 (Vt. 1999).

Barbaro, Michael. 2012. "In Largely Symbolic Move, N.A.A.C.P. Votes to Endorse Same-Sex Marriage." *New York Times,* May 19. http://www.nytimes.com/2012/05/20/us/politics/naacp-endorses-same-sex-marriage.html.

Bernstein, Mary. 1997. "Celebration and Suppression: The Strategic Uses of Identity by the Lesbian and Gay Movement." *American Journal of Sociology* 103 (3): 531–65.

BeyondMarriage.org. 2006. "Beyond Same-Sex Marriage: A New Strategic Vision for All Our Families and Relationships." http://www.beyondmarriage.org/full_statement.html.

Brown, Wendy. 2006. *Regulating Aversion: Tolerance in the Age of Identity and Empire.* Princeton, N.J.: Princeton University Press.

Chauncey, George. 2004. " 'What Gay Studies Taught the Court': The Historians' Amicus Brief in *Lawrence v. Texas.*" *GLQ* 10 (3): 509–38.

———. 2008. "How History Matters: Sodomy Laws and Marriage Reform in the United States." *Public Culture* 20 (1): 27–37.

Colbert Report. 2009. "The Colbert Coalition's Anti-Gay Marriage Ad." Comedy Central, April 16, 2009. http://www.colbertnation.com/the-colbert-report-videos/224789/april-16-2009/the-colbert-coalition-s-anti-gay-marriage-ad.

Collins, Patricia Hill. 2005. *Black Sexual Politics: African Americans, Gender, and the New Racism.* New York: Routledge.

Cott, Nancy. 2000. *Public Vows: A History of Marriage and the Nation.* Cambridge, Mass.: Harvard University Press.

Cowan, Reed. 2010. "8: The Mormon Proposition" (film).

de Certeau, Michel. 1984. " 'Making Do': Uses and Tactics." In *The Practice of Everyday Life.* Translated by Steven Rendall, 29–42. Berkeley: University of California Press.

D'Emilio, John. 1993. "Capitalism and Gay Identity." In *The Lesbian and Gay Studies Reader,* edited by Henry Abelove, Michele Aina Barale, and David M. Halperin, 467–76. New York: Routledge.

Dickenson, Tom. 2008. "Same-Sex Setback." *Rolling Stone Magazine,* December 11. www.rollingstone.com/politics/story/24603325/samesex_setback/print.

Dugan, Kimberly B. 2005. *The Struggle over Gay, Lesbian, and Bisexual Rights: Facing Off in Cincinnati.* New York: Routledge.

Duggan, Lisa. 2002. "The New Homonormativity: The Sexual Politics of Neoliberalism." In *Materializing Democracy: Toward a Revitalized Cultural Politics,* edited by Russ Castronovo and Dana Nelson, 175–94. Durham, N.C.: Duke University Press.

Economist. 2011. "The Decline of Marriage: For Richer, for Smarter." *The Economist,* June 23. http://www.economist.com/node/18867552.

———. 2012. "Gay Marriage: To Have and to Hold." *The Economist,* November 17. http://www.economist.com/news/international/21566626-trend-toward-giving-homosexuals-full-marriage-rights-gaining-momentum-have-and.

Edelman, Lee. 2004. *No Future: Queer Theory and the Death Drive.* Durham, N.C.: Duke University Press.

Egan, Patrick J., and Kenneth Sherrill. 2009. *California's Proposition 8: What Happened, and What Does the Future Hold?* San Francisco: Evelyn and Walter Haas, Jr. Fund and the National Gay and Lesbian Task Force. http://www.thetaskforce.org/downloads/issues/egan_sherrill_prop8_1_6_09.pdf.

Family Research Council. 2004. "The Slippery Slope of Same-Sex Marriage." *InFocus*. Washington, D.C.: Family Research Council.

———. 2008. "Happy Parent Number 1 Day." http://www.frc.org/get.cfm?i=WA08F28.

Ferguson, Roderick A. 2004. *Aberrations in Black: Toward a Queer of Color Critique*. Minneapolis: University of Minnesota Press.

Fineman, Martha Albertson. 1991. *The Illusion of Equality: The Rhetoric and Reality of Divorce Reform*. Chicago: The University of Chicago Press.

———. 1995. *The Neutered Mother, the Sexual Family, and Other Twentieth Century Tragedies*. New York: Routledge.

———. 2004. *The Autonomy Myth: A Theory of Dependency*. New York: The New Press.

———. 2008. "The Vulnerable Subject: Anchoring Equality in the Human Condition." *Yale Journal of Law and Feminism* 20 (1).

Firestone, Shulamith. 1970. *The Dialectic of Sex: The Case for Feminist Revolution*. New York: Bantam.

Foster, Frances Smith. 2010. *'Til Death or Distance Do Us Part: Marriage and the Making of African America*. Oxford: Oxford University Press.

Franke, Katherine. 2004. "The Domesticated Liberty of *Lawrence v. Texas*." *Columbia Law Review* 10: 1399–427.

Gallagher, Maggie. 2002. "What Is Marriage For? The Public Purposes of Marriage Law." *Louisiana Law Review* 62: 1–16.

———. 2004a. "(How) Will Gay Marriage Weaken Marriage as a Social Institution: A Reply to Andrew Koppelman." *University of St. Thomas Law Journal* 2 (1): 33–70.

———. 2004b. "Rites, Rights, and Social Institutions: Why and How Should the Law Support Marriage?" *Notre Dame Journal of Law, Ethics and Public Policy* 18 (2): 225–42.

Gamson, Joshua. 1997. "Messages of Exclusion: Gender, Movements, and Symbolic Boundaries." *Gender and Society* 11: 178–99.

Gamson, William A., and David Meyer. 1996. "Framing Political Opportunity." In *Comparative Perspectives on Social Movements*, edited by Doug McAdam, John D. McCarthy, and Mayer N. Zald, 275–90. Cambridge: Cambridge University Press.

Goldberg, Michelle. 2007. *Kingdom Coming: The Rise of Christian Nationalism*. New York: W.W. Norton and Co.

Goodridge v. Department of Public Health, 798 N.E.2d 941 (Mass. 2003).

Goodwin, Jeff, James M. Jasper, and Francesca Polletta. 2001. *Passionate Politics: Emotions and Social Movements*. Chicago: University of Chicago Press.

———. 2004. "Emotional Dimensions of Social Movements." In *The Blackwell Companion to Social Movements*, edited by David. A. Snow, Sarah A. Soule, and Hanspeter Kriesi, 413–32. Malden, Mass., and Oxford: Blackwell Publishing.

Guerra, Fernando, Jennifer Magnabosco, Stephen A. Nuño, and Mara Marks. 2008. "The Leavey Center for the Study of Los Angeles 2008 Exit Polls of the Presidential Primary and National Elections." The Thomas and Dorothy Leavey Center for the Study of Los Angeles.

Heath, Melanie. 2006. "Fighting for Marriage: Gender, Sexuality and Religion in the Contemporary Marriage Movement." Ph.D. diss., University of Southern California.

———. 2012. *One Marriage under God: The Campaign to Promote Marriage in America.* New York: New York University Press.

Herman, Didi. 1997. *The Anti-Gay Agenda: Orthodox Vision and the Christian Right.* Chicago: University of Chicago Press.

Hollingsworth v. Perry, 2012 U.S. LEXIS 9416, 81 U.S.L.W. 3324 (U.S. Dec. 7, 2012).

iProtectMarriage.com. 2008a. "Youth Quiz—Decide for Yourself: Question 6, 'Do You Think That It Is "Okay" to Say That Same-Sex Marriage Is Wrong?'—'No.'" Originally available at http://www.iprotectmarriage.com/the-issue/#health. On file with author.

———. 2008b. "Which Parent Doesn't Matter?" http://web.archive.org/web/20080828 230657/http://iprotectmarriage.com/.

Kaye, Kate. 2009. "How 'Yes on Prop 8' Campaign Took the Web by Storm." *ClickZ News, Politics and Advocacy,* April 6. http://www.clickz.com/clickz/news/1692996/how-yes-prop-campaign-took-web-storm.

Khan, Surina. 2009. "Tying the Not: How the Right Succeeded in Passing Proposition 8." *Public Eye* 24 (1): 1–9.

Kim, Richard. 2008. "Marital Discord: Why Prop 8 Won." *The Nation,* November 24. www.thenation.com/doc/20081124/kim/print?rel+nofollow.

Kintz, Linda. 1997. *Between Jesus and the Market: Emotions That Matter in Right-Wing America.* Durham, N.C.: Duke University Press.

———. 1998. "Clarity, Mothers and Mass-Mediated Soul." In *Media, Culture and the Religious Right,* edited by Linda Kintz and Julia Lesage, 115–40. Minneapolis: University of Minnesota Press.

LaGanga, Maria L. 2009. "The Prop. 8 Debate Is Loud—and Colorful." *Los Angeles Times,* March 6.

Lawrence v. Texas, 539 U.S. 558 (2003).

Lee, Rachel C. 2000. "Notes from the (Non)Field: Teaching and Theorizing Women of Color." *Meridians* 1 (1): 85–109.

McAdam, Doug. 1996. "The Framing Function of Movement Tactics: Strategic Dramaturgy in the American Civil Rights Movement." In *Comparative Perspectives on Social Movements,* edited by Doug McAdam, John D. McCarthy, and Mayer N. Zald, 338–56. Cambridge: Cambridge University Press.

Meyer, David. 2007. *The Politics of Protest.* Oxford: Oxford University Press.

Moore, Mignon. 2010. "Articulating a Politics of (Multiple) Identities: LGBT Sexuality and Inclusion in Black Community Life." *Du Bois Review: Social Science Research on Race* 7: 315–34.

———. 2011. *Invisible Families: Gay Identities, Relationships and Motherhood among Black Women.* Berkeley: University of California Press.

National Association for the Advancement of Colored People. 2012. "NAACP Passes Resolution in Support of Marriage Equality." National Association for the Advancement of Colored People, May 19. http://www.naacp.org/news/entry/naacp-passes-resolution-in-support-of-marriage-equality.

National Marriage Project. 2011. "Why Marriage Matters: Thirty Conclusions from the Social Sciences." Charlottesville: Center for Marriage and Families at the Institute for American Values and The National Marriage Project, University of Virginia. http://www.virginia.edu/marriageproject/pdfs/WMM_summary.pdf.

National Organization for Marriage. 2009a. "Gathering Storm." Originally accessed at http://www.nationformarriage.org/site/c.omL2KeNoLzH/b.5075663/k.A89C/ Religious_Liberty.htm. Available at http://www.youtube.com/watch?v=Wp76ly2_ NoI&feature=plcp.

———. 2009b. "National Organization for Marriage Board Update, 2008–2009." Released as "NOM Deposition Exhibition 25." In *National Organization for Marriage v. McKee*, No. 11-1196 (1st Cir. Jan. 31, 2012). Available at http://thecaucus.blogs .nytimes.com/2012/03/27/anti-gay-marriage-group-recommends-creating-tension -between-gays-and-blacks/?emc=eta1.

Ngai, Mae M. 2004. *Impossible Subjects: Illegal Aliens and the Making of Modern America*. Princeton, N.J.: Princeton University Press.

Nock, Steven L., Laura Ann Sanchez, and James D. Wright. 2008. *Covenant Marriage: The Movement to Reclaim Tradition in America*. New Brunswick, N.J.: Rutgers University Press.

Pateman, Carole. 1988. *The Sexual Contract*. Stanford, Calif.: Stanford University Press.

Perry v. Brown, 10-16696, 2012 WL 372713 (9th Cir. 2012).

Perry v. Schwarzenegger, 704 F.Supp. 2d 921 (2010).

Polikoff, Nancy D. 2008. *Beyond (Straight and Gay) Marriage: Valuing All Families under the Law*. Boston: Beacon Press.

ProtectMarriage.com. 2008a. "California Proposition 8—to Protect Children" (advertisement). http://www.youtube.com/watch?v=Y5qdOQ-yzFU.

———. 2008b. "Daddy, Where Do Babies Come From?" (advertisement). http://www .youtube.com/watch?v=75J3TN9Zzck.

———. 2008c. "Proposition 8 Made Simple" (advertisement). http://www.youtube.com/ watch?v=vI-GjWY-WlA.

———. 2008d. "Robb and Robin Wirthlin's Story" (advertisement). http://www.youtube .com/watch?v=WLHWBWSaW-4.

———. 2008e. "Yes on 8 TV Ad: It's Already Happened" (advertisement). http://www .youtube.com/watch?v=0PgjcgqFYP4.

Re: Marriage Cases, 43 Cal. 4th 757 (2008).

Roberts, Dorothy. 1997. *Killing the Black Body: Race, Reproduction, and the Meaning of Liberty*. New York: Vintage Books.

Rockwell, Norman. 1955. *Marriage License*, cover illustration. *Saturday Evening Post*, June 11. Image available at http://www.normanrockwellvt.com/Big.jpg/Marriage License.jpg.

Rupp, Leila J. 2001. "Toward a Global History of Same-Sex Sexuality." *Journal of the History of Sexuality* 10 (2): 287–302.

Ruskola, Teemu. 2005. "Gay Rights versus Queer Theory: What Is Left of Sodomy after *Lawrence v. Texas*." *Social Text* 23 (3): 235–49.

Russo, Mary. 1995. *The Female Grotesque: Risk, Excess and Modernity*. New York: Routledge.

Sandoval, Chela. 2000. *Methodology of the Oppressed*. Minneapolis: University of Minnesota Press.

Schubert, Frank, and Jeff Flint. 2009. "Passing Proposition 8." *Politics* 30 (2): 44–47.

Smith, Anna Marie. 2007. *Welfare Reform and Sexual Regulation*. Cambridge: Cambridge University Press.

Snow, David A. 2004. "Framing Processes, Ideology, and Discursive Fields." In *The Blackwell Companion to Social Movements*, edited by David A. Snow, Sarah A. Soule, and Hanspeter Kriesi, 380–412. Malden, Mass., and Oxford: Blackwell Publishing.

Snow, David A., and Robert D. Benford. 1992. "Master Frames and Cycles of Protest." In *Frontiers in Social Movement Theory*, edited by Aldon D. Morris and Carol McClurg Mueller, 133–55. New Haven, Conn.: Yale University Press.

Stevens, Jacqueline. 1999. *Reproducing the State*. Princeton, N.J.: Princeton University Press.

Tarrow, Sidney. 1993. "Modular Collective Action and the Rise of the Social Movement: Why the French Revolution Was Not Enough." *Politics and Society* 21: 69–90.

———. 1996. "States and Opportunities: The Political Structuring of Social Movements." In *Comparative Perspectives on Social Movements*, edited by Doug McAdam, John D. McCarthy, and Mayer N. Zald, 41–61. Cambridge: Cambridge University Press.

———. 1998. *Power in Movement: Social Movements and Contention Politics*. Cambridge: Cambridge University Press.

Taylor, Verta. 1995. "Watching for Vibes: Bringing Emotions into the Study of Feminist Organizations." In *Feminist Organizations: Harvest of the New Women's Movements*, edited by Myra Marx Ferree and Patricia Yancey Martin, 223–33. Philadelphia: Temple University Press.

———. 2000. "Emotions and Identity in Women's Self-Help Movements." In *Self, Identity, and Social Movements*, edited by Sheldon Stryker, Timothy J. Owens, and Robert W. White, 271–99. Minneapolis: University of Minnesota Press.

Taylor, Verta, Katrina Kimport, Nella Van Dyke, and Ellen Ann Andersen. 2009. "Culture and Mobilization: Tactical Repertoires, Same-Sex Weddings, and the Impact on Gay Activism." *American Sociological Review* 74: 865–90.

Taylor, Verta, and Leila J. Rupp. 1993. "Women's Culture and Lesbian Feminist Activism: A Reconsideration of Cultural Feminism." *Signs* 19 (1): 32–61.

———. 2002. "Loving Internationalism: The Emotion Culture of Transnational Women's Organizations, 1888–1945." *Mobilization: An International Quarterly* 7 (2): 141–58.

Taylor, Verta, Leila J. Rupp, and Joshua Gamson. 2004. "Performing Protest: Drag Shows as Tactical Repertoires of the Gay and Lesbian Movement." *Research in Social Movements, Conflicts and Change* 25: 105–37.

Taylor, Verta, and Nella Van Dyke. 2004. "'Get Up, Stand Up': Tactical Repertoires of Social Movements." In *The Blackwell Companion to Social Movements*, edited by David A. Snow, Sarah A. Soule, and Hanspeter Kriesi, 262–93. Malden, Mass., and Oxford: Blackwell Publishing.

Tilly, Charles, and Sidney Tarrow. 2007. *Contentious Politics*. Boulder: Paradigm Press.

United States v. Windsor, 2012 U.S. LEXIS 9413, 81 U.S.L.W. 3324 (Dec. 7, 2012).

U.S. Congress. Senate. Committee on the Judiciary. 2003. *What Is Needed to Defend the Bipartisan Defense of Marriage Act of 1996?: Hearing before the Subcommittee on the Constitution, Civil Rights and Property Rights*. 108th Cong., 1st sess., September 4.

Varnum v. Brien, 763 N.W. 2d 862 (Iowa 2009).

Warner, Michael. 1999. *The Trouble with Normal: Sex, Politics, and the Ethics of Queer Life.* New York: Free Press.

Whittier, Nancy. 2001. "Oppositional Emotions in the Movement against Child Sexual Abuse." In *Passionate Politics: Emotions and Social Movements,* edited by Jeff Goodwin, James M. Jasper, and Francesca Polletta, 233–50. Chicago: University of Chicago Press.

Williams, Juliet. 2009. "Loving or Leaving: On the Definition of Green Card Marriage Fraud." Unpublished paper.

Williams, Richard. 2004. "If Norman Rockwell Depicted the 21st Century." *MAD Magazine,* February. http://www2.warnerbros.com/madmagazine/files/onthestands/ots_438/rockwell.html.

Zald, Mayer N. 1996. "Culture, Ideology and Strategic Framing." In *Comparative Perspectives on Social Movements,* edited by Doug McAdam, John D. McCarthy, and Mayer N. Zald, 261–74. Cambridge: Cambridge University Press.

PART **III**   Marriage Activism

6 Mobilization through Marriage

The San Francisco Wedding Protest

Verta Taylor, Katrina Kimport, Nella Van Dyke,
and Ellen Ann Andersen

N 2004, SAME-SEX COUPLES ENGAGED in protests at marriage
licensing counters across the United States in connection with
the gay and lesbian movement's campaign to promote marriage
equality. Showing up at county clerks' offices, demanding marriage
licenses, and holding weddings in public places, gay couples challenged long-standing heteronormativity inscribed in laws that deny
marriage to same-sex couples. The largest protest occurred in San
Francisco, historically a center of gay and lesbian movement activity
(Armstrong 2002), where Mayor Gavin Newsom defied California's
Defense of Marriage Act (Proposition 22) by ordering the county clerk
to issue marriage licenses to same-sex couples. During the month-long
"winter of love," 4,037 couples obtained licenses and married at City
Hall, creating a public spectacle that drew widespread media attention. What were the origins of these protests and their significance?
And, no less important, what were the implications of these protests
for the marriage-equality movement more generally? We address these
questions by drawing from and building upon broader sociological understandings of contentious cultural performances, their attributes and
relational dynamics, and their varied potential impacts.

Social movement researchers increasingly view social movements
not as groups or organizations but as interactive performances or protest events in which collective actors make claims against elites, authorities, or some other group. This approach, which grew out of the work

of Tilly (2008, 2004, 1978) and his collaborators (McAdam 1982; Mc-Adam, Tarrow, and Tilly 2001; Tarrow 1998; Tilly and Tarrow 2007), has led to an interest in the performances and repertoires used by social movements to make collective claims (della Porta 2008; Jasper 2006; Tilly 2008; Walker, Martin, and McCarthy 2008). Tilly (2008) uses the metaphors of "performance" and "repertoire" to signal both the routine and limited forms of claim-making used by social movements in political contention and the tendency for claim-makers to innovate within limits set by the established repertoire and the cultural context.

While this formulation has been useful for understanding variations and changes in repertoires of contention, scholars working in the political process and contentious politics tradition have concentrated on a small range of claim-making performances, such as strikes, demonstrations, public meetings, petitions, and violence associated with the rise of the social movements of the nineteenth century (Tarrow 1998; Tilly 2008). Over the past decade, scholars concerned with the role of culture and consciousness in social protest have documented an even wider range of repertoires used in modern political contention (Bernstein 1997; Blee 2002; Earl and Kimport 2008; J. Gamson 1989; Jasper 1997; Mansbridge and Morris 2001; Pfaff and Yang 2001; Rupp and Taylor 2003; Staggenborg 2001; Staggenborg and Lang 2007). The core insight is that social movements often adapt, create, and use culture—ritual, music, street theater, art, the Internet, and practices of everyday life—to make collective claims.

Cultural performances certainly inspire solidarity and oppositional consciousness (Kaminski and Taylor 2008; Morris 1984; Roscigno and Danaher 2004; Taylor, Rupp, and Gamson 2004). Little attention, however, has centered on developing models that discern both the *dynamics* and *impact* of such performances. The same-sex marriage campaign provides an ideal case for addressing this gap in the literature. State-centered contentious politics and political process approaches frequently view the gay rights movement as a subcultural movement that embraces tactics that are expressive and internally oriented, rather than instrumental and externally oriented (Cohen 1985; Jenkins 1983; Kriesi et al. 1995; McAdam 1982; Tilly 1995). This distinction between expressive and instrumental action—or politics and culture—has, however, been overstated. To understand how social movements use cultural performances in political contention, it is necessary to look closely at the meaning and the relational dynamics of claim-making in particular contentious performances and to examine their potential mobilizing effects.

We use the 2004 San Francisco wedding protest to address two questions that are not only substantively meaningful but also theoretically important to general social movement scholarship. To what extent were the marriages used strategically and intentionally as a performance to make collective claims? And what effect did the month-long protest have on movement mobilization and subsequent actions directed at more conventional forms of political action? We begin with a theoretical discussion of tactics and repertoires, propose a model of cultural repertoires that bridges contentious politics approaches and social constructionist conceptions, and then offer a brief background on the 2004 San Francisco same-sex marriage protest. Our multimethod qualitative and quantitative analysis, which includes semistructured interviews with participants and leaders and a random survey of participants in the wedding protest, both documents the contentious nature of the marriages as a dynamic and multifaceted repertoire and highlights the consequences of the month-long wedding protest for other forms of political action after the participants' marriages were invalidated by the California Supreme Court.

CONCEPTUALIZING TACTICAL REPERTOIRES

We begin by building on the insights of two theoretical traditions in social movements—the contentious politics and social constructionist approaches—to understand the dynamics and consequences of cultural repertoires of contention. The contentious politics approach views social movements as a series of political campaigns that link claimants, their targets, and the public through contentious performances that cluster into repertoires (McAdam, Tarrow, and Tilly 2001; Tilly 2004, 2008; Tilly and Tarrow 2007). Repertoires of contention, according to Tilly (2008), are the recurrent, predictable, and narrow "tool kit" of specific protest tactics used by collective actors to express their interests and make claims on authorities. Like its theatrical counterpart, the term "repertoire" implies that the interactions between a movement and its antagonists are strategic performances or "established ways in which pairs of actors make and receive claims bearing on each other's interests" (Tilly 1995, 27).

Tilly (1986) initially introduced the repertoire concept to explain the rise in the nineteenth century of the social movement as a form of political contention directed at governments. The term repertoire is now used more broadly, however, to refer to "the culturally encoded ways in which people interact in contentious politics" or, more simply, "the forms of claim making that people use in real-life situations" (McAdam, Tarrow, and Tilly 2001, 16; see della Porta 2008; Walker et al. 2008).

Contentious performances and repertoires are critical to the emergence and endurance of social movements because they are occasions for collective actors to demand recognition, signal numerical strength, and promote goals (Tilly 2008, 121). Social movements, however, are more than contentious performances. Contentious political episodes influence subsequent campaigns and repertoires by creating social movement communities, submerged networks, and collective identity among participants that become the basis for further mobilization (Staggenborg and Lecomte 2009). Protest performances do not, in other words, simply morph into repertoires. Rather, as Staggenborg and Lecomte argue (2009), the ability of people to come together to engage in collective action requires explanation.

The social constructionist tradition in social movements provides insight into how repertoires diffuse (Jasper 1997; Staggenborg and Lang 2007). Social constructionists conceptualize movements as organizations, submerged networks, and ideologically structured challenges to a variety of different institutional authorities (Armstrong and Bernstein 2008; Melucci 1989; Polletta 2002; Snow 2004; Staggenborg and Taylor 2005; Zald 2000). We propose an integrated formulation of tactical repertoires—a formulation that bridges these varying conceptions of social movements by linking tactical repertoires to social movement networks and communities.

Our conception combines Tilly's attention to protest repertoires or claim-making routines with social constructionists' concern with the structure, meaning, and social psychological dynamics of political contention. We identify three features of tactical repertoires (for elaboration of the model, see Rupp and Taylor 2003; Taylor, Rupp, and Gamson 2004; Taylor and Van Dyke 2004). First, tactical repertoires are not spontaneous episodes, but *intentional and strategic* forms of claim-making (W. A. Gamson 1992; Jasper 2006; Klandermans 1997; McCarthy and Zald 1977; McPhail 1991; Tilly 2008). How culture is brought to bear in episodes of political contention is critical. Collective actors frequently use cultural rituals and performances intentionally and strategically to contest authorities and to pursue instrumental as well as cultural goals (Bernstein 1997; Blee 2002; Morris 1984; Rupp and Taylor 2003).

Second, tactical repertoires involve *contestation* in which bodies, symbols, identities, practices, and discourses are framed and deployed to target changes in multiple institutional arenas, including cultural codes and practices (Armstrong and Bernstein 2008; Van Dyke, Soule, and Taylor 2004). The body of work on framing by Snow and colleagues (1986) suggests that movements mobilize, in part, by drawing on identities, practices, beliefs, and symbols that are already meaningful in the dominant culture and placing them in another framework so that they are, as Goffman puts it, "seen by the participants to be something quite else" (1974, 43–44). The same-sex wedding protest illustrates how cultural repertoires, in particular, exhibit this process of cultural borrowing—borrowing wherein rituals and practices typically used to create moral attachment to the social order are, instead, mobilized in the interest of protest (Alexander, Giesen, and Mast 2006; Durkheim [1912] 1965; Pfaff and Yang 2001).

Finally, tactical repertoires mobilize supporters through the construction of *collective identity*. To consider collective identity as one of the defining features of a tactical repertoire is to acknowledge that contentious performances have both an external and an internal movement-building function (Bernstein 1997; Roscigno and Danaher 2004; Taylor and Van Dyke 2004; Taylor and Whittier 1992). Tactical repertoires serve both functions. They create solidarity, oppositional consciousness, and collective identity among participants, while also defining the relationship and boundaries between collective actors and their opponents (Klandermans and de Weerd 2000; Polletta and Jasper 2001; Rupp and Taylor 2003). Our analysis uses this model of tactical repertoires to demonstrate that the month-long same-sex wedding protest in San Francisco was a strategic collective action intended to challenge discriminatory marriage laws and practices.

To understand how cultural repertoires contribute to more conventional forms of political action, it is important to recognize that the dilemma for collective actors when strategizing about tactics is "whether to play to inside or outside audiences" (Jasper 2006, 10). This is precisely why scholars have often argued that cultural tactics detract from instrumental actions, because they privilege mobilization over tactics directed at external targets (Cohen 1985). However, this strategic choice is not mutually exclusive. Generally, movements that engage in expressive forms of action and identity deployment also aim to influence external targets (Bernstein 1997; Raeburn 2004; Staggenborg 2001; Whittier 1997). And tactical repertoires that target the state also create solidarity and collective identity (Jasper 1997; Klandermans, van Dertoorn, and van Stekelenburg 2008; Melucci 1989). While scholars increasingly recognize that cultural repertoires matter, very few have considered whether and how they influence subsequent mobilization.

CULTURAL PERFORMANCES, SPILLOVER, AND IMPACT

The body of literature on social movement spillover, which considers the effects of social movements on one another, allows us to understand how cultural performances and repertoires serve as a conduit for subsequent collective action directed at changing power structures and politics (McAdam 1995; Meyer and Whittier 1994; Whittier 2009). Prior research points to two spillover effects capable of creating new mobilizations and altering existing movements and campaigns: *spillover across movements* (McAdam 1988; Soule 2004; Taylor 1989;

Whittier 1995, 1997) and *diffusion within movements* or the spin-off of social movement tactics, frames, identities, and networks within the same campaign (Soule 1997, 2004).

Studies of movement-to-movement influence suggest that activism around one campaign affects participation in subsequent movements (McAdam 1988, 1989; Meyer and Whittier 1994; Soule 1997; Taylor 1989; Van Dyke 1998). McAdam (1988) describes how the civil rights movement spawned the student, antiwar, and women's movements; Meyer and Whittier (1994) demonstrate that the women's movement critically influenced the frames, tactics, and organizational forms of the peace movement; and Voss and Sherman (2000) provide evidence of how inter-movement exchanges of personnel revitalized labor unions.

Movements influence each other through tactical repertoires, collective identities, frames, and shared networks. Tactics from prior movements outline possibilities for activists in other movements (Soule 2004; Tilly 2008, 1995), and tactics deployed by one campaign spread to other locales and social movement organizations through network linkages and shared frames (Isaac and Christiansen 2002; Snow and Benford 1992; Soule 1997). And, of course, social movement communities in the larger social movement sector often supply the networks, master frames, and collective identities that allow new campaigns to emerge (McAdam 1988; Taylor 1989; Whittier 1995). Studies of diffusion processes within social movements suggest that the collective identity and solidarity fostered by participating in a single protest event with high symbolic impact can create activist networks with a "readiness" to participate in subsequent political actions (McPhail 1991; Soule 1997).

In the case of the 2004 same-sex marriage protest in San Francisco, there is considerable evidence that the campaign was a spin-off of earlier movements. The body of writings on tactical repertoires and social movement spillover leads us to expect that, for most participants, the mass matrimony at City Hall was not a one-shot deal. Rather, the "winter of love" fostered heightened mobilization through the formation of collective identity and networks that generated future actions aimed at challenging authorities and discriminatory legal practices that support heteronormativity.

THE CASE OF SAME-SEX MARRIAGE,
THE GAY AND LESBIAN MOVEMENT, AND
THE SAN FRANCISCO WEDDING PROTEST

Throughout recent U.S. history, same-sex couples have embraced marriage rituals as a politics of "recognition, identity, inclusion, and social support" (Hull 2006, 2), even in the absence of legal recognition. Disagreement over the desirability of marriage, however, kept it off the agenda of national lesbian and gay organizations until the mid-1990s (Andersen 2006). A vocal element of the movement opposed gay marriage, arguing that marriage constitutes "a normalizing process that assimilates queers to heteronormativity" (Green 2008, 10) and provides a stamp of legitimacy to the hegemony of heterosexuality by excluding other relationships (Badgett 2009; D'Emilio 2007; Hull 2006).

Few lesbian and gay organizations thus engaged in activism around the issue of same-sex marriage until 1993, when it seemed as though same-sex couples in Hawaii might win the right to marry in *Baehr v. Lewin.* The state legislature, however, reversed Hawaii's Supreme Court by amending the state constitution to define marriage as a relationship between a man and a woman (Andersen 2006).

Tina Fetner (2008) credits the Religious Right's opposition with catapulting same-sex marriage to the top of the agenda of the lesbian and gay movement. Opponents of gay marriage launched a nationwide mobilization that resulted in passage of the 1996 federal Defense of Marriage Act (DOMA), limiting the definition of marriage to a "legal union between one man and one woman as husband and wife" and allowing states to deny recognition of same-sex marriages. California, along with thirty-four other states, jumped on the bandwagon and passed mini-DOMAs. National and local lesbian and gay organizations responded by orchestrating campaigns to win legal recognition for same-sex marriage in receptive states, using litigation as the primary tactic (Andersen 2006; Pinello 2006).

The first inkling that the lesbian and gay movement would embrace same-sex marriage occurred in 1987 at the third national March on Washington for Lesbian and Gay Rights. Couples, Inc., a Los Angeles–based organization fighting for recognition of lesbian and gay couples in a movement that had its origins in a critique of traditional marriage, organized a collective wedding protest to contest the discriminatory laws and practices embedded in marriage (Ghaziani 2008). Several thousand gay and lesbian couples took part, blocking off an entire street in front of the Internal Revenue Service building. Since this first marriage protest in 1987, same-sex weddings have been deployed as street theater in connection with local gay pride demonstrations around the United States.

The campaign for same-sex marriage languished until a window of opportunity for mass mobilization opened in 2003, when the Massachusetts Supreme Judicial Court ruled it unconstitutional to deny same-sex couples the right to marry, making Massachusetts the first state to grant legal status to same-sex marriages. When then-President George W. Bush responded with a proposal for a federal constitutional amendment to ban same-sex marriage, Gavin Newsom, San Francisco's Democratic mayor, directed the assessor-recorder's office to begin issuing marriage licenses to gays and lesbians. This set off a wave of marriage protests around the country. A county clerk in Sandoval County, New Mexico, issued twenty-six licenses, and gay nuptials were performed on the courthouse lawn before the state attorney general stopped the marriages. In New York, the mayor of New Paltz married nineteen couples, and the mayor of Ithaca began accepting marriage license applications from same-sex couples. In March 2004, a collective action comparable in scope to the San Francisco wedding protest emerged in Portland, Oregon, where 3,022 couples managed to marry before a circuit court judge ordered a halt to the marriages.

After same-sex couples began marrying legally in Massachusetts, and the marriages in San Francisco, Portland, and other locales were overturned by court action, the same-sex wedding protests receded, although isolated protests at marriage counters continued to emerge across the country. In August 2007, same-sex marriage was declared legal for less than four hours in Polk County, Iowa. Although only one couple managed to marry before the county judge declared a halt to the marriages, twenty-seven same-sex couples filed applications for licenses. The largest instance of matrimony among lesbian and gay couples occurred in California in the summer of 2008, after the California

Supreme Court ruled it unconstitutional to exclude same-sex couples from marriage. Between June 17 and November 4, an estimated eighteen thousand couples married, until Proposition 8, passed by 52 percent of the voters, banned same-sex marriage in California. During the course of the "summer of love" it became evident that the Religious Right's campaign to ban same-sex marriage was gaining ground. As a result, the marriages took on an increasing political urgency. By the time the California Supreme Court upheld Proposition 8, denying same-sex couples the right to marry but allowing the existing marriages to stand, Connecticut, Iowa, Vermont, Maine, and, shortly afterward, New Hampshire had opened marriage to same-sex couples, making it clear that the battle had not ended.

Although California was at the forefront of the legal recognition of rights for same-sex couples, public opinion in the state over same-sex marriage has been divided. In 2000, voters approved Proposition 22, a ballot measure supported by a coalition of conservative and Religious Right groups, amending the Family Code to read, "Only marriage between a man and a woman is valid and recognized in California." Then in 2005, the California legislature granted domestic partners the state-conferred rights of marriage.

In San Francisco, the tactic of same-sex couples showing up at City Hall to demand marriage licenses originated on February 12, 1998, when the Lambda Legal Defense and Education Fund, a national organization of the lesbian and gay rights movement, sponsored "Freedom to Marry Day." Gay rights groups held small actions in more than forty cities that year. In San Francisco, Molly McKay and her partner Davina Kotulski went to the marriage counter at City Hall to request a marriage license. When they were denied, they decided to make it an annual protest. The spirited political contest over Proposition 22 led the two women to found Marriage Equality California (MECA), one of several fledgling grassroots organizations in California advocating for same-sex marriage. Through MECA, McKay and Kotulski ritualized the marriage-counter demonstration. Each year on Freedom to Marry Day, McKay donned a wedding dress and went to City Hall with a contingent of same-sex couples to render visible the discrimination that occurs at the marriage counter every day.

In addition to the annual marriage-counter protest, MECA coordinated rallies, marches, and other public actions to mobilize a broader base of support and to educate the public about same-sex marriage. Across the country, National Freedom to Marry Day regularly featured groups of same-sex couples dressed in wedding gowns and tuxedos strolling down city streets. The Lambda Legal Defense and Education Fund even published a "Strolling Wedding Party Guide" touting the efficacy of street theater for stimulating discussion of same-sex marriage.[1]

On February 12, 2004, demonstrators in San Francisco experienced a catalyzing moment. Same-sex couples went to City Hall to apply for marriage licenses, expecting to get turned down as usual. Instead, they received marriage licenses (Figure 6.1). The same-sex weddings, which began that day, were orchestrated by Mayor Gavin Newsom's staff, working with Kate Kendell of the National Center for Lesbian Rights (NCLR), Tamara Lange of the northern California chapter of

FIGURE 6.1. Hundreds of same-sex couples, waiting for marriage licenses, form a line around the block at San Francisco's City Hall.
Source: *Frederic Larson/San Francisco Chronicle/Corbis.*

FIGURE 6.2. Lesbian activists Phyllis Lyon and Del Martin, the first couple married in San Francisco's City Hall. *Source: Liz Mangelsdorf/San Francisco Chronicle/Corbis.*

the American Civil Liberties Union (ACLU), and Geoff Kors of Equality California (EQCA). Kendell suggested that Phyllis Lyon and Del Martin—partners for fifty-one years and historic figures in the gay and lesbian movement—be the first couple married (Figure 6.2), and the ACLU invited four other couples, chosen for their suitability as plaintiffs in the lawsuit anticipated when the licenses were invalidated.

Social movement organizations coordinated the initial stages of the protest by selecting the first couples to apply for licenses. The couples who went to City Hall for the annual marriage-counter protest were among the first to marry. Media attention, however, allowed the wedding protest to gain momentum. Soon throngs of gay men and lesbians arrived to take their place in a queue of couples sharing food, blankets, chairs, and friendship while waiting outside City Hall, and media coverage flooded the nation with images of the couples waiting in line, then emerging from City Hall waving marriage licenses. In an Internet-launched campaign of support known as "Flowers from the Heartland," people donated money to purchase flowers for the couples married at City Hall. A handful of crusading Christians opposed to gay marriage marched alongside the long line of couples. Passersby honked in support, sometimes handing out wedding bouquets and cakes. So many couples showed up that the city began scheduling appointments a month in advance. Showing her support for the protest, talk-show host Rosie O'Donnell flew to San Francisco to marry her longtime girlfriend, Kelli Carpenter-O'Donnell. By the time the California Supreme Court ordered San Francisco to cease issuing and recording same-sex marriage licenses, 4,037 same-sex couples had received marriage licenses and 3,095 had managed to have their marriages officially recorded.

What can we learn about the dynamics and impact of contentious cultural performances by examining the 2004 same-sex wedding protest in San Francisco? While the media portrayed the weddings as personally motivated, a social movement analysis suggests a different reading of the mass nuptials. In our analyses, we examine both how the weddings were a tactical repertoire used by participants to dramatize their claims to the rights of marriage and how the San Francisco wedding protest affected subsequent mobilization on behalf of marriage equality. This two-pronged focus—on marriage as a tactical repertoire and its implications—addresses an important gap in the social movement literature surrounding the dynamics of cultural repertoires and how they may facilitate future mobilization.

DATA AND MEASUREMENT

Most research on cultural repertoires is based on small and unsystematic samples (J. Gamson 1989; Rupp and Taylor 2003; Staggenborg 2001; Staggenborg and Lang 2007). Our analyses, in an effort to address some of these prior limitations, draws on survey data as well as semi-structured interviews and combines quantitative and qualitative analysis. Initially, we conducted a random survey of all participants in the San Francisco weddings.[2] Although the individual is the unit of analysis, we sampled at the couple level, sending two surveys to a sample of 1,000 households in October 2006, approximately two-and-a-half years after the San Francisco protests. We received at least one questionnaire from 311 households (37 percent), and 525 individuals (31 percent) responded.[3]

The survey consisted mostly of closed-ended questions about respondents' demographic attributes, family structure, couple's legal status, political attitudes, and social movement participation prior to and after the protest. Our analysis draws from the survey data and the rich set of controls it affords, particularly for the quantitative analysis described below. We also draw at length from one open-ended question: "When San Francisco started issuing marriage licenses to same-sex couples, why did you and your spouse decide to apply for a license?"

In-depth insight into the dynamics of and the mobilization effects of participating in the protest—the two core foci of our analyses—necessitated not only systematic surveying of participants and measurement of potentially important controls, but also depth that only qualitative data could provide. We therefore conducted semi-structured interviews with five key informant activists from marriage-equality organizations, as well as interviews with forty-two gay and lesbian individuals, representing twenty-seven couples, who participated in the weddings. On average, each interview lasted about 90 minutes. We transcribed and coded the interview data using Microsoft OneNote.

Although the sample of participants we interviewed was not obtained randomly but through snowball sampling, the respondents come close to representing the characteristics of all of the individuals who married in San Francisco on nearly all dimensions. According to the City of San Francisco, more than half (57 percent) of the participants were women, a trend mirrored by the same-sex marriages taking place in other locations during 2004 (Teng 2004),[4] and more than half (55 percent) were between the ages of thirty-six and fifty. Our survey data reveal that these couples had been together an average of twelve years, although nearly one-fourth of the couples had been in their relationship for sixteen years or more. The great majority (88 percent) of survey respondents identified as white, while 4 percent identified as Hispanic/Latino, 4 percent as Asian American, and less than 2 percent as African American. Most had a college degree or higher and a household income of $71,000 or higher. Although the protest drew same-sex

couples from forty-six states and eight foreign countries, the vast majority (91 percent) were from California (Teng 2004).

We use interview and open-ended survey data to analyze our first
question about the dynamics of protest in general, and weddings as
contentious performances in particular. We coded these data along the
three analytical dimensions of the theory: contestation, intentionality, and collective identity. We then turn to our second question about
impact, using the survey data along with qualitative data from the
participant and key informant interviews. Here we ask whether participation in the weddings and the protest following the nullification of
the marriages influenced an individual's subsequent participation in
the campaign for marriage equality. We expect that prior participation
in a variety of related movements will have a generative effect on the
marriage-equality movement by spinning off a new challenge through
relationships within the existing social movement sector and collective identities formed in prior campaigns (Isaac and Christiansen 2002;
McAdam 1995; Whittier 2001).

Dependent Variables: Subsequent Activism

While the first portion of our analyses centers on the dynamics of contention relative to contestation, intentionality, and collective identity,
and draws largely on the qualitative material, the second portion draws
more evenly from both quantitative and qualitative data and focuses
on impact and spillover. The first outcome is whether the individual
protested after the California Supreme Court invalidated the marriages.[5] Reactions to the invalidation took a number of forms (see Table
6.1). We then consider the effects of prior activism and participation in
marriage protests on whether the individual is a current lesbian, gay,
bisexual, transgender (LGBT) or marriage rights activist.[6] Among our
respondents, 58 percent are current activists. Table 6.2 reports descrip-
tives for these outcomes, as well as the predictors and controls used in
our modeling.

Explanatory Variables

Given that our theoretical argument predicts that participation in protest inspires subsequent activism, our quantitative modeling includes a

Table 6.1. Actions Taken in Response to Invalidation of Marriage Licenses

ACTIVITY	PERCENT
I have given money to an organization dedicated to fighting for marriage rights.	74.9
I have become more "out" about my marriage.	45.6
I have given money to a political party or candidate.	40.3
I have participated in a demonstration or protest on behalf of marriage rights.	38.8
I have written letters to public officials or other people of influence.	37.3
I have joined an organization dedicated to fighting for marriage rights.	30.4
I have spoken to or gone to see a public official or other people of influence.	14.8
None of the above	10.6

Note: N = 474. Respondents were able to select multiple activities, so percentages do not sum to 100.

dichotomous indicator of *prior activism,* including anti-war, civil rights, environment, women's rights, labor, pro- or anti-abortion rights, community concerns, and education. Although these movements have different goals, they are related in their challenge to the status quo and in fostering the creation of solidarity and an oppositional collective identity.

We also examine how participation in contention following the California Supreme Court's invalidation of the marriages influenced the participants' subsequent activism. We include a dichotomous variable coded 1 if individuals protested the invalidation of their marriage. Consistent with our theoretical argument, we expect that individuals who engaged in collective forms of protest that brought them into contact with other activists, fostering the development of social network ties and collective identity, will be more likely to be current activists (W. A. Gamson 1992; McAdam 1986). We include a series of dummy

Table 6.2. Descriptive Statistics for Variables in the Analysis

ACTIVITY	MEAN (SD)
Took action to protest dissolution	.891 (.308)
Current LGBT or marriage activist	.582 (.494)
Prior activism	.757 (.429)
Political motivation for marriage	.812 (.391)
Believe civil unions are not an acceptable alternative (4-point scale)	2.496 (1.117)

TYPE OF ACTION TO PROTEST DISSOLUTION	
Demonstrated	.388 (.488)
Joined an organization	.304 (.460)
Became more out about relationship	.456 (.499)
Gave money to an organization	.749 (.434)
Gave money to a politician	.406 (.491)
Met with a public official	.148 (.355)
Wrote letters	.373 (.484)

CONTROLS	
Experienced problems	.646 (.479)
Liberal (7-point scale)	5.751 (.989)
High political efficacy	.437 (.496)
Interest in government and public affairs	.772 (.420)
Female	.487 (.500)
Race (white)	.882 (.323)
Income (10 = $74,000–100,000)	10.289 (1.465)
Children	.293 (.456)
Employed full time	.709 (.455)
Age	47.2 (8.930)

Note: N = 474.

variables measuring distinct actions, including whether they demonstrated, joined an organization, became more out about their relationship, gave money to an organization, gave money to a politician, met with a public official, or wrote letters.

We include *intentionality* in our modeling to capture whether individuals participating in the weddings with an explicit and intentional political motivation differ from those who married solely for personal reasons. We expect participants who intended their marriage to make a political statement to be more likely to protest the dissolution of their marriage and to be current marriage activists.

Another survey question allows us to examine intentionality indirectly. We asked whether respondents felt that civil unions were an acceptable alternative to legal marriage and included a measure that ranges from 1 to 4, with a mean of 2.5, where higher values indicate less support for civil unions as a compromise measure.[7] We expect that respondents less willing to accept civil unions as an alternative to marriage would be more likely to protest the invalidation of their marriage licenses and to report ongoing involvement in the marriage-equality movement.

Controls

Based on prior work, we include a number of arguably important controls. Social movement scholars have found that grievances provide at least a partial explanation for protest participation (Jasper 1997; Klandermans, van Dertoorn, and van Stekelenburg 2008; Olzak 1992). Here, we include an indicator of whether individuals feel they have been disadvantaged by not having the legal protections offered to traditional families. Research also consistently demonstrates that receiving information about a protest facilitates activism (Klandermans 1997; Klandermans and Oegema 1987; Schussman and Soule 2005). We include a measure of how informed the individual is about government affairs. The variable is measured dichotomously.

Research on political engagement suggests that individuals with a greater sense of personal efficacy are more likely to take action in pursuit of social change (Ennis and Schreuer 1987; Klandermans, van Dertoorn, and van Stekelenburg 2008). Our measure captures a high feeling of personal efficacy based on two survey questions: "People like me don't have any say about what the government does" and "I feel that I could do as good a job in public office as most people." Respondents were coded 1 if they disagreed or disagreed strongly with the first statement and agreed or agreed strongly with the second. Our final attitudinal measure captures whether survey respondents consider themselves to be liberal (Schussman and Soule 2005), based on a 7-point scale ranging from extremely conservative (1) to extremely liberal (7).

Finally, research consistently finds that young people, those without full-time jobs, and people without children are more likely to participate in social movements (Klandermans and Oegema 1987; McAdam 1986, 1989; Schussman and Soule 2005). We thus include variables measuring age, full-time employment, and the presence of children, as well as race (1 = white), sex (1 = female), and income (in eleven categories).

ANALYTIC STRATEGY AND RESULTS

Our analyses proceed in two steps, each of which employs the rich, multimethod character of these data. We begin by addressing our first empirical question. Drawing on the tactical repertoires formulation discussed earlier, we analyze the weddings as contentious cultural performances. The survey data allow us to discern the intentions of a random sample of participants, and the qualitative interview data illuminate the meaning and dynamics of the weddings as a contentious performance.

The second component of the analyses addresses the impact of the wedding protest on subsequent political actions associated with the campaign for marriage equality. We begin with descriptive statistics regarding participation in the protests after the invalidation of the same-sex weddings to establish spillover as a cause. To examine the impact of the same-sex wedding protest, we rely on logistic regression as the principal technique.[8] The first model (Table 6.3) estimates the likelihood of protest participation following the invalidation of the marriages. The next two models (Table 6.4) predict current activism in the marriage movement. The first model includes a measure of whether they took any action to protest the dissolution of their marriage, while the second examines the effect of different forms of action. Importantly, these analyses integrate qualitative data as well, allowing us to elaborate on the processes and mechanisms through which contentious cultural performance leads to further protest and more conventional forms of political action.

Table 6.3. Results of Logistic Regression Model Predicting Response to Marriage License Invalidation

EXPLANATORY VARIABLES		
Prior activism	.422	(.347)
Political motivation for marriage	.620*	(.354)
Civil unions not viewed as acceptable alternative	.189	(.143)
CONTROLS		
Experienced problems	.763**	(.319)
Liberal	.112	(.162)
High political efficacy	.206	(.333)
Interest in government and public affairs	.046	(.375)
Female	.256	(.341)
Race (white)	.301	(.441)
Income	.180*	(.095)
Children	−.710*	(.354)
Employed full time	−.679*	(.405)
Age	.032*	(.019)
Intercept	−3.257*	(1.695)
−2 Log Likelihood	296.379	

Note: N = 474. Log odds; standard errors in parentheses.

* $p < .05$; ** $p < .01$; *** $p < .001$ (one-tailed test).

SAME-SEX MARRIAGE AS A TACTICAL REPERTOIRE

Contestation

Cultural rituals typically serve to affirm dominant relations of power. When used in the pursuit of change, however, cultural tactics imbue traditional symbols, identities, and practices with oppositional meaning and are often deployed in new ways that challenge and subvert the dominant order (Taylor, Rupp, and Gamson 2004). For most participants, the weddings were not meant to embrace the institution of marriage as traditionally defined. Rather, as sites of ritualized heterosexuality (Ingraham 2003), the weddings were an opportunity for same-sex couples to deploy identity publicly and strategically (Bernstein 1997) to gain visibility for their relationships, stake a claim to civil rights, contest discriminatory marriage laws, and challenge the institutionalization of heterosexuality.

The interview and open-ended survey data are remarkably consistent on these points. The overwhelming majority of participants considered their marriages acts of protest in which they were confronting the identity categories, values, and practices of heteronormative society (Jackson 2006) by enacting marriage outside the boundaries of state sanction. When asked "why did you and your spouse decide to apply for a license?" 81 percent of survey respondents characterized the weddings as politically motivated, describing their actions as "acts of civil disobedience," "a political statement," "a public statement," "a civil rights movement," and "a protest against discrimination." One woman admitted that she married entirely to make a "political statement." She said, "I was against the institution. I didn't want to be the same as straight people." Among interview respondents, 81 percent cited political motivations for their participation, including one man who said:

> Certainly for most people, the idea of being married has no connection whatsoever with making a political statement, but for us, obviously, it's unavoidable, inescapable. It's civil disobedience.

Participants sought to challenge stereotypes of lesbians and gays. As one interviewee reported, "I saw what we were doing as a form of political protest because it was counter to all the hegemonic messages of society." Individuals who married also aimed to remake the meaning of an institution that ritualizes heterosexuality. One woman explained, "We wanted into that institution to transform it from the inside." One interviewee opposed marriage but wed so she could "participate in a movement that was trying to change society's attitudes about homosexuality, more than anything else, to say that you can't deny lesbians and gay men the rights that you grant to everyone else." Among couples who indicated they married for political reasons, many were also motivated by the desire to obtain access to the plethora of state and federal rights and responsibilities associated with marriage (Andersen 2006).

Although the majority of respondents gave political justifications for their marriages, a significant number also described the weddings as an opportunity to publicly profess their love and offered deeply personal and emotional reasons for getting married. About one-third of both surveyed (36 percent) and interviewed (31 percent) respondents gave personal as well as political motives for marrying. One survey respondent emphasized the emotional significance of making a public expression of commitment to her partner of many years: "At first it was a spontaneous decision to participate in part of history, but quickly it became something much more significant for us emotionally and politically." An interview respondent who described his marriage as "a political statement" also acknowledged that the government of the City and County of San Francisco lifted "us up from a place of second-class citizenship to a place of equality. There we were, face to face, loving each other and committing to each other. It was very profound and moving." He went on to explain:

> We both grew up believing in government, believing it meant something. I just remember when the official said, "By the authority of the state of California, I pronounce you spouses for life." And there was this electric chill, physically. And it was the sense of feeling for the first time that we're actually fully equal in the eyes of the law and the government, something we had never imagined.

The 19 percent of survey respondents and interviewees who did not provide political reasons for their marriages offered mostly personal motivations that parallel those used by conventional heterosexual couples to justify marriage (Swidler 2001). Nonetheless, these motivations disputed the hegemonic constitution of love as heterosexual (Johnson 2005, 15). One interviewee argued, "People say two guys or two girls getting married is breaking the notion of marriage but, no, it's a question of love, a question of being together." No matter what individuals' motivations were for marrying, the spectacle created by thousands of same-sex couples lining up outside San Francisco's City Hall was itself a form of discursive politics that contested heterosexuality's monopoly on marriage, its associated emotions, and its attendant benefits.

Intentionality

The interview data suggest that the decision to use public same-sex weddings as contentious performances was linked to activists' experience with tactical repertoires from previous campaigns. According to one marriage-equality activist, the San Francisco weddings were "our generation's Stonewall." Kate Kendell, head of the NCLR, described her reaction when the mayor's office informed her that the city would begin issuing marriage licenses to gay couples: "Forget 'where you were when JFK was shot?' 'When did you find out about Gavin Newsom's decision to marry lesbian and gay couples?'" (Pinello 2006, 76).

Molly McKay, the founder of Marriage Equality California, borrowed the idea of the marriage-counter protest from the lunch-counter sit-ins used by the civil rights movement:

We were very inspired by the grassroots organizers in Greensboro, North Carolina, the four college students that sat in at the lunch counters, and rendered visible segregation and the ugliness of white-only lunch counters. And we thought the only way to render visible the discrimination that crosses across the marriage counter every single day is to go and request a marriage license. We'll do it with dignity. We'll do it very peacefully.

McKay emphasized the modularity of the tactic: "the great thing about it, it is a moment of civil disobedience where anyone can participate because there's a marriage license counter in every town no matter how big or small." By making their annual request for marriage licenses in mid-February, the couples were taking advantage of the cultural meaning of Valentine's Day as a holiday that celebrates love to call attention to the heartbreak experienced by same-sex couples denied access to marriage.

When City Hall began issuing marriage licenses, the couples assembled for the annual protest were among the first to marry. The survey and interview data provide clear evidence that, for the majority of participants, the marriages represented a strategic action with instrumental as well as cultural goals. Social movement actors anticipated that the weddings would be shut down quickly, and couples who married believed that the courts eventually would invalidate the marriages. The explanation provided by one respondent, when asked why he and his partner got married, illustrates this point:

> It was a historic moment that we wanted to be part of. We fully expected the courts to close it down, so we rushed over as soon as we could. We felt this was a way to participate in the activist efforts to bring marriage equality to all of us.

Participants saw the weddings, however, as more than a strategy to expand same-sex couples' access to marriage. The weddings were forms of collective action with highly symbolic impact intended to win media attention, with the aim of increasing the social status and worth of lesbians and gay men as a group. This idea is seen in one man's explanation of why he and his partner participated in the weddings: "We wanted to share our love with the world and work to end homophobia." Such responses indicate that the majority of participants viewed the weddings as a strategy to bring about legal and social recognition of same-sex relationships. This finding is consistent with previous research suggesting that even in contexts where same-sex marriage is legal, many couples marry to make a political statement about the rights of gay men and lesbians to full equality (Badgett 2009).

Collective Identity

Protest is one means by which challenging groups develop oppositional consciousness, solidarity, and collective identity. To consider collective identity as one of the defining features of a tactical repertoire acknowledges not only that protest tactics are directed to external targets but that they also have an internal, movement-building function (Roscigno and Danaher 2001; Taylor and Van Dyke 2004; Taylor and Whittier 1992). The San Francisco wedding protest facilitated the creation of new forms of solidarity and community related to the participants' adoption of an activist identity. Participants described their actions as part of a "civil rights movement." One interview respondent explained, "I feel responsible to my elders who fought so hard, all those people who spoke out, who pushed the issue forward, we owe it to them and then for the future generations to come so that they don't have to fight this barrier." Moreover, the collective scene at City Hall affected the participants' sense of themselves as part of a larger whole (see Figure 6.3). One man explained: "It was just a thrill to be sitting there where everybody's gay and everybody's there with the same purpose. And I thought, hmm, this is what straight people experience every day of their life."

FIGURE 6.3. Solidarity forms among couples waiting outside San Francisco's City Hall to marry on Valentine's Day. *Source: Kurt Rogers/San Francisco Chronicle/Corbis.*

The wedding protest countered the negative experiences of living in a heteronormative society by bringing so many gay men and lesbians together. One woman remembered standing in line for hours having "this emotional sharing of stories and dreams with all these strangers," and another found the "group support when you're coming in or going out to get married really amazing." A third woman put it this way: "This was the opposite of a homophobic culture. This was: we're embracing and celebrating you and excited about you and interested in you because you're gay." Indicative of the solidarity fostered by the weddings, couples borrowed each other's rings and served as witnesses for each others' marriages. The joy and camaraderie experienced by couples waiting to get married was so intense that several couples volunteered to come back to City Hall and assist with the marriages in order to remain connected to the oppositional community.

In summary, although weddings as ritual practices typically reinforce status hierarchies and symbolic codes, our data provide clear evidence that, for the overwhelming majority of the participants, the San Francisco same-sex weddings were not meant for that purpose. Rather, the weddings provided participants an opportunity to advance their claims for equal access to marriage. The individuals who married during the month-long protest considered their marriages acts of *contestation*. They used the public marriages strategically and *intentionally* to challenge discriminatory marriage laws that reinforce heteronormativity and to make demands for gay marriage rights, which also concern the right to love. Moreover, the marriage protest fostered a sense of solidarity and *collective identity* among participants that likely persisted long after the event's conclusion. The survey data demonstrate that these results hold true for a sizable segment of the couples, and the qualitative interviews provide depth and shed light on the deep emotional and symbolic character of the weddings. These findings demonstrate the utility of our theoretically grounded conception of tactical repertoires, which attends to actors' intentions and to the dynamic and relational aspects of political contention.

THE IMPACT OF THE MARRIAGE
PROTEST ON MOBILIZATION

The wedding protest not only functioned as a creative and strategic tactical repertoire, but also resulted from and then contributed to participation in activism. As Figure 6.4 shows, license applicants had an extensive activist history in a variety of movements. Prior participation in a range of related movements had a generative effect on the marriage-equality movement by spinning off a new challenge through relationships within the existing social movement sector (Isaac and Christiansen 2002; McAdam 1995; Whittier 2001). In turn, participation in the same-sex wedding protest had significant effects on subsequent activism in the campaign for marriage equality. The figures

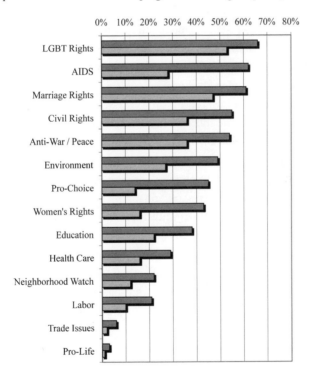

■ report involvement in movement at any point in time   ▣ report current involvement in movement

FIGURE 6.4. Participation in prior social movements.

in Table 6.1 indicate that an astoundingly high number of survey respondents (89 percent) engaged in some form of contentious political activity following the California Supreme Court's invalidation of the marriage licenses. The median number of political acts performed by protest participants subsequent to the voiding of the marriages was three; giving money to a social movement organization was the most common action (75 percent). Nearly a third of respondents (30 percent) reported joining an organization dedicated to fighting for marriage rights.

These survey data are corroborated by our interviews with leaders of social movement organizations, who consider the San Francisco marriage protest the catalyst that led to rapid and large-scale mobilization of the marriage-equality movement. One month after the marriage protest ended, the two major marriage-rights organizations in San Francisco, EQCA and MECA, merged under the Equality California (EQCA) banner to combine grassroots tactics with legislative and legal action; EQCA's staff increased from five to twenty-two.

Marriage participants also deployed confrontational actions in response to the court ruling (see Figure 6.5). Nearly 40 percent of respondents participated in subsequent demonstrations. In twenty-five counties, marriage rights organizations mobilized campaigns using emotion-laden direct-action tactics to win public sympathy. Same-sex couples, especially those with children, took to the streets, organizing demonstrations in parking lots, shopping malls, and other public places to express their reactions to the nullification of their marriages and to demand civil rights to protect their families.

Table 6.3 reports regression analyses predicting protest against the Supreme Court ruling. Coefficients reflect the log odds of respondents currently being marriage activists. We find that individuals who married as an intentional act of political protest were 86 percent more likely to participate in subsequent marriage dissolution protests.[9] As Table 6.3 reveals, neither prior activism nor support for civil unions predicts participation in the dissolution protest. In addition, two control variables are significant. Individuals who experienced problems related to the lack of legal protection were also more likely to engage in protest after their marriages were overturned. About 65 percent of respondents

FIGURE 6.5. Marriage Equality California leads an anti–Proposition 8 protest in San Francisco. *Source: AJ Alfieri-Crispin.*

indicated they had experienced problems such as difficulty visiting a partner during a medical emergency, been declared ineligible for coverage on a partner's health insurance, denied parenting rights, childcare benefits, or inheritance rights. Although some scholars question grievance-based explanations of social movements, our findings are also consistent with recent research that suggests that grievances sometimes provide a partial explanation for protest participation (Klandermans, van Dertoorn, and van Stekelenburg 2008; Olzak 1992).

Several of the significant control variables are also consistent with prior research on the role of biographical availability in predicting protest participation. Individuals without children and without full-time jobs, as well as older and higher-income individuals, were more likely to protest. The association between viewing the marriages as political acts and participating in subsequent activism is thus quite robust, even accounting for these arguably standard controls derived from the social movement literature.

Table 6.4 reports the impact of wedding protest participation on future involvement in the marriage rights movement, with notable results. Recall from Table 6.2 that 58 percent of respondents, surveyed almost three years after the marriage protest, indicated that they were currently active in the LGBT or marriage rights movement. Variables for prior activism and marriage dissolution protest, reported in Table 6.4, Model 1, are positive and significant, lending important weight to the possibility of spillover effects. For ease of interpretation, we convert log odds to odds here. The odds of current marriage activism are over 7 times higher for those who previously engaged in activism than for those who had not. Moreover, individuals who protested dissolution at an earlier point in time are more than 5 times as likely as those who did not to be marriage activists nearly three years later. These results show that the marriage rights protest was strongly influenced by participants' prior activism in earlier social movements, and protesting the dissolutions, in turn, inspired subsequent protest activity.

Consistent with our argument that participation in contentious action fosters the creation of collective identity and social networks that inspire further activism, respondents who participated in protest actions involving interaction with other activists are most likely to have continued their activism. Two-thirds of individuals who attended a demonstration after the invalidation of the marriages remained active in the marriage rights movement. The results of Model 2 suggest that individuals who joined an organization, participated in a demonstration, or met with a public official were most likely to be current marriage activists. The odds of being a current marriage activist are almost 3 times greater for those who joined an organization and 2.2 times greater for those who demonstrated or met with public officials. In short, individuals who participated in collective actions rather than individualized tactics, such as giving money to a political figure or becoming more "out" about their relationships, were more likely to be current activists.

Results from Model 2 are more complex with respect to the relationship between marrying for explicitly political motivations and current participation in the marriage-equality movement. Having a political motivation for participating in the weddings does not entirely explain

Table 6.4. Results of Logistic Regression Models Predicting Current Activism

	MODEL 1		MODEL 2	
Prior activism	2.011***	(.272)	1.895***	(.295)
Political motivation for marriage	.167	(.276)	.101	(.288)
Believe civil unions are not an acceptable alternative	.293**	(.099)	.179*	(.106)
Took action to protest dissolution	1.656***	(.384)	—	

TYPE OF ACTION TO PROTEST DISSOLUTION

	MODEL 1		MODEL 2	
Demonstrated	—		.791***	(.259)
Joined an organization	—		1.058***	(.295)
Became more out about relationship	—		.383	(.249)
Gave money to an organization	—		.564*	(.278)
Gave money to a politician	—		−.155	(.261)
Met with a public official	—		.799*	(.423)
Wrote letters	—		.551*	(.258)

CONTROLS

	MODEL 1		MODEL 2	
Experienced problems	.042	(.230)	−.060	(.244)
Liberal	−.032	(.119)	.001	(.128)
High political efficacy	.602***	(.231)	.432*	(.249)
Interest in government and public affairs	.675*	(.263)	.348	(.283)
Female	.089	(.232)	.234	(.254)
Race (white)	.896**	(.338)	.984**	(.365)
Income	−.178*	(.081)	−.121	(.087)
Children	−.022	(.255)	.140	(.281)
Employed full time	.178	(.250)	.232	(.266)
Age	−.010	(.013)	−.007	(.014)
Intercept	−2.827*	(1.387)	−2.973*	(1.460)
−2 Log Likelihood	514.412		465.417	

Note: N = 474. Log odds; standard errors in parentheses.

* $p < .05$; ** $p < .01$; *** $p < .001$ (one-tailed test).

the difference between individuals currently active in the movement and those who are not. This factor does help predict participation in marriage dissolution protests, and it is clear that participating in marriage dissolution protests predicts current activism. Another indirect way of measuring the relationship between political intentions and current activism is through attitudes about civil unions as an alternative to marriage. The wedding protest participants who would accept civil unions or domestic partnerships may have been more interested in the benefits of marriage than intentionally challenging the status quo. Results in Table 6.4, in fact, suggest that respondents who find civil unions an unacceptable alternative to marriage are more likely to be currently involved in marriage rights activism.

While the quantitative findings certainly demonstrate that marriage protests had an impact on subsequent activism, the rich qualitative data and our analysis of it delineate how. One respondent explained the mobilizing effect of the "month of marriages" at City Hall:

> I think we were actually in a bit of a lull at the time that the marriages happened. In a sense we were ripe to get re-energized. It wasn't like we hadn't been politically active before, but we were kind of recharging a bit. It was very opportune timing. We were ready to go.

It is significant that in no instance did interviewees report a lessening of their involvement in the movement after participating in the San Francisco wedding protests. Two-thirds of individuals reported that the collective wedding protest had a significant impact on their subsequent activism.

Nearly half of the individuals who participated in the same-sex weddings reported that after the weddings were invalidated, they channeled their activism away from other causes, such as LGBT and women's rights activism, into the marriage-equality movement to defend the legality of the San Francisco marriages in the face of antigay opposition. Citing both the court's invalidation of the marriages and the governor's veto of the gender-neutral marriage bill introduced the same day Mayor Newsom began the marriages, one respondent said:

It just really wasn't my hot-button issue. And then it was. You wake up one morning and realize that Arnold Schwarzenegger decides whether you get married or not and you get a little pissed off.

Among protest participants, 20 percent reported that the weddings were the catalyst that initiated their participation in activism around marriage equality. One couple's actions illustrate the wide range of tactics used in the campaign for marriage equality in the months following the weddings. The couple wrote a declaration with the American Civil Liberties Union and the National Center for Lesbian Rights; they were amicus parties to and plaintiffs in a lawsuit; they traveled to Washington on the marriage-equality caravan; and they engaged in lobbying, public speaking, and media appearances. Many other couples reported that, when the same-sex weddings provoked such strong opposition from Republicans and the Religious Right, they understood the necessity of using identity deployment as a strategy to educate others about marriage equality:

We've been very public since the events at City Hall, and very involved in trying to build networks with all the different people, so it really has been a way where the personal and political really dovetail together.

The ensuing court cases offer additional evidence of the ways in which the San Francisco weddings served as a springboard for policy change. Following the decision to void the marriage licenses, several couples initiated legal proceedings against the state, alleging that the ban on same-sex marriage constituted a violation of the state's equal protection clause. The City and County of San Francisco, too, filed legal proceedings against the State of California, and the social movement organizations that coordinated the same-sex weddings took part in the case. The legal director of NCLR, who had worked with Mayor Newsom on the plan to issue licenses, was one of the attorneys who argued before the court. The California Supreme Court's ruling in March 2008 opened access to same-sex marriage until the passage of

FIGURE 6.6. Thousands protest in San Diego after the
passage of Proposition 8. *Source: Grant Glidewell.*

Proposition 8. That new defeat set off a wave of large demonstrations
and movement mobilization both statewide and nationally (see Figures
6.6 and 6.7). Although our data do not allow us to assess the scope and
duration of these events, it is highly likely that the campaign for same-
sex marriage may result in the largest mass mobilization in the history
of the lesbian and gay movement.

Our findings regarding the impact of the protest highlight the
connection between cultural contention and more conventional political tactics. The quantitative results provide strong evidence that
individuals who had political motivations for participating in the San
Francisco weddings were more likely to engage in conventional political protests such as public demonstrations, joining organizations,
and lobbying policy-makers in response to the dissolution of their
marriages. Participation in dissolution protests, in turn, holds clear implications for current marriage activism. The qualitative data, which
afford us greater depth and breadth, are particularly useful for understanding how participants channeled their activism into new forms of
claim-making, as well as examining the wide range of tactics used in
the campaign for marriage equality in the months following the dis-

FIGURE 6.7. Thousands of Californians gathered on the steps of the State Capitol building in Sacramento to protest Proposition 8. *Source: Fritz Liess.*

solution of the marriages, including the initiation of legal proceedings against the state of California to overturn the state's Defense of Marriage Act.

CONCLUSIONS

Social movement scholars have long debated the role of culture in producing social and political change. Yet researchers have largely ignored cultural tactics and repertoires, in part because political process theorists have a narrow conception of what constitutes a protest event (e.g., Kriesi et al. 1995; Tarrow 1998; Tilly 2008) and in part because state-centered approaches hold that cultural tactics have no impact on policy change (Rucht 1988; Tilly 1995). This article confronts this debate more directly than previous studies by analyzing the attributes, dynamics, and impact of the 2004 same-sex wedding protest in San Francisco.

Drawing from a rich data set that integrates qualitative and quantitative analyses, we offer compelling evidence that cultural tactics do, indeed, matter in political contention. Our analyses demonstrate that the San Francisco weddings constituted contentious public performance used by actors intentionally and strategically to make collective claims. We also find that the month-long wedding protest sparked other forms of political action and mobilization on behalf of marriage rights, igniting a state-wide campaign for marriage equality in California. Together, these findings offer powerful evidence for moving beyond the rigid distinction between culture and politics that characterizes mainstream theorizing in social movements in order to consider the influence of cultural repertoires in political contention.

Our three-dimensional model of cultural repertoires has broad utility above and beyond our particular case in point and, we hope, offers other scholars a theoretical blueprint that more fully incorporates cultural repertoires into the study of social movements. This model combines the insights of contentious politics approaches (which define social movements as a series of public campaigns involving contentious performances or repertoires enacted between claimants and their targets) with social constructionist conceptions (which view movements as communities that create submerged networks and collective identity). We identify three features of cultural repertoires—contestation, intentionality, and collective identity—all of which interact in various ways. This formulation adds a qualitative component to research on protest events, which has been concerned mainly with documenting the diffusions of and variations in a relatively limited set of repertoires of contention. As our analyses reveal, the tactical repertoires model allows us to look inside cultural performances to discern their meaning and to examine the relational dynamics involved in political contention. The collective identity dimension of tactical repertoires captures both the internal movement-building function of cultural repertoires and the external targets of contentious performances, providing insight into how social movement tactics diffuse within and among movements.

Participation in one movement, even simply one high-profile demonstration, can clearly affect subsequent participation in protests through the generation of networks, solidarity, and collective identity

(Meyer and Whittier 1994). The couples who took part in the weddings in San Francisco had links to a variety of social movements, including the civil rights, AIDS, lesbian and gay, women's, and pro-choice movements. Movement-to-movement spillover helps to explain marriage-equality activists' initial adoption of marriage-counter protests as a strategy to make visible the civil rights denied to same-sex couples by virtue of the state's prohibition of same-sex marriage. These activists borrowed the repertoire from the direct-action tactics pioneered by the civil rights movement of the 1950s and 1960s, adapting it to the political street theater used by the AIDS and women's movements in the 1980s and 1990s.

Our results also provide evidence pertaining to other unresolved questions about the role of culture in political contention. These data challenge the position of scholars who argue that expressive tactics that foster collective identity are not also directed at influencing external targets (Kriesi et al. 1995). The qualitative analysis provides clear evidence that couples intentionally participated in the wedding protest not only to make identity claims but also to communicate their numerical strength and disruptive potential and to challenge the state. Scholars of social movements have, at times, faulted the gay and lesbian movement for its preference for tactics that rely on culture, performance, and identity deployment, arguing that these detract from the movement's broader political agenda (D'Emilio 2007; J. Gamson 1995). As our findings show, wedding protests used the trappings of the traditional white wedding—bridal gowns, tuxedos, bouquets, and wedding cakes—to dramatize and challenge the heteronormativity of traditional marriage. Such cultural performance was effective in mobilizing more traditional forms of political action.

One of our goals has been to demonstrate that the eruption of mass matrimony among lesbian and gay couples in 2004, when thirteen thousand same-sex couples received licenses to marry in San Francisco, Oregon, Massachusetts, and other locations around the country, was a tactical innovation that increased the pace of mobilization around the issue of gay marriage. During the month-long protest in San Francisco, images of gay and lesbian couples standing in line for marriage licenses, then marrying in civic buildings and other public locations, appeared on the evening news, front pages of newspapers, and covers of weekly news magazines, challenging the hegemonic interpretation of marriage as a relationship between a man and a woman. Politics is as much a discursive struggle as it is a contest over resources (Alexander, Giesen, and Mast 2006). As our findings show, not only do cultural repertoires play an important role in the internal life of social movements but cultural symbols, rituals, and practices can also be used to convey powerful political messages to the multiple targets of social movements and to mobilize actors to engage in other forms of political contention.

Although the lesbian and gay movement historically has been more likely than other social movements to deploy cultural performances and repertoires to assert identity claims and to promote particular goals, the use of cultural performances in political contention is not limited to this particular movement. Social movements on both the left and the right typically use a variety of cultural forms of political expression, including music, art, literature, and theater. Our findings raise questions about how contentious cultural performances in less public venues might be connected to larger campaigns. Prior research suggests, for example, that same-sex couples who elect to engage in public or private ceremonies to express their commitment frequently offer political reasons for their marriages (Badgett 2009; Lewin 1998). Similarly, Rupp and Taylor (2003) argue that drag performances in gay commercial establishments are tactical repertoires that have a long history in the gay and lesbian movement as forms of claim-making that create collective identity and contest heteronormative structures, identities, and practices. One of our central interests in this study is to extend the concept of tactical repertoires to embrace these understudied cultural forms of political expression. To understand how movements remain vital, how they connect to previous and future campaigns, and what types of impact they have, it is fundamental that scholars recognize the significant impact of culture performances and repertoires in political contention.

NOTES

This chapter was previously published as "Culture and Mobilization: Tactical Repertoires, Same-Sex Weddings, and the Impact on Gay Activism," *American Sociological Review* 74, no. 6 (December 2009): 865–90.

1. Lambda Legal Defense and Education Fund, "Strolling Wedding Party Guide: Street Theater for Your Community," http://www.lambdalegal.org/our-work/publications/page.jsp?itemID=32008446.

2. The data are part of a larger study of same-sex couples who married in 2004, including the 3,027 couples in Multnomah County, Oregon, and the 6,095 couples in Massachusetts.

3. Sixteen percent of the packets were returned with no forwarding address. We attempted to increase the response rate, but follow-up with nonrespondents revealed many were suffering survey fatigue. The City of San Francisco made names of those who married available to the public for a nominal fee, and they had been inundated with mail from researchers and businesses.

4. At 43 percent, men made up a greater proportion of couples who married in San Francisco than in Multnomah County, Oregon (29 percent) or Massachusetts (36 percent).

5. The survey sampled individuals who participated in the marriage protest. As a result, we are unable to run models predicting participation in the initial San Francisco weddings. A sample of nonparticipant gays and lesbians would be virtually impossible to obtain.

6. We obtained comparable results when we restricted our analysis to those currently active in the marriage-equality movement only.

7. The question wording was as follows: "Some people seeking to find a 'middle ground' in the debate over marriage equality have argued that same-sex couples should be given all the legal rights and responsibilities associated with legal marriage, but that their relationship should be called by another name, such as civil unions or domestic partnerships. If the government were to create civil unions, identical to marriage in everything but name, would that be acceptable to you?" The four possible answers ranged from "very unacceptable" to "very acceptable." We reversed the order of responses for the analysis, so that a higher value indicates less support.

8. Diagnostics suggest no problems with multicollinearity, with all v.i.f.'s below 1.3.

9. We calculated likelihoods by transforming coefficients using the formula $(\exp(b) - 1) \times 100$.

REFERENCES

Alexander, Jeffrey C., Bernard Giesen, and Jason L. Mast. 2006. *Social Performance: Symbolic Action, Cultural Pragmatics, and Ritual.* New York: Cambridge University Press.

Andersen, Ellen Ann. 2006. *Out of the Closets and into the Courts: Legal Opportunity Structure and Gay Rights Litigation.* Ann Arbor: University of Michigan Press.

Armstrong, Elizabeth. 2002. *Forging Gay Identities: Organizing Sexuality in San Francisco, 1950–1994.* Chicago: University of Chicago Press.

Armstrong, Elizabeth, and Mary Bernstein. 2008. "Culture, Power, and Institutions: A Multi-Institutional Politics Approach to Social Movements." *Sociological Theory* 26 (1): 74–99.

Badgett, M. V. Lee. 2009. *When Gay People Get Married: What Happens When Societies Legalize Same-Sex Marriage.* New York: New York University Press.

Bernstein, Mary. 1997. "Celebration and Suppression: The Strategic Uses of Identity by the Lesbian and Gay Movement." *American Journal of Sociology* 103 (3): 531–65.

Blee, Kathleen. 2002. *Inside Organized Racism: Women in the Hate Movement.* Berkeley: University of California Press.

Cohen, Jean. 1985. "'Strategy or Identity'? New Theoretical Paradigms and Contemporary Social Movements." *Social Research* 52: 663–716.

della Porta, Donatella. 2008. "Protest on Unemployment: Forms and Opportunities." *Mobilization* 3: 297–310.

D'Emilio, John. 2007. "Will the Courts Set Us Free? Reflections on the Campaign for Same-Sex Marriage." In *The Politics of Same-Sex Marriage*, edited by C. A. Rimmerman and C. Wilcox, 39–64. Chicago: University of Chicago Press.

Durkheim, Emile. [1912] 1965. *The Elementary Forms of Religious Life.* Translated by Joseph Ward Swain. New York: Free Press.

Earl, Jennifer, and Katrina Kimport. 2008. "The Targets of Online Protest: State and Private Targets of Four Online Protest Targets." *Information, Communication and Society* 11: 449–72.

Ennis, James G., and Richard Schreuer. 1987. "Mobilizing Weak Support for Social Movements: The Role of Grievance, Efficacy and Cost." *Social Forces* 66: 390–409.

Fetner, Tina. 2008. *How the Religious Right Shaped Lesbian and Gay Activism.* Minneapolis: University of Minnesota Press.

Gamson, Joshua. 1989. "Silence, Death, and the Invisible Enemy: AIDS Activism and Social Movement 'Newness.'" *Social Problems* 36: 351–67.

———. 1995. "Must Identity Movements Self-Destruct? A Queer Dilemma." *Social Problems* 42 (3): 390–407.

Gamson, William A. 1992. "The Social Psychology of Collective Action." In *Frontiers of Social Movement Theory*, edited by Aldon Morris and Carol McClurg Mueller, 53–76. New Haven, Conn.: Yale University Press.

Ghaziani, Amin. 2008. *The Dividends of Dissent: How Conflict and Culture Work in Lesbian and Gay Marches on Washington.* Chicago: University of Chicago Press.

Goffman, Erving. 1974. *Frame Analysis: An Essay on the Organization of Experience.* Cambridge, Mass.: Harvard University Press.

Green, Adam Isaiah. 2008. "Same-Sex Marriage: Lesbian and Gay Spouses Marrying Tradition and Innovation." Paper presented at the annual meeting of the American Sociological Association, Boston, Mass.

Hull, Kathleen E. 2006. *Same-Sex Marriage: The Cultural Politics of Love and Law.* Cambridge: Cambridge University Press, 2006.

Ingraham, Chrys. 2003. "Ritualizing Heterosexuality: Weddings as Performance." In *Sexual Lives: A Reader on the Theories and Realities of Human Sexualities*, edited by R. Heasley and B. Crane, 235–45. New York: McGraw Hill.

Isaac, Larry, and Lars Christiansen. 2002. "How the Civil Rights Movement Revitalized Labor Militancy." *American Sociological Review* 67: 722–46.

Jackson, Stevi. 2006. "Gender, Sexuality, and Heterosexuality: The Complexity (and Limits) of Heteronormativity." *Feminist Theory* 7: 105–21.

Jasper, James M. 1997. *The Art of Moral Protest: Culture, Biography, and Creativity in Social Movements.* Chicago: University of Chicago Press.

——. 2006. *Getting Your Way: Strategic Dilemmas in Social Life.* Chicago: University of Chicago Press.

Jenkins, J. Craig. 1983. "Resource Mobilization Theory and the Study of Social Movements." *Annual Review of Sociology* 9: 527–33.

Johnson, Paul. 2005. *Love, Heterosexuality, and Society.* New York: Routledge.

Kaminski, Elizabeth, and Verta Taylor. 2008. "'We're Not Just Lip-Synching Up Here': Music and Collective Identity in Drag Performances." In *Identity Work: Negotiating Sameness and Difference in Activist Environments,* edited by Rachel Einwohner, Daniel Myers, and Jo Reger, 47–75. Minneapolis: University of Minnesota Press.

Klandermans, Bert. 1997. *The Social Psychology of Protest.* Malden, Mass., and Oxford: Blackwell Publishers.

Klandermans, Bert, and Marga de Weerd. 2000. "Group Identification and Political Protest." In *Self, Identity, and Social Movements,* edited by Sheldon Stryker, Timothy J. Owens, and Robert W. White, 68–90. Minneapolis: University of Minnesota Press.

Klandermans, Bert, and Dirk Oegema. 1987. "Potentials, Networks, Motivations, and Barriers: Steps towards Participation in Social Movements." *American Sociological Review* 52: 519–31.

Klandermans, Bert, Jojanneke van Dertoorn, and Jacquelien van Stekelenburg. 2008. "Embeddedness and Identity: How Immigrants Turn Grievances into Action." *American Sociological Review* 73: 992–1012.

Kriesi, Hanspeter, Ruud Koopmans, Jan Willem Dyvendak, and Marco G. Giugni. 1995. *New Social Movements in Western Europe.* Minneapolis: University of Minnesota Press.

Lewin, Ellen. 1998. *Recognizing Ourselves: Ceremonies of Lesbian and Gay Commitment.* New York: Colombia University Press, 1998.

Mansbridge, Jane, and Aldon Morris, eds. 2001. *Oppositional Consciousness: The Subjective Roots of Social Protest.* Chicago: University of Chicago Press.

McAdam, Doug. 1982. *Political Process and the Development of Black Insurgency, 1930–1970.* Chicago: University of Chicago Press.

——. 1986. "Recruitment to High Risk Activism: The Case of Freedom Summer." *American Journal of Sociology* 92: 64–90.

——. 1988. *Freedom Summer.* Oxford: Oxford University Press.

——. 1989. "The Biographical Consequences of Activism." *American Sociological Review* 54: 744–60.

——. 1995. "'Initiator' and 'Spin-off' Movements: Diffusion Processes in Protest Cycles." In *Repertoires and Cycles of Collective Action,* edited by Mark Traugott, 218–39. Durham, N.C.: Duke University Press.

McAdam, Doug, Sidney Tarrow, and Charles Tilly. 2001. *Dynamics of Contention.* Cambridge: Cambridge University Press.

McCarthy, John D., and Mayer N. Zald. 1977. "Resource Mobilization and Social Movements: A Partial Theory." *American Journal of Sociology* 82: 1212–41.

McPhail, Clark. 1991. *The Myth of the Madding Crowd.* New York: Aldine de Gruyter.

Melucci, Alberto. 1989. *Nomads of the Present: Social Movements and Individual Needs in Contemporary Society.* London: Hutchinson Radius.

Meyer, David S., and Nancy Whittier. 1994. "Social Movement Spillover." *Social Problems* 41: 277–98.

Morris, Aldon. 1984. *The Origins of the Civil Rights Movement: Black Communities Organizing for Change.* New York: Free Press.

Olzak, Susan. 1992. *The Dynamics of Ethnic Competition and Conflict.* Stanford, Calif.: Stanford University Press.

Pfaff, Steven, and Guobin Yang. 2001. "Double-Edged Rituals and the Symbolic Resources of Collective Action: Political Commemorations and the Mobilization of Protest in 1989." *Theory and Society* 30: 539–89.

Pinello, Daniel R. 2006. *America's Struggle for Same-Sex Marriage.* Cambridge: Cambridge University Press.

Polletta, Francesca. 2002. *Freedom Is an Endless Meeting: Democracy in American Social Movements.* Chicago: University of Chicago Press.

Polletta, Francesca, and James Jasper. 2001. "Collective Identity and Social Movements." *Annual Review of Sociology* 27: 283–305.

Raeburn, Nicole. 2004. *Changing Corporate America from Inside Out: Lesbian and Gay Workplace Rights.* Minneapolis: University of Minnesota Press.

Roscigno, Vincent, and William Danaher. 2001. "Media and Mobilization: The Case of Radio and Southern Textile Worker Insurgency, 1929 to 1934." *American Sociological Review* 66: 21–48.

———. 2004. *The Voice of Southern Labor: Radio, Music, and Textile Strikes, 1929–1934.* Minneapolis: University of Minnesota Press.

Rucht, Dieter. 1988. "Themes, Logics and Arenas of Social Movements: A Structural Approach." *International Social Movement Research*, vol. 1, *From Structure to Action* 1: 305–28.

Rupp, Leila J., and Verta Taylor. 2003. *Drag Queens at the 801 Cabaret.* Chicago: University of Chicago Press.

Schussman, Alan, and Sarah A. Soule. 2005. "Process and Protest: Accounting for Individual Protest Participation." *Social Forces* 84: 1083–1106.

Snow, David A. 2004. "Framing Processes, Ideology, and Discursive Fields." In *The Blackwell Companion to Social Movements*, edited by David A. Snow, Sarah A. Soule, and Hanspeter Kriesi, 380–412. Malden, Mass., and Oxford: Blackwell Publishing.

Snow, David A., and Robert D. Benford. 1992. "Master Frames and Cycles of Protest." In *Frontiers in Social Movement Theory*, edited by Aldon D. Morris and Carol McClurg Mueller, 133–55. New Haven, Conn.: Yale University Press.

Snow, David A., E. Burke Rochford, Jr., Steven K. Worden, and Robert D. Benford. 1986. "Frame Alignment Processes, Micromobilization, and Movement Participation." *American Sociological Review* 51 (4): 464–81.

Soule, Sarah A. 1997. "The Student Divestment Movement in the United States and Tactical Diffusion: The Shantytown Protest." *Social Forces* 75: 855–83.

———. 2004. "Going to the Chapel? Same-Sex Marriage Bans in the United States, 1973–2000." *Social Problems* 51: 453–77.

Staggenborg, Suzanne. 2001. "Beyond Culture versus Politics: A Case Study of a Local Women's Movement." *Gender and Society* 15: 507–30.

Staggenborg, Suzanne, and Amy Lang. 2007. "Culture and Ritual in the Montreal Women's Movement." *Social Movement Studies* 6: 177–94.

Staggenborg, Suzanne, and Josee Lecomte. 2009. "Social Movement Campaigns: Mobilization and Outcomes in the Montreal Women's Movement Community." *Mobilization* 14: 405–27.

Staggenborg, Suzanne, and Verta Taylor. 2005. "Whatever Happened to the Women's Movement?" *Mobilization* 10: 37–52.

Swidler, Ann. 2001. *Talk of Love: How Culture Matters*. Chicago: University of Chicago Press.

Tarrow, Sidney. 1998. *Power in Movement: Social Movements and Contention Politics*. Cambridge: Cambridge University Press.

Taylor, Verta. 1989. "Social Movement Continuity: The Women's Movement in Abeyance." *American Sociological Review* 54: 761–75.

Taylor, Verta, Leila J. Rupp, and Joshua Gamson. 2004. "Performing Protest: Drag Shows as Tactical Repertoires of the Gay and Lesbian Movement." *Research in Social Movements, Conflicts and Change* 25: 105–37.

Taylor, Verta, and Nella Van Dyke. 2004. "'Get Up, Stand Up': Tactical Repertoires of Social Movements." In *The Blackwell Companion to Social Movements*, edited by David A. Snow, Sarah A. Soule, and Hanspeter Kriesi, 262–93. Malden, Mass., and Oxford: Blackwell Publishing.

Taylor, Verta, and Nancy E. Whittier. 1992. "Collective Identity in Social Movement Communities: Lesbian Feminist Mobilization." In *Frontiers in Social Movement Theory*, edited by Aldon Morris and Carol McClurg Mueller, 104–30. New Haven, Conn.: Yale University Press.

Teng, Mabel. 2004. "Demographic Breakdown of Same Gender Marriage." http://www.alicebtoklas.org.

Tilly, Charles. 1978. *From Mobilization to Revolution*. Reading, Mass.: Addison-Wesley.

———. 1986. *The Contentious French*. Cambridge, Mass.: Belknap Press.

———. 1995. "Contentious Repertoires in Great Britain, 1758–1834." In *Repertoires and Cycles of Collective Action*, edited by Mark Traugott, 15–42. Durham, N.C.: Duke University Press.

———. 2004. *Social Movements, 1768–2004*. Boulder, Colo.: Paradigm.

———. 2008. *Contentious Performances*. Cambridge: Cambridge University Press.

Tilly, Charles, and Sidney Tarrow. 2007. *Contentious Politics*. Boulder, Colo.: Paradigm.

Van Dyke, Nella. 1998. "Hotbeds of Activism: Locations of Student Protest." *Social Problems* 45: 205–19.

Van Dyke, Nella, Sarah A. Soule, and Verta A. Taylor. 2004. "The Targets of Social Movements: Beyond a Focus on the State." *Research in Social Movements, Conflicts, and Change* 25: 27–51.

Voss, Kim, and Rachel Sherman. 2000. "Breaking the Iron Law of Oligarchy: Union Revitalization in the American Labor Movement." *American Journal of Sociology* 106: 303–49.

Walker, Edward T., Andrew W. Martin, and John McCarthy. 2008. "Confronting the State, the Corporation, and the Academy: The Influence of Institutional Targets on Social Movement Repertoires." *American Journal of Sociology* 114: 35–76.

Whittier, Nancy. 1995. *Feminist Generations: The Persistence of the Radical Women's Movement.* Philadelphia: Temple University Press.

———. 1997. "Political Generations, Micro-Cohorts, and the Transformation of Social Movements." *American Sociological Review* 62: 760–78.

———. 2001. "Emotional Strategies: The Collective Reconstruction and Display of Oppositional Emotions in the Movement against Child Sexual Abuse." In *Passionate Politics: Emotions and Social Movements,* edited by Jeff Goodwin, James M. Jasper, and Francesca Polletta, 233–50. Chicago: University of Chicago Press.

———. 2009. *The Politics of Child Sexual Abuse: Emotion, Social Movements, and the State.* New York: Oxford University Press.

Zald, Mayer. 2000. "Ideologically Structured Action: An Enlarged Agenda for Social Movement Research." *Mobilization* 5 (1): 1–16.

7 The Long Journey to Marriage

Same-Sex Marriage, Assimilation, and Resistance in the Heartland

Melanie Heath

I N FEBRUARY 2004 I had just embarked on a road trip from California to Oklahoma to undertake an ethnography of the state's initiative to promote heterosexual marriage—a policy that uses welfare money to provide "marriage education" skills to poor single mothers as a means to lift them out of poverty (see Heath 2012)—when the news hit. Back in California a different form of marriage promotion was taking place. San Francisco Mayor Gavin Newsom, asserting authority under the equal protection clause of California's constitution, had released a directive to the city-county clerk to issue marriage licenses to same-sex couples. Soon same-sex couples from Oklahoma would embark on the reverse of the journey I was making to marry in California and then return to their homes in Oklahoma. Others would go to Oregon, and still others went and were planning trips to Massachusetts and Canada. As these couples made their respective pilgrimages to marry legally, the political climate in Oklahoma was heating up to position the "marriage debate" as a central concern of the 2004 election; voters ultimately passed a constitutional amendment to ban same-sex marriage.

The battle over marriage in Oklahoma parallels the broader political and legal contests in the United States over the question of legal recognition of same-sex marriage. Historian George Chauncey remarks that same-sex marriage is the latest phase in an extensive debate over equality for lesbians and gay men. The history of marriage, however, "has given this debate special significance for all sides because the freedom to marry, including the right to choose one's partner in marriage, has come to be regarded as a fundamental civil right and a powerful symbol of full equality and citizenship" (2004, 165). Those in opposition—most vocally members of the Religious Right—frequently argue that same-sex marriage is not a civil rights issue because marriage is a universal institution that joins together a man and a woman for the purpose of procreation, whether this purpose is realized or not. It has been at the forefront of a massive grassroots mobilization to successfully pass legislation to ban same-sex marriage. In this political climate, the lesbian and gay movement has been pulled by the Religious Right's activism to prioritize the fight for marriage equality as a powerful marker of the social and moral worth of lesbians and gay men (Fetner 2008).

Below the surface of this unified mobilization for marriage equality, however, are internal debates within the lesbian, gay, bisexual, transgender, and queer (LGBTQ) community concerning the potential benefits of legalized marriage. A central concern is whether organizing for same-sex marriage is inherently an assimilationist endeavor that will establish the value of same-sex relationships based on the dominant cultural norms of heterosexual marriage, including its historical relation to patriarchy (Ettelbrick 1992; Polikoff 1993; Vaid 1995; Walters 2001). A related concern is whether fighting for same-sex marriage will devalue the diverse formation of relationship and kinship patterns that have occurred in the lesbian and gay community due to the lack of legal marriage, and will further discriminate against the marginalized—both heterosexuals and nonheterosexuals—who are not legally married (Polikoff 2008; Weston 1991).

To examine whether same-sex marriage represents resistance to or an accommodation of the dominant norms of heterosexual marriage, scholars have studied same-sex commitment rituals to analyze their potential political power (Hull 2006; Lewin 1998; Stiers 1999). Sociologist Kathleen Hull (2006) argues that the very act of participating in a public ritual in which family, friends, and clergy act as witnesses amounts to symbolic political resistance because it makes lesbian and gay relationships visible in a social environment where invisibility is the status quo. These acts count as political resistance in the form of cultural performance. As an act of protest, same-sex commitment rituals are highly personal acts that form an alternative legality outside the boundaries of the law (Hull 2006; Rupp and Taylor 2003; Taylor et al., chapter 6 herein). These rituals hold "promise as well as danger for LGBT families" in potentially protecting them from harm and discrimination, while potentially excluding relationships that do not fit the dominant model of heterosexual marriage (Bernstein and Reimann 2001, 14).

Taylor et al. (2009) build on the literature that studies the relationship between cultural performance and oppositional consciousness in their innovative study of the month-long 2004 same-sex wedding protest in San Francisco. Drawing together theories on contentious politics and social constructionist understandings of social movements, they demonstrate that cultural repertoires—characterized by contestation, intentionality, and collective identity—offer a window into an expanded definition of what counts as protest. Lesbian and gay couples viewed their weddings as intentional contentious public performances that facilitated strategic collective claims about rights and inclusion. Their research on cultural forms of political expression points to how scholars might transcend debates over the extent to which wedding mobilizations are assimilationist or oppositional. Taylor et al., however, do not specifically consider how the concept of assimilation might be challenged or reinforced through such mobilizations.

This chapter addresses the question of how the act of participating in a same-sex marriage in the context of political contestations over its legal status can be assimilationist and/or transgressive. Incorporating a "multi-institutional political framework" for understanding social movements (Armstrong and Bernstein 2008), I analyze the same-sex marriages among Oklahomans who participated in a same-sex marriage outside their state to argue that the symbolic struggles over marriage must be understood in relation to local, state, and cultural ideologies that shape what resistance can mean. The nascent research on same-sex rituals and political mobilizations has concentrated on large metropolitan and urban areas: San Francisco (Taylor et al. 2009), Chicago (Hull 2006), and the Netherlands (Badgett 2009). Given the nature of American federalism, however, states vary considerably in

their laws and regulation of family composition, and more conservative states have some of the most stringent laws. Moreover, the cultural
and social context of different states can mean different institutional
practices. My study of Oklahoma is the first to examine the impact of a
hostile climate on resistance practices within the specific social context
of a conservative state. The political climate and laws in Oklahoma
were essential to shaping the reasons and responses of same-sex couples
to marriage.

Also important to a "multi-institutional political framework" is
a consideration of the changing nature of social institutions. While
many studies have taken into account the ways queer families create
multiple sites of resistance, these have theorized resistance based on
commitment rituals with couples who most closely approximate their
heterosexual counterparts—in particular monogamous, marriage-like,
same-sex relationships. In contrast, research on gay male relationships
has revealed a great variety of sexual pathways and innovations toward
intimacy and commitment that do not necessarily rely on monogamy
(Adam 2006; Dowsett 1996; Green 2010; Ringer 2001; Stacey 2005).
My examination of the political nature of same-sex couples' wedding
mobilizations considers the relationship between cultural repertoires
and context in the debate over assimilation and resistance.

OKLAHOMA AND THE FUNDAMENTALS
OF CHRISTIANITY

On February 29, 2004, two Oklahoma couples made front-page news
in the *Tulsa World* with the headline: "Same-Sex Weddings Planned."
The article featured their approaching trip to join the "thousands of
gay men and lesbians who are getting married in San Francisco, knowing their controversial unions won't be recognized when they come
home" (Barber 2004). Between April and November 2004, I conducted
in-depth interviews, first with these two couples, and then, through
snowball sampling, with an additional twelve couples, for a total of
twenty-eight participants—four gay male and ten lesbian couples. The
greater number of lesbian couples in this sample parallels preliminary
data in eight states where a larger percentage of female couples have

entered a legal status than male couples (Badgett and Herman 2011). Hull (2006), in her assessment of why more lesbian couples participate in public rituals, offers three factors that play a role: gender socialization, parenting status, and cultural differences in lesbian and gay communities. I have given pseudonyms to all participants except six who requested that I use their real names. These six said that they viewed participating in this study as part of their activism to educate others and to improve the lives of lesbians and gay men in Oklahoma (see Stein 2010 for a good discussion of the possible benefits of using real names in ethnography). I made contact with these couples after the two who married in San Francisco initiated a listserv of same-sex couples who had traveled out of state to marry. Other contacts were made through lesbian and gay–affirming churches.

Of the fourteen couples, eleven had traveled to another city, state, or country that either had legalized same-sex marriage or was issuing legal marriage licenses to same-sex couples in 2004. One couple obtained a marriage application from the Cherokee Nation and was married in Oklahoma. One had participated in a "holy union" in Arkansas and did not desire to travel out of state to marry. And, finally, one did not see the need to marry. Twelve couples are white, one is African American, and one is interracial—Latino and white. Their ages range from 25 to 65. Most of them are university educated (five have only a high school diploma) and reported earning a yearly combined income in the range of $40,000 to $80,000. I also interviewed five prominent lesbian and gay activists who organized against the state constitutional amendment to ban same-sex marriage. The semi-structured interviews lasted between one and three hours, with an average of two hours, and were based on a standardized interview guide to ask about relationship history and reasons for marrying, as well as views on activism. All interviews were audiotaped, transcribed, and coded using the procedures of grounded theory (Strauss and Corbin 1998).

Oklahoma politics have long been involved in conservative causes, and the dominance of conservative Christianity has significantly influenced policy outcomes (Bednar and Hertzke 1995; Morgan and Meier 1980; Satterthwaite 2007). Many Oklahomans dub their state the "buckle of the Bible Belt," with justification. Almost 60 percent of registered voters say they attend church regularly, compared to the national average of 40 percent, making Oklahoma the sixth highest in the nation for church attendance. Nearly two-thirds of these identify as born-again or evangelical (Campbell 2002). The largest denomination is Southern Baptist; one in five Oklahomans are affiliated, making the state third in the nation for this denomination. The state accommodates several large conservative Christian ministries, including Oral Roberts University and Rhema Church and Bible Training College. The Oklahoma Family Policy Council, associated with James Dobson's Focus on the Family, puts out an election-year voter's guide that provides candidate responses to election issues of import to those who embrace "family values" (many Democratic candidates do not respond to these surveys). The Baptist General Convention is also a vital religious player in Oklahoma politics, actively supporting or opposing state ballot initiatives and legislation according to their interests.

Oklahoma has a long history of legislating against lesbians and gay men (Satterthwaite 2007). In 1978 the state passed a statute stating that any teacher who is "advocating, soliciting, imposing, encouraging, or promoting public or private homosexual activity" may be "rendered unfit for his [sic] position," a measure that was struck down by the U.S. Supreme Court in 1985 (Tugend 1985). Oklahoma legislators worked at the national and state level to pass the federal law to deny recognition of same-sex marriages performed in other states, the Defense of Marriage Act, that was signed into law by President Clinton in 1996. A Republican state senator drafted a state version that was signed into law by former Governor Keating in the same year. One of the state's more draconian laws was passed in 2004: a bill that required birth certificates issued to children adopted by same-sex couples outside the state to carry the name of only one parent. The Lambda Legal Defense and Education Fund, which worked to overturn the law, described it as so extreme that it might have left children adopted by same-sex couples in other states orphans in the eyes of the law when in Oklahoma. Elizabeth Birch, former president of the Human Rights Campaign, said of the political climate when she visited the state: "Oklahoma representatives cost my organization a lot of money, because we have to spend a lot of money to fight against what they want to do. We need a better atmosphere in this state for gays and lesbians" (Overall 1996).

The debate over same-sex marriage became a call to arms among religious conservatives. Terry Gatewood, cofounder of Cimarron Alliance Foundation—a political action committee with a goal to advance equality for LGBT Oklahomans—explained how back in 1995 he attended a Human Rights Campaign conference in Chicago where the leaders were discussing strategies to fight for legalizing same-sex marriage in Hawaii. He described raising his hand to say:

> "I am sure this is well intended, but could you please explain to many of us (in which I would frankly use the term, the rest of us) how we are talking about marriage when we still have sodomy laws; we don't have job-place protection; we don't have parental rights." What I meant by parental rights was the right of a lesbian mother to keep her own child type thing! I wasn't talking adoption yet. She was like, "Oh well, we need to . . ." I said, "No, you are going to scare the hell out of my"—and I used the term *my*—"fundamentalists back in Oklahoma, and you are going to galvanize them. What are you thinking?" Gosh. I think now, what a prophetic . . . Before this train leaves the station, if you think you are going to pull the rest of us along by getting marriage in Hawaii or whatever, that ain't going to happen.

Terry expressed frustration as conservative states such as Oklahoma took the brunt of the backlash against efforts to legalize same-sex marriage. In the first few months, Oklahoman legislators introduced ten measures to ban it. One bill brought by Republican State Representative Bill Graves sought to deny recognition of same-sex marriages or civil unions, declaring such relationships "shall be considered repugnant to the public policy of the state." In a television interview, he told reporters that the legislation "is just showing that that sort of activity is repulsive. I think it is and a lot of other people do, too." A coalition of government officials, churches, and parachurch organizations joined together to campaign against same-sex marriage, and several rallies

were held at the state Capitol. Finally, in April 2004, conservative legislators were able to put Oklahoma State Question 711 on the November
ballot, which ultimately passed with 76 percent of the votes in favor.

This pervasive anti–lesbian and gay climate has meant that many
lesbian and gay Oklahomans stay in the closet for fear of losing their
jobs or of complete ostracism by family and friends. This is especially
true in rural parts of the state. Terry expressed the difficulty of organizing and making progress for lesbian and gay rights:

> Sometimes it feels like you are lucky to keep your head above
> water here in Oklahoma. Sometimes you feel like you've made
> some progress, and then . . . I'm a very visual person. In my head,
> I saw myself as a kid in a pool. I'm doing pretty good. I'm mov-
> ing; I'm going to get there. Then, all of a sudden, hit the deep
> end, and oh, crap, now what do I do. It feels like, right now, we
> are in the deep end. I kind of go back and forth as to how glum
> I think things are.

Terry's description of the difficulty of living as a gay man or lesbian
in Oklahoma was echoed throughout my interviews. Yet in these dire
circumstances a number of same-sex couples in Oklahoma made decisions to travel to other states to marry.

A SYMBOLIC JOURNEY

Karen Weldin, a fifty-year-old white lesbian, grew up in a Southern
Baptist family and attended Oklahoma Baptist University. In our interview, she explained the stages of coming out to herself and others. During college, she had had a couple of sexual experiences with women.
She lived with a woman for five years; for the first six months their relationship was sexual, but then Karen panicked and told the woman she
was not gay. After that, they lived together as roommates for the next
four and a half years. After admitting to herself she was a lesbian, she
remained closeted in her next relationship out of fear that she might be
fired from her first professional job as a therapist at an alcohol and drug

counseling center. One of her colleagues was fired after he came out as gay. Even though she remained closeted, she was eventually fired for being a lesbian. She brought a lawsuit against the agency and settled out of court. After losing her job, she went into private practice but remained closeted over concern that her business would fail. During this time she met Suzanne.

Suzanne Bain, sixty-three and white, had dated boys in high school and in college had a flirtation with a woman. After their first kiss, Suzanne described never feeling that way before. Both women were dating men but shared a single room in an apartment with two other friends in a second room. After graduating, she moved to Dallas to be near the man she had been dating. She said to herself: "You know, I can't do this with a woman. That is not what I'm supposed to do. I'm supposed to graduate, work for a little while, then get married and have a family, and that's what I have to do." She married and had two sons. After twenty-five years and with an empty nest, the marriage fell apart. At forty-nine, she moved to Oklahoma City and got her own apartment. In 1989, Suzanne began to see Karen as a counselor until they fell in love. She says, "Scared me to death!" It took Suzanne many years to finally come out to her sons, and when she did, the younger one said, "Mom, we knew that!"

After nearly fourteen years together, Suzanne gave Karen a red plastic heart on Valentine's Day with a piece of paper inside that read, "Will you marry me?" The two had discussed a "holy union" but felt that didn't really make sense for them. Instead, they considered traveling to Canada or Massachusetts to marry legally. Then Mayor Newsom gave his directive to issue marriage licenses to same-sex couples, and their minister, Leslie Penrose, e-mailed them to ask if they would be interested in going to San Francisco to marry. Leslie, who had resigned from the United Methodist denomination in 1999 after being charged with violating church law for conducting holy unions for same-sex couples, had refused to officiate at civil ceremonies for heterosexuals because she couldn't do so for lesbians and gay men. Karen and Suzanne agreed that this was the perfect way to honor their relationship.

Karen, who by this time worked for Soulforce—an LGBT civil

rights organization that promotes understanding in the religious com-munity—explained how she came "barreling out of the closet" and that Suzanne had not been in that place. They had many heart-to-heart talks about it. After they decided to marry in San Francisco, Karen called the local newspaper. Suzanne said that this made her a little nervous, but she wasn't too concerned, because Karen had issued many press releases with Soulforce in Oklahoma that didn't get much re-sponse. She recalled:

> So, sure enough, when we got to the airport that day there were two news channels from Tulsa. And of course the newspaper—and I knew it was going to be in the paper. I called both of my kids and my mother and told them. . . . Well, Lord, I never imag-ined it was going to be on the front page of the *Tulsa World*!

Her mother, who was ninety-one years old, asked, "Why do you need to do this?" Suzanne said that she just "flipped over it" when it came out on the front page of the paper. The public act of marrying took on new meaning as it became newsworthy and challenged family members to come to terms with their own increased public scrutiny as parents or siblings of a lesbian.

While few couples who had participated in commitment rituals viewed their decision in political terms, most of the couples I inter-viewed who traveled out of state to marry, including Karen and Su-zanne, expressed the view that the personal act of marrying had political implications, relating to the feminist notion that the personal is political (Hull 2006). Karen, for example, told a reporter, "It's signifi-cant that we are dissenters of an unjust law, but this is a personal step for us—not a political act" (Barber 2004). The personal was apparent in the vows they wrote to each other and in the rituals of lighting candles and playing special music for each other when their minister married them at City Hall. Yet both of them recognized a political dimension in their willingness to represent their relationship visibly to the outside world. A picture of the couple together with their minister featured prominently on the front page of the Sunday *Tulsa World*. Similar to the findings of Taylor et al. (2009), they saw the act of marrying as an intentional form of contestation against the injustice of banning them from marriage.

Fernando Este and Don Glass were the second couple that traveled with Karen, Suzanne, and their minister to marry in San Francisco. Fernando had been born and raised in Venezuela in a very religious Catholic family. He knew he was gay from a young age and tried to rid himself of homosexuality, even going through an exorcism. At eighteen, he was involved in missionary work in the church and met a woman whom he came out to right away and who became his closest friend. He went to seminary to become a priest but realized the life of celibacy was not for him. He married this woman when he was twenty-five, and they began to build a life together. A year after their marriage, she died of liver cancer. At this point, Fernando realized that he wanted to be with a man. He began working as a safety engineer for the oil industry in Venezuela, and the company sent him to a seven-week seminar in Norman, Oklahoma. He met an "Okie" and began a relationship with him. This man followed Fernando to Venezuela, and they eventually moved back to Oklahoma, where Fernando received a master's degree in occupational and environmental health from the University of Oklahoma. After this relationship ended, he had another relationship before meeting Don at a Pride picnic. They began as friends, started dating, and over time Don became his soul mate.

Don was raised in a white Southern Baptist family in Van Buren, Arkansas, where religion was a central component of their lives. He also knew he was gay from a young age but tried to suppress it. He recounted, "Like through high school and early college, I said, 'I'm gay and I know it, and nobody else is going to know it,' and I told myself I can never do anything with a guy." He attended architecture school at the University of Arkansas. During his final semester, Don shared an apartment with a man who made a pass at him, and they eventually began a relationship. After graduating, he went back to Van Buren and tried to break off this relationship. While Don was away on a trip to Washington, D.C., his ex-lover called and outed him to his mother. When Don returned, his dad told him what had happened, and Don denied it, telling his father this man must be crazy. He eventually began a relationship with another man that lasted for six and a half years;

they moved together to Tulsa so Don could become a partner in an architecture firm. When he finally decided to break off the relationship because he felt his partner was too controlling, he feared that he would be outed again and decided to come out to his parents before this could happen. Don said of the experience, "You know how you have the *ooh* feeling in your body like everything slows down and I thought, I can't do this." But he did, and his parents—his mother more so than his father—ended up being fairly supportive despite their fundamentalism. When Don met Fernando, he wanted a relationship more quickly, but they began slowly as friends because Fernando was just coming out of a difficult relationship.

Five years later, Fernando at forty-six and Don at thirty-nine had discussed marriage. When Fernando received a call from Karen, whom he knew through Soulforce, to ask if he and Don would like to marry in San Francisco, he was excited. Don, however, needed a day to process the idea. He described feeling scared: "It was just like zero to sixty from marriage as a theoretical thing we might do in a few months . . . and now it's like let's get on the Internet and buy tickets!" Don also knew there would be press coverage and that he should tell his parents in Arkansas, but he put it off and decided to tell them when he got back. However, the story was featured in his parents' local paper, and his mother cut it out before Don's father could see it. His father had had bypass surgery, and she was afraid it would upset him. She asked Don not to tell him the news.

For both Don and Fernando, getting married in San Francisco was about a personal commitment and taking a stand against discrimination. Don said, "It's like we're both interested in politics, and this is an opportunity to be part of something and kind of throw in our lot with this train that's going. So, I think that's how we looked at it, you know, [to] be a part of history." Fernando echoed the sentiment that their journey was a political *and* a personal statement:

> You declare your love for each other, you're changing the universe. I believe in that. And hearing the state of California say, "I declare you spouses for life," was something that I didn't think I was going to be able to witness or go through in my life.

To reporters, he expressed his political stance in terms of assimilation: "We got together for the same reasons as any other couple. We have the same interests, the same values, and we both know what we want to accomplish with our lives" (Barber 2004). Yet their very public journey to marry offers a challenge to the "normality" of marriage. Fernando explained to me that he sees an important distinction between church and state:

> We wanted to be able to have access to a stable marriage with all the rights and duties that come with marriage and also with our faith community. But we always saw [these two] as separate issues. Religious institutions have the right to celebrate marriage—whatever they want to say, but I think the government cannot—should not keep two people from getting married. That's not the role of the government.

The interviews reflected the idea that the resistance strategies in marrying as a civil rights strategy are more than purely a means of assimilation. For both couples, marriage meant a public declaration of further "coming out" to challenge state and governmental practices that limit their rights. In addition to the news covereage, a videographer—a friend of Fernando—recorded their story, which became a half-hour documentary about the marriage debate that was shown on public television in Colorado.

The political climate in Oklahoma directly shapes resistance strategies. The stories above, as well as those recounted by other couples I interviewed, reflect the struggles of coming out in a local environment of invisibility and religious censure. The other couples I interviewed similarly viewed their marriages in terms of taking a stand against the injustice in their own state by going out of state to marry. Upon returning to Oklahoma, many of the couples expressed their commitment to continue activism to change the climate for lesbians and gay men in Oklahoma. Karen, for example, told me that, even though living in Oklahoma means a constant battle against discrimination, she "would not want to live any other place right now." When I asked what it was like being a married lesbian in Oklahoma, she replied: "In a lot of ways it's fun to me. I always wanted to be a missionary." She joked, "I'm serious," and went on to describe her feeling of fulfillment in her claim to marriage as a means of compelling others "to stretch" their beliefs and values. For couples who married out of state, the act of participating in a legal marriage gave them a new sense of legitimacy and equality that the ban on same-sex marriage in Oklahoma could not eradicate. Despite the hostile political climate, the journey to marriage felt like a courageous act that redefined their relationship to the state.

The couples found ways to publicly declare their marriages when returning, even while politics within the state were seeking to ensure their marriages would never be recognized. The mayor of Tulsa said: "If you are wanting to be married in a gay relationship, you better get on a plane or in your car and drive hundreds of miles to San Francisco, because it's not going to happen in Tulsa. Not with this mayor. Not going to happen" (Barber 2004). The couples incorporated core features of cultural repertoires—contestation, intentionality, and collective identity—in their efforts to declare their marriages publicly and to organize with others who had participated in a same-sex marriage outside the state in order to educate others about the right to marry. As stories of same-sex Oklahoman marriages circulated on websites, blogs, and in the news, conservative activists in the campaign against same-sex marriage drew on them as proof of the need for a constitutional state amendment. Thus, being located in a conservative state was essential to shaping the particular dynamics of these campaigns.

MARRYING UNDER A SOVEREIGN NATION INSIDE A STATE

The California Supreme Court halted same-sex weddings on March 11, 2004. By May, a new wrinkle in the battle over same-sex marriage was taking place in Oklahoma, a novel opportunity for resisting state law. Leslie Penrose, the minister who married the couples in San Francisco, had mobilized with a Cherokee gay activist, Samuel Crittenden, to obtain a license to perform marriages certified by the Cherokee Nation. Samuel had studied tribal sovereignty statutes and found a mandate that Native American marriages be recognized by states. The Cherokee Nation, similar to other Native American tribes, is a federally recognized sovereign nation, and can thus create its own policy around marriage for same-sex couples. Samuel believed that a same-sex couple could conceivably circumvent laws to establish a marriage that was not approved by the state. Kathy Reynolds and Dawn McKinley, both citizens of the Cherokee Nation, went to Tahlequah, Oklahoma—the capital of the Nation—on May 13 to obtain a marriage application. As the clerk handed them the application, she said she had no problem giving it to them but they probably wouldn't be able to find anyone to perform the ceremony, unaware that Leslie Penrose had already obtained a license certified by the Nation. The next day, the Chief Justice of the Cherokee Nation District Court initiated a memorandum preventing any further same-sex couples from obtaining marriage certificates.

On May 18, Dawn and Kathy held their wedding ceremony on Cherokee land at a Tulsa park with Leslie officiating. Samuel began with a native ceremony for blessing the couple. Family and friends attended, as well as several reporters and activists. Leslie performed a service that honored "the traditional Cherokee spirituality." She said a prayer for the couple to repeat that incorporated earth, fire, wind, and water: "Creator God, We honor all you created as we pledge our hearts and lives together. We honor earth and ask for our marriage to be abundant and grow stronger through the seasons." They took some of the red earth that Samuel had gathered from the Cherokee land at Mohawk Park and threw it in the wind. "We honor fire and ask that our union be warm and full of passion." One of the attendees presented a candle for the couple to sweep their hands over. "We honor wind and ask for wisdom as we struggle and grow this marriage together." Another attendee blew soap bubbles to signify water. "We honor water and ask that our marriage may never thirst for commitment or care." The water was from a sacred spring that had been flown in from the Cherokee homeland. I later asked Samuel where the homeland was, and he replied it was Blue Springs, Georgia, close to the internment camp where many of their ancestors lost their lives. Leslie finished, "Creator God, We honor all you created as we pledge our hearts and lives together. Amen." Honoring Cherokee tradition, the ceremony embraced a non-Christian, non-Eurocentric understanding of marriage.

After the ceremony, I drove with the wedding party to Tahlequah to file the application. When we arrived we were told that there was a moratorium on accepting marriage applications. At this point, Justice Stacy Leeds entered to address us: "Justice Dowty, the thirteenth [Chief] Justice [of the Cherokee Nation], has issued a moratorium on all marriages. Heterosexual, same-sex, all marriages, and I understand that there will be some changes coming from the council at some point." Several of us asked questions about procedure, and Justice Leeds kept reiterating the moratorium. Dawn angrily protested: "The court clerk issued that to us, and now you are going to hold it and stop us from filing it until you change your laws? Then, when you change your law, this is not going to be valid anymore. We had the right before the law changed." Justice Leeds told us that she would be sitting on the case and could not comment on the law. Leslie requested a letter documenting that Dawn and Kathy had come to file the application and that they were refused. Leslie asked Dawn and Kathy if they had anything to say. Kathy began but ended up in tears, so Dawn spoke up:

> We're good enough to be on your roll, but not good enough to be married in the eyes of the tribe, and where does that leave us? That's saying that we are not as equal, and that's not right, because the laws of the tribe are set out to serve everyone. It doesn't say anywhere in that because you are homosexual you don't deserve the same rights as the heterosexual people in our tribe. You know, it's bad enough our state won't recognize us, but for our own tribe—for our own people to turn against us. We are good enough to be tribal members, and shame on those people who are in office and don't want us to have any rights. I've always been very proud to be a part of the Cherokee people. I am very proud of my heritage. Today, I am very ashamed of it, because of the conduct of the people in office. You know what, shame on them! Shame on them!

Dawn identified her membership within the tribe as a powerful reason for recognition, even though the Nation was unwilling. Her words commenced their long struggle with the Nation to recognize the application, a battle that would receive international attention.

In June, the Tribal Council unanimously passed a measure to exclude same-sex couples from marrying within their jurisdiction. However, under Cherokee law, the measure is not retroactive and did not impact Kathy and Dawn's marriage application. Other measures needed to be taken to nullify their marriage. On June 16, Todd Hembree, a lawyer for the Cherokee Tribal Council, filed a petition seeking to have Dawn and Kathy's marriage held invalid. In the next months, Kathy and Dawn sought throughout Oklahoma for a lawyer to take their case. Those they contacted either were opposed to the marriage or did not want to alienate the tribe and the lucrative tribal contracts handed out to law firms. Dawn told a reporter: "There were about 35 lawyers on the list of those permitted to argue in tribal court, and one day I went down the whole list and couldn't find anyone willing to take the case. . . . One guy laughed and hung up on me" (Romano 2005). Dawn and Kathy were forced to represent themselves, finally securing the representation of the San Francisco–based National Center for Lesbian Rights after the case had worked its way up to the highest Cherokee court. In September 2005, the Judicial Appeals Tribunal of the Cherokee Nation ruled that Hembree had no standing to sue. Then a group of elected tribal councillors filed a new court challenge that was also found to have no standing because the council members could not prove that they were individually harmed or affected by the marriage. In the same month, the court administrator, who is responsible for recording marriage licenses, filed a third lawsuit challenging the validity of the couple's marriage, which is still pending as of 2012.

During our interview in 2004, Kathy, then twenty-seven, and Dawn, thirty-two, described being pulled into activism with little knowledge of the struggle ahead. They had experienced their share of discrimination as a couple. When Kathy was hospitalized with back problems, the staff did not allow Dawn to visit her because the institution recognized them only as roommates—even though they had been living together for years and were parenting Dawn's eleven-year-old daughter. This was a big part of their reason for seeking to legally marry.

Neither, however, had any idea of the extent of the activism they would need to embrace. Kathy said: "We were so naïve. We had no idea it would be like this. . . . With the marriage certificate, we just thought we've bought some marriage certificate, get married, and it would be done. In our heads it wasn't going to be a big deal." Dawn echoed this sentiment, saying that she felt a very rosy picture had been painted about what would happen and they were unaware of the impending fight:

> We're very quiet kind of people. We live in the suburbs, we pretty much mind our own business and it was just like, "What do you mean?" We never even thought about being activists. We sign petitions and do stuff like that but to actually get out and fight for a cause was just never—wasn't something we did. We kind of stood on the sidelines like most people.

Both had been somewhat apolitical before the marriage. Kathy described how frustrated she felt by people who said they were doing this for political gain. "Honestly, we didn't. It didn't start out as that anyway." She described her evolution in thinking that eventually saw this as an opportunity to help others: "At some point, it occurred to us that we did this so maybe the other couples that are interested they can go ahead and get married too. And then it became a bigger idea to us that that could be a gateway to get it legal in Oklahoma. [But] we kind of had our doubts about that being possible." This evolution represents the awakening of political consciousness and a broader collective identity.

Kathy and Dawn's marriage within a sovereign nation in a state that defines marriage as exclusively heterosexual offers a glimpse into the multilayered forms resistance can take. Dawn and Kathy wanted to be like others who are able to live out their married lives in privacy. Yet their political awakening came as they began to recognize the kinds of discrimination they faced as a couple. I asked Kathy about whether she and Dawn had considered moving to another state. She responded: "There've absolutely been days when it just sounds so awesome to go be in a place that accepts you for who you are and welcomes you for that, because it's difficult. I never realized, I don't think, until all of this how difficult it is, how openly the world rejects our relationship."

While their case sparked off a debate that led to a consolidation of power in the tribe to define marriage as exclusively heterosexual, Kathy and Dawn's marriage became not only a legal battle but also a symbolic fight for the tribe's recognition of their marriage.

ADDING GAY MEN AND LESBIANS
TO THE MARRIAGE STEW

In her assessment of the potential benefits of same-sex marriage, Suzanna Danuta Walters expresses skepticism that it will transform the institution:

> It is not at all clear that adding lesbians and gays to the marriage stew will necessarily alter its flavor just as it is not clear that allowing gays to serve in the military would alter the structure of the military. . . . True, no institution is impenetrable or completely inelastic to change. Nevertheless, powerful and hierarchical ones such as the military or marriage are not going to be easily transformed. (2001, 352)

On the one hand, Walters is right about the power of marriage as an institution, but on the other her assessment does not fully take into account the fundamental transformations in family life that have already taken place over the last half-century. Her worry echoes that of Michael Warner concerning assimilation: "Marriage sanctifies some couples at the expense of others. It is selective legitimacy" (2000, 82). From this perspective, incorporating lesbians and gay men into marriage will redraw the lines of discrimination between those who have sex inside marriage and all other sexual "deviants." Are the symbolic practices of resistance that lesbians and gay men perform in marrying better thought of as acquiescence to the heterosexual norm?

This is a fraught question. I believe that the cases above offer some evidence that same-sex marriage has the potential to challenge social environments like the one in Oklahoma where organized efforts are made to quell rights for lesbians and gay men. Simultaneously, one wonders how willingly these men and women would blend in to the dominant family model if they were given the opportunity. Since legalized same-sex marriage is such a new phenomenon, there is little research to evaluate the transgressive potential of same-sex marriage. Research on same-sex relationships has uncovered their innovative potential as constituting "families of choice" (Weston 1991). In addition to promoting family relationships outside biological or marital ties, other research has examined the practice of nonmonogamy among same-sex couples. Ringer (2001) conducted in-depth interviews with thirty gay male couples to theorize their "relational ideologies" as constituting practices that do not require monogamy. Other studies of gay male couples have also confirmed the importance to many same-sex couples of constructing relationships outside the constraints of monogamy (Adam 2006; Bech 1997; Ringer 2001; Stacey 2005). More recently, one study in Canada has actually examined relationship innovation among married same-sex couples. Green (2010; chapter 11 herein) conducted in-depth interviews with thirty married lesbians and gay men in Ontario to find that half of same-sex spouses (predominantly gay male) reported partaking in a practice of nonmonogamy.

One of the couples I interviewed offered more preliminary evidence that adding gay men to the marriage stew can change the flavor. Similar to the other couples I interviewed, Gary, a thirty-eight-year-old white gay male, and Oscar James-Wright, sixty and white, did not set out to transform marriage. Oscar had grown up in a small town in Oregon and completed his Ph.D. on the East Coast. He took a position at Oklahoma State University in 1981 and is now a professor of history. At age twenty-three, he had had numerous sexual encounters with boys and men, but social pressures led him to marry heterosexually and the couple had two sons. After ten years the marriage disintegrated, and Oscar entered a relationship with a younger man, which lasted for eight years. When they split up, Oscar decided that being a single bachelor had its benefits and that sex would mean no strings attached. Gary, born and raised in Canada, had dated girls platonically in high school and came out in college. He'd had three relationships, which he described as dysfunctional. The two met at a bar in Vancouver, and they became, as each termed it, "soul mates."

After a year of a very intense relationship, they made a decision to open their relationship for separate sexual encounters as well as adventures together. Gary had resisted at first but described his change of heart:

> I wanted to find my prince charming. I had a very pedestrian notion of what a relationship was, I guess. It was a full year that Oscar and I were together before he broached the topic of having a nonexclusive relationship. I finally just said fuck it, why not? Everything else I had tried didn't work. They all cheated on me or I cheated on them. Let's try it.

Gary's reluctance soon faded. After several years of an open relationship, he said he couldn't imagine it any other way. Oscar described his need for nonexclusivity: "I needed very much to have this. My libido is very high. I like a great deal of sex and I am very sexually active." Gary, on the other hand, didn't have the same drive. He told me: "Oscar is far more sexual than I am. I have my moments. I am quite jealous of that sometimes. I wish I were so comfortable in my skin. He seems to be extremely comfortable and at ease with himself sexually." Surprisingly, Oscar—who had more encounters with other men—was actually the one who became jealous at times. He said:

> At first, I was very jealous. It was fine for me to go have sex, but if he did I wasn't sure because I was afraid he was going to leave me. He would find someone he liked to have sex with, that had a bigger cock, or was better in bed. My own insecurities were coming out. I don't feel that way anymore. I'm much calmer about it.

As a couple they maintained complete honesty about their encounters, and Gary described how sexy it was when Oscar recounted his adventures.

In 2003, Gary and Oscar traveled to Canada to marry legally. They made this decision for immigration purposes, because the two were considering moving there. Oscar had tired of the antigay atmosphere that pervaded Oklahoma. According to Oscar, marriage didn't change anything about their relationship or commitment. However, Gary expressed feeling different afterward:

> It makes a huge difference. I am kind of shocked at myself for saying this. I felt very different after having gone through that ceremony and having them pronounce us as married. I didn't feel . . . there was no quantitative increase to my attachment to Oscar but qualitatively it just resonated differently.

Gary was shocked because he was somewhat critical of the institution of marriage. He described his parents' marriage as none too happy, and that he didn't see any reason for gay men to emulate heterosexual unions. However, the symbolic dimensions of publicly announcing his commitment made a difference. The two felt strongly about challenging the heterosexual assumption of marriage, and both changed their last names to a hyphenated combination: James-Wright.

Marriage may have changed the way Gary felt, but it didn't change the agreement the two had to be nonexclusive. Oscar explained:

> To make love is one thing, to have sex is another. We make love, and sometimes we have sex too, but the level of intimacy when we are just in bed holding each is much more intimate than anybody I'm having sex with. It's just touching each other. It's hard to explain.

The idea of separating love and sex relates to broader transformations in intimacy where trust is no longer taken for granted but negotiated (Giddens 1992). Gary discussed contemplating such a move as possibly beneficial to their relationship. Living in Oklahoma, however, the couple found that the gay community often condemned their nonmonogamous marriage. Gary said: "I get a lot of shit from people about how dare you proclaim that you are married and have sex with other people. I think that just offends people. You get accused of having a double standard and being a sellout, and all of this stuff." Others, according to Gary, mess around but are not honest about it, and in his view it is this behavior that is hurtful and unethical. Ironically, as noted at the beginning of this chapter, activists and scholars have leveled a queer critique of "being a sellout" at lesbian and gay couples in long-term monogamous relationships viewed as mirroring heterosexual patterns of marriage and monogamy. In the context of conservative Oklahoma, being a sellout is defined as the opposite practice of nonmonogamy.

Gary and Oscar's nonmonogamous marriage offers another interesting wrinkle in the debate over resistance and assimilation. Gary describes the expressive elements of being married in terms similar to those of other couples whom I interviewed. However, these two have fashioned a relationship that works for them based on ideas very different from dominant heterosexual norms. This couple may be an anomaly given that their reason for marrying was predicated on possible future emigration. Gay male couples who prefer nonmonogamy may predominantly self-select as the non-marrying type. However, Green's (2010) research on male same-sex spouses suggests that nonmonogamous couples may represent a more dominant pattern that complicates the simple equation of assimilation and resistance. Thus, while nonmonogamy among same-sex spouses is still an important area for future investigation, there is some evidence that it will, along with activist accounts of reasons for marrying, advance a more nuanced picture of the debate over assimilation.

CONCLUSION

Same-sex couples who traveled to other cities, states, or countries to marry legally returned to a social environment that rejected their marriages in culture and law. State actors and Religious Right activists organized to consolidate the meaning of marriage as exclusively heterosexual to circumvent the kind of challenge that same-sex couples marrying elsewhere might bring. The hostile environment for lesbians and gay men in Oklahoma leads one to wonder why these couples would travel outside the state to marry when these marriages will remain unrecognized in their home state. For these couples, the symbolic act of marriage became an important form of activism. As Taylor et al. (2009) theorize, the symbolic act of marrying consolidates cultural repertoires that transform a private and personal event into a public and political

form of activism. Rather than using marriage as a way to simply assimilate into dominant heterosexual culture, lesbian and gay couples
viewed the act of marrying as a form of political testimony to resist
the conservative backlash and discrimination that was pervasive in
Oklahoma.

The resistance practices of these same-sex couples were often a
double-edged sword. Dawn and Kathy, who fought their battle in the
interstices between tribal and state authority, were disappointed at how
quickly Cherokee leaders consolidated power to give marriage an exclusionary definition. On the one hand, resistance created increased
visibility of the issues for same-sex couples like Dawn and Kathy, who
face discrimination on an everyday basis. The media coverage of out-
of-state and tribal same-sex marriages offered a human face to stories
of discrimination and exclusion, in contrast to the negative stereotypes
perpetuated by the Religious Right. The complex relationship between
heterosexual and queer cultures, same-sex marriage, and practices of
nonmonogamy such as those performed by Oscar and Gary points to
the ways that same-sex marriages might foster the diversity that is the
landmark of transformations of intimacy (Giddens 1992). On the other
hand, these practices also point to the ways that resistance strategies
can feed into the doxa of the Religious Right, who use out-of-state marriage activism and practices of nonmonogamy to publicize the need to
"protect" heterosexual marriage. Thus, the broader political implications for same-sex couples who marry must be conceptualized in connection to the cultural constraints of location and history.

Are same-sex marriage resistance practices nothing more than a
road toward assimilation and acceptance by the dominant heterosexual culture? My ethnographic research in Oklahoma challenges the
simplistic either/or construction of the question between assimilation
and transformation. Oklahoma's hostile environment shaped resistance
practices as the symbolism of out-of-state same-sex marriages represented both personal and political motives, and public marriage took
on specific meanings given a social location where being more fully
"out" could have severe consequences. Would out-of-state same-sex
unions that originated in a state without legal marriage but with domes-

tic partnership rights for same-sex couples have the same implications for debates over assimilation? While this remains an important question for future research, I would venture to speculate that the meanings attributed to assimilation would differ with greater acceptance. Future research should also examine what such resistance practices mean for lesbians and gay men who are even more marginalized by race and class. Most of the couples who participated in out-of-state same-sex marriages were white and middle- to lower-middle-class, leaving open the question of how fighting for same-sex marriage might leave out the needs and interests of more marginalized others. Given the argument of this chapter concerning the importance of social location and historical context in creating the very possibilities of what can count as assimilation or transformation, it will be important to consider other social contexts and marginalized identities. Bernstein (2002) found similar shifting, multidimensional, and complex negotiations taking place in how LGBT movements over time have interacted with essentialist identities, where the meanings and embrace of a lesbian and gay fixed identity varied depending on resources, networks, and political conditions, particularly in connection to the rise of the Religious Right. Contextual and nuanced arguments such as these will offer rich possibilities for theorizing the relationship between social movements and progressive social change.

REFERENCES

Adam, Barry. 2006. "Relationship Innovation in Male Couples." *Sexualities* 9 (1): 5–26.

Armstrong, Elizabeth, and Mary Bernstein. 2008. "Culture, Power, and Institutions: A Multi-Institutional Politics Approach to Social Movements." *Sociological Theory* 26 (1): 74–99.

Badgett, M. V. Lee. 2009. *When Gay People Get Married: What Happens When Societies Legalize Same-Sex Marriage.* New York: New York University Press.

Badgett, M. V. Lee, and Jody L. Herman. 2011. "Patterns of Relationship Recognition by Same-Sex Couples in the United States." The Williams Institute, UCLA School of Law. http://williamsinstitute.law.ucla.edu/research/marriage-and-couples-rights/patterns-of-relationship-recognition-by-same-sex-couples-in-the-united-states/.

Barber, Brian. 2004. "Same-Sex Weddings Planned." *Tulsa World*, February 29.

Bech, Henning. 1997. *When Men Meet: Homosexuality and Modernity.* Chicago: University of Chicago Press.

Bednar, Nancy L., and Allen D. Hertzke. 1995. "Oklahoma: The Christian Right and

Republican Realignment." In *God at the Grassroots: The Christian Right in the 1994 Elections*, edited by Mark J. Rozell and Clyde Wilcox, 91–107. Lanham, Md.: Rowman and Littlefield.

Bernstein, Mary. 2002. "Identities and Politics: Toward a Historical Understanding of the Lesbian and Gay Movement." *Social Science History* 26 (3): 531–81.

Bernstein, Mary, and Renate Reimann, eds. 2001. *Queer Families, Queer Politics: Challenging Culture and the State*. New York: Columbia University Press.

Campbell, Kim. 2002. "Can Marriage Be Taught?" *The Christian Science Monitor*, July 18. http://www.csmonitor.com/2002/0718/p01s02-ussc.html.

Chauncey, George. 2004. *Why Marriage? The History Shaping Today's Debate over Gay Equality*. New York: Basic Books.

Dowsett, Gary. 1996. *Practicing Desire*. Stanford, Calif.: Stanford University Press.

Ettelbrick, Paula. 1992. "Since When Is Marriage a Path to Liberation?" In *Lesbian and Gay Marriage: Private Commitments, Public Ceremonies*, edited by Suzanne Sherman, 20–26. Philadelphia: Temple University Press.

Fetner, Tina. 2008. *How the Religious Right Shaped Lesbian and Gay Activism*. Minneapolis: University of Minnesota Press.

Giddens, Anthony. 1992. *The Transformation of Intimacy: Sexuality, Love and Eroticism in Modern Societies*. Cambridge: Polity Press.

Green, Adam Isaiah. 2010. "Queer Unions: Same-Sex Spouses Marrying Tradition and Innovation." *Canadian Journal of Sociology* 35: 399–436.

Heath, Melanie. 2012. *One Marriage under God: The Campaign to Promote Marriage in America*. New York: New York University Press.

Hull, Kathleen E. 2006. *Same-Sex Marriage: The Cultural Politics of Love and Law*. Cambridge: Cambridge University Press.

Lewin, Ellen. 1998. *Recognizing Ourselves: Ceremonies of Lesbian and Gay Commitment*. New York: Columbia University Press.

Morgan, David R., and Kenneth J. Meier. 1980. "Politics and Morality: The Effect of Religion on Referenda Voting." *Social Science Quarterly* 61: 144–48.

Overall, Michael. 1996. "Rights Activist Addresses Senate Bills Affecting Gays." *Tulsa World*, September 8.

Polikoff, Nancy D. 1993. "We Will Get What We Ask For: Why Legalizing Gay and Lesbian Marriage Will Not 'Dismantle the Legal Structure of Gender in Every Marriage.'" *Virginia Law Review* 79 (7): 1535–50.

———. 2008. *Beyond (Straight and Gay) Marriage: Valuing All Families under the Law*. Boston: Beacon Press.

Ringer, R. Jeffrey. 2001. "Constituting Nonmonogamies." In *Queer Families, Queer Politics: Challenging Culture and the State*, edited by Mary Bernstein and Renate Reimann, 137–51. New York: Columbia University Press.

Romano, Lois. 2005. "Battle over Gay Marriage Plays Out in Indian Country." *Washington Post*, August 1.

Rupp, Leila J., and Verta Taylor. 2003. *Drag Queens at the 801 Cabaret*. Chicago: University of Chicago Press.

Satterthwaite, Shad B. 2007. "Oklahoma: A Battle of Good versus Evil." In *The Values Campaign? The Christian Right and the 2004 Election*, edited by John C. Green,

Mark J. Rozell, and Clyde Wilcox, 199–215. Washington, D.C.: Georgetown University Press.

Stacey, Judith. 2005. "The Families of Man: Gay Male Intimacy and Kinship in a Global Metropolis." *Signs* 30 (3): 1911–35.

Stein, Arlene. 2010. "Sex, Truths, and Audiotape: Anonymity and the Ethics of Exposure in Public Ethnography." *Journal of Contemporary Ethnography* 39 (5): 554–68.

Stiers, Gretchen A. 1999. *From This Day Forward: Commitment, Marriage, and Family in Lesbian and Gay Relationships.* New York: St. Martin's Press.

Strauss, Anselm, and Juliet Corbin. 1998. *Basics of Qualitative Research: Techniques and Procedures for Developing Grounded Theory.* 2nd ed. Thousand Oaks, Calif.: Sage Publications.

Taylor, Verta, Katrina Kimport, Nella Van Dyke, and Ellen Ann Andersen. 2009. "Culture and Mobilization: Tactical Repertoires, Same-Sex Weddings, and the Impact on Gay Activism." *American Sociological Review* 74: 865–90. Reprinted herein as chapter 6.

Tugend, Alina. 1985. "Homosexuality Law Weighed by Court." *Education Week,* January 23. http://www.edweek.org/.

Vaid, Urvashi. 1995. *Virtual Equality: The Mainstreaming of Gay and Lesbian Liberation.* New York: Anchor.

Walters, Suzanna Danuta. 2001. "The Marrying Kind? Take My Domestic Partner, Please: Gays and Marriage in the Era of the Visible." In *Queer Families, Queer Politics: Challenging Culture and the State,* edited by Mary Bernstein and Renate Reimann, 338–57. New York: Columbia University Press.

Warner, Michael. 2000. *The Trouble with Normal: Sex, Politics, and the Ethics of Queer Life.* Cambridge, Mass.: Harvard University Press.

Weston, Kath. 1991. *Families We Choose: Lesbians, Gays, Kinship.* New York: Columbia University Press.

8 Being Seen through Marriage

Lesbian Wedding Photographs and the Troubling of Heteronormativity

Katrina Kimport

AT ABOUT NOON ON THURSDAY, February 12, 2004, Gavin Newsom, the mayor of San Francisco, directed the county clerk to begin issuing marriage licenses to same-sex couples. Only weeks into his first term as mayor, Newsom chose this course of action with intentionality, aiming to publicly oppose what he perceived as discriminatory comments by then-President George W. Bush that encouraged the restriction of marriage to different-sex couples. Many of the specifics came together very quickly (Chasnoff 2004). Those who were involved in the whirlwind planning did not expect that the license-granting to same-sex couples would last; most assumed the courts would quickly intervene and put a stop to San Francisco's actions. But the courts did not intervene immediately, and San Francisco issued marriage licenses to same-sex couples for the rest of that afternoon, all of the next day, and through the weekend. As word got out, same-sex couples from near and far traveled to the city and lined up for their opportunity to apply for a marriage license. By the Friday of the following week, the city switched to an appointment system, and granting same-sex marriage licenses became part of City Hall's business as usual. Nearly one month later, on March 11, the Supreme Court of California halted the license-granting, pending a review of the legality of the mayor's actions. All told, more than 4,000 same-sex couples received marriage licenses during that time, and those licenses remained legally valid while the court considered the case.

Recent scholarship on social movements has called for attention to cultural performances as a means by which social movements make collective claims (della Porta 2008; Jasper 2006; Rupp and Taylor 2003; Taylor, Rupp, and Gamson 2004; Tilly 2008; E. Walker, Martin, and McCarthy 2008). Prior research has suggested that the large-scale same-sex wedding demonstrations that took place in the United States in 2004, such as the San Francisco and Portland weddings, were a tactical innovation that quickened the pace of collective action around same-sex marriage (Taylor et al. 2009). Certainly the weddings had significant effects on the contest over same-sex marriage, both through mobilization and the strong opposition they provoked from the Religious Right. A growing body of research documents the ways in which social movements draw upon dominant cultural forms to make political claims. Through performances and practices, from music (Kaminski and Taylor 2008; Roscigno and Danaher 2001) to theater (Taylor, Rupp, and Gamson 2004), social movements draw on and adapt conventional cultural meanings, practices, and rituals to both embrace and contest dominant meanings. In this chapter, I am interested in the ways that couples' performances of marriage rituals were deployed by participants in these protests to play with, mix up, and question the gender and sexual meanings associated with the ritual and institution of marriage.

The meaning of marriage in the United States has steadily evolved over the past two centuries (Coontz 2004, 2005), but despite these changes, its role in the (re)production of normative sex, gender, and sexuality has persisted (Cott 2000). Although weddings are frequently constructed as private events, they have very public effects. For example, because marriage carries with it more than one thousand federal benefits (General Accounting Office 2004), the exclusion of same-sex couples effectively rewards only one form of sexuality—heterosexuality. In turn, this perpetuates the construction of heterosexuality as normal and natural. Scholars refer to this as heteronormativity (Warner 1993), wherein heterosexuality is privileged above other sexual identities. Scholars of critical heterosexuality studies argue that the reach of heteronormativity extends beyond policing sexuality to include instituting normative gender (Ingraham 2005); because heterosexuality is

premised on two mutually exclusive, oppositionally constructed genders, privileging heterosexuality both produces and is dependent on
normative gender. In this way, heteronormativity is about both sexual
and social roles (Ingraham 2005).

While much attention has been paid to the ways same-sex marriage challenges heteronormative ideals about sexuality (Badgett 2009;
Hull 2006; Josephson 2005), less attention has been paid to its effect on
social roles. Exceptions to this pattern include Mary Bernstein (2001),
who argues that same-sex marriage, by definition, undermines normative assumptions about gender and sexual categories and practices, and
William Eskridge (1996), who predicts that same-sex marriage will
disrupt not only the marginalized status of gays and lesbians but the
contemporary gender system as well. While these scholars may foresee
transformative outcomes of same-sex marriage for social roles, others
are less sanguine. Lisa Duggan (2002), for example, anticipates that
same-sex couples will come to mirror heteronormativity in marriage,
and Mariana Valverde (2006) characterizes marriage as an institution
that will compel same-sex couples to mimic the values of different-
sex couples, leading to a loss of queerness. Here I add to the body of
scholarship on gender and social movements that has been concerned
with the effects of social movement tactics on gender practices and
relations (Taylor 1999; Taylor and Van Dyke 2004; Taylor and Van Willigen 1996).

In this chapter, I look at ways that photographs of the same-sex weddings in San Francisco contest and/or reify normative meanings of gender. As scholars working in the growing interdisciplinary field of visual
culture contend, the visual is centrally cultural and inextricably linked
to social discourses (Kozol 2005; Mirzoeff 2002). Wedding photographs
in particular have functioned to build group cohesion, culture, and history (Bourdieu [1965] 1990), making them a useful site for examining
the meanings the San Francisco same-sex weddings dually embraced
and contested. These weddings grabbed attention around the world,
landing on the front page of major newspapers in the United States
and elsewhere, cable news shows, and broadcast television's nightly
news segments. Images of same-sex newlyweds and their stories blanketed the media and, arguably, came to represent the face of same-sex

marriage across the nation and the globe, speaking and making claims in ways that the personal narratives gay couples have produced cannot, particularly to non–English-speaking audiences.

These photographs pose questions about the meaning of same-sex marriage to normative gender ideals. The central question is, how do images of the nonnormative San Francisco weddings (i.e., same-sex weddings) make, un-make, and re-make normative social assumptions about sex and gender that operate through weddings and marriage? I address this question by looking closely at four wedding portraits from the San Francisco weddings that were published as part of an online album by the *San Francisco Chronicle*. These photographs are publicly accessible and, through their association with the major local newspaper, were presumably well disseminated. All four images chosen for in-depth consideration depict a couple with one subject who presents as gender normative and one subject who does not. In appearance, these couples conform to the (heteronormative) wedding standard of a different-gendered couple but, because both subjects are of the same sex, only one is gender normative. In the *Chronicle* album, only lesbian couples depict gender difference; none of the men in the photographs presented in non–gender normative ways. This is an intriguing occurrence, and it points to the existence of markedly different visual conventions for men and women and for gay men and lesbians. Since the focus of this chapter is on how same-sex marriage may contest gender normativity, I restrict my analysis here to lesbian wedding photographs, finding that, in some ways, these cultural artifacts echo contemporary gender expectations of married couples and/or women. In other ways, they upend normative conventions, disputing the assumed association between sex and gender.

Following Stephen Valocchi's (2005) call to situate discursive power in institutional processes, I argue that the challenge made by these images of lesbian couples to normative gender and sexuality is inextricably tied to the institution of marriage. These performances in the context of the institution of marriage challenge assumptions about normative sex, gender, *and* sexuality; they force the viewer to read the individuals as parts of a couple. When a feminine-looking woman is read paired with another woman, for example, her lesbian sexuality is made visible. Moreover, through her participation in the lifelong institution of marriage—as the photographs document—she is placed beyond the possibility of "reform" into normative heterosexuality. Taken together, these analyses suggest that same-sex wedding photographs can challenge heteronormative assumptions about gender as well as sexuality. Simultaneously, these images, and the online album as a whole, may reify marriage as normative. I analyze ways in which these photographs also conform to heteronormative expectations about the institution of marriage. Finally, using personal accounts and interview data, I close my analysis by questioning easy assumptions about the inevitability—or lack thereof—of gay marriage's challenge to heteronormativity.

Studying these events addresses an additional aspect of social movement theorizing: the ongoing challenge of identifying and articulating the cultural consequences of social movements. As a field, social movement scholars have generally failed to engage the question of how social movements accomplish cultural change, even as cultural change is often identified as a key goal and outcome of movements (Burstein et al. 1995; Earl 2000, 2004). This chapter's focus on the manipulation of meanings around gender and marriage contributes to our thinking about the process of cultural change via contentious politics.

NORMATIVE SEX, GENDER, AND SEXUALITY

As Candace West and Don Zimmerman (1987) argue in their seminal piece on gender, gender is not something we *are*, it is something we *do*. We are held accountable for our gender, reaping social rewards for appropriate gendered behavior, appearance, and so on, and earning social punishments, from slights to violence, for our failure to fit into normative gendered expectations. We often use appearance and behavior to discern a subject's membership in the categories of sex, gender, and sexuality (West and Zimmerman 1987). Normative discourse presumes an a priori existence of sex, gender, and sexuality that induces particular forms of expression (signs) that can, in turn, be read back as evidence of a subject's sex, gender, and sexuality (the signified).

Similarly, feminist and queer theorists have documented the production and reification of normative sex, gender, and sexuality, arguing that despite social understandings of the three characteristics as "natural" and "fixed," they are neither (Butler 1993, 1997b). All three share a similar binary construction that exclusively and exhaustively sorts all bodies: a body is either a woman or a man, always one and never both (Lorber 1996); sexuality is presumed permanently and uniquely either heterosexual or homosexual (Butler 2004; Foucault 1978; Lorber 1996). Further, one's identity in one category is linked to one's identity in another. Bodies sexed as female, for example, are presumed to have a feminine gender identity and sexually desire bodies sexed as male with masculine gendered identities. Thus evidence of a body's gender is taken as evidence of the body's sex and sexuality as well, evidence of a body's sex is read as proof of gender and sexuality, and so on. Barbara Ponse (1978) refers to this as the principle of consistency. The construction of these categories is erased in public life and each category is discursively produced as "natural" through, for example, language (Butler 1997a; Irigaray 1985; Wittig 1992), clothing and taste (Bourdieu 2001; Segal 1996), and state institutions such as welfare (Orloff 1996) and marriage (Cott 2000).

There are exceptions to this principle of consistency. Historically, for example, the mannish lesbian is a familiar character (Newton 1984). Turn-of-the-century sexologists explained this phenomenon through theories of inversion: the mannish lesbian is a woman who misidentifies as a man and, because of this, desires feminine women (Ellis 1895; Krafft-Ebing [1886] 1965). The reason she is attracted to women is that she is confused. In other words, the woman-desiring, masculine woman was understood as a gender invert: her mismatched sex and gender led to an inappropriate, or at least non-"normal," sexual desire (Newton 1984). Of course, the gender invert only described women-desiring women who adopted masculine dress and mannerisms—what we would today term "butch"—and not the "femme." The femme is not confused about her gender but nonetheless desires someone with a masculine gender performance (L. Walker 1993). Historically, feminine women who had romantic relationships with other women were usually considered confused heterosexuals.

To this day, perceived gender is implicated in sexuality. Calhoun (1995) asserts that public appearance marks some women as lesbians.

In her conceptualization, presumed sexuality is assigned based on the viewer's perception of a match between sex and gender. A person whose visual presentation betrays a mismatch between sex (female) and gender (masculine)—a butch—is understood as a lesbian while a person whose presentation appears to conform—a femme—is understood as heterosexual. Scholars have noted the invisibility of the femme (Carolin and Bewley 1998; Halberstam 1998a; Nestle 1992; L. Walker 1993; Whatling 1998). It seems that the butch is the only socially visible lesbian (Rich 1986).

However, during the 2004 San Francisco weddings, same-sex couples of all kinds were on display, their images captured and beamed around the world. What meanings did those images convey?

REPRESENTATIONS OF THE SAN FRANCISCO WEDDINGS

During and after the 2004 San Francisco weddings, the *San Francisco Chronicle* compiled a photo album of images. Some photos were submitted by the individuals involved and some came from the *Chronicle's* own photographers. In all, hundreds of images were published on the newspaper's website.[1] The *Chronicle's* online images depict a range of couples. All of the images contain at least the two participants (the two brides or the two grooms), and a significant portion also include the officiate, a City Hall official, and/or additional family members, such as parents or siblings of the brides or grooms or the couple's own children. The images capture a variety of points in the marriage process, from candid pictures of couples waiting in line outside City Hall, exchanging vows, or emerging triumphant from the government building, to more formal, staged compositions commemorating the couples' participation in this rite of passage. At the most basic level, these images are commemorative of a social ritual: a wedding.

By producing these images, these couples conform to current social convention and, indeed, historical social convention—wedding photographs were sometimes the only photographs possessed by early-twentieth-century families (Bourdieu [1965] 1990)—marking weddings as important occasions to document and as symbolic of individuals' position in society and relationships to others (Peters and Mergen 1977).

But these are also documents of a protest event (Taylor et al. 2009) and, as such, offer insight into what claims participants made and how.

There is a cultural standard for the composition of wedding photographs, a standard that has evolved over time and offers a window into cultural and social history (Peters and Mergen 1977). Wedding photographs tend to be formal and consciously staged, with the couple generally centered in the frame and with most of their bodies captured in the image, as opposed to a head or head-and-shoulder shot (Norfleet 1979). The photographs are often in black and white. The couple is generally dressed formally, usually with the bride in a white dress and the groom in a suit or tuxedo. The groom often has his arms around the bride, standing slightly behind her. In addition to the couple, wedding photographs frequently include the active display of symbols of marriage, including wedding and engagement rings and religious or civil licensing documents. Of particular relevance to the analysis presented here, by convention wedding photographs depict clear gender difference. Although gendered standards of presentation and dress have relaxed over time, wedding photographs remain sites of clear gender distinction between men's and women's bodies.

Women's bodies in particular are subject to elaborate expectations. Although women routinely wear pants, no makeup, and unstyled hair, brides almost uniformly wear an expensive dress, professional makeup, and professionally styled hair. A brief glance at the considerable bridal industry, which includes magazines, television shows, and websites, reveals further gendered expectations of women's bodies during weddings, including expectations about their thinness, skin color and clarity, and the whiteness of their teeth.

The broad cultural standard for wedding photographs was in evidence in the photographs included in the *Chronicle*'s online album of the San Francisco same-sex weddings. Many of the photographs conform to the conventions of how weddings are captured on film, using poses, settings, and gestures common to the genre of wedding portraits. The online album contained images of 351 couples, representing roughly 9 percent of the more than 4,037 couples who received marriage licenses during the month-long events. The photographs are about evenly split between lesbian couples (53 percent) and gay men

(47 percent), and several trends hold across both groups. For example, both groups are captured in a range of settings—from waiting in line outside City Hall, to their ceremony in City Hall's dramatic rotunda, to celebrations in locales other than City Hall, which often suggest a formal ceremony—and in similar framings, with the couples generally facing either the camera or each other. There are women in white dresses and men in dark suits. There are women in suits, too, sometimes marrying a woman in a white dress, but no men who presented in non–gender normative ways. As noted above, because only lesbian couples depicted gender difference with one subject conforming to gender expectations while the other did not—in some ways conforming to a heteronormative wedding standard—this analysis will focus on photographs of lesbian couples. These gender-different couples, who depict and deviate from gender normativity at the same time, offer the most useful case for investigating what challenge, if any, same-sex marriage poses to gender normativity.

Looking more closely at the photographs of lesbian couples, I find that most (61 percent) depict two women of similar gender presentation—whether that presentation be highly feminine, masculine, or somewhere in between—but a substantial minority (39 percent) contain two women with different gender presentations, as signified through dress, body positioning, hair, and makeup. This diversity of presentation begs investigation. Valverde (2006) has commented on the presence of lesbian couples in which both wear wedding dresses (i.e., displaying sartorially similar gender) in San Francisco and of more muted butch presentations among lesbian couples marrying in Toronto. Scholars have yet to investigate, however, the significant number of images of mixed gender presentation among marrying lesbian couples. Given concerns by queer activists that marriage represents a loss of queerness and conformity to heteronormativity (Duclos 1991; Duggan 2002; Ettelbrick 1989; Valverde 2006), images of gender difference—especially insofar as heteronormativity is premised on the presumption of gender difference—within marrying couples are an important site for querying what some have termed the "homonormativity" (Duggan 2002) of lesbian marriage.

Although this second set of photographs most fully epitomizes the standard for contemporary wedding photographs, both in their composition and in their depiction of gender difference within a couple, this analysis is not restricted to lesbian couples displaying different gender presentations. I will illustrate how it holds for couples with similar gender presentation, including femme-femme and butch-butch couples.

CHALLENGING ESSENTIALIZED SEXUALITY

In the first pair of photographs I consider here, the lesbian couples exhibit a high degree of gender difference, so much so that, with only a short glimpse, one might take them for different-sex couples. In Figure 8.1, we find two subjects captured in black-and-white in a romantic garden setting. The bridal gown and tuxedo mark the couple as bride and groom. The gowned woman has long hair, pulled away from her face, consistent with signs signifying a woman. Meanwhile, the tuxedoed woman has short, spiky hair, which generally signals a man. The masculine woman occupies the center of the frame and appears to have her arm around the waist of the feminine woman, in a gesture that is both protective and possessive. Any physical curves of the masculine figure are obscured because of her central and forward-facing placement in the frame. Not so for the feminine figure, whose position in profile to the camera makes the rise of her breasts visible. Here, one figure is read as masculine, perhaps even male, based on clothing, position in the frame, and protective relationship to the other figure, and the other figure, with discernible female body parts and dress, signifies femininity.

The second portrait (not pictured here) depicts many of the same conventions: one woman with a masculine presentation (short hair, suit, and tie) and one woman with feminine presentation (long

FIGURE 8.1. Same-sex couple displaying gender difference.

hair and jewelry). Both face the camera and are smiling. This photograph, unlike Figure 8.1, is more documentary than staged. It is set indoors, in a commercial-looking room, suggesting not the romantic ideal of a garden but a more pragmatic, governmental tone. The short-haired woman is slightly set back in the frame, with her arm around the long-haired woman. The long-haired woman reciprocally has her arm around her spouse, but her arm is at a lower angle and more casually placed. The short-haired woman proudly displays their marriage license and the long-haired woman holds a red-and-white bouquet—while the former holds an item associated with government, the latter holds decorative flowers. In general, relationships with the state and the public sphere are coded male while domestic, ephemeral, and private relationships are coded female. Thus the items the figures hold contribute to their gender presentation: the first communicates masculinity and the second, femininity.

In these two images, the figures signify gender difference in their clothing, hairstyles, and positioning in the photographs. According to social conventions linking gender signs and a body's sex, these figures imply difference in biological sex through their presentation of gender difference. However, the placement of these photographs in an album of same-sex wedding pictures upends that implication, suggesting instead that the figures are similar. While normative expectations of sex, gender, and sexuality assert that difference in biological sex produces gender difference and sexuality is premised on both biological sex and gender difference, the publication context of these two images reveals that they depict a different equation. In these photographs, gender difference does not signify difference in biological sex. Further, while sexuality appears associated with presented gender difference—one desires someone of a different gender—it is not tied here to implied difference in biological sex since the context (a same-sex wedding album) suggests that the subjects are biologically alike.

What these images demonstrate is the possibility that lesbian couples can appear like different-sex couples. Just as the drag queens Taylor, Rupp, and colleagues (Rupp and Taylor 2003; Taylor, Rupp, and Gamson 2004) studied deployed different gender identities during their stage performances, the masculine members of these lesbian couples perform gender in ways that are not explicitly feminine in their wedding photographs. With couples like that of Figure 8.1, the presumption that the performance of gender stems from a body's immutable character is upended because lesbian couples can look like different-sex couples. These performances challenge the presumed connection between sex and gender, portraying a gender difference without difference in biological sex and disrupting what Ponse (1978) terms the principle of consistency—the assumed contingency between sex and gender. This is a direct violation of the normative assumption that gender is an expression of a priori biological sex (Butler 1991). These images bring into question claims of gender as original or natural: if anyone can perform masculinity, the claim that gender derives from a preexisting sexed subject is untenable.

Simultaneously, however, these photographs continue the representation of marriage as a union predicated on gender difference, supporting claims that same-sex marriage will perpetuate heteronormativity (Duggan 2002; Valverde 2006). The subjects assume the traditional trappings of the gendered subjectivities of marriage: they wear specific, formal clothing and are positioned in certain ways in the frame. The images may challenge expectations of relationships between sex and gender but, insofar as they conform to expectations of gender roles in marriage (Cott 2000), they reify normative assumptions. The perpetuation of normative marital roles, despite the subjects' nonnormative sexuality, portends what Valverde (2006) describes as the advent of the "respectable same-sex couple," a couple that is notably asexual and, like mainstream culture, is concerned centrally about family and finances. Nonetheless, to the extent that hegemonic understandings of marriage retain its definition as a sexual institution, the participation of same-sex couples in marriage can also be read as a statement about their intention to have homosexual sex. When marriage is understood as a sexual institution, same-sex marriage necessarily challenges heteronormativity (Bernstein 2001). I turn next to images that, I argue, not only disrupt assumptions about the linear relationship between sex and gender, but also offer readings that dispute the expectation that marriage is premised on normative gender roles.

THE IMPACT OF INSTITUTIONAL CONTEXT

In the second pair of photographs the depicted couples would not be read as different-sex couples, although the individuals nonetheless signify some gender difference in their dress and style. In these images, the two subjects signify as female—as being biologically women—but with different degrees of masculinity and femininity. The marital context, cued through signs denoting a wedding, forces the viewer to recognize the lesbian sexuality of the subjects—they cannot be read as simply friends since marriage is premised on a sexual relationship (Goldfarb 1998)—bringing their disruption of normative contingencies among sex, gender, and sexuality into relief.

In the first portrait (not pictured here), a woman with long hair, wearing an elegant white dress and makeup, epitomizes a feminine bride. The second figure wears a dark suit and collared shirt. The suited figure encircles her bride with her arms in an assertive manner while her bride gently lays her hand on the other's suited forearm. In gesture and dress, the suited figure signals masculinity and the gowned figure, femininity. However, the masculine figure has long hair and her pose suggests breasts beneath her suit. Although they communicate signs of gender difference, the two figures also communicate signs of gender similarity: their hair and bodies are visibly similar, despite differences in attire and presentation.

The second photograph (Figure 8.2) contains an analogous combination of similarity and difference. The left-hand figure wears a white, low-cut dress, jewelry, and a wrap, with her long hair falling around her shoulders in a soft, feminine way. Embracing her, her partner wears a suit. Beyond her clothing, however, the suited figure is not masculine. She has long hair, shaped eyebrows, and wears a women's-cut dress shirt. She mixes signs, visibly feminine in some ways but wearing the suit of a man and proudly displaying a garter—associated with bridal vestments—around her upper arm, its nontraditional and unconcealed placement perhaps suggesting it is a trophy from her bride—a masculine behavior. The subjects display both gender difference and gender similarity. They are identifiable as a lesbian couple, but each embodies a distinct gender presentation.

FIGURE 8.2. Same-sex couple displaying a combination of gender similarity and difference.

There is no gender ambiguity in the figures in these two images; their gender presentation largely matches their presumed sex category. However, these images nonetheless challenge heteronormative gender assumptions in regard to the relationship of gender to sexuality. As wedding photographs, these images adopt heterosexual iconography, but do so in ways that defy discursive assumptions. The couples participate in the institution of marriage but refuse one of its assumed requirements—oppositionally gendered participants—creating the paradox of homosexuals participating in a heterosexual practice, while they explicitly retain other meanings of marriage: love and commitment.

By marrying, these couples imply a long-term romantic and sexual relationship. They make a public commitment to a lesbian relationship and assert the permanence of same-sex relationships; they cannot be "rescued" from homosexuality because marriage is intended to be a permanent union. It is important here that the masculine partner is read as a woman; because of this reading, these images make nonnormative sexuality visible. When the masculine figure is read as a woman, the feminine figure can no longer be read as straight. The marital context of these images forces the viewer to read the figures in relation to each other and undoes the assumption of heterosexuality for women who display normative gender.

Similarly, they remake the meaning of marriage, revising its meaning as an institution that produces specific gender roles (Cott 2000). Although practices from weddings (Ingraham 1999) to prom (Best 2000) are heterosexually structured, with their signs of gender similarity, the couples in these images do not allow for readings as heterosexual. Work by contemporary scholars suggests that some same-sex couples consciously remake the gendered meaning of marriage as they participate in the institution and challenge generalized heteronormative assumptions that devalue same-sex relationships (Hull 2006; Nicol and Smith 2008; Smart 2008). The subjects of these portraits appear to embrace marriage, likely in its contemporary meaning as an act of love (Coontz 2005), while ignoring assumptions normatively embedded in the institution, specifically that marriage is for different-sex couples.

LESBIAN VISIBILITY

If we shift our consideration from the couples to the subjects as individuals, we see that these images also pose broader challenges to normative readings of women's bodies that apply to the wedding photographs depicting gender-similar couples. Outside of a wedding setting, the consequences of their gender performances are different for each member of the couples. Of the two members of each couple, one is marked as a lesbian through her masculine presentation and the other is not (Calhoun 1995; L. Walker 1993).

The photographs under consideration, however, are of *couples* and each individual must be read with consideration of her partner. By conforming to many of the standard conventions of wedding photographs, these images depict their subjects as intimately related to each other; these couples are married, not "just friends." In images signaling marriage, both subjects signal lesbian sexuality, even if they may be read differently on their own. For these brides with different gender performances, same-sex marriage explicitly couples the femme with the butch and makes visible her nonnormative sexuality: we have the visible lesbian and the *rendered visible* lesbian. As an individual, the femme's gender and sex presentation may cause her to be read as heterosexual (Carolin and Bewley 1998; Halberstam 1998a; L. Walker 1993; Whatling 1998), but the institutional context of marriage to a woman marks her body explicitly as lesbian. The combination of her nonnormative sexuality with her normative gender display disrupts heteronormative assumptions and complicates discursive assumptions about the readability of appearance and the obviousness of "difference."

The significance of the institution of marriage for lesbian visibility extends beyond just same-sex couples who display gender difference. Through marriage, femme-femme pairs, in which each member may individually pass as straight, are also explicitly marked as lesbian. Through participation in the institution of marriage, the femme as well as the butch is socially visible.

Scholars have argued that the confusion over the proper category for the feminine lesbian reveals the fluidity of boundaries (Tyler 2003; L. Walker 1993). Not only does presumed sexuality fail to line up evenly with gender displays, these bodies occupy liminal spaces that exceed categorization. They are categorized by the viewer sometimes in one way and sometimes in another. The signs of sex, gender, and sexuality become context-specific and can no longer be assumed immutable. If a viewer's perceptions of sex, gender, and sexuality can change based on the subject's context, then sex, gender, and sexuality can no longer be understood as the expression of some foundational truth of the subject.

Portraying (at least) two distinct gender presentations for lesbians, the women in these four images complicate assumptions that sex and gender are causally related. The subjects are understood as sexually similar, but they present gender difference. Because sex is assumed to determine gender, the multiplicity of genders performed by individuals on a single category of sex disrupts assumptions not only about how gender is expressed, but also about the "truth" of sex. The butch and the femme are alternatives to normative womanliness (Case 1988). With evidence that lesbian women can perform more than one gender—presenting as both butches and femmes, for example—the variation in gender performance challenges the presumption of a one-to-one relationship between sex and gender that is often read through sexuality. Although a heterosexual woman is assumed to have a certain sex (female) and sexuality (directed toward a different sex), the observed dual combinations of characteristics for lesbian women—butch as masculine females who desire women and femme as feminine females who desire women—immediately expands the field of possibility for all women (Case 1988). The diversity of lesbian gender identification disrupts the heteronormative chain (female–feminine–desires masculine men) and exposes the arbitrary relations among its links.

These photos also indicate the permanence of this border-crossing state. By celebrating marriage, these images show lesbian couples explicitly placing themselves outside of normative gender (for the non-feminine subject) and sexuality (for both). Although divorce is prevalent, contemporary marriage is still culturally associated with lifelong commitment (Coontz 2005); every couple thinks they are going to last. More important, cultural norms dictate that outsiders should treat marriages as though they will last. By marrying, lesbians signal their intention to be sexual with another woman and compel others to read this sexual identity as permanent; it is not a stage they will grow out of. They will not be returned to a feminine gender and reeducated into heterosexuality. The two figures are tied to each other; neither is available to be reappropriated into normative gender displays.

WEDDINGS AS PROTEST: CONSCIOUSLY CHALLENGING HETERONORMATIVITY

While the women in these photographs have not been interviewed about the intentions of their performances of gender and sexuality, there is evidence both in published accounts of same-sex marriage and in interview data I collected from couples married during these wedding events that lesbians consciously deploy the power of the marital institution to signify and render visible gender and sexual identities that challenge heteronormative practices and structures (see also Taylor et al. 2009). In Suzanne Sherman's (1992) edited volume of personal stories of lesbian and gay marriage, Nora cites same-sex marriage as a way of being "out": "For me this was a very political thing to do. You can't be more 'out' about who you are . . . than to get married" (as quoted in Sherman 1992, 114). And Nina's story evidences the cultural meaning of marriage as a permanent union. In describing her family's reaction to her wedding plans, she explained:

> My sister wrote and said, "This is my last chance to try to talk you out of being a lesbian." I'd been a lesbian for fifteen years before this relationship, and she'd known all my lovers, but to her this meant the final commitment to lesbianism rather than to a particular person. (quoted in Sherman 1992, 113)

In these women's accounts, marriage forces others to read them through their partners and, in turn, signals them as lesbians. These women acknowledge and intentionally embrace the power of the institution of marriage and its ritual practices in order to disrupt normative assumptions.

In my own interviews with forty-two participants in the San Francisco same-sex weddings, several respondents commented on the way in which marriage—and the public association of themselves with their same-sex partner—was a way of being "out." Sonia used her marriage as an opportunity to make sure everyone knew she was gay:

> I actually sent out an e-mail. I felt like I really—all those people in my life—I came out very late in life—and all those people who didn't know, weren't sure, thought maybe, I wanted to clarify. So I sent out an e-mail [telling them I got married].

Like the feminine-appearing women in the images discussed above whose sexuality is revealed through their presence in an album of same-sex wedding pictures, Sonia came out through identifying herself as a participant in the San Francisco same-sex weddings.

Deirdre's experience more specifically relates to the analysis of the third and fourth images. Deirdre passes as heterosexual and so actively uses her partner—and her marriage—to signal her homosexuality:

> I kind of have this strategy about being out in my life where I just make sure everybody—'cause I don't code typically, like you wouldn't guess looking at me that I'm a lesbian, right? Most

people assume I'm straight because most people assume you're straight unless you do something that's obviously coded as otherwise. My strategy is I just find a way to come out, usually within the first five minutes that I'm in a room, say "my partner," "my wife," mention my son: "his other mom and I blah, blah, blah." I just get it out there.

These women's stories provide some evidence that the challenge to heteronormativity that I have read in these images is intended by the participants.

Queer scholars have cautioned against unequivocal support of same-sex marriage and identified ways in which the gay and lesbian community has downplayed its "queerness"—its deviation from social norms—in the attempt to secure marriage rights (Valverde 2006). Yet for some lesbians the act of getting married is motivated in part by this same goal of disrupting normative assumptions about their gender and sexuality (Lewin 1998; Nicol and Smith 2008; Smart 2008). This finding is consistent with research that suggests that same-sex marriage, at least at this historical moment, can be understood as a form of protest to gain visibility for same-sex couples and as an act of political contestation intended to communicate the injustices associated with lack of access to the benefits of marriage (Pinello 2006; Taylor et al. 2009). The photographs analyzed in this chapter are visual representations of this cultural ritual that some have deployed to make that challenge intentionally.

CONCLUSION

The photographs of same-sex couples who married during the 2004 San Francisco protest events (Taylor et al. 2009) constitute cultural performances that must be understood as a form of claim-making to render lesbian sexuality visible and as part of a broader critique of normative gender, as accomplished through traditional heterosexual marital relationships. These pictures *are* wedding pictures—and they look like wedding pictures, citing discursive expectations of wedding photography—but they confound discursive expectations about the meaning of gender signs. By looking at these documents of a social ritual, I offer insight into the ways social movements use public performances of protest to challenge and resist gender norms and practices (Taylor and Van Dyke 2004; Taylor and Van Willigen 1996). This study also adds to our understanding of the role of social movements in cultural change more generally, which has been an understudied aspect of social movements (Burstein et al. 1995; Earl 2000, 2004).

The women in the photographs considered here illustrate disconnections in the principle of consistency: some appear masculine but are really women, some would be presumed heterosexual but are revealed as lesbian. Whether they are read as "straight" or as "men," the signs do not signal the assumed signifieds; there is no linearity between sex, gender, and sexuality as social convention contends. Images such as these have the potential to expose the arbitrary quality of normative presumptions of stable, a priori gender on a large scale. As drag performers have long shown, one body can perform more than one gender (Butler 1990; Halberstam 1998b; Rupp and Taylor 2003). These performances, however, remain marginalized, while, in the mainstream context of the institution of marriage, the San Francisco weddings and their attendant images blanketed the global media and continue to resurface as the issue of gay marriage remains politically contentious. Through the San Francisco weddings, the diversity of gender performances by same-sex couples has entered the mainstream and can play a more active role in the negotiation of the meaning of sex, gender, sexuality, and, indeed, marriage.

In these photographs, we see that bodies can successfully mix and match sex, gender, and sexuality categories. In contemporary society, the more visible the lesbian is—whether through presentation as part of a couple or as an individual—and the more varied her gender displays are, the less stable are the heterosexual project and social assumptions about essentialized sex, gender, and sexuality. Although these couples display signs of gender difference, these signs do not further signify difference in biological sex. Similarly, although the femme bodies in the photos may signal heterosexuality when alone, when framed in the institution of marriage in relation to a partner of the same sex, the gender signs are exposed as failing to signify heterosexuality. According to their personal accounts, for at least some lesbians, this relational coming out through marriage is intentional. Marriage takes on a political component, becoming a transgressive act that contests heteronormativity (Taylor et al. 2009).

An important consideration is the extent to which these performed identities are constrained by the institution of marriage, even as they play with, mix up, and question the categories it implies. In order to signal their participation in marriage, these subjects have participated at least partially in the discursive expectations of marriage. What is clear is that we cannot simply argue one way or another—that same-sex marriage always challenges or never challenges heteronormativity. Instead, I have sought to unpack some of the ways in which, by their very citing of marital conventions, these images disrupt normative assumptions about bodies and identity and to provide a complement to work that has insisted on the nondisruptive consequences of gay marriage (Duggan 2002; O'Brien 2004; Valverde 2006).

Marriage has long been understood by scholars as a public ritual that helps create and solidify the group (Bourdieu [1965] 1990; Durkheim [1912] 1995); these photographs draw on that existing social meaning to signal long-term commitments, love, and a sexual relationship, even as they remake its meaning as a heterosexual practice. They cite and speak back to cultural discourses on marriage and normative discourses on sex, gender, and sexuality that presume their naturalness and interrelationship, negotiating the meaning of these categories through recourse to and revision of the institutional meaning of marriage. In depicting lesbian women as sexual couples, they engage the cultural performance of marriage in claim-making that challenges normative assumptions about who counts as a couple.

NOTE

1. This website is no longer live. A locally saved version of the site content is available from the author upon request.

REFERENCES

Badgett, M. V. Lee. 2009. *When Gay People Get Married: What Happens When Societies Legalize Same-Sex Marriage.* New York: New York University Press.

Bernstein, Mary. 2001. "Gender, Queer Family Policies, and the Limits of the Law."

In *Queer Families, Queer Politics: Challenging Culture and the State*, edited by Mary Bernstein and Renate Reimann, 420–46. New York: Columbia University Press.

Best, Amy L. 2000. *Prom Night: Youth, Schools, and Popular Culture*. New York: Routledge.

Bourdieu, Pierre. [1965] 1990. *Photography: A Middle-Brow Art*. Reprint. Stanford, Calif.: Stanford University Press.

———. 2001. *Masculine Domination*. Translated by Richard Nice. Stanford, Calif.: Stanford University Press.

Burstein, Paul, Rachel Einwohner, and Jocelyn A. Hollander. 1995. "The Success of Political Movements: A Bargaining Perspective." In *The Politics of Social Protest: Comparative Perspectives on States and Social Movements*, edited by J. Craig Jenkins and Bert Klandermans, 275–95. Minneapolis: University of Minnesota Press.

Butler, Judith. 1990. *Gender Trouble*. New York: Routledge.

———. 1991. "Imitation and Gender Insubordination." In *Inside/Out*, edited by Diana Fuss, 13–31. New York: Routledge.

———. 1993. *Bodies That Matter: On the Discursive Limits of "Sex."* New York: Routledge.

———. 1997a. *Excitable Speech: A Politics of the Performative*. New York: Routledge.

———. 1997b. *The Psychic Life of Power: Theories in Subjection*. Stanford, Calif.: Stanford University Press.

———. 2004. *Precarious Life: The Powers of Mourning and Violence*. New York: Verso.

Calhoun, Cheshire. 1995. "The Gender Closet: Lesbian Disappearance under the Sign 'Women.'" *Feminist Studies* 21: 7–34.

Carolin, Louise, and Catherine Bewley. 1998. "Girl Talk: Femmes in Discussion." In *Butch/Femme: Inside Lesbian Gender*, edited by Sally R. Munt, 109–22. London: Cassell.

Case, Sue Ellen. 1988. "Toward a Butch-Femme Aesthetic." *Discourse* 11: 55–73.

Chasnoff, Debra. 2004. "One Wedding and a Revolution." Film. San Francisco: Women's Educational Media.

Coontz, Stephanie. 2004. "The World Historical Transformation of Marriage." *Journal of Marriage and the Family* 66: 947–79.

———. 2005. *Marriage, a History: From Obedience to Intimacy, or How Love Conquered Marriage*. New York: Viking.

Cott, Nancy. 2000. *Public Vows: A History of Marriage and the Nation*. Cambridge, Mass.: Harvard University Press.

della Porta, Donatella. 2008. "Protest on Unemployment: Forms and Opportunities." *Mobilization* 3: 297–310.

Duclos, Nitya. 1991. "Some Complicating Thoughts on Same-Sex Marriage." *Law and Sexuality* 1: 31–61.

Duggan, Lisa. 2002. "The New Homonormativity: The Sexual Politics of Neoliberalism." In *Materializing Democracy: Toward a Revitalized Cultural Politics*, edited by Russ Castronovo and Dana Nelson, 175–94. Durham, N.C.: Duke University Press.

Durkheim, Emile. [1912] 1995. *The Elementary Forms of Religious Life*. Translated by K. E. Fields. Reprint. New York: Free Press.

Earl, Jennifer. 2000. "Methods, Movements, and Outcomes: Methodological Difficulties in the Study of Extra-Movement Outcomes." *Social Movements, Conflicts and Change* 22: 3–25.

———. 2004. "The Cultural Consequences of Social Movements." In *The Blackwell Companion to Social Movements*, edited by David A. Snow, Sarah A. Soule, and Hanspeter Kriesi, 508–30. Malden, Mass., and Oxford: Blackwell Publishing.

Ellis, Havelock. 1895. "Sexual Inversion in Women." *Alienist and Neurologist* 16: 141–58.

Eskridge, William, Jr. 1996. *The Case for Same-Sex Marriage: From Sexual Liberty to Civilized Commitment*. New York: Free Press.

Ettelbrick, Paula. 1989. "Since When Is Marriage a Path to Liberation?" *Out/Look* 6: 9.

Foucault, Michel. 1978. *The History of Sexuality: An Introduction*. Translated by R. Hurley. New York: Pantheon Books.

General Accounting Office. 2004. "Defense of Marriage Act: Update to Prior Report." http://www.gao.gov/new.items/d04353r.pdf.

Goldfarb, Sally F. 1998. "Family Law, Marriage, and Heterosexuality: Questioning the Assumptions." *Temple Political and Civil Rights Law Review* 7: 285.

Halberstam, Judith. 1998a. "Between Butches." In *Butch/Femme: Inside Lesbian Gender*, edited by Sally R. Munt, 57–66. London: Cassell.

———. 1998b. *Female Masculinity*. Durham, N.C.: Duke University Press.

Hull, Kathleen E. 2006. *Same-Sex Marriage: The Cultural Politics of Love and Law*. Cambridge: Cambridge University Press.

Ingraham, Chrys. 1999. *White Weddings: Romancing Heterosexuality in Popular Culture*. New York: Routledge.

———. 2005. "Introduction: Thinking Straight." In *Thinking Straight: The Power, the Promise, and the Paradox of Heterosexuality*, edited by Chrys Ingraham, 1–14. New York: Routledge.

Irigaray, Luce. 1985. *This Sex Which Is Not One*. Translated by C. Porter. Ithaca, N.Y.: Cornell University Press.

Jasper, James M. 2006. *Getting Your Way: Strategic Dilemmas in Social Life*. Chicago: University of Chicago Press.

Josephson, Jyl. 2005. "Citizenship, Same-Sex Marriage, and Feminist Critiques of Marriage." *Perspectives on Politics* 3 (2): 269–84.

Kaminski, Elizabeth, and Verta Taylor. 2008. "'We're Not Just Lip-Synching Up Here': Music and Collective Identity in Drag Performances." In *Identity Work: Negotiating Sameness and Difference in Activist Environments*, edited by Rachel Einwohner, Daniel Myers, and Jo Reger, 47–75. Minneapolis: University of Minnesota Press.

Kozol, Wendy. 2005. "Miss Indian America: Regulatory Gazes and the Politics of Affiliation." *Feminist Studies* 31: 64–94.

Krafft-Ebing, Richard von. [1886] 1965. *Psychopathia Sexualis*. Translated by Franklin S. Klaf. Reprint. New York: Bell Publishing.

Lewin, Ellen. 1998. *Recognizing Ourselves: Ceremonies of Lesbian and Gay Commitment*. New York: Columbia University Press.

Lorber, Judith. 1996. "Beyond the Binaries: Depolarizing the Categories of Sex, Sexuality, and Gender." *Sociological Inquiry* 66: 143–59.

Mirzoeff, Nicholas. 2002. *The Visual Culture Reader.* New York: Routledge.

Nestle, Joan. 1992. "The Femme Question." In *The Persistent Desire: A Femme-Butch Reader,* edited by Joan Nestle, 138–46. Boston: Alyson Publications.

Newton, Esther. 1984. "The Mythic Mannish Lesbian: Radclyffe Hall and the New Woman." *Signs* 9: 557–75.

Nicol, Nancy, and Miriam Smith. 2008. "Legal Struggles and Political Resistance: Same-Sex Marriage in Canada and the USA." *Sexualities* 11: 667–87.

Norfleet, Barbara. 1979. *Wedding.* New York: Simon and Schuster.

O'Brien, Jodi. 2004. "Seeking Normal: Considering Same Sex Marriage." *Seattle Journal for Social Justice* 1: 459–73.

Orloff, Ann. 1996. "Gender in the Welfare State." *Annual Review of Sociology* 22: 51–78.

Peters, Marsha, and Bernard Mergen. 1977. "'Doing the Rest': The Uses of Photographs in American Studies." *American Quarterly* 29: 280–303.

Pinello, Daniel R. 2006. *America's Struggle for Same-Sex Marriage.* Cambridge: Cambridge University Press.

Ponse, Barbara. 1978. *Identities in the Lesbian World: The Social Construction of Self.* Westport, Conn.: Greenwood Press.

Rich, B. Ruby. 1986. "Review: Feminism and Sexuality in the 1980s." *Feminist Studies* 12: 525–61.

Roscigno, Vincent, and William Danaher. 2001. "Media and Mobilization: The Case of Radio and Southern Textile Worker Insurgency, 1929 to 1934." *American Sociological Review* 66: 21–48.

Rupp, Leila J., and Verta Taylor. 2003. *Drag Queens at the 801 Cabaret.* Chicago: University of Chicago Press.

Segal, Eric J. 1996. "Norman Rockwell and the Fashioning of American Masculinity." *The Art Bulletin* 78: 633–46.

Sherman, Suzanne. 1992. *Lesbian and Gay Marriage: Private Commitments, Public Ceremonies.* Philadelphia: Temple University Press.

Smart, Carol. 2008. "'Can I Be Bridesmaid?' Combining the Personal and Political in Same-Sex Weddings." *Sexualities* 11: 761–76.

Taylor, Verta. 1999. "Gender and Social Movements: Gender Processes in Women's Self-Help Movements." *Gender and Society* 13: 8–33.

Taylor, Verta, Katrina Kimport, Nella Van Dyke, and Ellen Ann Andersen. 2009. "Culture and Mobilization: Tactical Repertoires, Same-Sex Weddings, and the Impact on Gay Activism." *American Sociological Review* 74: 865–90.

Taylor, Verta, Leila J. Rupp, and Joshua Gamson. 2004. "Performing Protest: Drag Shows as Tactical Repertoires of the Gay and Lesbian Movement." *Research in Social Movements, Conflicts and Change* 25: 105–37.

Taylor, Verta, and Nella Van Dyke. 2004. "'Get Up, Stand Up': Tactical Repertoires of Social Movements." In *The Blackwell Companion to Social Movements,* edited by David A. Snow, Sarah A. Soule, and Hanspeter Kriesi, 262–93. Malden, Mass., and Oxford: Blackwell Publishing.

Taylor, Verta, and Marieke Van Willigen. 1996. "Women's Self-Help and the Reconstruction of Gender: The Postpartum Support and Breast Cancer Movements." *Mobilization* 1: 123–42.

Tilly, Charles. 2008. *Contentious Performances.* Cambridge: Cambridge University Press.

Tyler, Carole-Anne. 2003. *Female Impersonation.* New York: Routledge.

Valocchi, Stephen. 2005. "Not Yet Queer Enough: The Lessons of Queer Theory for the Sociology of Gender and Sexuality." *Gender and Society* 19: 750–70.

Valverde, Mariana. 2006. "A New Entity in the History of Sexuality: The Respectable Same-Sex Couple." *Feminist Studies* 32 (1): 155–63.

Walker, Edward T., Andrew W. Martin, and John McCarthy. 2008. "Confronting the State, the Corporation, and the Academy: The Influence of Institutional Targets on Social Movement Repertoires." *American Journal of Sociology* 114: 35–76.

Walker, Lisa. 1993. "How to Recognize a Lesbian: The Cultural Politics of Looking Like What You Are." *Signs* 18: 866–90.

Warner, Michael. 1993. Introduction to *Fear of a Queer Planet: Queer Politics and Social Theory*, edited by Michael Warner, vii–xxxi. Minneapolis: University of Minnesota Press.

West, Candace, and Don Zimmerman. 1987. "Doing Gender." *Gender and Society* 1: 125–51.

Whatling, Clare. 1998. "Femme to Femme: A Love Story." In *Butch/Femme: Inside Lesbian Gender*, edited by Sally R. Munt, 74–81. London: Cassell.

Wittig, Monique. 1992. *The Straight Mind and Other Essays.* Boston: Beacon Press.

PART **IV** The Impact of the
Marriage-Equality
Movement

9 Normalization, Queer Discourse, and the Marriage-Equality Movement in Vermont

Mary Bernstein and Mary C. Burke

OR THE PAST DECADE AT LEAST, the fight for same-sex marriage has arguably been the top priority for the lesbian and gay movement. Lesbian and gay rights activists view extending the right to marry to same-sex couples as a simple matter of equality. In this view, the extension of civil marriage would give same-sex couples the same rights as different-sex couples and would help legitimate gay men and lesbians and the families they form. Queer activists, on the other hand, view the act of extending the right to marry to same-sex couples as simply expanding current conceptions of what is normal and acceptable to include same-sex married couples. Same-sex marriage would not ultimately challenge the very notions of normality that define lesbian and gay people as other and thus would offer no support to people with nonnormative family structures.

In sociological terms, this is a debate over movement outcomes; but thus far, these questions over whether or not the movement for same-sex marriage has normalized "traditional" family structures at the expense of other family forms or has led to a greater recognition of diverse family forms have rarely been addressed sociologically (see Bernstein and Naples 2010 for an exception). In this chapter, we argue that while the sociolegal literature provides a cogent critique of rights-based litigation strategies, this literature assumes, rather than empirically demonstrates, that advocating for same-sex marriage has deleterious normalizing effects. Here we examine the discursive impact of the marriage-equality movement as one aspect of the internal movement debate about normalization. We examine this impact through a study of queer discourse in the media during the course of the Vermont campaign for same-sex marriage that resulted in the passage of civil unions in 2000.[1] Contrary to much of the literature that critiques legal strategies for being normalizing, we find that there is nothing about court decisions per se that precludes queer debates of the issue. Instead, court decisions can set the terms of the debate and, in cases where the decision is ambiguous, can actually spark critically reflective talk. Thus, our study suggests that under certain circumstances both the general marriage-equality movement and its more specific outcomes, such as relevant court decisions, can actually foster critical discourse about marriage and make queer debates over marriage visible to the broader public.[2]

SOCIOLEGAL AND LESBIAN AND GAY COMMUNITY DEBATES

Sociolegal scholars have questioned the merits of litigation strategies for social movements for decades (Bauman 2002; Halley and Brown 2003; Rosenberg 1991; Scheingold [1974] 2004; Unger 1983).[3] Most recently, queer scholars and queer legal studies theorists argue that advocating in the name of a lesbian/gay subject results in a hierarchical ordering that marks the homosexual subject as different from and less than the heterosexual subject and fails to challenge heteronormativity or systemic prejudices (Bower 1997; Brandzel 2005; Cain 1993; Dennis 1997; Halley 1994; Stychin 2003). These analysts suggest that the movement for same-sex marriage constitutes a move toward normalizing monogamous lesbian and gay couples at the expense of other constellations of intimate relationships (Boellstorff 2007; Butler 2002; Case 1993; C. J. Cohen 1997; Polikoff 1993; Walters 2001; Warner 1999a, 1999b). In this way, the threat of diverse sexualities can be contained within conventional forms of monogamous commitment.

Queer theorists argue that sexuality is used as a means of social control (Ingraham 1996). Heterosexuality is privileged as the benchmark by which to judge all other forms of sexuality. In this sense, the issue is not simply straight/gay, but also normal/deviant and insider/outsider. Framing the issue in this manner, queer theorists point out that winning the right to marry might improve the lot of same-sex couples who wish to enter into such unions, but overall it will simply redraw the line between normal and deviant a little further in one direction. In other words, simply by demanding this right, same-sex marriage proponents contribute to the normalizing discourse on sexuality. While they struggle to place themselves within the normal, insider category, they further reify both the dichotomies and others' positions within them (C. J. Cohen 1997; Duggan 2003, 2004; Gamson 1995; Walters 2001; Warner 1999a, 1999b).

Within the lesbian and gay community, activists have long shared similar concerns. In her now-famous exchange with activist Tom Stoddard (1989) nearly twenty-five years ago, lesbian and gay rights activist Paula Ettelbrick (1989) called for a variety of ways of recognizing families, rather than simply focusing on marriage (see also Duggan and Kim 2005; Fineman 1995). In the mid-2000s consolidated opposition to the marriage goal became increasingly visible. For instance, a new organization of academics and activists calling themselves "Beyond Marriage.org" formed in response to growing dissatisfaction with the emphasis on marriage equality taking hold in the LGBT movement (Hartocollis 2006). Decrying the focus in the same-sex marriage movement on the privileges of marriage as a way to secure a series of benefits such as social-security survivor benefits or health insurance through an employed spouse, BeyondMarriage.org states on its website that "we believe the LGBT movement should reinforce the idea that marriage should be one of many avenues through which households, families, partners, and kinship relationships can gain access to the support of a caring civil society" (BeyondMarriage.org 2006). San Francisco's Gay Shame Collective echoes this sentiment in more pointed language in their "End Marriage" statement, writing:

> What we are calling for is an abolishment of State sanctioned coupling in either the hetero or homo incarnation. We are against any institution that perpetuates the further exploitation

of some people for the benefit of others. Why do the fundamental necessities marriage may provide for some (like healthcare) have to be wedded to the State sanctioned ritual of terror known as marriage? (Gay Shame Collective, 2009)

While passionately argued, the issue of whether or not the debate over same-sex marriage has contributed to the normalization of some family forms at the expense of others has not been examined empirically. In other words, has the move toward same-sex marriage occurred at the expense of the recognition of diverse family forms? In what other ways could normalization be examined?

As Jennifer Earl (2004) points out, there are very few examples of how to operationalize changes in discourse or cultural practices. Steven Epstein's (1996) research on the AIDS movement shows that the movement changed the practices by which new drugs were tested and brought to the market. Kelly Moore (1999) illustrates that activists within the scientific community and antiwar activists changed the norms of knowledge production, which included increased access for the public to information about the dangers and benefits of new technologies. While these are some important ways to understand the cultural consequences of social movements, none of these conceptions of cultural change address the issue of normalization.

Though they do not focus on the issue of normalization, a few theorists of cultural outcomes have examined changes in language (Mansbridge and Flaster 2007) or the media as a way to understand shifts in discourse. Thomas Rochon (1998) along with William Gamson and Andre Modigliani (1989), for example, take patterns of media coverage as indicators of value change. In order to analyze discourse on same-sex marriage in terms of normalization, we build on Paul Lichterman's (1999) insights in his study of queer and gay rights organizing. Lichterman defines the "forum" quality of a group as the "interactional space identity groups allow for discussing opinions freely, and for discussing critically the varied identities that activists claim" (1999, 104). Thus, in Lichterman's interpretation, a group contains a forum to the degree that it values critically reflective discussion. Myra Marx Ferree and colleagues (2002) and William Gamson (2005) argue that the mass media constitute a "master" forum, where political contests over meaning take place and discourse is presented to the public in a selective form. Building on Lichterman, we term the presence of critical minority viewpoints "critically reflective discourse." In our case, the extent to which queer arguments are present or absent will indicate how much the same-sex marriage movement has normalized or troubled the issue of relationship recognition. Our goal is to understand the extent to which critically reflective discussion about the issues raised by queer activists takes place both within broadly defined LGBT communities and in the mainstream media. The latter is particularly important given that some scholars find that newspapers are highly influential in shaping public opinion about important issues (Palmgreen and Clarke 1977; Walgrave and Van Aelst 2006).

In order to assess normalization as a possible cultural outcome of the same-sex marriage movement, we examine the extent to which discourse that is critical of marriage as an institution or that promotes the recognition of a variety of family forms is covered in the media. We investigate cultural outcomes of the same-sex marriage movement in Vermont by looking at the discourse produced in two Vermont newspapers: a mainstream Vermont newspaper, the *Burlington Free Press* (*BFP*), and a lesbian and gay Vermont paper, *Out in the Mountains* (*OITM*). Comparing discourse across both mass and movement-linked media outlets allows us to examine the ways in which activists engage or do not engage with queer discourse.

METHODS

For this chapter, we employ ethnographic qualitative content analysis. Ethnographic content analysis involves a more reflective and contextual analysis of documents (Altheide 1987) that allows us to examine the process of meaning making and to draw connections among LGBT movement frames, the work of opposing movements (Bernstein 1995), and events taking place in judicial and policy arenas.

The Newspapers

The *Burlington Free Press* was selected to represent "mainstream" coverage because its circulation is the largest of all Vermont state newspapers. The *BFP* publishes editions seven days a week, with a daily circulation of 51,000 and a Sunday edition circulation of 62,000. We analyze coverage in this newspaper to examine the extent to which a discussion of queer perspectives on marriage occurs, and what forms that discussion takes. *Out in the Mountains* (*OITM*) was chosen to represent LGBT press coverage because of its position as the only statewide LGBT newspaper produced in Vermont. *OITM*, while no longer being printed in its original form, was published on a monthly basis and had a circulation of 6,000 during the years under study. We examine *OITM* in order to provide a gauge of what the LGBT movement concerns and issues are and to allow for an analytic comparison between mass media and alternative media coverage.

Dataset

The dataset used contains all coverage related to marriage equality, civil unions, and LGBT families that appeared in the two newspapers between 1996 and 2002. These seven years can be broken down into three periods. The first period, 1996–1999, represents discourse starting from the landmark same-sex marriage court case in Hawaii and the passage of the Defense of Marriage Act (DOMA) to the Vermont Supreme Court ruling *Baker v. State of Vermont* in favor of same-sex marriage rights in December 1999. The second period, 2000, represents discourse surrounding the creation and implementation of the civil union law. The third period, 2001–2002, represents discourse after the passage and implementation of the civil union law.

All relevant available coverage, including news briefs and letters to the editor, was included in the analysis. *BFP* articles were searched using an electronic database and *OITM* articles were found through manual searches of print and electronic versions of each issue. The dataset included 403 *BFP* documents and 376 *OITM* documents. Of these 779 documents, 670 were articles. The remaining 109 documents consisted of letters-to-the-editor sections, containing a total of 498 letters.

Thus, a total of 1,168 articles and letters to the editor are included in the larger study from which this analysis is drawn. For the purposes of this chapter, we considered each "Reader's Forum," the *BFP*'s title for the letters-to-the-editor section, to be one document and then coded each letter writer as one speaker, where relevant. Thus, the term *document* will refer to both articles and letters-to-the-editor sections throughout the following discussion.

Coding

All documents were scanned, converted into individual text files, and transferred into the QSR NVivo 7 program. For this chapter, we focus on documents that engage with queer arguments in any way. To achieve external validity, we developed an initial list of indicators to represent queer perspectives, based on our reading of queer theory and queer critiques of marriage. These terms included mentions of topics such as alternative family forms, benefits for other family and partner relationships, critiques of marriage as an institution, and ambivalence toward wanting to get married. Once we identified which articles engaged with queer perspectives in any way, we then further coded these articles for the types of queer arguments presented. These types of arguments, discussed below, emerged from the data as each coauthor read and reread the arguments. The term "warranting" explains how we assessed the reliability of our codes (Wood and Kroger 2000). We compared our evaluations of types of queer arguments, reached agreement, developed a final coding scheme, and coded accordingly. In critical discourse analysis, reliability is ascertained by multiple readings and coding of the text by at least two researchers. Here, both authors coded each speaker who addressed queer arguments in any way and then compared codes.

In both newspapers, we coded for the perspective of each speaker mentioned who engaged with queer arguments. Even if a speaker was mentioned multiple times in the article, we coded that speaker only once. We took this approach because we are interested in the ways in which speakers engaged with queer arguments in relation to their overall views expressed. In the case of letters to the editors, we coded each letter in its entirety to represent the views of one speaker within a specific letters-to-the-editor document. We present the results in terms of documents and, where the documents contained multiple speakers engaging with queer arguments, we provide that information as well.

In the process of coding engagements with queer arguments, eight themes emerged (see Table 9.1). Two types of articles took a pro-queer perspective. Speakers that we coded as *queer* included full-length queer critiques of marriage as well as expressions of general or personal ambivalence toward getting married. Common themes in queer articles included antipathy to marriage; concern with the negative impact of marriage, such as possessiveness and violence in relationships; critiques of the wish to marry as desiring assimilation to the dominant heterosexual cultural paradigm and thus losing the uniqueness of being queer; and concern about the impact of same-sex marriage on relationship recognition policies more generally. The latter included fears that same-sex marriage would damage existing domestic partnership policies, would promote marriage over alternative family forms, or

Table 9.1. Queer Documents in *OITM* and *BFP*

	TOTAL	TOTAL *BFP*	TOTAL *OITM*
Queer	17	5	10
Civil unions are NOT marriage	4	1	3
Refutation	3	0	4
Queer harms	3	0	4
Queer conversion	4	1	3
Unity through diversity (rights)	14	2	9
Unity through diversity (queer)	3	1	2
Mixed	5	3	2
Total queer documents	53	13	37
Total number of documents	779	403	376
Queer as percent of all documents	6.8	3.2	9.8

would be unfair to bisexuals, single people, and polyamorists. A related pro-queer position included the view that *civil unions are not marriage*; but this was considered not a problem but a good thing because queers could create a new institution that did not carry the "baggage" of marriage.

Arguments that were pro-same-sex marriage and simultaneously anti-queer took three forms, which we call *refutation, queer harms,* and *queer conversion*. Refutation speakers actively confronted and challenged queer perspectives. Queer-harms speakers went even further to contend that queer arguments could harm the cause of same-sex marriage and that queer proponents were no better than the movement's homophobic opponents in that both seek to limit choices for lesbian and gay people. Queer conversion stories were another version of this argument, presenting what can be termed a "post-queer" perspective. In these articles, speakers recounted tales of their own previously queer politics, such as a commitment to nonmonogamy or their previous critiques of marriage. In each queer conversion article, the speaker was moved by the campaign for same-sex marriage and began to support opening up access to what they once viewed as an institution of dubious value.

The next two themes that emerged reflect what Elizabeth Armstrong (2002) views as the logic of the lesbian and gay movement, "unity through diversity." Armstrong argues that the gay/lesbian freedom parades' theme "unity through diversity" illustrates that the movement had coalesced around what she calls an "identity political logic," defined as a logic that tries to overcome alienation through creating and affirming collective identities. In our analysis, *unity-through-diversity (rights)* arguments took the form of politely acknowledging the internal diversity of the LGBT community with regard to the issue of marriage, while supporting same-sex marriage. Unity-through-diversity (rights) arguments did not engage at all with the substance of queer critiques of marriage, but merely asserted that everyone should be allowed to marry even if some would choose not to do so. Similarly, *unity-through-diversity (queer)* arguments also politely acknowledged internal diversity within the LGBT movement while supporting nonmarital relationships such as polyamory. Finally, some of the speakers contained diversity within their own views, supporting both rights and queer perspectives. We coded these speakers as *mixed*.

Ebbs and flows in attention to queer perspectives can be directly linked to marriage-equality activism. In 1996 *OITM* gave some attention to queer perspectives, with 16 percent of documents (six speakers) addressing queer arguments in 1996 (see Table 9.2). Four out of the six speakers directly referenced the impending same-sex marriage court decision in Hawaii or the federal DOMA; a fifth speaker, D. B. Skeeter Sanders (1996), began his article saying, "Suddenly, everybody's talking about legalizing same-sex marriage" with an oblique reference to Hawaii and DOMA, while the sixth speaker responded to Sanders. In 1997, after DOMA's passage in 1996 and a lack of news from Hawaii, no speakers addressed queer issues. In short, it was the marriage-equality movement itself that opened up public dialogue over queer critiques of marriage within LGBT communities.

Movement activity increased again as the Vermont Freedom to Marry Task Force and its lawsuit gained momentum in 1998 when argu-

Table 9.2. Queer Documents in *OITM* by Year

	1996	1997	1998	1999	2000	2001	2002
Queer	1	0	4	3	2	0	0
Civil unions are NOT marriage	0	0	0	0	2	0	1
Refutation	1	0	1	0	2	0	0
Queer harms	1	0	1	1	1	0	0
Queer conversion	0	0	0	1	1	0	1
Unity through diversity (rights)	2	0	3	2	2	0	0
Unity through diversity (queer)	0	0	0	1	1	0	0
Mixed	1	0	0	0	0	0	1
Total	6	0	9	8	11	0	3
Total number of documents	38	7	53	49	131	40	58
Queer as percent of all documents	15.8	0.0	17.0	16.3	8.4	0.0	5.2

ments were heard in the Vermont Supreme Court, making the issue of same-sex marriage more salient in Vermont. Coverage was comparable in 1998 and 1999 with, respectively, 17 percent and 16 percent of documents engaging with queer debates. In 2000, the year that the Vermont legislature was determining a remedy for the inequities in benefits between same-sex and different-sex couples in accordance with *Baker*, coverage dropped to 8 percent. While the absolute number of documents engaging queer arguments did not change significantly, coverage of same-sex marriage nearly tripled in 2000, leading to the decrease in the relative attention given to queer arguments. As social movement activity regarding same-sex marriage subsided in 2001, there were no queer arguments in *OITM*, and in 2002, only 5 percent of documents engaged at all with queer arguments.

Collectively, these data show that social movement activity both nationally and locally led directly to a discussion of queer perspectives in *OITM*. Whether or not this critically reflective talk genuinely opened space or simply necessitated a reaction on the part of queer activists is a matter of interpretation. For our purposes, the point is that discourse emerged to question the value of marriage in response to the marriage-equality movement, providing an occasion to challenge an institution that had hitherto been uncontested.

The *BFP* devoted sixty documents to the same-sex marriage debates from 1996 to 1999, the years prior to the *Baker* decision (see Table 9.3). However, engagement with queer arguments of any sort was completely absent in the *BFP* until after the Vermont Supreme Court reached its landmark *Baker* decision in late December 1999. While same-sex marriage proponents had standing in the *BFP*, queer viewpoints did not. Once it became clear from the decision that the Court had charged the legislature with creating a remedy that would give same-sex couples the rights and benefits of marriage and that this charge included the possibility of enacting alternatives to marriage such as a comprehensive domestic partnership scheme, speakers in the *BFP* began to engage with queer arguments. Thus it was the *Baker v. State* decision that helped give queer arguments credibility and therefore standing in a way that they had not been able to garner prior to the decision.

So rather than produce normalizing results, as queer legal theory

Table 9.3. Queer Documents in *BFP* by Year

	1996–1999, PRE-*BAKER*	2000	2000 SPEAKERS	2001–2002, POST-*BAKER*
Queer	0	5	11	0
Civil unions are NOT marriage	0	1	1	0
Refutation	0	0	0	0
Queer harms	0	0	0	0
Queer conversion	0	1	1	0
Unity through diversity (rights)	0	2	2	0
Unity through diversity (queer)	0	1	1	0
Mixed	0	3	7	0
Total	0	13	23	0
Total number of documents	60	300		43
Queer as percent of all documents	0.0	4.3		0.0

would expect, the *Baker v. State of Vermont* decision itself opened the door to considering a critique of marriage and queer arguments supporting alternative forms of relationship recognition. We are not arguing that queer arguments usurped normalizing arguments or that legal activism gave queer arguments equal standing. Nonetheless, the Court's decision, which resulted from social movement activity, actually opened the door for the *BFP* to consider queer perspectives for the first time. Thus, the *Baker* decision increased both the credibility of queer arguments and the standing of those questioning the value of marriage in a newspaper whose operating procedures gave strong credence to the Court's decision.

ENGAGEMENT WITH QUEER ARGUMENTS

In addition to the different patterns of coverage of queer arguments, the ways in which activists and other social actors engaged with queer arguments—that is, the frames they used—also varied over time. In this section, we examine queer arguments in *OITM* and in the *BFP* and then we explain the differences that we find. The examination of *OITM* provides a basis of comparison for our discussion of the *BFP* by allowing us to illustrate the range of queer voices and critiques as well as the types of debates over marriage in which the LGBT movement was engaged.

Out in the Mountains

In total, thirty-seven documents from *OITM* spoke to queer issues. Of those, ten were explicitly queer and thirteen expressed support for both queer and rights positions via unity-through-diversity arguments or mixed arguments. Eleven documents (30 percent) directly refuted queer arguments, argued that queer arguments harm the cause of lesbian and gay rights, or repudiated their own formerly queer convictions (see Table 9.1).

The ten speakers/documents that we labeled "queer" challenged the institution of marriage as well as the pursuit of marriage as a goal of the lesbian and gay movement for a variety of reasons. For example, regular *OITM* columnist D. B. Skeeter Sanders (1996) argues:

> On the contrary, most of my life I have advocated the complete abolition of marriage, and I submit that the "queer" community is making a huge mistake agitating to be included in an institution that is falling apart from its own rot. . . . Anyone, regardless of whether they're gay, straight, or bi, who wants to get married in this day and age when even the British Royal Family can't stay out of divorce court has lost their marbles, as far as I'm concerned.

Sanders also expressed concern over what would happen to domestic partnerships that provided a legal alternative to marriage. Another queer advocate argued, "Can't we instead celebrate the diversity that makes up our lives; including our chosen families that don't always 'fit' the traditional monogamous model?" (Heiwa 1998). Thus queer voices expressed a variety of critiques of marriage and of marriage equality as a goal of the LGBT movement in the pages of *OITM.*

Another ten speakers actively repudiated others' queer arguments (refutation) or their own previously queer positions (queer conversion) or went even further to argue that queer arguments harm the cause of same-sex marriage (queer harms). In an article in *OITM* that expressly refuted some queer arguments, Beth Robinson (1996), one of the lead attorneys in *Baker v. State of Vermont* and co-coordinator of Vermont Freedom to Marry, argued that the same-sex marriage debate would not adversely affect policies for recognition of alternative relationships. She contended, "The debate about marriage can only raise everyone's consciousness of the legal and economic privileges associated with the marital relationship—a consciousness that will likely promote rather than undermine the drive for domestic partnership benefits and more inclusive governmental policies towards everyone's families" (Robinson 1996). Yet Robinson, while she stopped short of cutting off the debate, also came close to claiming that queer arguments would harm the cause of same-sex marriage:

> There is no question that mixing the age-old debate about whether we should marry into the current public debate about whether we should be allowed to marry will confuse the issue for many, provide fodder for those who will argue (as if it matters) that we as a community don't even have our own act together on this issue, and undermine our collective efforts to advance all of our civil rights. I'm not saying that we should cut off debate about the merits of marriage, but we need to realize that most of the straight world is now seriously considering, for the first time ever, treating many of our families and relationships as legally equal to their own. . . . That's a huge deal. Let's not blow it. (1996)

Ending on a cautionary note, Robinson (1996) implied that, while important, the movement should focus more time on battling with opponents rather than continuing with internal debate. Others claimed that same-sex marriage was indeed radical because it challenged the gender roles associated with marriage (Shamas 2000). These counterframes thus engaged each other in critically reflective debate opened up by the marriage-equality movement.

Queer harms perspectives also challenged queer critics of the same-sex marriage movement. But these challenges went even further, equating queer critics with homophobic anti-same-sex marriage activists. For example, Carolyn Ashby (2000) asks:

> What is the difference between "all gay people are sick, promiscuous, radical and want to destroy traditional social and political systems" and "all gay people who work within the system, take action that puts them in leadership roles, and believe in marriage rights are assimilationist, conservative, elitist, and white?"

Finally, queer conversion arguments also presented some critiques of marriage, but told of their own maturing process. For example, in discussing her own prior commitment to nonmonogamy, Crow Cohen (1999) argues:

> It didn't work for me. I remember a few years ago sitting at my kitchen table with a young lesbian friend of mine as I described this non-monogamous theory so many of us dykes in Burlington swore by when we were all flying around under the banner of "sisterhood is powerful." She said, "Yeah? How did it go?" I burst out laughing and couldn't stop. It was like describing the events leading up to World War II and casually being asked, "Yeah? How did it go?" The prolonged laughter was obviously a release of years of accumulated pain.

Such critically reflective discourse was possible in *OITM* because of its close connections with the LGBT movement and the standing given to queer perspectives and was sparked by the marriage-equality movement.

While queer advocates challenged marriage as an institution and the lack of attention to other types of relationships, and their opponents engaged them in critical debate, nearly half of the speakers/documents (n = 22) simply acknowledged the internal diversity of the LGBT movement while expressing support for same-sex marriage, queer positions, or both simultaneously. These unity-through-diversity arguments reflect Armstrong's (2002) view that the lesbian and gay movement was able to sustain itself by viewing diversity as a strength rather than as a weakness. As Armstrong would expect, unity-through-diversity speakers clearly showed that the movement was not united in its views on marriage or the desirability of seeking same-sex marriage as a political goal. The rights version of this view was commonly expressed by prominent same-sex marriage activists and allies. For example, the Vermont American Civil Liberties Union (ACLU), a longtime supporter of and advocate for LGBT rights (Bernstein 2002), stated that the "ACLU recognizes that there are differences within the gay and lesbian community—as there are within the heterosexual community about the value of marriage, but supports the right of individuals to have access to the benefits and responsibilities of state-sanctioned marriage" (ACLU-Vermont 1996). Bari Shamas (1998), writing a column on behalf of Vermont Freedom to Marry, acknowledged, "It's worth noting that not all members of the Task Force embrace the institution of marriage; some do and some don't. The core values that unite the Task Force are the beliefs that gay and lesbian Vermonters should have the same legal choices as our heterosexual counterparts and that laws which treat us and our relationships as second class denigrate all of us, regardless of our desire to marry." In short, same-sex marriage advocates were careful to acknowledge a diversity of views toward the institution of marriage in the lesbian and gay community. However, from the point of view of cultural changes seen through critically reflective talk, unity-through-diversity arguments allowed speakers to avoid actually engaging with the substance of queer critiques of marriage or, more important, with their claims for the recognition of alternative family forms.

These diverse arguments showed distinct temporal patterns. The most critically reflective discussions took place in the pages of *OITM* during the phase before civil unions were enacted (i.e., before mid-2000). Queer arguments were debated by speakers directly and by speakers who changed their own perspective or averred that queer arguments harmed the advancement of lesbian and gay rights.

After the legislative enactment of civil unions in 2000, which effectively put *Baker* to rest, there is very little engagement of any sort with queer arguments. The only exceptions are a new trend that started after civil unions were established in which some speakers lauded the benefits of civil unions and the fact that civil unions were distinct from marriage. As a different institution, same-sex couples could make something new and, presumably, better than marriage. One speaker poignantly claimed, "But all of this is new. We are creating new rituals, ceremonies and ways of celebrating our commitment to each other. We don't have to rely on what someone else has done. We are creating new memories that will be shared with those who follow us. Not hidden out of sight, but in full view of history" (Goslant 2002). Thus queer sentiment remained at least partially visible when some speakers expressed the view that civil unions, as a unique and different institution from marriage, were a positive benefit of not having been granted marriage. A "mixed" speaker talked about protecting gay culture from governing bodies while also seeing civil unions as not good enough, thus supporting both rights and queer perspectives. Queer conversion arguments were also present after the civil unions resolution. These accounts suggested that for these speakers there was a logical evolution from experimenting with radical politics and alternative family forms to supporting civil unions and/or same-sex marriage, portraying queer sentiments as the artifacts of misguided or idealistic youth.

Burlington Free Press

In 2000, thirteen documents (twenty-three speakers) addressed or presented queer arguments (see Table 9.3). Five documents (eleven speakers) expressed doubts about the institution of marriage. Three documents/speakers took a unity-through-diversity perspective, while three documents (seven speakers) were mixed, expressing doubts about marriage and support for the right to marry at the same time. One speaker/document presented a queer conversion frame. What is most striking is that, with the exception of the story of personal evolution, in contrast to *OITM*, none of the speakers in the *BFP* challenged queer arguments at all. They simply let others' doubts about marriage go un-addressed. Why, with the exception of the one queer conversion argu-ment, did none of the speakers in the *BFP* challenge queer arguments in contrast to the speakers in *OITM*?

Explaining Differences between *OITM* and the *BFP*

In order to understand the differences between queer discourse in *OITM* and the *BFP*, it is first important to understand the overall prom-inence of queer arguments compared to other arguments. Table 9.4 presents the total number of text units containing pro- and anti-same-sex marriage arguments as a percentage of the total number of text units containing arguments in each of the respective newspapers. First, pro arguments were featured almost 25 percent more in *OITM* than in the *BFP*. Second, while in the *BFP* pro argument frames appeared only 10 percent more often than anti argument frames, in *OITM* pro argu-ments appeared over 60 percent more often than anti argument frames. These differences in standing accorded to speakers espousing different types of arguments help explain how activists engaged with the media. We suggest that the types of actors granted standing and the argument frames that they employ affect the choices that actors make with the opportunities afforded to them in the media.

In *OITM*, advocates for same-sex marriage/LGBT rights and pro-same-sex marriage arguments were featured far more prominently than in the *BFP*. In the *BFP*, advocates for same-sex marriage had to con-tend far more often with opponents' speakers and frames. Therefore, in *OITM* pro arguments and speakers were more normative than in the *BFP*, where the idea of marriage or even marriage rights for same-sex

Table 9.4. Distribution of Pro- and Anti-Same-Sex Marriage Argument Types by Newspaper

	BFP*	OITM**
Pro	55%	79%
Anti	45%	21%

*n = 2605; **n = 1065

couples was more suspect. This means that advocates of same-sex marriage were more free in *OITM* to acknowledge and discuss the place and importance of queer critiques.

On the other hand, in the *BFP*, same-sex marriage opponents were given higher standing than in *OITM*. Actors were therefore more engaged with and more concerned about combating countermovement claims. In fact, it is likely that queer arguments were so seldom advocated or even mentioned in the *BFP* because of fears of pandering to or providing fodder for countermovement actors. For instance, in the *BFP* there were countermovement actors who drew on the slippery-slope analogy in order to posit same-sex marriage as a sort of gateway drug to greater social ills such as polygamy and the further destruction of the American family. In this context, it becomes risky to expand the challenge beyond the inclusion of same-sex couples because this could be interpreted as an affirmation of prominent anti frames and arguments. However, in *OITM*, where these anti arguments appear very seldom and are likely not taken seriously by the readers, actors can disengage themselves slightly from the opponents of same-sex marriage, thus freeing up energy to consider the issues raised by queer theorists and activists.

Such was the case for Beth Robinson, one of the key players in the civil union debate. An out lesbian and member of a same-sex couple, she represented the plaintiffs in *Baker* and was active in several social movement organizations advocating for same-sex marriage rights in Vermont. In the *BFP*, where she had to compete for limited standing with a variety of other actors, many staunchly opposed to same-sex marriage and relatively few who ever questioned the institution, she never acknowledged or engaged with queer critiques of marriage. However, in *OITM*, where she was provided with higher standing and the additional outlet of a monthly column, and where queer positions on marriage were featured more prominently, she acknowledged divisions over marriage in the LGBT community and also actively engaged with queer critiques of marriage (Murray and Robinson 2000; Robinson 1996 [see quotation above]). Thus activists make strategic choices based on the relative standing of opponents and minority views within their own social movement.

CONCLUSION

Much debate has centered on whether or not court decisions and legal campaigns themselves are inherently normalizing. In this study, we have examined the impact of the marriage-equality movement in Vermont in opening up critically reflective discourse among LGBT communities as well as the broader public. We have found that in an LGBT newspaper, activists engage each other in dialogue over the institution of marriage and the wisdom of pursuing same-sex marriage as a goal. Significantly, it was the marriage-equality movement that actually made the debate visible. In the broader public, discussion of queer issues emerged as a result of *Baker*, which increased the standing of those questioning the value of marriage as an institution. The lower standing given to same-sex marriage opponents in *OITM* compared to the *BFP* freed up space for more critically reflective talk about the value of the institution of marriage and the wisdom of pursuing marriage equality as a goal. In the *BFP*, the prominence of opposing movement frames led activists to avoid engaging with the substance of queer critiques and to devote more time to countering the opposition's rhetoric.

In contrast to much of the literature that critiques legal strategies for being normalizing, we have argued that there is nothing about court decisions per se that preclude critically reflective talk. Instead, court decisions can set the terms of the debate and, with an ambiguous decision like *Baker*, can spark critically reflective debate. Our analysis also suggests, however, that court decisions that mandate marriage may not open up space for critically reflective debate in the same way. Furthermore, our data do not allow us to assess the long-term impact of this expanded discourse. Finally, Vermont is a very liberal state, so it is possible that the mainstream media in Vermont may have been more open to queer discourse than media in other states would be. However, given that queer voices emerged in the *BFP* only after the *Baker* decision, we believe this was the result of the court decision, which granted some momentary legitimacy to queer voices within the mainstream press rather than being the result of the liberal politics of Vermont alone.

Nonetheless, to fully test this issue, future research would have to examine whether or not a court decision similar to *Baker* had a similar impact in more conservative states.

NOTES

1. Vermont eventually legalized same-sex marriage in 2009.
2. We do not make claims about how this expansive discourse is received by the broader public. Although this is an important question, it is beyond the scope of this study.
3. For example, sociolegal theorists have argued that engagement with the law siphons off important movement resources, including time and money from the political battles that need to be won. Worse yet, legal decisions absent political mobilization could lead to severe backlash, thus harming progressive causes. They argue that the nature of the law and legal institutions preclude any progressive social change. Given that judges themselves operate under majoritarian constraints, they are unlikely to be far ahead of public sentiment. Therefore, social movements would do better to engage in targeted political campaigns, rather than fritter away their time engaging in lawsuits that would at best necessitate prolonged political battles to implement. For responses to these critiques, see McCann (1991, 1994, 1998, 2004; for a recent review, see Bernstein, Marshall, and Barclay 2009). These critiques as applied to the same-sex marriage movement have been debated by a number of theorists (e.g., Andersen 2005; Pierceson 2005). In this chapter, we limit our analysis to an aspect of the issue of normalization, something that has not yet been addressed by this literature.

REFERENCES

ACLU-Vermont. 1996. "ACLU-Vermont Opposes DOMA." *Out in the Mountains* 11 (8) (November): 2.

Altheide, David L. 1987. "Ethnographic Content Analysis." *Qualitative Sociology* 10: 65–77.

Andersen, Ellen Ann. 2005. *Out of the Closets and into the Courts: Legal Opportunity Structure and Gay Rights Litigation.* Ann Arbor: University of Michigan Press.

Armstrong, Elizabeth. 2002. *Forging Gay Identities: Organizing Sexuality in San Francisco, 1950–1994.* Chicago: University of Chicago Press.

Ashby, Carolyn. 2000. "Working within the System Is Inherently Radical." *Out in the Mountains* 15 (1). http://www.mountainpridemedia.org/oitm/issues/2000/feb2000/oe_radical.htm.

Bauman, Richard W. 2002. *Ideology and Community in the First Wave of Critical Legal Studies.* Toronto: University of Toronto Press.

Bernstein, Mary. 1995. "Countermovements and the Fate of Two Morality Policies: Consensual Sex Statutes and Lesbian and Gay Rights Ordinances." Paper presented at the annual meeting for the American Political Science Association, Chicago, Illinois.

———. 2002. "The Contradictions of Gay Ethnicity: Forging Identity in Vermont." In *Social Movements: Identity, Culture, and the State*, edited by David S. Meyer, Nancy Whittier, and Belinda Robnett, 85–104. New York: Oxford University Press.

Bernstein, Mary, Anna-Maria Marshall, and Scott Barclay. 2009. "The Challenge of Law: Sexual Orientation, Gender Identity, and Social Movements." In *Queer Mobilizations: LGBT Activists Confront the Law*, edited by Scott Barclay, Mary Bernstein, and Anna-Maria Marshall, 1–17. New York and London: New York University Press.

Bernstein, Mary, and Nancy A. Naples. 2010. "Sexual Citizenship and the Pursuit of Relationship Recognition Policies in Australia and the U.S." *Women's Studies Quarterly* 38 (1–2): 132–56.

BeyondMarriage.org. 2006. "Beyond Same-Sex Marriage: A New Strategic Vision for All Our Families and Relationships." http://www.beyondmarriage.org/full_state ment.html.

Boellstorff, Tom. 2007. "When Marriage Falls: Queer Coincidences in Straight Time." *GLQ* 13 (2–3): 227–48.

Bower, Lisa. 1997. "Queer Problems/Straight Solutions: The Limits of 'Official Recognition.'" In *Playing with Fire: Queer Politics, Queer Theories*, edited by Shane Phelan, 267–91. New York: Routledge.

Brandzel, Amy L. 2005. "Queering Citizenship? Same-Sex Marriage and the State." *GLQ* 11 (2): 171–204.

Butler, Judith. 2002. "Is Kinship Always Already Heterosexual?" *Differences: A Journal of Feminist Cultural Studies* 13 (1): 14–44.

Cain, Patricia A. 1993. "Litigating for Lesbian and Gay Rights: A History." *Virginia Law Review* 79 (7): 1551–1641.

Case, Mary Anne. 1993. "Couples and Coupling in the Public Sphere: A Comment on the Legal History of Litigating for Lesbian and Gay Rights." *Virginia Law Review* 79 (7): 1643–94.

Cohen, Cathy J. 1997. "Punks, Bulldaggers, and Welfare Queens: The Radical Potential of Queer Politics?" *GLQ* 3: 437–65.

Cohen, Crow. 1999. "On Non-Monogamy." *Out in the Mountains* 3 (9). http://www .mountainpridemedia.org/oitm/issues/1999/jan99/crow.htm.

Dennis, Dion. 1997. "AIDS and the New Medical Gaze: Bio-Politics, AIDS, and Homosexuality." *Journal of Homosexuality* 32 (3–4): 169–84.

Duggan, Lisa. 2003. *The Twilight of Equality? Neoliberalism, Cultural Politics, and the Attack on Democracy*. Boston: Beacon Press.

———. 2004. "Holy Matrimony!" *The Nation*, March 15. http://www.thenation.com/ doc/20040315/duggan.

Duggan, Lisa, and Richard Kim. 2005. "Beyond Gay Marriage." *The Nation*, July 28. http://www.thenation.com/doc/20050718/kim.

Earl, Jennifer. 2004. "The Cultural Consequences of Social Movements." In *The Blackwell Companion to Social Movements*, edited by David A. Snow, Sarah A. Soule, and Hanspeter Kriesi, 508–30. Malden, Mass., and Oxford: Blackwell Publishing.

Epstein, Steven. 1996. *Impure Science: AIDS, Activism, and the Politics of Knowledge.* Berkeley: University of California Press.

Ettelbrick, Paula. 1989. "Since When Is Marriage a Path to Liberation?" *Out/Look* 6: 9.

Ferree, Myra Marx, William A. Gamson, Jürgen Gerhards, and Dieter Rucht. 2002. *Shaping Abortion Discourse: Democracy and the Public Sphere in Germany and the United States.* Cambridge: Cambridge University Press.

Fineman, Martha Albertson. 1995. *The Neutered Mother, the Sexual Family, and Other Twentieth Century Tragedies.* New York: Routledge.

Gamson, William A. 1995. "Constructing Social Protest." In *Social Movements and Culture,* edited by Hank Johnston and Bert Klandermans, 85–106. Minneapolis: University of Minnesota Press.

———. 2005. "Movement Impact on Cultural Change." In *Culture, Power, and History,* edited by Stephen Pfohl, Aimee Van Wagenen, Patricia Arend, Abigail Brooks, and Denise Leckenby, 103–25. Boston: Brill Publishers.

Gamson, William A., and Andre Modigliani. 1989. "Media Discourse and Public Opinion on Nuclear Power: A Constructionist Approach." *American Journal of Sociology* 95 (1): 1–37.

Gay Shame Collective. 2009. "End Marriage." www.gayshamesf.org/endmarriage.

Goslant, Keith. 2002. "I Do Hereby Recognize, Certify and Celebrate." *Out in the Mountains* 16 (6) (July): 9.

Halley, Janet E. 1994. "Reasoning about Sodomy: Act and Identity in and after *Bowers v. Hardwick.*" *Virginia Law Review* 79: 1721–80.

Halley, Janet E., and Wendy Brown, eds. 2003. *Left Legalism/Left Critique.* Durham, N.C.: Duke University Press.

Hartocollis, Anemona. 2006. "For Some Gays, a Right They Can Forsake." *New York Times,* July 30. http://www.nytimes.com/2006/07/30/fashion/sundaystyles/30 MARRIAGE.html?scp=2&sq=%22For+Some+Gays%2C+A+Right+They+Can+ Forsake%22&st=nyt.

Heiwa, Jesse. 1998. "In Defense of Queer." *Out in the Mountains* 3 (3). http://www .mountainpridemedia.org/oitm/issues/1998/jul98/queer.htm.

Ingraham, Chrys. 1996. "The Heterosexual Imaginary: Feminist Sociology and Theories of Gender." In *Queer Theory/Sociology,* edited by Steven Seidman, 168–93. Cambridge, Mass.: Blackwell Publishing.

Lichterman, Paul. 1999. "Talking Identity in the Public Sphere: Broad Visions and Small Spaces in Sexual Identity Politics." *Theory and Society* 28: 101–41.

Mansbridge, Jane, and Katherine Flaster. 2007. "The Cultural Politics of Everyday Discourse: The Case of 'Male Chauvinist.'" *Critical Sociology* 33: 627–60.

McCann, Michael W. 1991. "Legal Mobilization and Social Reform Movements: Notes on Theory and Its Application." *Studies in Law, Politics, and Society* 11: 225–54.

———. 1994. *Rights at Work: Pay Equity Reform and the Politics of Legal Mobilization.* Chicago: University of Chicago Press.

———. 1998. "How Does Law Matter for Social Movements?" In *How Does Law Matter,* edited by Bryant G. Garth and Austin Sarat, 76–108. Evanston, Ill.: Northwestern University Press.

———. 2004. "Law and Social Movements." In *The Blackwell Companion to Law and Society*, edited by Austin Sarat, 506–22. Malden, Mass.: Blackwell Publishing.

Moore, Kelly. 1999. "Political Protest and Institutional Change: The Anti–Vietnam War Movement and American Science." In *How Social Movements Matter*, edited by Marco Giugni, Doug McAdam, and Charles Tilly, 97–115. Minneapolis: University of Minnesota Press.

Murray, Susan, and Beth Robinson. 2000. "Toward Equality." *Out in the Mountains* 15 (2). http://www.mountainpridemedia.org/oitm/issues/2000/mar2000/oe_toward.htm.

Palmgreen, Philip, and Peter Clarke. 1977. "Agenda-Setting with Local and National Issues." *Communication Research* 4: 435–52.

Pierceson, Jason. 2005. *Courts, Liberalism, and Rights: Gay Law and Politics in the United States and Canada*. Philadelphia: Temple University Press.

Polikoff, Nancy D. 1993. "We Will Get What We Ask For: Why Legalizing Gay and Lesbian Marriage Will Not 'Dismantle the Legal Structure of Gender in Every Marriage.'" *Virginia Law Review* 79 (7): 1535–50.

Robinson, Beth. 1996. "Marriage: For Better or Worse." *Out in the Mountains* 1 (30). http://www.mountainpridemedia.org/oitm/issues/1996/0708julyaug1996/pro marri.htm.

Rochon, Thomas R. 1998. *Culture Moves: Ideas, Activism, and Changing Values*. Princeton, N.J.: Princeton University Press.

Rosenberg, Gerald N. 1991. *The Hollow Hope: Can Courts Bring about Social Change?* Chicago: University of Chicago Press.

Sanders, D. B. Skeeter. 1996. "If You Get Married, You Ain't Queer." *Out in the Mountains* 1 (3). http://www.mountainpridemedia.org/oitm/issues/1996/0708julyaug1996/anti marr.htm.

Scheingold, Stuart. [1974] 2004. *The Politics of Rights: Lawyers, Public Policy, and Political Change*. Reprint. Ann Arbor: University of Michigan Press.

Shamas, Bari. 1998. "Vermont Freedom to Marry Task Force Column." *Out in the Mountains* 2 (11). http://www.mountainpridemedia.org/oitm/issues/1998/apr98ftm tfcol.htm.

———. 2000. "Radical Shifts." *Out in the Mountains* 15 (8). http://www.mountainpride media.org/oitm/issues/2000/sep2000/oe04_shift.htm.

Stoddard, Thomas. 1989. "Why Gay People Should Seek the Right to Marry." *Out/Look* 6: 9.

Stychin, Carl F. 2003. *Governing Sexuality: The Changing Politics of Citizenship and Law Reform*. Oxford: Hart Publishing.

Unger, Roberto. 1983. "The Critical Legal Studies Movement." *Harvard Law Review* 96: 561–675.

Walgrave, Stefaan, and Peter Van Aelst. 2006. "The Contingency of the Mass Media's Political Agenda Setting Power: Toward a Preliminary Theory." *Journal of Communication* 56: 88–109.

Walters, Suzanna Danuta. 2001. "The Marrying Kind? Take My Domestic Partner, Please: Gays and Marriage in the Era of the Visible." In *Queer Families, Queer*

Politics: Challenging Culture and the State, edited by Mary Bernstein and Renate Reimann, 338–57. New York: Columbia University Press.

Warner, Michael. 1999a. "Normal and Normaller: Beyond Gay Marriage." *GLQ* 5 (2): 119–71.

———. 1999b. *The Trouble with Normal: Sex, Politics and the Ethics of Queer Life.* New York: Free Press.

Wood, Linda A., and Rolf O. Kroger. 2000. *Doing Discourse Analysis: Methods for Studying Action in Talk and Text.* Thousand Oaks, Calif.: Sage Publications.

10 What Happens When You Get What You Want?

The Relationship between Organizational Identity and Goals in the Movement for Same-Sex Marriage

Kristine A. Olsen

O
N OCTOBER 10, 2008, Connecticut's Supreme Court decided that it was unconstitutional to deny same-sex couples equal access to the institution of marriage. As a result of the ruling in *Kerrigan v. Commissioner of Public Health*, marriage was opened to gay and lesbian couples on November 12 of that year. For Connecticut's most prominent gay and lesbian rights organization, Love Makes a Family (LMF), the outcome marked the end of a decade-long struggle for marriage equality. LMF witnessed a series of successes over the years, including the passage of co-parent adoption and the blocking of a discriminatory DOMA, or "defense of marriage amendment," in 2000. The organization was a repeat player before the state legislature, and along with the group's lobbyist, Betty Gallo & Company, maintained a long-standing and productive relationship with key legislators, including the cochairs of Connecticut's judiciary committee. Over the years, in addition to growing its membership each consecutive year, LMF also increased public support for its cause. Despite a record of successful lobbying, the establishment of routine access to the polity, growing public support for their cause, a large group of committed constituents, and a skilled leadership, in November 2009, just a year after winning marriage, LMF closed its doors for good.

LMF's closure came as a surprise to much of its constituency; its leadership concluded that, with marriage finally secured, the group lacked a clear, defining goal. Other states that have legalized same-sex marriage—such as Massachusetts in 2004 and Vermont in 2009—have retained state-based LGBT rights organizations since winning marriage. Some of the so-called umbrella organizations, such as Mass-Equality, take on multiple and diverse LGBT causes, while others are single-issue organizations focused on expanding marriage equality, such as Vermont Freedom to Marry, whose website proclaimed, "As long as Vermont couples are discriminated against outside our borders and within our state by the federal government, our work for marriage equality continues."[1] While similar preeminent state-based gay and lesbian rights organizations have diversified their objectives, LMF defined its work as done.

Same-sex marriage has become the focal point of the gay and lesbian rights movement in the United States. On the one hand, supporters of same-sex marriage point to their exclusion from an institution that automatically confers myriad benefits, including inheritance rights, financial and medical benefits, and legal decision-making capabilities to recipients, but they also argue that marriage is an important cultural institution from which they are excluded. On the other hand, queer activists have challenged the predominance of same-sex marriage as a movement goal, arguing that expansion of the institution would force gay and lesbian relationships into a heteronormative mold; they have advocated alternative avenues to state-sanctioned benefits, such as alternative relationships and forms of relationship recognition. A recurrent queer concern is that the achievement of same-sex marriage is analogous to the full assimilation of gays and lesbians into society, thus marking the end of a need for activism.

In this chapter, I argue that the relationship between organizational identity and valued goals, as they are defined by activists, plays a significant role in determining when a social movement organization (SMO) defines its work as done. After outlining and evaluating two well-established explanations for SMO continuity and decline—a *resource dependency model* and an *institutionalization model*—I suggest that a third, complementary yet presently underdeveloped *identity model* helps to explain the closure of LMF. Though each model can partially explain the closure of LMF, the resource dependency and institutionalization explanations cannot explain it alone. The identity model attends to the ways that activists define goals that coincide with their shared beliefs, values, and ideological commitments. LMF attracted like-minded individuals to the organization, maintaining a relatively homogenous understanding of the social significance of marriage and, more broadly, the meaning of gay and lesbian equality. For LMF, the construction of same-sex marriage as the pinnacle of movement "success" and a symbol of gay and lesbian equality meant that the organization could define its work as done.

Social movement scholarship addresses the question of organizational decline in three main ways, each with different underlying assumptions about organizational survival and extinction. First, the resource dependency model views the extent to which organizations within the same organizational field compete or cooperate with each other as the primary determinant of the survival of an SMO. Thus, any social movement will face extinction once an organizational field becomes overcrowded and finite resources become too scarce to support the abundance of organizations. Second, the institutionalization model defines social movement success as the establishment of routine access to the polity and treats desired legal outcomes and official recognition of aggrieved groups as success and the endpoint of activism. As applied to the gay and lesbian rights movement, the achievement of same-sex marriage as a form of regular access to state-distributed rights and benefits means formal legal recognition and thus institutionalization, marking the logical end of the movement. A third identity model suggests that the construction of collective identity is necessary not only for mobilization, as it translates individual into group interests, but also for the definition of shared values and goals, and, ultimately, decisions regarding the need for continued demands. The identity boundaries of a given organization are related to the definition of some goals as valued and privileged over others, and whether or not certain goals are even intelligible as such.

DATA AND METHOD

This research is based on fifteen in-depth interviews with key activists involved in the pro-same-sex marriage organization Love Makes a Family (LMF) of Connecticut. Although I do not draw formally on participant observation in this analysis, I volunteered in LMF's Hartford office for approximately one year while the organization was working on its same-sex marriage campaign, and during this period I was able to connect with several key leaders, as well as office employees and volunteers. These initial contacts led to my first interviews with members of the organization. Additional interviewees were selected using snowball sampling procedures, which yielded interviews with leaders of coalition member organizations, and insight into the negotiations that take place when divergent interests are brought to the table.

The interviews were conducted at a location of the interviewee's choosing (mostly private homes, restaurants, coffee shops, and places of employment), and lasted between one and two-and-a-half hours. Although I altered my line of questioning slightly depending on the role of the activist in the organization, interviewees were asked questions related to the same broad topics, including the history of her or his involvement with LMF; ideological commitments to the group and its objectives; strategic preferences; conflict and cooperation among leadership and coalition members; perceptions about the impact of organized opposition; funding decisions and dispersion; diversity within the organization (including race, class, gender identity, and sexual orientation/preference); and, finally, how the participant was involved with and felt about the closing of the organization.

All interviews were fully transcribed and analyzed with the qualitative data analysis software NVivo. My analysis of the interviews was guided especially by social movement scholarship in the areas of identity and strategy, interorganizational dynamics, and coalitions. Using these areas of scholarship as a guide, I designed a preliminary coding scheme and then allowed emergent themes to shape and refine my final categories of analysis, which inform the arguments advanced in this chapter.

THE FORMATION OF LMF

LMF emerged as a coalition of the Connecticut Women's Education and Legal Fund (CWEALF), the Connecticut Civil Liberties Union (now the Connecticut affiliate of the American Civil Liberties Union), the Connecticut Conference of the United Church of Christ, the Permanent Commission on the Status of Women, and the Connecticut Coalition for LGBT Civil Rights. Margaret,[2] a member of one of the founding organizations of the LMF coalition, was highly involved with the Connecticut Coalition for LGBT Civil Rights, an organization that lobbied for and ultimately witnessed the passage of an antidiscrimination bill in 1991. In 1993, LGBT residents would come under attack with the case of "Baby Z," a 1993 court ruling that prevented a lesbian mother's partner from adopting a child that was being raised by both of them. The LMF coalition was formed in response to Baby Z, and it established the family focus of the organization at the outset.

In 2000, not only was LMF victorious in the overturning of the Baby Z decision, effectively implementing co-parent adoption in the state, but also the group lobbied successfully for the extension of a considerable number of rights and benefits for the partners of state employees. At a time when national and international attention was turning to LGBT families, same-sex marriage seemed like the next logical step, according to Margaret. In 2005, the same-sex marriage bill supported by the organization failed to achieve majority support in the state's legislature, but a compromise civil union bill, which LMF opposed because of its treatment of gays and lesbians as "second-class citizens," was passed in its place. Then in 2008, after years of lobbying and gaining support in the legislature, LMF witnessed the final ruling in *Kerrigan*, a court case spearheaded by the national organization Gay and Lesbian Advocates and Defenders (GLAD), and the legalization of same-sex marriage in Connecticut.

After winning marriage in Connecticut, LMF struggled to find a new focus. The organization polled its constituents, but came up empty-handed; though there was some interest in supporting issues like HIV/AIDS, transgender advocacy, and antigay bullying in schools, no clear, defining purpose emerged. After hiring a consultant and communicating with coalition members, the founders of LMF decided it was best to distribute its remaining funds to existing LGBT organizations in the state and disband. In the next section, I examine theoretically why LMF closed its doors.

THE RESOURCE DEPENDENCY MODEL

Those working in the resource mobilization tradition have long recognized the importance of material resources to the operation of SMOs. With the insight that grievances are relatively constant, the resource dependency model suggests that resources, which are best utilized by formalized, professional organizations, are the key to sustained mobilization. Translated into assumptions about organizational survival, as long as a steady supply of financial resources and skilled movement entrepreneurs persists, we should expect an SMO to thrive (Jenkins 1983; McCarthy and Zald 1973, 1977, 1987; Minkoff 1997).

Through empirical investigation, the list of "resources" has been expanded to include not only funding, but also skilled leadership, effective strategies and tactics, constituent support, technology (communications, electronic innovations, etc.), and access to the media, among other things (Haider-Markel 1997; Koopmans 1993; McCarthy and Zald 2001, 536–37; Minkoff 1994, 1995; Soule and King 2008; Zald and McCarthy 1980). LMF arguably had all of these resources in abundance. The president and later executive director of the organization was an Ivy League–educated and highly skilled (though she humbly denies it) public debater with years of experience working for nonprofit organizations. All of the original leaders of member organizations who would eventually staff LMF's board of directors came to the group with considerable experience in nonprofit organization management, and all were college-educated, many having advanced degrees and certifications related to law and public policy.

LMF had highly skilled leadership, a necessary condition of the resource dependency model. The leaders also influenced a string of legal successes, from an early antidiscrimination bill to co-parent adoption, to employee benefits, to civil union and same-sex marriage. With all of these resources available, why did the organization close? One of the most important resources in the resource dependency model is funding. In addition to member donations, the largest source of funding for LMF's legal endeavors came from national LGBT organizations interested in supporting the same-sex marriage battle in key states, especially in the northeast. GLAD, in particular, provided grants to help fund LMF's efforts in Connecticut. Larger, well-funded national organizations help to shape the trajectories of state-based organizations by selecting when and why they will provide additional financial support. LMF activists assessed the national landscape and determined that same-sex marriage *could* become a reality in Connecticut. "Same-sex marriage was due" in Connecticut, as one leader put it. However, it is unlikely that LMF could have retained the same level of funding that it had received from the national organizations for the marriage issue. When I asked about whether other issues, such as antigay bullying or antidiscrimination, could draw such funds, members almost unanimously agreed that they could not, given the current national excitement around and legal emphasis on same-sex marriage.

One major limitation of resource mobilization theory is that it assumes that conflict and competition over resources drive protest cycles (Levitsky 2007), and thus the likelihood that a given organization will close. Some of this competition is alleviated by the division of a crowded social movement field into industries and specialized sectors (McCarthy and Zald 1987, 153). However, eventually competition peaks in a "competitive spiral," in which initiating organizations generally decline, and successor organizations take over (Minkoff 1997, 782, 793; Meyer 1993; Meyer and Imig 1993).

A recent expansion of the resource dependency model suggests that SMOs within the same field may strategically cooperate rather than compete with one another. The niche hypothesis (Levitsky 2007) recognizes that social movements are not homogenous entities, but groups of diverse organizations working together to achieve the same broad goal by targeting multiple social institutions simultaneously (Benford 1993; Haines 1984). For instance, the gay and lesbian rights movement works to achieve greater equality for sexual minorities, but is composed of a multitude of organizations with diverse goals—from legal and policy change to cultural change, to institutional reform—and strategies—from direct action and protest to advocacy, lobbying, and litigation. Niche activism mitigates the weaknesses in the resource dependency model. Recognizing the scarcity of resources, SMOs occupying the same organizational field may strategically cooperate with one another, prioritizing different goals and distributing external resources as they see fit (Levitsky 2007).

Though there were ideological differences between the founding members of LMF, for the most part activists were in agreement that marriage should be the defining issue. LMF worked alongside CWEALF, the Connecticut TransAdvocacy Coalition (CTAC), the Connecticut chapter of Parents, Families, and Friends of Lesbians and Gays (PFLAG), and the Connecticut chapter of the American Civil Liberties Union (ACLU), and all four organizations maintained a member on LMF's board, the main decision-making arm of the organization. Board members whom I spoke with suggested that same-sex marriage was the next logical step in a succession of gay and lesbian rights victories that they had built upon over the years. One apparent advantage of having multiple, single-issue organizations versus one umbrella organization was that each could work relatively independently of the others, applying focused attention and expertise to a range of LGBT issues simultaneously, but then join forces with peer organizations when necessary to combine their strengths and amplify their political power.

Consistent with the niche hypothesis (Levitsky 2007), LMF worked side-by-side with other gay and lesbian rights organizations as they occupied different, complementary spheres of the broader movement. Even though they privileged marriage as a movement goal, my interviewees quickly agreed that since winning marriage there was "still work to be done." Gender-identity antidiscrimination, an issue that was taken up by LMF later in its career but never passed in the legislature, was left unfinished when LMF closed its doors. When asked who would continue this struggle, members pointed to other organizations that were now "better situated" than LMF, they said, to take up these causes. Activists conjured an image of taking turns when they described LMF's time at the top of Connecticut's gay and lesbian rights movement. The organization had had its turn, and, with its main objective achieved, it could step back and allow other LGBT organizations the coveted spot they had occupied. "Well, we still had CTAC," Carolyn explained. "With LMF out of the picture, they could come to the forefront." Margaret concurred with this view. "They [CTAC] really took a back seat while we were working on marriage," she explained. With LMF's objective achieved, CTAC could focus attention on gender-identity antidiscrimination, the next pressing LGBT issue.

Commenting on the degree of organizational specialization she observed, board member Anna suggested that every important LGBT issue already had its own advocacy organization.

> You know, for the schools you have True Colors, you have PFLAG, and they do a great job that we could never have done. . . . And there's CTAC to work on the trans stuff, and there's CWEALF to do gender discrimination . . .

With such a high degree of organizational specialization, LMF leadership felt they could rest assured that all other significant LGBT issues would be sufficiently handled after LMF's closure.

LMF coalition members were keenly aware of the ways in which the political landscape contributed to the prioritization of certain goals over others. With marriage secured, Margaret was certain that the gender-identity antidiscrimination legislation would finally get the attention it deserved. As Margaret predicted, after the organization disbanded, Connecticut did pass gender-identity antidiscrimination legislation, suggesting that institutional constraints had dictated, in part, which LGBT issues would come before the state's legislature and when. Carolyn explained that the legislature would only move on one "gay bill" per session, and that member organizations had decided early on that marriage was the most important one on the table. Once same-sex marriage became a reality and LMF saw its work as done, they distributed their remaining funds, primarily to CWEALF and CTAC. As the niche hypothesis suggests, these organizations within the same field cooperated instead of competing with one another.

THE INSTITUTIONALIZATION MODEL

The institutionalization model views social movements as extrainstitutional actors seeking access to or concessions from a centralized authority or body of decision makers, typically in the form of a state or government. In William Gamson's ([1975] 1990) classic definition, "success" is achieved when activists gain official recognition for new identities, or when they are granted concessions from the state, such as legal and policy gains. In this model, the achievement of routine access to the polity is the desired outcome. Doug McAdam, Sidney Tarrow, and Charles Tilly's (2001) more recent "polity model" suggests that successful social movements ultimately become polity insiders themselves. Once this type of access is established and claim-makers are able to play a regular role in the decision-making process, grievances subside, and the need for an organized extrainstitutional entity declines.

Gaining access to mainstream channels for redress calls for less controversial strategies. LMF spent a considerable amount of time and effort tailoring its strategies to be as nonconfrontational as possible so that the organization could maintain access to key legislators. As Mary Bernstein (1997) argues, when activists seek access to dominant social and political institutions, they choose uncontroversial strategies that emphasize their sameness to the majority, in this case, heterosexuals. Applied to organizational continuity and decline, those organizations that seek reform rather than radical change, and those that have the most broadly appealing, least controversial plans of action are those that have the best life chances (Minkoff 1993, 890; Staggenborg 1988). Institutional conformity is a "survival advantage," according to Debra Minkoff (1993), that ensures that an SMO will continue to maintain elite support. The consequences of seeking access to mainstream social institutions are important to consider. Queer activists and scholars alike see the law as a conservatizing force in the gay and lesbian rights movement that assimilates gays and lesbians while leaving dominant norms intact and pushing other issues affecting the LGBT population to the margins (Bernstein 2001).

By all accounts, LMF maintained a level of institutional support achieved by few other comparable organizations, and its uncontroversial strategies were credited by its members for much of this gain. The organization's ongoing campaign theme of "telling our stories" highlighted the real struggles of gay and lesbian couples and families as they faced discrimination because of their inability to marry. Public judiciary committee hearings on same-sex marriage provided an opportunity for proponents of same-sex marriage to share their experiences with legislators. Although a lottery system was used to select the order of presenters in the daylong hearing, Margaret revealed that LMF ensured that the most compelling testimonials were moved to the head of the line. These hand-selected couples and individuals were chosen because the challenges they faced as a result of their exclusion from marriage and the stories they told resonated most powerfully with legislators. Margaret described the presenter selection process, and how LMF carefully selected couples whose lives would underscore the similarities between gay and straight couples.

> We wanted couples who had been together for a long time, couples with kids. . . . They really personalized and embodied, if you will, quite nicely, the arguments that we were making at the time.

Margaret referred to the strategy of pro-same-sex marriage activists sharing personal experiences with legislators as the "embodiment" of the argument that love, rather than the sexual orientation of members, makes a family. Because its purpose was to evoke sympathy, personalized testimony was both unthreatening and uncontroversial. Activists adopted such strategies in order to gain and to maintain institutional access.

THE IDENTITY MODEL

The identity model focuses on how the organizational structure, strategies, and goals of SMOs resonate with the activists' sense of who they are and what they value. A collective identity is a shared sense of "we-ness" (Hunt and Benford 2004) that is reinforced through movement participation, and "the shared definition of a group that derives from members' common interests, experiences, and solidarity" (Taylor and Whittier 1992, 170; see also Polletta and Jasper 2001). While resource mobilization and collective identity explain different aspects of organizational proliferation, each perspective maintains a different focus. Although both resources *and* reaffirmation of personal values sustain SMOs, we can't fully understand the trajectories of SMOs without attending to the ways that activists' identities and values align with SMO goals.

The identity approach considers the ways activists themselves define and interpret goals, and it can be applied to how and why they respond to shifts in the political landscape. Social movements may seek policy and mobilization outcomes, but they may also exclusively or simultaneously seek cultural outcomes (Bernstein 2003; Earl 2004; Levitsky 2007; Staggenborg 1995), including shifts in values or belief systems, the creation of new collective action frames, tactics, and collective identities, or changes in institutional cultures and practices (see, for instance, Katzenstein 1999), all cultural elements that are beyond the scope of the resource dependency model or the institutionalization model (Goodwin and Jasper 1999; Polletta 1999). Bernstein (2002; Armstrong and Bernstein 2008) argues that the definition of activism as political or cultural is constructed by activists and changes over time. Understanding how activists interpret the importance of different goals, then, is crucial for explaining when and why they respond or not to shifts in the external political environment. When it comes down to it, activists are the ones who construct the meaning associated with their activism and its outcomes.

DEFINING SUCCESS: THE RELATIONSHIP
BETWEEN VALUES AND GOALS

Prior to our interview, which she invited me to conduct in her spacious suburban home, Margaret introduced me to Carol, her partner of over fifteen years, who was hurriedly attending to the couple's two toy poodles. "This is my wife, Carol," she exclaimed with a wide smile. "For a long time I said 'partner,' but I have to be conscientious about referring to her as my wife," she explained, suggesting that using the new terminology available to gay and lesbian couples is an important way to reinforce their newly won equal marital status. Though I did not officially gather information from my interviewees pertaining to socioeconomic status, nearly all of the leadership I encountered could be described as middle or upper middle class. Many had advanced degrees, and were or had been credentialed professionals. Though the constituency of LMF was considerably more diverse along these lines than its leadership, the relationship between racial and class privilege and the prioritization of marriage over other sorts of goals warrants attention.

Diversity is something that LMF struggled with throughout its career. The organization was charged with being "elitist" by other LGBT organizations in the state. As a result it attempted to diversify its board, committees, and constituency by reaching out to working-class gays and lesbians and the transgender and gay Latina/o communities; the latter two groups felt marginalized by LMF, but the organization sought them as allies. After participating in a diversity training program, LMF invited members of Conn-Bi-Nation, a bisexual advocacy group, and CTAC to sit in on its board meetings. Activists agreed that this was a good move, but that it was probably "too little, too late" to do much in the way of diversifying the same-sex marriage movement in Connecticut.

Challenges to heteronormativity posed by queer activists represent another tension within the gay and lesbian rights movement. When presented with queer critiques of the institution of marriage, LMF activists generally responded by constructing same-sex marriage as a challenge to heteronormativity. Although most of LMF's leadership was familiar with queer critiques of marriage, including the argument that marriage is a heterosexist, patriarchal institution, they treated this understanding of marriage as problematic. Instead, marriage was upheld by members as a resounding success for the LGBT community. It makes sense, then, that with same-sex marriage secured by *Kerrigan,* the organization was able to collectively define its work as done.

LMF's goals were circumscribed by the early framing of the organization's purpose, to fight for the equality of gay and lesbian families.

Though they later focused exclusively on marriage, the organization had also supported antidiscrimination initiatives, employee benefits, and co-parent adoption. Still, according to the founding members, marriage was always the focus, and the other issues were constructed as stepping-stones. The organization's title, Love Makes a Family, was narrowly tailored to this issue. The phrase was borrowed, Margaret explained, from a mid-nineties traveling photo display that highlighted diverse family forms, including gay and lesbian families, single-parent families, and extended families. The name was favored by all of the founding members. Once adopted, however, it imposed its own set of limitations on the definition of goals; in Margaret's estimation, though, the name was uncontroversial and unthreatening, which worked to LMF's advantage in the legal arena. "Love Makes a Family" spoke to an apparently universal need as a foundational social institution. Margaret explained that she once longed for the organization to have a more "political" name, like "Connecticut Equality," or "Connecticut Freedom to Marry Coalition," but that the choice to go with "Love Makes a Family" was strategically beneficial in the end because it carefully and cautiously introduced gay and lesbian couples and families to citizens who claimed to lack exposure to them.

> [T]he name ended up being a huge asset to us. . . . "Love Makes a Family" really disarmed, not just opponents, but even more, sort of people who hadn't thought about the issue. Very non-threatening, and it was very, not only non-threatening, but a very positive message.

The "disarming" qualities of "Love Makes a Family" served to legitimate gay and lesbian families, depicting them as acceptable family forms. Members of LMF explained that "family" was a universal concept that everyone could understand and identify with, and in this way the organization's name drew an explicit connection between gays and lesbians and everyone else. Active member John spoke of the increasing diversity of family forms in society, but noted that underneath the superficial differences, all families provide members with the same sorts of support.

Love Makes a Family, well, of course everyone has a family. . . . [T]hey might look a little bit differently, but we all want to have that support, and safety, and security . . . we deserve it. . . . And so that's really what we wanted to drive home.

In defining the organization narrowly around marriage, LMF played on uncontroversial notions of family meant to emphasize the similarities between gay and lesbian families and their straight counterparts.

The goals of LMF were also circumscribed by its focus on marriage through the organization's definition of same-sex marriage as the ultimate gay and lesbian rights victory. Activists viewed the path to marriage as a logical progression of legal gains that could be achieved in a favorable political climate with lawmakers amenable to instituting the desired changes. Antidiscrimination protection was sought first, followed by parental rights and, finally, relationship recognition. The analogy implied by leaders of LMF was one of a hierarchy of family-related rights and benefits, with same-sex marriage at the top, standing as the final hurdle to gay and lesbian equality. Board member Anna explained that when it came to recognizing gay and lesbian families, incremental changes were necessary to gradually gain the support of lawmakers. Once antidiscrimination and co-parenting legislation had passed, marriage was the next logical objective. She explained,

We had done every kind of legal thing you could do to address LGBT civil rights in Connecticut. And so marriage . . . was the issue left, and it was, you know, a really big issue I think for the gay community because they had done all these other things . . . and it was like, just go attack the big issue. . . . We'd done the civil rights bill, we'd done second parent adoption, you know, and I think it was also clear to us how many things we were having to do to, you know, to scaffold our rights . . . for marriage.

The analogy of earlier gay and lesbian rights victories as a "scaffold" for same-sex marriage is particularly revealing, as it suggests that the

360 • Kristine A. Olsen

leadership saw themselves, at least in retrospect, as building a foundation of legal gains in anticipation of the ultimate goal of marriage. Margaret considered this ordering of legal gains to be logical, given the local and national political context.

"Marriage was certainly on our minds," she explained.

> Do you do marriage first, [or] do you do adoption first? I think that in a lot of European countries they did marriage first. . . . I think because the practical needs of parents—same-sex parents—who are adopting kids become clear so quickly, I think that probably . . . [that was] why adoption came first and was happening in different courtrooms around the country. . . . It just, it was before us and we needed to deal with that . . .

Like Anna, Margaret saw a clear chronology of legal victories for the LGBT community. In the case of Connecticut, it made sense to activists to pursue antidiscrimination, then adoption, and finally marriage as the pinnacle of success for the organization.

The closure of LMF at the height of its success suggests that the organization not only defined its work as done, but that it perceived no real threat to its newly won victory. According to leaders, the decision to close an organization at the peak of a win is unusual, but all saw it as exiting the political arena "on a high note," as one member put it. Anna explained how she conversed with the executive directors of several other local progressive political groups to get a sense of how LMF might proceed once same-sex marriage was legalized. She revealed that LMF was considering closing its doors to get their input.

> I mean, I talked to other [executive directors] when it actually happened and they were like, "Wow," because nobody does it. They all fight to the bitter, bitter end until they have like two dollars left and then they're like okay, now close the doors. . . . It was like you were sucking wind. . . . And we did, we went on out on a high, which doesn't happen very often. I was really excited that we did it that way.

Although the decision to close LMF was based in part on the perceived ability of the organization to secure future funding, Patricia constructed marriage to be the high point of LMF's collective work. Carolyn saw the timing of the closing as "fitting," and a great way to exit the legal arena. "We won," she said, "and we can take that away with us."

The strategies adopted by LMF reflected both their narrow organizational identity and their definition of what constituted appropriate expressions of activism, and thus appropriate activists. Throughout the course of its same-sex marriage campaign, LMF used uncontroversial strategies aimed at gaining legislative support. Their emphasis on education was based on the assumption that lawmakers could be persuaded to support same-sex marriage if they could only see gays and lesbians as real people, who experienced all the joys and challenges of life faced by their heterosexual peers, but lacked the legitimacy and legal protections that the lawmakers themselves enjoyed. One of the most successful efforts the organization undertook in its campaign involved holding house parties for legislators at members' homes so that they could see firsthand just how "normal" same-sex couples were. Camila explained,

> If you can connect with them on a personal level; if they can put a face to it, it's much more difficult for them to say, "I'm going to deny you these rights that I have."

It is not surprising, then, that members of LMF commonly expressed a distaste for more radical challenges to culture and the state, including visible displays of disruption and political protest. Camila spoke about the distaste she had for the attention-getting strategies of SMOs like Act Up, a grassroots HIV/AIDS group known for its use of shocking public displays in order to gain media attention and challenge politics as usual. When activists talked about their strategic preferences, I pushed them to define the boundaries of what constituted an appropriate response to the exclusion of gays and lesbians from the institution of marriage. Camila was attracted to LMF because of its uncontroversial methods and the "positive reputation" that the group had achieved in the media and through its activities around the state. To provide a point of contrast, Camila recalled watching same-sex marriage activists on television who were disruptive in order to gain media attention. Referring to a group of activists featured in the news for their public "make out" session, she griped,

> That doesn't jibe with me, 'cause when I'm the person on this side of the TV watching people do that, you usually see a relatively small group of people that are engaged in that, and yeah, it may make the news for a minute or two, but I think it shuts out a person that might really be open to whatever it is you're doing.

Camila clearly sees protest activity that draws attention to the issue of same-sex marriage by shocking its audience as counterproductive. While she admits it gains attention, in her estimation it has no productive long-term effect, and in fact might exclude would-be supporters who could further grow the movement.

Rhonda, a former community organizer, also indicated that she was drawn to LMF because of the organization's philosophy of using education to "change hearts and minds," as she put it. "[T]hat's what attracted me to Love Makes a Family," she recalled as she reflected on her decision to become more involved in the organization's steering committee, the group responsible for the direction of the organization. Like Camila, Rhonda viewed radical tactics as antithetical to movement progress. As she saw it, this sort of strategy dissuaded potential supporters. She also expressed support for the educational approach taken by LMF, a strategy that resonated with her on a personal and emotional level.

LMF probably also dissuaded queer activists from becoming involved with the organization. When the organization closed, it sent all existing members information about other local gay and lesbian rights organizations that they could support, including CTAC, CWEALF, the ACLU of Connecticut, the Connecticut AIDS Resource Coalition, Connecticut Latina/os Achieving Rights and Opportunities, Conn-Bi-Nation, the Gay, Lesbian and Straight Education Network, Pride at Work, and True Colors, an organization dedicated to supporting LGBT youth. However, when I asked Carolyn how many of LMF's constituents had actually joined these organizations as a result, she estimated, "only a couple." This again suggests that same-sex marriage narrowly defined the members' purpose in the movement. It is likely that LMF attracted and retained constituents with similar views of LGBT equality, and that LMF's prioritization of marriage further reinforced the primacy of this goal.

Although LMF's board members claimed that most decisions regarding the direction of the organization were arrived at amicably and democratically, when the group opened its meetings to include members of the transgender and bisexual communities, tensions arose between same-sex marriage advocates and critics. Representatives from CTAC and Conn-Bi-Nation, an organization that promoted advocacy around and visibility of bisexuals, were potential allies who stood to diversify the organization, but were peripheral to LMF's progress on the marriage campaign. Anna described her frustration with meeting attendees who did not stick to the same-sex marriage agenda. In the following passage she recalls a particularly vocal individual who warned that LMF was too exclusive and elitist, and that its focus on marriage marginalized sexual minorities who did not identify as "gay" or "lesbian." At meetings, these attendees hindered deliberations.

> [Fred] would typically slow things down, like if we had an item that we really needed to discuss and that was the priority, and here I am after already a long day, you know, and he would be like . . . if you said "gay and lesbian," he would chime in with, "and bi" . . . we're trying to get something accomplished and he's correcting speech.

When LMF turned its full attention to marriage, Fred charged that the organization had lost its subversive character. Anna recalled that at that point, "[W]e still had people who were trying to be kind of grassrootsy, and for me it was exhausting." These challenges illustrate not only the exclusivity that comes with prioritizing marriage, but also the apparent retreat from subversive politics that stems from seeking access to, rather than challenging, a dominant social institution such as marriage.

Critiques of marriage, by and large, were deemed nonproductive among the activists I interviewed. At the same time that they defined marriage as the most important objective of the gay and lesbian rights movement, activists both sympathized with and expressed frustration over the efforts of others to critique marriage. While most activists were aware of queer critiques of marriage as a patriarchal, heterosexist, monogamous institution, they expressed little or no direct support for this position, seeing it as counterproductive to their cause.

Rather than dispute queer critiques of marriage, many of my interviewees constructed marriage, and their involvement in the same-sex marriage movement generally, as a challenge to the existing gender order and to heteronormativity. In this way they were able to position themselves as participating in a form of subversive politics, which had the effect of making queer critiques appear extreme or extraneous. Margaret shared her thoughts on the criticisms of marriage that came from within the gay and lesbian community:

> I think that there were certainly segments of the community, and I think those tended to be . . . the more traditional feminist segments who felt like marriage was a bad institution, it was a patriarchal institution. . . . That it was oppressive, heteronormative, all of those things, and why would we want to replicate an institution that had been so detrimental to women.

She then suggested that gays and lesbians stood to redefine marriage and gender relations from the inside out.

> My feeling was always that . . . having gay and lesbian people as a part of marriage would actually help diminish a lot of those sexual stereotypes and gender roles, and I think that it is starting to do that.

Mark expressed a similar view of same-sex marriage as a challenge to heteronormativity. After admitting that he was aware of struggles to make "alternative" relationships visible, he went on to explain how he felt his own heterosexual marriage challenged traditional gender roles, which reflected the view of the same-sex marriage movement that institutions could be meaningfully transformed from the inside out.

> I get it [the queer critique of marriage], but then I also have a personal experience of being now in a fifteen-year marriage that works remarkably well that is, I think, antisexist, and where I think if you came in our house and you followed us around you would see . . . a complete absence of gender roles.

John was in partial agreement with the queer critique of marriage as a heterosexist, patriarchal institution that should be challenged rather than reinforced. However, he also viewed the critique as impractical or even nonproductive, considering the current trajectory of the gay and lesbian rights movement. He explained that while he could support the rejection of the institution of marriage "in theory," in practice there was little value in challenging marriage "for the sake of it." He had been instrumental in organizing religious leadership in support of same-sex marriage, and described the symbolic importance of having clergy involved as part of the "culture-building" that was necessary groundwork for passing same-sex marriage in the state. He struggled, however, to conceive of a social movement that sought to critique or deconstruct marriage: "[I]f there was a way for that to be [*pauses, laughs*], for a political movement to develop around that," he mused, "I might get involved, if I thought it was going to be effective, but I think I only have so much time on this earth, and we're not going to get rid of marriage."

In defining same-sex marriage as a challenge to the existing gender order, some LMF members both expressed guarded support for and simultaneously distanced themselves from queer critiques of marriage.

John also suggested that some queer critiques of heterosexual and monogamous relationships may reinforce, rather than challenge, gender inequality. For instance, he expressed his disapproval of polyamory, or intimate relationships with more than one partner simultaneously, which he viewed as analogous to polygamy, which he stated was oppressive to women. Peter recalled when a representative from Conn-

Bi-Nation approached LMF about pursuing an alternative to marriage that would legally recognize polyamorous relationships. His thoughts on this prospect are telling; he likens the arguments of Conn-Bi-Nation to those of the Family Institute of Connecticut (FIC), a longtime vocal opponent of same-sex marriage in the state.

> We said we'd consider it [supporting polyamorous relationships], but, um, in my view it would be totally destructive of what we were trying to accomplish to argue for those things because that's just what we hear from the likes of Brian Brown,[3] that this is a slippery slope that . . . [will lead to] a bunch of things including polyamory and multi-spouse marriage and bestiality and all the rest.

Including polyamory in its agenda would undoubtedly delegitimize LMF's claims to marriage. Both John and Peter could not understand the purpose of embracing polyamory, since they see it as being at odds with the purpose of marriage. Their disavowal of alternative relationship forms and embrace of the state-sanctioned relationship of marriage reveals the continued tension between queer and gay and lesbian rights activism.

Generally, the LMF leadership expressed the belief that society's institutions should be reformed rather than radically altered or rejected. Activists explained the desire to reform marriage as a matter of giving all citizens equal access, whether or not individuals chose to participate. Karen explained her desire to see marriage broadened to include gays and lesbians in a way that did not explicitly reject the critiques, but reoriented the matter to be about choice:

> [W]e needed to view it similarly to the fight against Don't Ask, Don't Tell, you know, not everybody wants to be in the military, not everybody supports the military, but, you know, as citizens LGBT people need to have the choice.

In emphasizing "choice," some activists alleviated the tension between supporters and critics of marriage by arguing that, even if you criticized the institution of marriage, as a citizen you still were entitled to the choice.

Although LMF probably attracted and retained like-minded individuals, it is also likely that the group's views on the significance of marriage influenced constituents. One activist in my sample expressed more explicit disdain for same-sex marriage, but maintained her support for LMF's work nonetheless, suggesting that the group's definition of valued goals affected the members' commitments to the group's agenda, even when it did not expressly fit with their own values. Amanda recalled that she was more dedicated to and active in an earlier campaign for co-parent adoption than the campaign for same-sex marriage. She attributed this in part to her disappointment with LMF's single-issue focus on marriage, which invalidated alternative relationships and forms of relationship recognition, or even the preference to remain unmarried. "I mean, I'm not a huge fan of marriage," she said.

> I'm kind of [from] the old school where marriage was created to help us protect our stuff, and so, . . . instead of figuring out how people can protect their stuff within this socially prescribed union thing, maybe we should look at how we can ensure that people have access to needs and whatever, and don't have to actually get married to do it.

Despite her critique of marriage and desire for an alternative, Amanda defined the achievement of same-sex marriage as an important goal for the gay and lesbian movement as a whole. Significantly, she also expressed disappointment over LMF's closing, and explained that she wished the group had used its influence to bring much-needed attention to other LGBT issues. She envisioned the organization as an umbrella gay and lesbian rights group for the state of Connecticut, overseeing the activities of other, smaller gay and lesbian rights organizations. Notably, when she worked with LMF, Amanda was also the most instrumental in heading transgender antidiscrimination initiatives, a cause that, unlike marriage, she felt she could commit to and wholeheartedly support.

LMF's focus on marriage not only circumscribed its goals, but also, in the view of its members, helped the organization to be influential among public officials, especially those legislators who were so-called fence-sitters and likely to be persuaded by unthreatening strategies. Instead of directly opposing queer critiques that challenge or deconstruct mainstream social institutions, activists chose to define their support for marriage as a challenge to the institution that had the potential to transform it from the inside out.

STRATEGY, IDENTITY, AND ORGANIZED OPPOSITION

Social movement scholars have researched the myriad ways that opposing social movements influence one another (e.g., Dugan 2004; Esacove 2004; Fetner 2001; Hull 2001; McCaffrey and Keys 2000; Rohlinger 2002). The FIC, LMF's most vocal opponent in the legislative arena, provided a foil against which they could further legitimize their claims and win the support of public officials. While the challenge presented by the FIC might have provided a reason for LMF to remain active in the political arena, its failure to provide any real threat left the group confident that the organization could not repeal the gains that had been made. In fact, the FIC's perceived extremism was an asset to LMF, whose claims, as a result, were legitimized.

The FIC emerged shortly after the founding of LMF and created its political action and lobbying arm in 2004, the year that LMF saw the introduction of a marriage-equality bill. The FIC opposed not only same-sex marriage, but also any form of legal recognition for same-sex couples and their families. The organization gained support from a large number of Connecticut voters and was perhaps most successful in mobilizing opponents of same-sex marriage through the church. A 2005 rally at the state's Capitol reportedly drew thousands, as FIC planned its protest on a Sunday so that churchgoers could be bused directly from Sunday services to the state Capitol in Hartford.

Despite winning the support of a large number of Connecticut residents, however, the FIC failed to garner much support in the state legislature. My respondents suggested that the FIC's religious opposition to same-sex marriage and general disavowal of gay civil rights was off-putting to many legislators. Members of LMF explained that the

FIC's generally unpopular position in the legislature helped to further legitimate their own cause. As Carolyn explained,

> [T]he fact is that they're not well respected at the Capitol. I mean, they're sort of viewed as a crazy group, except by the other crazy legislators, but most legislators are like, "These guys are nuts!"

Other members echoed this view, arguing that the FIC helped rather than hurt their cause. The FIC's opposition to LMF enhanced the effectiveness of LMF's uncontroversial strategies and further solidified their image as families that were "just like everyone else." "They gave us a great nemesis," said Anna.

> They embodied the worst of the opposition, and their director [Brian Brown] was hideous. . . . I thought it was easier in some ways to bring people around to our side because when you saw the opposition, you said, "Oh my God, I am not them!"

Camila agreed, indicating that the presence of the FIC helped to polarize the debate, positioning LMF as the victim, and therefore deserving of defense.

> They were good because if we hadn't had a good vocal opponent, it would have been harder to separate the good guys from the bad guys.

The FIC's relative extremism helped LMF's cause, further legitimizing their claims that gay and lesbian families were just like heterosexual families and thus entitled to the same rights and benefits.

Margaret explained that the FIC had tried to challenge the notion that love alone makes a family, but suggested that this counterframe did not advance their arguments against same-sex marriage. The FIC, she recounted, argued that if love alone made a family, by this logic the government should also allow siblings who love one another to marry, or allow three people who love one another to marry, the so-called slippery slope argument. In her opinion, this approach did not sway many legislators on the issue. Instead they were more inclined to sympathize with the idea that, because of their similarities to heterosexual families, gay and lesbian families were deserving of similar sorts of rights, benefits, dignity, and legitimacy.

Though LMF no longer exists as a formal organizational entity, former members expressed little concern over the future activities of the FIC. Specifically, since same-sex marriage was defined as the ultimate marker of gay and lesbian equality, once it was secured, the FIC no longer posed a threat. "I guess we felt like they're sort of irrelevant now," Carolyn explained.

> I think they're still trying to be relevant, but they're trying to find a reason to exist because there's nothing to oppose anymore.

Amanda's assessment of the FIC's potential future impact was similar. "Yeah, I mean they're making some noise but nobody's really listening," she said. "Nobody important, anyway." Activists agreed that when LMF was in its prime, the FIC helped them to further their cause. Since they narrowly defined same-sex marriage as equivalent to gay and lesbian equality, when LMF closed, the FIC ceased to be relevant.

CONCLUSION

Queer concerns over the assimilationist tendencies of contemporary gay and lesbian politics, especially those pertaining to the same-sex marriage movement, have garnered considerable attention from scholars. My findings show that the assimilation/deconstruction dichotomy, which equates same-sex marriage with the promotion of heteronormativity, lacks an understanding of the diverse ways that activists define subversive politics. Social movement scholarship can shed light on this matter by recognizing that the movement for marriage equality is about much more than reinforcing *or* challenging heteronormative institutions; it's also about the ways that activists construct their work as meaningful under a given set of institutional opportunities and constraints. Although activists were uncritical of the institution of marriage, they also defined efforts to achieve same-sex marriage as subversive, either by arguing that marriage could be transformed from the inside out, as more diverse couples wed, or by arguing that marriage and queer critiques of marriage were not necessarily incompatible. While LMF intentionally utilized uncontroversial strategies that emphasized lesbian and gay similarities to the straight majority, they simultaneously sought to challenge stereotypes about gays and lesbians through the redefinition of gender roles and hierarchies.

In seeking to approximate heterosexual relationships, however, the same-sex marriage movement has simultaneously marginalized other sexual minorities, such as transgender and bisexual individuals, as well as poor gays and lesbians, and gay people of color. Perhaps the issue of greatest concern is that the achievement of same-sex marriage became the apparent endpoint of organization-based LGBT activism for nearly all of LMF's constituents. With marriage secured, members were not moved to take up other pressing LGBT causes. The relationship between individual values and organizational values is likely reciprocal: LMF attracted like-minded individuals, while its intensified focus on marriage further influenced its members' priorities.

In terms of social movement scholarship, this research suggests that resources and institutional access only partially explain organizational continuity and decline. The relationship between identity and valued goals shows us that the ways that activists justify their priorities helps to explain how they determine when their work is done. A fruitful direction for future research would involve comparing the trajectories of LGBT organizations like LMF that closed once achieving their goals with those that have revised their objectives after successfully reaching previous goals. Through such an analysis we can isolate political, cultural, and institutional factors that affect organizational continuity and decline.

NOTES

1. See http://www.vtfreetomarry.org/.
2. All names are pseudonyms.
3. Brian Brown is the former executive director of the Family Institute of Connecticut. He is currently the president of the National Organization for Marriage.

REFERENCES

Armstrong, Elizabeth, and Mary Bernstein. 2008. "Culture, Power, and Institutions: A Multi-Institutional Politics Approach to Social Movements." *Sociological Theory* 26 (1): 74–99.

Benford, Robert D. 1993. "Frame Disputes within the Nuclear Disarmament Movement." *Social Forces* 71: 677–701.

Bernstein, Mary. 1997. "Celebration and Suppression: The Strategic Uses of Identity by the Lesbian and Gay Movement." *American Journal of Sociology* 103 (3): 531–65.

———. 2001. "Gender, Queer Family Policies, and the Limits of the Law." In *Queer Families, Queer Politics: Challenging Culture and the State*, edited by Mary Bernstein and Renate Reimann, 420–46. New York: Columbia University Press.

———. 2002. "The Contradictions of Gay Ethnicity: Forging Identity in Vermont." In *Social Movements: Identity, Culture, and the State*, edited by David S. Meyer, Nancy Whittier, and Belinda Robnett, 85–104. New York: Oxford University Press.

———. 2003. "Nothing Ventured, Nothing Gained? Conceptualizing Social Movement 'Success' in the Lesbian and Gay Movement." *Sociological Perspectives* 46 (3): 353–79.

Dugan, Kimberly B. 2004. "Strategy and 'Spin': Opposing Movement Frames in an Anti-Gay Voter Initiative." *Sociological Focus* 37: 213–33.

Earl, Jennifer. 2004. "The Cultural Consequences of Social Movements." In *The Blackwell Companion to Social Movements*, edited by David A. Snow, Sarah A. Soule, and Hanspeter Kriesi, 508–30. Malden, Mass., and Oxford: Blackwell Publishing.

Esacove, Anne W. 2004. "Dialogic Framing: The Framing/Counterframing of 'Partial-Birth' Abortion." *Sociological Inquiry* 74: 70–101.

Fetner, Tina. 2001. "Working Anita Bryant: The Impact of Christian Anti-Gay Activism on Lesbian and Gay Movement Claims." *Social Problems* 48: 411–28.

Gamson, William A. [1975] 1990. *The Strategy of Social Protest*. 2nd ed. Belmont, Calif.: Wadsworth.

Goodwin, Jeff, and James M. Jasper. 1999. "Caught in a Winding, Snarling Vine: The Structural Bias of Political Process Theory." *Sociological Forum* 14: 27–54.

Haider-Markel, Donald P. 1997. "Interest Group Survival: Shared Interests versus Competition for Resources." *Journal of Politics* 59: 903–12.

Haines, Herbert. 1984. "Black Radicalization and the Funding of Civil Rights: 1957–1970." *Social Problems* 36 (1): 31–43.

Hull, Kathleen E. 2001. "The Political Limits of the Rights Frame: The Case of Same-Sex Marriage in Hawaii." *Sociological Perspectives* 44: 207–32.

Hunt, Scott A., and Robert D. Benford. 2004. "Collective Identity, Solidarity, and Commitment." In *The Blackwell Companion to Social Movements*, edited by David A. Snow, Sarah A. Soule, and Hanspeter Kriesi, 433–57. Malden, Mass., and Oxford: Blackwell Publishing.

Jenkins, J. Craig. 1983. "Resource Mobilization Theory and the Study of Social Movements." *Annual Review of Sociology* 9: 527–33.

Katzenstein, Mary Fainsod. 1999. *Faithful and Fearless: Moving Feminist Protest inside the Church and Military*. Princeton, N.J.: Princeton University Press.

Koopmans, Ruud. 1993. "The Dynamics of Protest Waves: West Germany, 1965 to 1989." *American Sociological Review* 58: 637–58.

Levitsky, Sandra R. 2007. "Niche Activism: Constructing a Unified Movement Identity in a Heterogeneous Organizational Field." *Mobilization* 12: 271–86.

McAdam, Doug, Sidney Tarrow, and Charles Tilly. 2001. *Dynamics of Contention*. Cambridge: Cambridge University Press.

McCaffrey, Dawn, and Jennifer Keys. 2000. "Competitive Framing Processes in the Abortion Debate: Polarization-Vilification, Frame Saving, and Frame Debunking." *The Sociological Quarterly* 41: 41–61.

McCarthy, John D., and Mayer N. Zald. 1973. *The Trend of Social Movements in America: Professionalization and Resource Mobilization*. Morristown, N.J.: General Learning Press.

——. 1977. "Resource Mobilization and Social Movements: A Partial Theory." *American Journal of Sociology* 82: 1212–41.

——. 1987. "The Trend of Social Movements in America: Professionalization and Resource Mobilization." In *Social Movements in an Organizational Society: Collected Essays*, edited by Mayer N. Zald and John D. McCarthy, 337–91. New Brunswick, N.J.: Transaction Books.

——. 2001. "The Enduring Vitality of the Resource Mobilization Theory of Social Movements." In *Handbook of Sociological Theory*, edited by Jonathan H. Turner, 533–65. New York: Springer.

Meyer, David S. 1993. "Protest Cycles and Political Process: American Peace Movements in the Nuclear Age." *Political Research Quarterly* 46 (3): 451–79.

Meyer, David S., and Douglas R. Imig. 1993. "Political Opportunity and the Rise and Decline of Interest Group Sectors." *Social Science Journal* 3: 253–70.

Minkoff, Debra. 1993. "The Organization of Survival: Women's and Racial-Ethnic Voluntarist and Activist Organizations, 1955–1985." *Social Forces* 71: 887–908.

——. 1994. "From Service Provision to Institutional Advocacy: The Shifting Legitimacy of Organizational Forms." *Social Forces* 72: 943–69.

——. 1995. "Interorganizational Influences on the Founding of African American Organizations, 1955–1985." *Sociological Forum* 10: 51–79.

——. 1997. "The Sequencing of Social Movements." *American Sociological Review* 62: 779–99.

Polletta, Francesca. 1999. "Snarls, Quacks, and Quarrels: Culture and Structure in Political Process Theory." *Sociological Forum* 14: 63–70.

Polletta, Francesca, and James Jasper. 2001. "Collective Identity and Social Movements." *Annual Review of Sociology* 27: 283–305.

Rohlinger, Deana A. 2002. "Framing the Abortion Debate: Organizational Resources, Media Strategies, and Movement-Countermovement Dynamics." *The Sociological Quarterly* 43: 479–507.

Soule, Sarah A., and Brayden King. 2008. "Competition and Resource Partitioning in Three Social Movement Industries." *American Journal of Sociology* 113 (6): 1568–1610.

Staggenborg, Suzanne. 1988. "The Consequences of Professionalization and Formalization in the Pro-Choice Movement." *American Sociological Review* 53: 585–606.

———. 1995. "Can Feminist Organizations Be Effective?" In *Feminist Organizations: Harvest of the New Women's Movement*, edited by Myra Marx Ferree and Patricia Yancey Martin, 339–55. Philadelphia: Temple University Press.

Taylor, Verta, and Nancy E. Whittier. 1992. "Collective Identity in Social Movement Communities: Lesbian Feminist Mobilization." In *Frontiers in Social Movement Theory*, edited by Aldon Morris and Carol McClurg Mueller, 104–30. New Haven, Conn.: Yale University Press.

Zald, Mayer N., and John D. McCarthy. 1980. "Social Movement Industries: Competition and Cooperation among Movement Organizations." In *Research in Social Movements, Conflict and Change*, edited by Louis Kriesberg, 3: 1–20. Greenwich, Conn.: JAI Press.

11 Debating Same-Sex Marriage

Lesbian and Gay Spouses
Speak to the Literature

Adam Isaiah Green

S AME-SEX CIVIL MARRIAGE is increasingly a legal reality for lesbian and gay couples throughout North America and Western Europe. And yet, if there is a dearth of empirical attention to same-sex marriage, there has been no lack of speculation on the topic as activists and social critics contemplate the social consequences of same-sex marriage from a wide spectrum of cultural and political standpoints. Typically, these standpoints are marked by distinct forecasts regarding the effects of same-sex marriage on same-sex couples and on the larger society. Ranging from optimistic to apocalyptic, competing forecasts of the effects of state-sanctioned same-sex marriage have produced a lively field of contentious debate, but have done far less to shed light on same-sex marriage as a lived institution.

In this chapter, I draw on thirty in-depth interviews of same-sex spouses residing in and around Toronto, Canada, to explore how actual same-sex marriages relate to this field of debate. Taken as a whole, these cases defy reduction to the forecasts of either the proponents or opponents of same-sex marriage but instead present a more complex sociological picture of assimilation and innovation than has been developed in the literature. In sociological terms, the complexity of these marriages is perhaps not surprising, since North American lesbians and gay men are *dually* socialized, first in the dialectic of a dominant "meaning-constitutive" tradition (Gross 2005) that valorizes (heterosexual) marriage and kinship, and second, in a "queer meaning-constitutive" tradition based in sexual freedom and nontraditional gender relations (Herdt 1992; Weeks, Heaphy, and Donovan 2001). In this sense, one important sociological question for the future is whether the availability of same-sex marriage will transform the dialectic, eroding the structural conditions that underpin a distinctive queer meaning-constitutive tradition and, in turn, same-sex marital innovation.

Below, I outline three broad positions that dominate the discourse on state-sanctioned same-sex marriage, including social conservative, critical feminist/queer, and lesbian and gay assimilationist positions, and highlight their respective forecasts regarding the effects of same-sex marriage. A methods section outlines the sampling and data analysis procedures of this study. Then, two data sections draw attention to the ways in which actual same-sex marriages both consolidate and subvert the "traditional" marital form of twentieth-century, middle-class North America—that is, a marital relation with norms and practices that include monogamy, reproduction, and a gendered division of labor (Coontz 2000; Cott 2000). A final discussion compares the findings of this study to the extant debates on the topic and advances important lines of inquiry derived from the study's conclusions.

FORECASTING SAME-SEX MARRIAGE: DEBATES IN THE LITERATURE

State-sanctioned marriage is a protean institution with a contentious history marked by competing claims of inclusion and citizenship (Josephson 2005). Forecasts regarding the effects of same-sex marriage, including how same-sex married couples will affect and be affected by the institution of marriage, have been no less divided. Here, "pro" and "con" positions on same-sex marriage are distinguished not only by divergent prognostications of what will become of the institution should lesbians and gays be granted civil marriage, but also, in some instances, by opposing normative evaluations of the same forecast.[1] While individual positions within this debate are irreducible to political, religious, or academic affiliation, it is possible to identify at least three broad perspectives within the activist and academic literature, including social conservative, critical feminist/queer, and lesbian and gay assimilationist positions. Below, I offer a selective review of these positions in order to provide a context for their respective predictions of the effects of same-sex marriage.[2]

Social Conservative and Critical Feminist/Queer: Critics of Same-Sex Marriage

Within the activist and academic literature, social conservatives and critical feminist/queer theorists represent an internally differentiated contingent deeply critical of same-sex marriage. Social conservatives worry that same-sex marriage will undermine the stability of traditional, nuclear families and the sanctity of marriage, while critical feminist/queer theorists are concerned that same-sex marriage will reinforce patriarchal and heteronormative[3] relations. They thus advance opposing forecasts of the effects of same-sex marriage even as they both reject the institution for lesbians and gays.

Social conservatives regard heterosexual marriage as the foundation of society. Based in gender complementarity, monogamous partnership, and nuclear families, heterosexual marriage is believed to constitute the optimal condition for raising healthy, moral children and, in turn, a healthy, moral society (Dobson 2004; Elshtain 1991; Lutzer 2004). Same-sex marriage, by contrast, cannot serve this function, in part because, while the heterosexual libido can be "tamed" by the institution of marriage, homosexuals are themselves incapable of or unwilling to subscribe to marital fidelity. Grounded in reproduction (Christensen 2004; Dobson 2004), the heterosexual marital bond "civilizes" men by channeling sexual desire into a reproductive bounty and establishing paternity, both of which stabilize the dyad and the social order. Same-sex marriage, by contrast, will set a bad precedent for susceptible heterosexual youth because "unisex marriage" decouples childbearing from marriage and undermines traditional norms and practices associated with marital monogamy. Thus Maggie Gallagher (2003) worries: "I am sure unisex marriage will dramatically affect the cultural norms and values of the next generation in ways that will encourage divorce and disconnect marriage further from childbearing." And Stephen Baskerville (2006) posits that same-sex marriage will end fatherhood and, in turn, destabilize civilization. In this sense,

heteronormative
patriarchal
bullshit

opposition to same-sex marriage represents an impassioned battle for the very salvation of civilization: "Marriage turns a man from a sperm donor into a parent, and thus creates paternal authority. . . . [I]t is the presence of the father that creates both the intact family and, by the same measure, the civil institution itself" (Baskerville 2006).

By contrast, where social conservatives see in same-sex marriage the downfall of patriarchal relations and the demise of civilization, a contingent of feminists and queer theorists see the opposite: the consolidation of patriarchal relations, the bolstering of a social order organized around sexism and gender inequality, and the disciplining of a new, assimilated queer subject. While these feminist and queer discourses are not interchangeable, their mutual critique of heteronormativity contains an important element of correspondence regarding same-sex marriage.

That a contingent of feminists—what Jyl Josephson refers to as "lesbian feminists" (2005, 274)—would be critical of same-sex marriage is perhaps not surprising, given the more general feminist criticism of the institution of marriage as a fundamental source of women's oppression (Bevacqua 2004; Rich 1980).[4] Thus it is not a huge leap to imagine same-sex marriage as a "sell out" (Baird and Rosenbaum 1997, 11), a tool of male domination incapable of rehabilitation (Saalfield 1993) and unworthy of queer struggle (Ettelbrick [1989] 1997). "For feminists, the question of lesbian and gay marriage is, or should be, inextricably bound to the ongoing critique of marriage as an institution" (Bevacqua 2004, 36).

Historical considerations aside, feminists critical of same-sex marriage forecast that the institution will colonize gays and lesbians, producing institutionalized gender-role-differentiated marriages and a new kind of same-sex, nuclear "patriarchal family" based in monogamy, parenthood, and the conception of partners as property (Auchmuty 2004; Lehr 1999; Walters 2001). Hence, Gust Yep, Karen Lovaas, and John Elia (2003, 56) write: "[I]t is reasonable to believe that same-sex marriages might reproduce conventional gender roles . . . [and] the kind of containment and control that has been so much a part of heterosexuality."

In a related analysis, queer theorists (who may be feminist-identified, too) regard the institution of marriage as a governing relation by which the state transforms docile liberal subjects into self-regulating domestic citizenry (Butler 2002; Duggan 2002; Warner 1999). Marriage is not only a site of sexual regulation and social control but, more important, it is an institution of normalization in which the married are rendered "normal," healthy and moral, and the unmarried "abnormal," unhealthy and deviant.[5] Like feminists before them, queer theorists envision an emancipatory project rooted in resistance to normalization through practices that defy normative intimate life. Thus Paula Ettelbrick ([1989] 1997) writes: "Being queer means pushing the parameters of sex, sexuality and family, and in the process transforming the very fabric of society." In a similar vein, Duggan (2002, 176), alarmed by the prospect of same-sex marriage and the broader politics of queer assimilation, advances the term *homonormativity* to signal a hegemonic lesbian and gay culture now wholly unmoored from its roots in the radical liberationist politics of the 1970s. And Mariana Valverde (2006) "half jokingly but half seriously" (156) finds in same-sex marriage the birth of the "respectable same-sex couple" (156)—a new social entity composed of same-sex individuals for whom the radical marginality of homosexuality is now long gone. "Bank loans, florists' bills, joint bank accounts, renovated gentrified downtown homes, and worries about the relatives are the pieces that make up the new, post-homosexual entity that Canadian jurisprudence has helped to fabricate: the respectable 'same-sex' couple" (Valverde 2006, 162).

Lesbian and Gay Assimilationists: Proponents of Same-Sex Marriage

Proponents of same-sex marriage typically advance a liberal, rights-based discourse in support of extending the institution to same-sex couples. Here, marriage is understood to confer a wide range of benefits to which lesbian and gay couples are entitled, including those related to inheritance, health benefits, taxation, parenting, and childcare (Eskridge and Spedale 2006). Lesbian and gay assimilationists regard same-sex marriage as an especially important entitlement because the institution is predicted to bring stability to the same-sex dyad. Recalling some of the virtues attached to heterosexual marriage by social conservatives, lesbian and gay assimilationists forecast that same-sex marriage will strengthen same-sex relationships by reining in the libido and promoting monogamy (Hausknecht 2003; Rotello 1997; A. Sullivan 1996). In fact, Hausknecht argues that, without the right to marry, gay men are propelled into "disorderly" sexual careers characterized by high rates of multiple sexual partners: "If marriage does discipline sex, then those denied its benefits can more easily drift into a life of disorderly promiscuous sex. This is precisely the situation of gay men" (2003, 9). Similarly, Andrew Sullivan (1996, 254) employs the metaphor of an "anchor" to describe the stabilizing effects of marriage for same-sex couples. Rooted in norms of monogamy, same-sex marriage is said to promote marital fidelity when "human virtue" fails.

To conclude, forecasts regarding the effects of state-sanctioned same-sex marriage take a variety of forms and are distinguished, in part, either by divergent predictions or by diverging normative evaluations of the same prediction.

METHODS

This study is based on thirty semi-structured in-depth interviews of legally married lesbian and gay spouses residing in two urban centers in Ontario, Canada. Fifteen lesbians and fifteen gay men were recruited between 2005 and 2007 through public advertisements and solicitations at local lesbian and gay organizations. Each respondent had been married to a same-sex partner for at least one year. Respondents were between twenty-six and sixty-one years old. With the exception of two spouses, the same-sex spouses of this study identified as white.[6] Most of the sample is university educated; they characterized themselves as earning a yearly combined income of $80,000 (Canadian) and above. Female same-sex couples had been together for an average of ten years, with a range from four to thirty-two years; male same-sex couples had been together for an average of thirteen years, with a range from five to forty years. Most couples had been married for approximately two years, which is not surprising given that same-sex marriage was legalized in Ontario in 2003.

The semi-structured interviews lasted from 1.5 to 2.5 hours, and were organized by a standardized interview guide that elicited a general relationship history, beginning in adolescence and ending with the current marital relationship. In an effort to understand the substance and character of same-sex civil marriages, I focused on questions related to the marital relationship, including how the partners met, the development of their relationship, the character of their relationship before and after marriage, the decision to marry, the meaning of marriage, the content and meaning of the civil and wedding ceremonies, the couple's relationship to family and in-laws, the reception of the marital couple at work and in the broader community, the decision (or not) to parent, and future expectations regarding the marital dyad.

All interviews were audiotaped and transcribed. The transcriptions were analyzed using the coding procedures of grounded theory (Strauss and Corbin 1998). The coding schema began with open codes to establish general categories, and then axial coding to establish dimensions among the open codes. Analytic memos were created from the open and axial codes to establish patterned themes across respondents. A final analytic process compared study findings from the analytic memos with key themes from the literature, including issues around the impact of marriage on dyadic commitment, perceived social legitimacy, the relationship of marital status to social support from family, friends, and coworkers, and the sexual norms and practices of the marital relationship.

Below I use data from this study to provide a preliminary examination of the ways in which actual same-sex marriages compare with the prognostications advanced by social conservative, critical feminist/queer, and lesbian and gay assimilationist positions. Rather than present the data as an exhaustive catalogue of same-sex marital relations within the sample, instead I highlight patterns in these relationships and how they relate to the literature. The present study is designed as an exploratory investigation that uses the voices and experiences of same-sex spouses to "speak back" to major themes in the same-sex marriage literature. It is therefore not intended to draw definitive inferences to a wider population of same-sex spouses. Nevertheless, the marital relations in this study may share structural similarities with a broader set of same-sex marriages (Badgett 2009; Eskridge and Spedale 2006; Lannutti 2005).

SAME-SEX MARRIAGE: CONSOLIDATING THE NUCLEAR FAMILY AND THE INSTITUTION OF MARRIAGE

To the extent that social conservatives extol the virtues of (heterosexual) marriage in terms of deepening commitment between partners, increased social support, and the facilitation of a reproductive, nuclear family, these effects are consistent with the ways in which same-sex married spouses experience, conceive of, and talk about their marriages. Perhaps more than any other sentiment, growing "commitment" to the dyad following marriage is ubiquitous throughout their narratives. This commitment is then linked to increased dyadic stability. Frank, for instance, found that even after six years with his partner, including a public commitment ceremony, the act of getting married in the seventh year brought a new sense of commitment and, in turn, stability.

> I think that prior to being married . . . if you were in disagreement about something, you know, there was always an easier way out. Whereas the commitment is definitely more . . . I think it's just the sense of commitment that you feel. You've made a vow and, it's hard to describe, it definitely feels different than prior to.　　　　　—*Frank, thirty-two years old*

For Hillary, marriage itself imparts a narrative of dyadic continuity that maps the partners' commitment to each other into late adulthood and even death.

> It really is life-changing and relationship-altering. It advances a relationship so much higher. . . . There's just, the marriage has just made the commitment even more solid. We talk about where we will be buried together and stuff [*laughs*], where we will retire, and what our retirement will be like.
> 　　　　　—*Hillary, forty-five years old*

While civil marriage includes rights and privileges that same-sex couples covet, its impact on relationships is often articulated in other terms. Premised on lifelong partnership, marriage is perceived as a psychological resource that "cements" the relationship above and beyond other more "tangible" benefits.

> I think it's only partially intellectual but there's something emotional as well. I think it's a partnership. A partnership of trust. And security, not financial security, [but a] kind of emotional security. . . . Yeah, about cementing the relationship and declaring it to one another.   —*Greg, thirty-two years old*

Not uncommonly, same-sex spouses had been coupled with their partners for many years prior to the legalization of civil marriage, which makes the consolidating impact of marriage on the relationship all the more surprising to Ava:

> It's funny, I wouldn't have thought that it would, but I think that it has a huge psychological thing going on. Confidence. I feel more relaxed. It's weird . . . just going through the ritual just helped me feel even after all those years, more comfortable in our relationship. Like, ok, she's going to stay [*laughs*]. She's not going anywhere.   —*Ava, fifty-five years old*

If marriage consolidates and deepens one's sense of commitment to the dyad, it may also serve as an important institutional bridge of legitimation to family. For some, the event of the wedding ceremony itself provides an occasion that pushes families of same-sex spouses to confront unresolved issues around the same-sex relationship. Jen, for example, had been in a relationship with Jackie for nearly thirty years. Still, over three decades, her family had been blissfully ignorant, choosing not to overtly recognize the relationship. The announcement of her marriage and the ceremony itself, however, initiated a significant shift in family reception, perhaps most importantly in her mother.

> We sat her down at the kitchen table, because we had never really come out to her. We sat her at the kitchen table and gave her a wedding invitation. She looked forward and she frowned and

she said, "What's this?" I said, "Well, Jackie and I want to get married." We gave her the whole spiel. . . . And she said, "Well, you know, I'm an old-fashioned girl and I don't understand all of this stuff." . . . But she did the whole thing, walked down the aisle like the mother of the bride. . . . And apparently she did say to my sister that we'd been together a long time and it was the right thing to do.　　　　　—*Jen, fifty-six years old*

For Larry, too, marriage increased emotional support from family and friends:

They started recognizing, wow, this isn't just a gay relationship —this is a relationship. . . . We would have had a strong relationship regardless of being married or not, but what we've learned from the process of being in marriage to each other and how it has affected the people around us, is that the support group has become magnified in terms of their acceptance of us.
　　　　　—*Larry, forty-eight years old*

And Clark takes great comfort that his civil marriage is the same marital form of his parents and grandparents:

[J]ust knowing she [Clark's mother] sees us as equally married as my family, like we're not just roommates or not just partners or not just common-law—we're *married*. And when you say that, it's not a civil union, it's marriage, just like your marriage, Mom and Dad, Nana and Grandpa.　　　—*Clark, thirty-six years old*

The legitimating effect of civil marriage for same-sex spouses, and the added social support they perceive to follow, is by no means limited to the domain of family and friends. In fact, because of the social intelligibility of marriage—that is, its normativity in the wider society— same-sex spouses find that their marital status helps them fit in with and garner the support of coworkers and employers. For instance, now that he is married, Greg perceives himself to be a socially recognizable, "real person" by his employer. His marriage provides a social status to which his heterosexual employer can relate.

> I went to dinner with my boss and his nephew . . . and his nephew was planning his wedding. And they asked me if I was married and I told them to a guy. And they started asking me about my experience and about the restaurant and the invitation or whatever, and it really validated that I had something in common, that I was a real person. As much as it was completely ridiculous and childish, it made me feel good that I wasn't a freak, that my relationship was as valid as theirs.
>
> —*Greg, thirty-two years old*

For Eric, too, being identified as part of a married couple provides advantages in the sphere of informal work interactions, where one's personal life structures work identity, network affiliations, and professional rapport. Here, Eric contrasts his marital status with some of the unmarried "gay village boys" at work. His discussion reflects the particular importance marital status may hold for gays and lesbians who otherwise hold a marginal position in the social structure (cf. Berlant and Warner 1998).

> There are honestly work benefits for us being married. When I interact with the partners [of the firm] in general . . . it's probably more comfortable if they had us over for dinner. We could get invited as a couple. It's a different comfort aspect to it . . . even how people interact and so on, even the signs of stability which is important to them when you get to the next level. . . . And in contrast to the gay village boys that are at work who might even be at the same career level [but] can't talk about their [partners] at all. . . . For sure, there's a difference, the whole perception of stability is different between the two. . . . And part of the way you develop rapport with anyone is to talk about your personal life: "Are you married and do you have kids?" It's the standard small-talk question.   —*Eric, thirty-three years old*

Like Greg and Eric, Izzy felt that her marriage announcement affected her social reception at work. Even among those who seemed to have the least regard for her relationship, marriage garnered some semblance of support: "I took her to the company picnics and company gatherings . . . [and] even the people that were most tight-assed were like 'congratulations!'"

If marriage transforms perceptions of legitimacy, integration, and social support within family and work domains, it can also produce a more abstract but perhaps no less significant perception of credibility in the day-to-day interactions of married spouses. That is, as in the realm of work, marriage is perceived to confer social recognition upon lesbians and gay men who acquire the legitimating status of "spouse" in the larger society. Subsequently, following civil marriage, informal interactions on the street, in the grocery store, or at the bus stop are perceived to change because one's self-concept has changed.

> [Civil marriage] has not changed the day-to-day of life in any way whatsoever. What it has changed is my internal feelings of being socially accepted. So, I meet you and we're at the bus stop and you say, "hi," and we're chatting. And you say, "So, you have a family?" . . . And I say, "Yep, I'm married with children." That validates me. I feel like in society I can say that I'm married with children. And for me, who is a lifetime lesbian, being able to somewhat be part of the norm is so unusual. I love it! I'm part of the norm: I'm married with children! I just happen to be a lesbian . . . it changed something in my head.
>
> —*Barbara, fifty-two years old*

Same-sex spouses also conceive of civil marriage as an institution conferring both social and legal benefits conducive to parenting. These spouses associate family formation and parenting with the context of a marital relationship and the familial, community, and state resources that accrue from marriage. Thus, Izzy conceives of marriage as a status in which the larger society will be held "accountable" to the needs of her reproductive family:

One of our first conversations was about how neither of us believed in the concept of marriage or were planning on getting
married. . . . And then we started talking about families and
about the fact that we wanted to get married. . . . The big ceremony was literally to show everybody who we were and to be a
couple and . . . because we also planned on having a family and
we wanted some sort of accountability.

—*Izzy, twenty-nine years old*

Among male same-sex partners, the context of marriage and the security it imparts may be particularly consequential because acquiring a
child requires extensive planning and concerted effort. Eric regards his
marriage as the foundation of a "package arrangement" (Green 2006)
that will likely include children and a larger house in the suburbs in
the coming years. Here, he articulates a marital trajectory that incorporates parenthood and domesticity in the near future: "I hope we find a
friendly suburb that we can move to. . . . Kids: one versus two!? I like
the idea . . . We're kind of waiting to see if we can afford a nanny versus
daycare."

To conclude, among the respondents of this study, civil marriage is
regarded as an institution that bears in significant ways upon the self,
the dyad, family formation, and one's relationship to the larger social
order. In total, these perceptions suggest that same-sex civil marriage
reproduces and consolidates the traditional institution of marriage and
the nuclear family more generally. That is, contrary to the predictions
of social conservatives, but consistent with the predictions of feminist/
queer critics and lesbian and gay assimilationists, same-sex marriage
may indeed establish a new "homonormativity" anchored, in part, in
the norms and traditions of heteronormativity.

However, while same-sex marriage may encourage same-sex relationships that replicate and thereby reinforce aspects of traditional
marriage, the marital forms in this study also depart in important ways
from heteronormativity and cannot, therefore, be reduced to "homonormativity." I explore this theme below with special attention to marital sexual norms and practices and the division of domestic labor.

SAME-SEX MARRIAGE: DYADIC INNOVATION AND
DEPARTURES FROM TRADITIONAL MARRIAGE

If same-sex marriage is a conservative phenomenon that reproduces the traditional, Western, twentieth-century family ideal, it is also the case that same-sex spouses in this study do not uniformly embrace traditional principles of marriage—including marital monogamy and a gendered division of labor—but instead hold a variety of views and engage in a range of intentional practices that depart from traditional marriage.[7]

One of the most pronounced ways in which the same-sex married spouses of this study depart from traditional marital conventions is through the adoption of nonmonogamous norms and practices. While nearly 100 percent of U.S. heterosexual married partners were found to expect sexual exclusivity from their partners (Laumann et al. 1994), and support for marital monogamy among the American public has actually *increased* in the last three decades, with 92 percent of respondents reporting that extramarital sex is "always wrong" or "almost always wrong" in 1998 (Cherlin 2002)[8]—two-thirds of same-sex spouses (40 percent female, 60 percent male) in this study do not believe that marriage need always be monogamous. What is more, nearly half of male same-sex spouses (47 percent) report an *explicit* policy of nonmonogamous practice, as did one female same-sex spouse. In fact, of this latter group (eight spouses), three reported that they became nonmonogamous only *after* civil marriage. Finally, monogamous practice itself is not typically taken for granted by either male or female same-sex spouses but instead emerges in a reflexive process (Giddens 1992) organized more by the personal needs and wants of the partners than by the heavy hand of heteronormative tradition.

Among the same-sex spouses with open marital relations, Giddens's notion of "plastic sexuality" is seen in the decoupling of sex and love (in which the former is distilled from the latter). In this regard, while marriage should be based in love, it need not preclude extramarital sexual relations.

[Q]uite honestly, I always found it very erotic that somebody else would find my partner sexually appealing. I just found that a real turn-on. I wasn't jealous. If anything, I was really proud. . . . But I always realized that it was sex. I've always been able to put sex and love in two categories. . . . One of the things I used to say to people was that you can have sex with your hand—it's ok. You don't fall in love with it, though. . . . So you can really keep it in perspective. And I really do think people do make a huge mistake confusing sex and love. —*Henry, sixty years old*

Conversely, perhaps counterintuitively, some couples remain monogamous *until* they are married. For example, Karl and his spouse find that marriage creates a level of dyadic commitment that makes sexual exploration outside the dyad possible:

The fact that we are legally married to each other is a completely different ballgame for opening up the relationship. I would not have felt comfortable to do it, not being legally married. So, it sounds kind of backwards to the traditional model, but the fact that we're legally married to each other and permanently committed makes us both feel very secure about doing this.

—*Karl, forty-seven years old*

And for Laura, the stability of marriage creates new sexual choices:

In the beginning . . . we talked about monogamy . . . and it sort of came up, on and off. . . . And then about three and a half years into our marriage, it came up again, and she said, "I want a chance to take a look at it." . . . And so I said, "Okay, let's try it." . . . And I have some straight friends that were like, "Oh my God, I would totally freak out, I would totally just say no!" . . . I feel like marriage allowed us to be . . . ironically, through all the fear around it, it actually made Lanna feel safe enough to bring it up in a very honest way. . . . She could actually be

completely honest. . . . Because we were married and she felt I
made a commitment to her that meant that I wouldn't be like,
"see ya!"   —*Laura, thirty-four years old*

If intentional and negotiated marital nonmonogamy represents an
innovation in the conventions of traditional marriage, then the norms
that same-sex spouses articulate around marital monogamy also represent a sharp departure. In this study, of those with explicitly monogamous marriages (73 percent), half of these latter respondents (roughly
equal by gender) believe that it is acceptable for marriages to be nonmonogamous, while over one-fifth (22 percent of the monogamous
males and 9 percent of the monogamous females) remain open to
the possibility that their own marriages may one day become nonmonogamous.

For instance, Candy rejects a hard-line approach to marital fidelity.
Asked if she felt marriage should always be monogamous, Candy draws
from her own positive experience with an open relationship, finding
the latter to have a therapeutic quality.

No, I have to say. My little thing I had a few years ago was very
pleasant. Because my self-esteem was so low, being with this . . .
wonderful, beautiful woman who was interested in me [and]
treated me very nicely. Not a person I wanted to spend the rest
of my life with, that I knew from the beginning. But I got that
little hint of that I was special. And it was really, really pleasant.
                              —*Candy, sixty years old*

Monogamous spouses, too, are often unwilling to categorically reject nonmonogamous marriage, even when they cannot imagine it for
themselves. Ava, for instance, has always had a monogamous relationship with her spouse and has no interest in an open marriage. Nonetheless, she approaches the principle of marital monogamy with suspicion
because it precludes the particular needs of the partners involved:

[We] are always monogamous. I just can't see it [nonmonog-
amy]. I can't, for me, I can't . . . it's too complicated [*laughs*]. I

can't be intimate, or I can't be sexual without being intimate, so it would, so I wouldn't want to, first of all, it just would feel like a betrayal. . . . But at the same time, I respect other people's life choices. . . . I guess it depends on the couple. And you know, consenting adults, what makes them happy, what they need.

—Ava, thirty-six years old

Ian, too, is committed to monogamy in his own marriage, though this commitment arises from an individual, reasoned choice rather than from adherence to religious proscriptions or dominant norms of marital fidelity. "I don't [think] marriage should always be necessarily [monogamous]. . . . They should be faithful by whatever definition the people involved chose to define fidelity."

Moreover, monogamous marital arrangements in the present do not preclude a different future arrangement. Instead, like the pure relationship described by Giddens (1992), these partners are willing to renegotiate needs over the course of the marriage. Thus, when asked if their marriage will always be monogamous, Alex states:

We don't know that, and . . . at the moment we are very happy with that. I don't think either of us thinks about going the other way. We have everything we want at the moment. In other words, it's not like "forever and ever," just let's do it and it works, so let's keep doing it. *—Alex, fifty-five years old*

In the same way that these spouses reject traditional norms of marital monogamy for a more democratic negotiation of sexual needs and wants, they also commonly report negotiating the domestic division of labor and authority. In fact, the majority of same-sex spouses describe a highly egalitarian domestic division of labor organized by individual interests and desires, rather than predetermined, role-differentiated tasks.[9] While these accounts cannot be assumed to reflect actual practices (Carrington 1999), and more research will be required to validate such accounts, they are nonetheless consistent with a larger body of research on the egalitarian character of housework among same-sex couples relative to their heterosexual counterparts (Blumstein and

Schwartz 1983; Patterson 1995). Moreover, in those cases where partners describe an unequal division of domestic labor, it is not ossified gender roles that guide who does what but, rather, fluid and pragmatic considerations associated with time and financial earnings. For instance, Ava—whose spouse has a considerably more high-powered occupation than she—divides house and yard work according to her and her partner's respective likes and dislikes:

> She cooks, I do the dishes. I clean the house, she gets the groceries [laughs]. We share yard work and, generally, she's the person who fixes things. Although, I usually do the technical stuff—the television, the computer stuff. . . . Like I hate doing laundry, so she does the laundry and I'll clean the bathroom because she hates cleaning the bathroom. So that's pretty much how it balances out. . . . It seems to work pretty well. We've got our routine down pat. But it's not rigid. If she doesn't feel like doing something or I don't feel like doing something, that's ok.
>
> —Ava, thirty-six years old

With multiple children, the domestic division of labor becomes even more complex. Kate and Kristina, for example, have a more traditional arrangement in which Kate stays home and Kristina works full-time. Nevertheless, though Kate does more housework than Kristina, this couple shares the care of their three children and many of the day-to-day household tasks:

> [I] think we're unique in a lot of different ways. We're very egalitarian and share pretty much everything fifty-fifty—be it from childcare to household stuff. . . . Pretty much it's what we're good at. Like, I do all the finances. I'd say I do the majority of the house stuff because I'm home and she's working. When it comes to the kids, we're fifty-fifty. She probably does more with the two-year-old than with the baby. . . . Like if one of the kids gets up in the middle of the night and we listen to the cry then if it's Mandy—which is the older one—then Kristina gets

up. . . . We both make dinners, we both do dishes. . . . It's just very equal. —*Kate, thirty-four years old*

The egalitarian and negotiated character of domestic labor to which these respondents refer is a theme repeated by many same-sex spouses. While some spouses attribute this to the absence of gender-differentiated roles in a same-sex relationship, others attribute it to the fact that same-sex partners experience the same gender socialization. In short, the couple's shared gendered expectations appear to level the playing field.

If the same-sex marriages of this study have a pronounced egalitarian character in terms of the domestic division of labor, they also tend to be egalitarian in terms of control of household finances. Faith, for example, discusses in detail the equitable financial arrangements of her household. When asked if their finances are integrated, Faith states:

Yes and no. We have a joint account, which is the household account, and we each contribute a certain amount into that account, and that covers monthly expenses, which is the household expenses. As well, we have an account, a mutual fund account for our property taxes, so what happens is a certain amount is pulled out of our household account into a mutual account bi-weekly, and when the property tax bill comes it gets paid out of our mutual funds account. We have two credit cards in both our names, and when the bill comes, unless it's a personal item for me or her, the bills are divided evenly and we pay that. . . . [But] not everything is blended; we have our own personal accounts [too]. —*Faith, forty-nine years old*

And Ben and Barry have switched financial roles organically as their respective careers have ebbed and flowed over time. Upon combining their expenses into one household bill, this couple pays expenses in proportion to their shifting relative incomes, rather than according to a predetermined set of expectations or gender roles.

[T]he money comes in, the money goes out, and it pays all the bills no matter whose bills they are. And it's been that way for some time. Initially, when we first were together, I would pay my bills and he would pay his bills, and I was working. We really switched roles from the time we met. Barry was working full-time and I was working part-time. . . . And so he was the major breadwinner and it's, since we've been in the city . . . my income has outstretched his so I've become the major breadwinner. But the money comes in, the money goes out, and all the bills get paid.   *—Ben, forty-four years old*

For many same-sex spouses, decision-making authority, too, has a marked, negotiated, give-and-take quality. Hence, Jen and her partner take turns playing "boss":

We built our own house. . . . We found that we'd get bogged down on stupid things. . . . If there were two opinions, you couldn't get two out of three because there were only two. So we would be boss for the day, and if you were boss for the day, you got to decide that stupid question. If it was something really serious, then we'd both have to decide, but for something that didn't matter, we'd take turns being boss for the day. We still can do that sometimes: if something comes up that's not important, we say, "who's boss for the day?" . . . That's just another negotiation that we developed.   *—Jen, fifty-six years old*

To conclude, these findings do not support the queer position that predicts a uniform homonormativity organized around marital fidelity and the exaltation of monogamous norms. Moreover, the negotiated quality of the domestic division of labor and authority across same-sex married couples does not align with the critical feminist prediction that marriage will assimilate lesbian and gay spouses into role-differentiated marriages that reproduce power inequities found in traditional heterosexual marriages. Conversely, while these findings cannot be construed to *promote* nonmonogamous marriages among heterosexuals, they do coincide with the social conservative prediction that same-sex marriages will be less likely to retain traditional norms of marital monogamy. The findings also coincide with the social conservative forecast that same-sex marriage will erode gender-differentiated roles of traditional marriage and the concomitant domestic division of labor.

DISCUSSION

In this chapter, I have used the voices of legally married same-sex spouses to "speak back" to a now voluminous, speculative literature on the effects of civil marriage on the same-sex dyad. Taken as a whole, the marital arrangements of this study defy reduction to the forecasts of either proponents or detractors of same-sex marriage. On the one hand, same-sex spouses in this study discuss assimilating to, reproducing, and thereby consolidating a traditional, idealized marital form premised on lifelong partnership, the adoption and valorization of marital identities (e.g., husband, wife, spouse), and, in some cases, the formation of reproductive nuclear families. Consistent with the lesbian and gay assimilationist and critical feminist/queer positions, but contrary to the social conservative position, same-sex marriage is experienced in this study as a superior arrangement that strengthens the bonds of the dyad, promotes deeper commitment and stability, and ties the same-sex marital family to larger networks of social support vis-à-vis extended family and work settings, thereby consolidating the marital dyad itself.

On the other hand, same-sex spouses in this study depart from and innovate upon the traditional marital ideal by adopting *explicit* nonmonogamous sexual norms and practices and through a highly negotiated domestic division of labor. In fact, the majority of spouses in this study reject a universal norm of marital fidelity; more than one-fifth of those in monogamous marriages remained open to the possibility of nonmonogamous marriage in the future, and nearly half of the male study participants had intentional, negotiated open marriages, along with one female participant. In these latter cases, interestingly, nearly half of those with open marriages became nonmonogamous only *after* getting married. That is, civil marriage provided a structure of permanence that these men regarded as a secure context in which to explore sexual pleasures outside the dyad. Indeed, monogamous practice, where it occurs, is a consequence more of personal needs and wants than the heavy hand of marital tradition. To be sure, to the extent that male spouses are less invested in monogamous *practice* than their female counterparts, the meanings that male and female same-sex spouses build around marriage are not reducible to being the same. Nevertheless, taken as a whole, the findings call into question the lesbian and gay assimilationist and critical feminist/queer forecasts—both of which predict that civil marriage will produce a new homonormativity organized around the uniform adoption of heteronormative monogamous norms and practices. Conversely, these dyadic arrangements coincide, in part, with the social conservative prediction that same-sex marriages will be organized by norms other than marital fidelity. In addition, the majority of same-sex spouses organize the domestic division of labor not around preestablished gender roles, but around the principles of interest, practical economic considerations, and egalitarianism. It would appear that a process of negotiation, rather than binary gender roles, determines who does what in the household. These latter findings are not predicted by critical feminist/queer theorists, who anticipate that marriage will produce internally stratified, role-differentiated relations, but confirm the worries of social conservatives, who abhor the de-differentiation of gender roles.

The fact that the spouses in this study have constructed marriages that in part reproduce traditional marriage and the nuclear family is perhaps not surprising, since they, like their heterosexual counterparts, are socialized in a regulative tradition that confers superior status upon this marital form. That is, following Neil Gross (2005), even as lifelong, internally gender-stratified marriages are on the decline, and even as those who deviate from such marital forms suffer diminishing consequences, North American intimate life nevertheless remains embedded within a "meaning-constitutive tradition" of romantic love (Gross 2005, 288). This tradition, like all meaning-constitutive traditions, is an objective source of subjectification wherein identities, subjectivities, and life projects are constituted by the particularities of history and culture. Thus, Gross (2005) likens meaning-constitutive traditions to a Durkheimian social fact:

[L]anguage and cultural traditions are the most fundamental example of a Durkheimian social fact, for they not only preexist the individual and hence are external to her, but beyond being constraining, are actually constitutive of her. (Gross 2005, 295)

Anchored to heteronormativity, the dominant meaning-constitutive tradition of contemporary North American culture imparts an idealized (if unrealized) narrative of self-fulfillment in the context of married, lifelong dyadic commitment and the reproductive nuclear family (Cherlin 2004). Indeed, even as divorce rates have increased dramatically since the 1960s in the United States and Canada (Ambert 1998; Laumann et al. 1994), and the age of marriage has increased while rates of fertility have dropped (Laumann et al. 1994; Statistics Canada 2004), marital fidelity is quite high (Laumann et al. 1994), and the idealization of marriage and the nuclear family as the superior familial arrangement for relational happiness and child raising continues to prevail (Seccombe 1993; Waite and Gallagher 2000)—that is, marriage continues to be "the capstone" of adult personal life (Cherlin 2004, 850). "Detraditionalization," argues Gross (2005), has indeed occurred over the course of the past century, insofar as nearly half of marriages in the United States end in divorce and traditional, internally gender-stratified marriages are waning. Nevertheless, it does not follow that romantic norms and ideals that underpin traditional marriage are anachronistic. Indeed, as Gross notes, they may continue to play an important role in shaping intimate life.

[W]hile those who deviate from the practice of LISM (lifelong, internally stratified marriage) are subject to fewer and less intensive social sanctions than in the past, the image of the form of couplehood inscribed in the regulative tradition of LISM continues to function as a hegemonic ideal in many—perhaps most—American intimate relationships. American intimacy also remains beholden to the tradition of romantic love, a cultural form that has its origins in 11th- and 12th-century Europe. These forms of indebtedness to tradition impose cultural

constraints on intimate practices that theorists of detraditionalization have largely ignored. (Gross 2005, 288)

In this cultural context, it is no wonder that a significant contingent
of same-sex spouses would conceive of, experience, and talk about marriage in a manner that idealizes the traditional marital form and associates it with increased commitment, lifelong dyadic stability, social
support and integration, and a child-rearing, nuclear family. Indeed,
it was William Simon and John Gagnon (1967) who, forty years ago,
made the seminal social constructionist observation that the sociological study of homosexuality cannot *but* begin with an analysis of the
larger social order in which homosexuals are embedded. In this regard,
the marriages that same-sex spouses create should not be exoticized or
essentialized, or conceived of as a sui generis dyadic form without context or precedent. Homosexuals live with and alongside heterosexuals
and heteronormativity, and are, in significant measure, subject to the
latter's socializing properties.

Yet, conversely, the fact that same-sex spouses adopt norms and
practices that depart from traditional marital sexual relations and the
domestic division of labor is also not surprising. Indeed, if contemporary lesbians and gays are subject to heteronormativity, they are also,
by dint of their outsider status as homosexuals, subject to a *"queer
meaning-constitutive tradition."* Emerging out of a historical dialectic marked by the exclusion from marriage and its concomitant relational norms and practices, this queer meaning-constitutive tradition
effects a resocialization process situated outside of and in opposition to
heteronormativity and the nuclear family (Green 2006; Herdt and
Boxer 1992).

[Y]oung gays and lesbians must both overcome the cultural stereotypes of homosexuality and give up previously internalized
heterosocial life goals. This identity change may involve some
"grief work" and mourning as previously held expectations for
marriage, heterosexual parenthood, etc., are replaced with new
expectations, ideals and ambitions. (Herdt and Boxer 1992, 19)

Perhaps nowhere is a queer meaning-constitutive tradition more fully realized than in the development of "sex-positive" (Becker 1984) queer cultures in large Western cities over the past four decades. These cultures strongly promote sexual freedom and celebrate sexual pleasure (Altman 1982; Weeks 1988). In this context, heteronormative assumptions regarding the tight coupling of sex and love, dyadic commitment and monogamy, are subject to a *"transformational process"* (Herdt 1992, 30) whereby the dominant meaning-constitutive romantic tradition identified by Gross (2005) is "unlearned" (Herdt 1992, 30) and reworked (Adam 2006). In its place, a queer meaning-constitutive tradition imparts an "ethics of relating" centered on the negotiation of sexual needs and wants (Weeks, Heaphy, and Donovan 2001, 148). In their study of gay men, David Woolwine and E. Doyle McCarthy find no single moral code around sexual fidelity, but rather a kind of queer "morally pragmatic stand" (2005, 400) arising in the historical context of anti-homosexual sentiment and associated stigmatization (399). Similarly, while most lesbian couples prefer monogamy, Susan Johnson (1990) finds that it is not uncommon for lesbian relationships to enter into phases of negotiated nonmonogamy. In sum, monogamy, even when practiced, is not a taken-for-granted dyadic norm, but is instead an outgrowth of the needs, desires, and reflexive communication of spouses.

This historical dialectic in meaning-constitutive traditions, and the *dual* socialization process that follows, is perhaps nowhere more clear than in contemporary same-sex marriage. On the one hand, lesbian and gay spouses are socialized within the dominant, heteronormative meaning-constitutive tradition, which includes discourses of romantic love and the idealization of matrimony and the nuclear family (Hull 2006). On the other hand, for the majority of their lives, these same lesbian and gay spouses have been excluded from access to the institution of marriage, and socialized, by contrast, in a queer meaning-constitutive tradition organized around sexual freedoms, dyadic innovation, and support for gender nonconformity (Adam 2006). Thus contemporary lesbians and gay men arrive at the institution of marriage in the context of discordant meaning-constitutive traditions. Put another way, with one foot anchored in heteronormativity and the other in homosexuality, today's same-sex married spouses are likely to express the cultural contradictions of their lives in the form of complex marital arrangements that bring together tradition and innovation, with the effect of both reproducing and subverting traditional marriage.[10] These are, indeed, *queer* unions.

And yet, because contemporary lesbian and gay spouses create marital forms against the waning historical backdrop of exclusion from the institution, they may represent less the future of same-sex marriage than a generational anomaly. That is, it is unclear if the radical dimensions of same-sex marriage will endure or if, instead, these elements will slowly erode as younger lesbian and gay spouses are socialized into the dominant meaning-constitutive tradition without the mediating effects of a competing, queer meaning-constitutive tradition. This is conceivable insofar as future lesbian and gay adults who grow up in the context of same-sex marriage provisions will have a different experience with the structures of kinship than the generation of queers who came of age in earlier times. In this sense, the idea that lesbians and gays will change the institution of marriage—as set forth by Josephson (2005)—may itself be both true and false. In the short run, the dual socialization of lesbian and gay spouses in both a heteronormative meaning-constitutive tradition *and* a queer meaning-constitutive tradition may provide the contradictory cultural conditions upon which a substantial contingent of "first-generation" same-sex spouses will re-imagine the marital form. But in the long run, the increasing availability of same-sex marriage may transform the historical dialectic outlined above, eroding the distinctiveness of what it means to be lesbian and gay and, in turn, queer and married. New generations of lesbians and gay men brought up with a same-sex marriage option may find a more "normalized" gay sexual subculture, accompanied by a "homonormativity" (Duggan 2002, 2003) grounded in the dominant, heteronormative meaning-constitutive tradition. Under these conditions, while surely not all lesbian and gay spouses will become marital traditionalists, they will also no longer encounter the structural conditions that underpin a queer marital innovation. If this were true, so the forecasts of critical feminists and queer theorists may be prescient, after all.

NOTES

1. For more on the complexity of characterizing the same-sex marriage debate, see Clarke and Finlay (2004).

2. As with all categorical exercises, these positions are necessarily abbreviated here in order to highlight only those elements of the debates with direct relevance to the analytic objectives of the present chapter. For an expanded discussion of these debates the reader may wish to see Josephson (2005), Yep, Lovaas, and Elia (2003), and Young and Boyd (2006).

3. "Heteronormativity" refers to the dominant set of mutually reinforcing norms, practices, and institutions that include heterosexuality, marriage, monogamy, and the nuclear family. As a concept, heteronormativity is analogous to Neil Gross's formulation of the contemporary, romantic "meaning-constitutive tradition" in the West (2005). For the original use of the term, see Warner (1991).

4. But see feminists Calhoun (2000), Cox (1997), and Graff (1997)—each of whom suggest that same-sex marriage will have a positive transformative effect on the institution itself. In this sense, Peel and Harding (2004) argue that some "pro" and "anti" feminist same-sex marriage positions are reconcilable. See Eskridge and Spedale (2006) and Nan Hunter (1991) for a related position. For some notable feminist sociological exceptions, however, see Waite and Gallagher (2000) on the overall value of marriage for women, and Stets (1991) on marital protection against violence for women.

5. Some lesbian and gay assimilationists articulate shared concerns with feminists regarding the misogynistic history of marriage, and in this regard, these positions overlap.

6. Despite the diversity of sample starting points in Toronto, and a wide distribution of recruitment materials to websites and community centers, I was able to recruit only two visible minorities: among two marriages, one female partner identified as Aboriginal and another female partner identified as Asian. In addition, nearly all respondents were middle class. This may be emblematic of the population of same-sex married spouses in North America which, according to some critics, will strongly favor a white, middle-class constituency (see, for example, Warner 1999). Given the paucity of demographic research on same-sex married couples in North America, the racial and class composition of these marriages is still not known.

7. The spouses of this study had little to say about their religious affiliation with respect to their marriages. This may be an artifact of the Canadian context, where religiosity is comparatively lower than in other jurisdictions that offer same-sex marriage.

8. Unfortunately, no comparable Canadian data exists, with the exception of a World Values Survey conducted in 1990. In this survey, nearly three-quarters of Canadian respondents reported that a marital affair was either never justifiable or rarely justifiable.

9. For related findings, see Dunne (2000) and M. Sullivan (2004).

10. It may also be the case that the first generation of married same-sex couples will

have been together for a longer period of time prior to marriage relative to future generations. In this sense, the institution of marriage may have less of an effect on this first generation of married couples than future generations.

REFERENCES

Adam, Barry. 2006. "Relationship Innovation in Male Couples." *Sexualities* 9 (1): 5–26.

Altman, Dennis. 1982. *The Homosexualization of America*. New York: St. Martin's Press.

Ambert, Ann-Marie. 1998. "Divorce: Facts, Causes and Consequences." Toronto: The Vanier Institute of the Family's Contemporary Family Trends.

Auchmuty, Rosemary. 2004. "Same-Sex Marriage Revived: Feminist Critique and Legal Strategy." *Feminism and Psychology* 14 (1): 101–26.

Badgett, M. V. Lee. 2009. *When Gay People Get Married: What Happens When Societies Legalize Same-Sex Marriage*. New York: New York University Press.

Baird, R. M., and S. E. Rosenbaum. 1997. *Same-Sex Marriage: The Moral and Legal Debate*. Amherst, Mass.: Prometheus.

Baskerville, Stephen. 2006. "The Real Danger of Same-Sex Marriage." *The Family in America, Online Edition* 20 (5–6). http://www.profam.org/pub/fia/fia.2005.6.htm.

Becker, G. 1984. "The Social Regulation of Sexuality: A Cross-Cultural Perspective." *Current Perspectives in Social Theory* 5: 45–69.

Berlant, Lauren, and Michael Warner. 1998. "Sex in Public." *Critical Inquiry* 24: 547–66.

Bevacqua, Maria. 2004. "Feminist Theory and the Question of Lesbian and Gay Marriage." *Feminism and Psychology* 14 (1): 36–40.

Blumstein, Phillip, and Pepper Schwartz. 1983. *American Couples: Money, Work, Sex*. New York: William Morrow.

Butler, Judith. 2002. "Is Kinship Always Already Heterosexual?" *Differences: A Journal of Feminist Cultural Studies* 13 (1): 14–44.

Calhoun, Cheshire. 2000. *Feminism, the Family, and the Politics of the Closet: Lesbian and Gay Displacement*. Oxford and New York: Oxford University Press.

Carrington, Christopher. 1999. *No Place Like Home: Relationships and Family Life among Lesbians and Gay Men*. Chicago: University of Chicago Press.

Cherlin, Andrew. 2002. *Public and Private Families: An Introduction*. New York: McGraw-Hill.

———. 2004. "The Deinstitutionalization of American Marriage." *Journal of Marriage and Family* 66 (4): 848–61.

Christensen, Bryce. 2004. "Why Homosexuals Want What Marriage Has Now Become." *The Family in America, Online Edition* 18 (4). http://www.profam.org/pub/fia/fia_1804.htm.

Clarke, Victoria, and Sara Jane Finlay. 2004. "Editors' Introduction: Lesbian and Gay 'Marriage': Personal, Political and Theoretical Perspectives." *Feminism and Psychology* 14 (1): 17–23.

Coontz, Stephanie. 2000. *The Way We Never Were: American Families and the Nostalgia Trap*. New York: Basic Books.

Cott, Nancy. 2000. *Public Vows: A History of Marriage and the Nation*. Cambridge, Mass.: Harvard University Press.

Cox, B. 1997. "A (Personal) Essay on Same-Sex Marriage." In *Same-Sex Marriage: The Moral and Legal Debate*, edited by Robert M. Baird and Stuart E. Rosenblum, 27–29. Amherst, Mass.: Prometheus Books.

Dobson, James. 2004. *Marriage under Fire: Why We Must Win This Battle.* Sisters, Ore.: Multnomah.

Duggan, Lisa. 2002. "The New Homonormativity: The Sexual Politics of Neoliberalism." In *Materializing Democracy: Toward a Revitalized Cultural Politics*, edited by Russ Castronovo and Dana Nelson, 175–94. Durham, N.C.: Duke University Press.

———. 2003. *The Twilight of Equality? Neoliberalism, Cultural Politics, and the Attack on Democracy.* Boston: Beacon Press.

Dunne, Gillian A. 2000. "Opting into Motherhood: Lesbians Blurring the Boundaries and Transforming the Meaning of Parenthood and Kinship." *Gender and Society* 14: 11–35.

Elshtain, Jean Bethke. 1991. "Against Marriage—II: Accepting Limits." *Commonweal* 1 (118): 685–86.

Eskridge, William, Jr., and Darren Spedale. 2006. *Gay Marriage: For Better or for Worse? What We've Learned from the Evidence.* Oxford: Oxford University Press.

Ettelbrick, Paula. [1989] 1997. "Since When Is Marriage a Path to Liberation?" In *Same-Sex Marriage: Pro and Con*, edited by Andrew Sullivan, 118–24. New York: Vintage.

Gallagher, Maggie. 2003. "The Divorce Thing: A Diversion in the Marriage Debate." *National Review Online*, August 13.

Giddens, Anthony. 1992. *The Transformation of Intimacy: Sexuality, Love and Eroticism in Modern Societies.* Cambridge: Polity Press.

Graff, E. J. 1997. "Retying the Knot." In *Same-Sex Marriage: Pro and Con*, edited by Andrew Sullivan, 134–38. New York: Vintage.

Green, Adam Isaiah. 2006. "Until Death Do Us Part: The Impact of Differential Access to Marriage on a Sample of Urban Men." *Sociological Perspectives* 49: 163–89.

Gross, Neil. 2005. "The Detraditionalization of Intimacy Reconsidered." *Sociological Theory* 23 (3): 286–311.

Hausknecht, Murray. 2003. "Gay Marriage and the Domestication of Sex." *Dissent* 50 (4): 8–10.

Herdt, Gilbert. 1992. "Coming Out as a Rite of Passage: A Chicago Study." In *Gay Culture in America: Essays from the Field*, edited by Gilbert Herdt, 29–67. Boston: Beacon Press.

Herdt, Gilbert, and Andrew Boxer. 1992. "Introduction: Culture, History, and Life Course of Gay Men." In *Gay Culture in America: Essays from the Field*, 1–28. Boston: Beacon Press.

Hull, Kathleen E. 2006. *Same-Sex Marriage: The Cultural Politics of Love and Law.* Cambridge: Cambridge University Press.

Hunter, Nan. 1991. "Marriage, Law and Gender: A Feminist Inquiry." *Law and Sexuality* 9: 18–19.

Johnson, Susan E. 1990. *Staying Power: Long-Term Lesbian Couples.* Tallahassee, Fla.: Naiad Press.

Josephson, Jyl. 2005. "Citizenship, Same-Sex Marriage, and Feminist Critiques of Marriage." *Perspectives on Politics* 3 (2): 269–84.

Lannutti, Pamela J. 2005. "For Better or Worse: Exploring the Meanings of Same-Sex

Marriage within the Lesbian, Gay, Bisexual and Transgendered Community." *Journal of Social and Personal Relationships* 22: 5–18.

Laumann, Edward O., John H. Gagnon, Robert T. Michael, and Stuart Michaels. 1994. *The Social Organization of Sexuality: Sexual Practices in the United States.* Chicago: University of Chicago Press.

Lehr, Valerie. 1999. *Queer Family Values: Debunking the Myth of the Nuclear Family.* Philadelphia: Temple University Press.

Lutzer, Erwin. 2004. *The Truth about Same-Sex Marriage.* Chicago: Moody Publishers.

Patterson, Charlotte J. 1995. "Families of the Lesbian Baby-Boom: Parents' Division of Labor and Children's Adjustment." *Developmental Psychology* 31: 115–23.

Peel, Elizabeth, and Rosie Harding. 2004. "Divorcing Romance, Rights and Radicalism: Beyond Pro and Anti in the Lesbian and Gay Marriage Debate." *Feminism and Psychology* 14 (4): 588–99.

Rich, Adrienne. 1980. "Compulsory Heterosexuality and Lesbian Existence." *Signs* 5 (4): 631–60.

Rotello, Gabriel. 1997. *Sexual Ecology: AIDS and the Destiny of Gay Men.* New York: Dutton.

Saalfield, C. 1993. "Lesbian Marriage . . . (k)not!" In *Sisters, Sexperts, Queers: Beyond the Lesbian Nation,* edited by Arlene Stein, 187–95. New York: Penguin.

Seccombe, W. 1993. *Weathering the Storm: Working-Class Families from the Industrial Revolution to the Fertility Decline.* London: Verso.

Simon, William, and John Gagnon. 1967. "Homosexuality: The Formulation of a Sociological Perspective." *Journal of Health and Social Behavior* 8: 177–85.

Statistics Canada. 2004. *Report on the Demographic Situation in Canada.* Statistics Canada, Demography Division.

Stets, Jan. 1991. "Cohabiting and Marital Aggression: The Role of Social Isolation." *Journal of Marriage and the Family* 53: 669–80.

Strauss, Anselm, and Juliet Corbin. 1998. *Basics of Qualitative Research: Techniques and Procedures for Developing Grounded Theory.* 2nd ed. Thousand Oaks, Calif.: Sage Publications.

Sullivan, Andrew. 1996. "Here Comes the Groom: A (Conservative) Case for Gay Marriage." In *Beyond Queer: Challenging Gay Left Orthodoxy,* edited by Bruce Bawar, 252–58. New York: Free Press.

Sullivan, Maureen. 2004. *The Family of Women: Lesbian Mothers, Their Children, and the Undoing of Gender.* Berkeley and London: University of California Press.

Valverde, Mariana. 2006. "A New Entity in the History of Sexuality: The Respectable Same-Sex Couple." *Feminist Studies* 32 (1): 155–63.

Waite, J. Linda, and Maggie Gallagher. 2000. *The Case for Marriage: Why Married People Are Happier, Healthier, and Better Off Financially.* New York: Doubleday.

Walters, Suzanna Danuta. 2001. "The Marrying Kind? Take My Domestic Partner, Please: Gays and Marriage in the Era of the Visible." In *Queer Families, Queer Politics: Challenging Culture and the State,* edited by Mary Bernstein and Renate Reimann, 338–57. New York: Columbia University Press.

Warner, Michael. 1991. "Introduction: Fear of a Queer Planet." *Social Text* 9 (29): 3–17.

———. 1999. *The Trouble with Normal: Sex, Politics and the Ethics of Queer Life.* New York: Free Press.

Weeks, Jeffrey. 1988. "Male Homosexuality: Cultural Pespectives." In *Diseases in the Male Homosexual*, edited by Michael Adler, 1–14. London: Springer-Verlag.

Weeks, Jeffrey, Brian Heaphy, and Catherine Donovan. 2001. *Same Sex Intimacies: Families of Choice and Other Life Experiments*. New York: Routledge.

Woolwine, David, and E. Doyle McCarthy. 2005. "Gay Moral Discourse: Talking about Identity, Sex and Commitment." *Studies in Symbolic Interaction* 28: 379–408.

Yep, Gust A., Karen E. Lovaas, and John P. Elia. 2003. "A Critical Appraisal of Assimilationist and Radical Ideologies Underlying Same-Sex Marriage in LGBT Communities in the United States." *Journal of Homosexuality* 45 (1): 45–64.

Young, Claire, and Susan Boyd. 2006. "Losing the Feminist Voice? Debates on the Legal Recognition of Same-Sex Partnerships in Canada." *Feminist Legal Studies* 14: 213–40.

Contributors

Ellen Ann Andersen is associate professor of political science and women's and gender studies at the University of Vermont. She is the author of *Out of the Closets and into the Courts.*

Mary Bernstein is professor of sociology at the University of Connecticut. She is coeditor of *Queer Families, Queer Politics: Challenging Culture and the State* and *Queer Mobilizations: LGBT Activists Confront the Law* and author or coauthor of thirty articles and book chapters.

Mary C. Burke is a lecturer of sociology and women's and gender studies at the University of Vermont.

Adam Isaiah Green is associate professor of sociology at the University of Toronto.

Melanie Heath is assistant professor of sociology at McMaster University, Ontario. She is the author of *One Marriage under God: The Campaign to Promote Marriage in America.*

Kathleen E. Hull is associate professor of sociology at the University of Minnesota. She is the author of *Same-Sex Marriage: The Cultural Politics of Love and Law.*

Katrina Kimport is a research sociologist in the Advancing New Standards in Reproductive Health (ANSIRH) program at the University of California, San Francisco.

Jeffrey Kosbie is a J.D./Ph.D. candidate in the Department of Sociology and School of Law at Northwestern University.

Katie Oliviero is an American Council of Learned Societies New Faculty Fellow and visiting assistant professor of women's and gender studies at the University of Colorado, Boulder.

Kristine A. Olsen is a Ph.D. candidate at the University of Connecticut.

Timothy A. Ortyl is a Ph.D. candidate in the Department of Sociology at the University of Minnesota.

Arlene Stein is professor of sociology and on the graduate faculty of the Women's and Gender Studies Program at Rutgers University. She is author of three books and editor of two essay collections, including *The Stranger Next Door: The Story of a Small Community's Battle over Sex, Faith, and Civil Rights* and *Sex and Sensibility: Stories of a Lesbian Generation.*

Amy L. Stone is associate professor of sociology at Trinity University in San Antonio, Texas. She is the author of *Gay Rights at the Ballot Box* (Minnesota, 2012).

Verta Taylor is professor of sociology and an affiliated faculty member in feminist studies at the University of California, Santa Barbara. She is author or editor of fifteen books, including *Drag Queens at the 801 Cabaret* (with Leila J. Rupp).

Nella Van Dyke is associate professor of sociology at the University of California, Merced. She is coeditor of *Strategic Alliances: Coalition Building and Social Movements.*

Index